HUMOR AND POWER IN ALGERIA, 1920 TO 2021

PUBLIC CULTURES OF THE MIDDLE EAST AND NORTH AFRICA
Paul A. Silverstein, Susan Slyomovics, and Ted Swedenburg, editors

HUMOR AND POWER IN ALGERIA, 1920 TO 2021

―⚏―

ELIZABETH M. PEREGO

INDIANA UNIVERSITY PRESS

This book is a publication of

Indiana University Press
Office of Scholarly Publishing
Herman B Wells Library 350
1320 East 10th Street
Bloomington, Indiana 47405 USA

iupress.org

© 2023 by Elizabeth Perego

All rights reserved

No part of this book may be reproduced or utilized in any form or by any means, electronic or mechanical, including photocopying and recording, or by any information storage and retrieval system, without permission in writing from the publisher. The paper used in this publication meets the minimum requirements of the American National Standard for Information Sciences—Permanence of Paper for Printed Library Materials, ANSI Z39.48-1992.

Manufactured in the United States of America

Library of Congress Cataloging-in-Publication Data

Names: Perego, Elizabeth M., author.
Title: Humor and power in Algeria, 1920 to 2021 / Elizabeth M. Perego.
Other titles: Public cultures of the Middle East and North Africa.
Description: Bloomington, Indiana : Indiana University Press, [2023] | Series: Public cultures of the Middle East and North Africa | Includes bibliographical references and index. |
Identifiers: LCCN 2023029140 (print) | LCCN 2023029141 (ebook) | ISBN 9780253067609 (cloth) | ISBN 9780253067616 (paperback) | ISBN 9780253067623 (pdf)
Subjects: LCSH: Algerian wit and humor—Political aspects—History. | Algerian wit and humor—Social aspects—History. | Wit and humor—Political aspects—Algeria. | Algeria—Politics and government—20th century. | Algeria—Politics and government—21st century. | BISAC: SOCIAL SCIENCE / Anthropology / Cultural & Social | HUMOR / Topic / Cultural, Ethnic & Regional
Classification: LCC DT294.5 .P465 2023 (print) | LCC DT294.5 (ebook) | DDC 965.04—dc23/eng/20230627
LC record available at https://lccn.loc.gov/2023029140
LC ebook record available at https://lccn.loc.gov/2023029141

CONTENTS

List of Illustrations   vii

Acknowledgments   xi

Note on Transliteration   xv

Introduction: The Price of Humor in Algeria's "Time of Terrorism"   1

1. Side-Splitting While Nation-Forming, 1914 to the 1980s   31
2. Humor in Rebellion and Uncertain Times, 1988 to 1992   76
3. Laughing at Victims and Assailants through Popular Jokes from the Black Decade   117
4. Drawing Lines through the Ambiguity of Terror, 1992 to 1997   150
5. Cartoons "Dancing on Coffins" and Drumming Up Memory during Reconciliation, 1997 to 2005   191

Conclusion: Remembering Algeria's 1990s Conflict and Humor over Time   232

Bibliography   247

Index   263

ILLUSTRATIONS

Figure 1.1. Playbills/pamphlets circulated by playwright Mahieddine Bachtarzi in the 1930s. *46*

Figure 1.2. A magazine produced by France's Army of Africa directed toward its Maghribi soldiers that tells the story of a pro-Ally Juḥā. *50*

Figure 1.3. A December 1959 FLN publication includes a cartoon of President de Gaulle presumably calling someone outside of Algeria to let them know that he is very "tied up" with the war. *54*

Figure 1.4. Slim's imagining of the Casbah during the Battle of Algiers in *Moustache et les frères Belgacem* (Mustache and the Belgacem brothers). *61*

Figure 1.5. Slim cartoon from *Algérie-Actualité*, March 13–19, 1980, 5. *64*

Figure 2.1. Algerian president Chadli Bendjedid in his skivvies. *100*

Figure 2.2. Fathy's April 1990 drawing for the "democratic" newspaper *Alger républicain*. *103*

Figure 2.3. A smurf, most likely standing in for the FLN, informs Abassi Madani, "Your importance is finished. Thank you for the work."

A vulture over the tank responds, "That is the important thing." The other vulture adds, "The important thing is that the path to democracy continues." 104

Figure 2.4. Melouah's representations of "Islamist" partisans, complete with clubs. 106

Figure 2.5. Cartoon by FIB. 108

Figure 4.1. "The Game of Seven Errors." "Hardcore Islamist." "Moderate Islamist." 167

Figure 4.2. Algeria is depicted as a police officer heroically fending off an attack from a bearded man coming from the "East." 169

Figure 4.3. Ayoub seems to dismiss any question of "who is killing whom" / "qui tue qui." 173

Figure 4.4. Algeria's "voice of youth" makes fun of the *qui tue qui* inquiry. 174

Figure 4.5. Dilem's death figure orders civilians "to go" as one would a meal from a restaurant worker with an "Islamist" behind the counter. 175

Figure 4.6. The state, boarded up, leaves civilians to fend for themselves amid the savage attacks that Dilem ascribes to his "Islamist/rebel" characters. 179

Figure 4.7. The "Sant'Egidio" meeting to develop a peace agreement to end violence through dialogue is listed among "cholera" and "famine" as an unhappy potential outcome for participants in this "game." 181

Figure 4.8. Armed groups appear menacing as they propose peace over the bodies of dead civilians. 181

Figure 5.1. "The 'terrorists' come down from the mountains." 193

Figure 5.2. "The repentant ones return home." 203

Figure 5.3. "Here, the people are really divided [on the referendum]." 207

Figure 5.4. "One year ago, Algerians voted for the Civil Concord." 210

Figure 5.5. "Madani Mezrag supports the Charter for Peace [and Reconciliation]." *214*

Figure 5.6. "200,000 graves desecrated." *216*

Figure 5.7. The "repentant ones" from the AIS sing the national anthem with skulls pinned to their chests in place of medals. *217*

Figure 5.8. "First March 8th of the Civil Concord." *219*

Figure 5.9. "My friend the cobbler asked for news about the emir [the name given to armed groups' leaders] and his beloved." *221*

Figure 5.10. "From national arms to national reconciliation." *223*

ACKNOWLEDGMENTS

THIS PROJECT WAS SPARKED BY a joke that a friend told me in 2009 during my first trip to Algeria. I could never have imagined how research into the topic of political humor in Algeria would put me on a path to meeting some of the most incredible individuals I have had the honor of knowing and whose support, encouragement, and friendship would so greatly influence this work. Their assistance has been invaluable as I have sought to do the best I can to bring the utmost respect and reverence to an important topic and to the individuals whose ideas and lives I attempt to portray here.

This book would never have seen the light of day without the assistance of many individuals to whom I am deeply indebted and who guided me through the long hours of research and writing. First, at the Ohio State University, Ousman Kobo offered invaluable counsel as I worked on this project. I am immensely thankful for his humor and steady guidance. Ahmad Sikainga and Sabra Webber mentored me through the research process and provided crucial feedback on this work. Discussions with several members of Ohio State's Departments of History and Near Eastern Studies greatly shaped who I am as a student of the Maghribi past. These members include Claire Robertson, Jane Hathaway, Sarah Van Beurden, Thomas McDow, Judy Tzu-Chun Wu, Daniel Rivers, Joseph Zeidan, Geoffrey Parker, Clayton Howard, Tyran Steward, Libby Marvel, Sanja Kadrić, Amy Archer, Ayse Baltacıoğlu-Brammer, Ali Gibran Saddiqi, Isacar Bolaños, Andrew Skabelund, Lauren Henry, John Perry, Brandy Thomas, Jamie Goodall, Patrick Scharfe, David Hadley, Frank Blazich, Dawn Miles Chisebe, Maria Potter, Hussam Arouri, Henryatta Balla, Reyna Esquival, Dani Anthony, Hyun-Joo Mooney, and Stephanie Honchell, among many others.

The American Institute for Maghrib Studies; the Council of Overseas American Research Centers; the Library of Congress's Swann Foundation; Ohio State University's Office of International Affairs, Merson Center, and Department of History; the West Virginia Humanities Council; and Shepherd University's Professional Development Fund all provided the support necessary for me to spend several years in France and Algeria to conduct research for this project. I am very grateful for their dedication to promoting humanities and social sciences research. Colleagues at Shepherd University and Appalachian State University provided me with ample space to complete this study and friendly conversation when I needed a break. I especially thank Samuel Greene, Xi He, Scott Relyea, Jason White, and Kristen Baldwin-Deathridge. I am grateful as well to Princeton University's Institute for the Transregional Study of the Contemporary Middle East, North Africa, and Central Asia, especially its director Bernard Haykel, and the Department of Near Eastern Studies for helping provide me with the space, time, and support that I needed as I worked toward finishing this manuscript. Additionally, instructing excellent students at these institutions such as Thomas McLamb and Ines Aitsahalia has provided me with great joy over the last few years as they have pushed me to think differently about research and writing.

In Algeria, Robert Parks and Karim Ouaras of the Centre d'études maghrébines en Algérie provided me with generous guidance as I navigated many trips to Algeria and with a forum for presenting my work to Algerian communities in Oran. The Glycines Center for Diocesan Studies offered a welcoming home in Algiers for the first part of my research there and instruction in Algerian dialects of Arabic that were critical for this project. I was also able to present a part of the manuscript to an audience at the Glycines, which helped me make invaluable contacts. Librarians and archivists at Algeria's National Library and *El Watan*'s, *El Khabar*'s, and *Liberté*'s archives patiently assisted me as I waded through the country's postindependence print culture. Friends from around Algeria and the Algerian diaspora whom I met while conducting research in Algiers made the experience of living there nothing short of amazing. I would especially like to thank Sofiane Zouggar, Saadia Gacem, Nabila Kalache, Zineb Sedira, Miloud Yabrir, Mourad Berra, El-Hadi Gasdira, Nassim Balla, and Atef Berredjem for their companionship. In France, the staff and librarians of the Algerian Cultural Center shared their collection of materials on comics and media culture from Algeria's postindependence era. Staff and archivists at the Archives Nationales d'Outre-Mer in Aix-en-Provence equally assisted me with uncovering material related to humor under colonial occupation.

Workshops at the Center for Middle East Studies at the University of California, Berkeley; the Center for Jewish History in New York; Cambridge University's Centre for Research in the Arts, Social Sciences, and Humanities; and the University of Maryland's Department of History challenged me to think in different ways and more broadly about the topic of Algerian humor in the twentieth century. I thank the organizers and participants of these meetings, especially the American Institute for Maghrib Studies, David Stenner, Sami Everett, Rebekah Vince, Mourad Yelles, and Peter Wien. Alice Conklin invited me to present a portion of the manuscript to faculty and students at Ohio State, and I thank her and them for their helpful feedback. An earlier version of chapter 3 of this book appeared in the *Journal of North African Studies* in a special issue organized by Jill Jarvis and Brahim El Guabli on "Violence and the Politics of Aesthetics: A Postcolonial Maghrib without Borders." Collaborating with them for this initiative allowed me to refine that chapter.

I can never thank the oral history narrators who participated in this project enough for their time and patience as they opened up to me about different periods of their lives and taught me about humor in Algeria's past. This project would not have been possible without their assistance as well as the insight of the many scholars and journalists in Algeria who have written about humor or related topics, including but certainly not limited to Mustapha Benfodil, Hadj Miliani, Lazhari Labter, Sihem Benmalek, Ameziane Ferhani, Hiyem Cheurfa, and Ouissal Harize. Theirs is the expertise that forms the foundation of this work. Any mistakes in interpretation are my own.

Over the years, I have enjoyed forging friendships with fellow students and scholars of the Maghrib. Vish Sakthivel, Gareth Smail, Sarah Ghabrial, Idriss Jebari, Sara Rahnama, Arthur Asseraf, Sandra Rousseau, Charlotte Courreye, Saphia Arezki, Malika Rahal, Samuel Anderson, Andrew Bellisari, Terry Peterson, Christopher Silver, Muriam Haleh Davis, Natalya Vince, Brahim Rouabah, Martin Evans, Tahir Kilavuz, Caroline Angle, Edward McAllister, Aili Mari Tripp, Mary Anne Lewis Cusato, and Alice Kaplan have contributed their knowledge and often a good laugh to the research and writing process for this book. Christiane Marie Abu-Sarah and Joshua Cole generously shared documents from French archives when the world shut down during the COVID-19 pandemic.

Susan Slyomovics, Paul Silverstein, and Ted Swedenburg selected this manuscript for their series on the Public Cultures of the Middle East and North Africa. I could not envision a better home for this work. Sophia Herbert and Bethany Mowry shepherded me through the review and editing and publication process with grace and wisdom. Neil Belakhdar and Jessica Stilwell assisted with transliterations and editing. I would like to also thank the anonymous reviewers for their most helpful feedback, which helped make this book a better and more solid piece of scholarship. Any remaining errors in this manuscript are mine.

Finally, I thank friends, family, and four-legged companions who saw me through this process and tolerated my frequent forays into what one friend calls "history world." To them my debt is endless. My loving partner and our baby daughter are the center of my real world. Their love is the ship that brings me back from the at times tumultuous waters of research and writing. I look forward to sharing this work with them.

NOTE ON TRANSLITERATION

FOR ALL ARABIC TEXTS, BOTH those in Modern Standard Arabic and Algerian dialects of Arabic, I have used the *International Journal of Middle East Studies* guidelines for transliteration. Algerian dialects of Arabic can be difficult to transliterate, as the pronunciations of some words can differ from region to region within the country. I have tried to stay as true to the sounds of the original sources as possible while transliterating texts from these dialects. For text in Tamazight, I have followed the conventions for transliteration set out by J. M. Dallet in his *Dictionnaire français-kabyle*. All translations are my own unless otherwise noted.

HUMOR AND POWER IN ALGERIA, 1920 TO 2021

INTRODUCTION

The Price of Humor in Algeria's "Time of Terrorism"

IN THE 1990S, SAÏD MEKBEL was one of Algeria's most-followed editorialists. A playful writer, he often infused his work with humor. Yet, on a cold morning in December 1994 on the back of popular French-language paper *Le Matin*, he published the following solemn words:

> The Thief Who
> The father who advises his children not to talk in public about the nasty job that he does, it is him.
> This bad citizen who hangs around in court waiting to go before the judges, it's him. This individual, grabbed in a neighborhood roundup and who a big hit with a baton propels to the back of a paddy wagon, it is him.
> It is he who, in the morning, leaves his house, unsure that he will arrive at work, and he who, at night, leaves his work unsure that he will arrive back home. This vagabond who doesn't know where to spend the night anymore, it's him.
> It's he who one threatens in the secrets of a government office, the witness who must swallow what he knows, this naked and distraught citizen...
> This man who wishes not to die with his throat slit, it's him. It's him who doesn't know how to do anything with his hands, nothing else but craft his little pieces of writing.
> He who hopes against everything because, is it not true, rose bushes grow well in piles of manure. He who is all of these things and who is simply a journalist.
>
> *Ce voleur qui*
> *Ce père qui recommande à ses enfants de ne pas dire dehors le méchant métier qu'il fait, c'est lui.*

> *Ce mauvais citoyen qui traîne au palais de justice, attendant de passer devant les juges, c'est lui. Cet individu, pris dans une rafle de quartier et qu'un coup de crosse propulse au fond du camion, c'est lui.*
>
> *C'est lui qui, le matin, quitte sa maison sans être sûr d'arriver à son travail et lui qui quitte, le soir, son travail sans être sûr d'arriver à sa maison. Ce vagabond qui ne sait plus chez qui passer la nuit, c'est lui.*
>
> *C'est lui qu'on menace dans les secrets d'un cabinet officiel, le témoin qui doit ravaler ce qu'il sait, ce citoyen nu et désemparé...*
>
> *Cet homme qui fait le vœu de ne pas mourir égorgé, c'est lui. C'est lui qui ne sait rien faire de ses mains, rien d'autres que ses petits écrits.*
>
> *Lui qui espère contre tout parce que, n'est-ce pas, les rosiers poussent bien sur les tas de fumier. Lui qui est tout cela et qui est seulement journaliste.*[1]

Mekbel went to work that morning at Algiers's Maison de la Presse, a walled-in compound minutes from bustling downtown Algiers that served as headquarters for a number of the country's lead newspapers. He left the office toward noon to have lunch with a friend. As was the habit of most journalists at the time, according to reports, Mekbel sat at a table facing the front entrance of the eatery. Why? By this point, December 3, 1994, the journalist renowned for his often-satirical column Mesmar J'ha (*mismār Juḥā*) had witnessed the murder of thirty-two of his fellow Algerian journalists. These losses were devastating, as media workers numbered at most a few hundred. The assassinations took place as armed, self-proclaimed "Islamist" organizations were then engulfed in a bloody revolt against the military-controlled regime that lasted approximately ten years and is now known as the *Black Decade* (*décennie noire* or *al-'ashariyya as-sawdā'*) or *Time of Terrorism* (*waqt al-irhāb*), among other names. This bloody civil conflict disrupted journalism and threatened journalists. Some of these rebel groups accused journalists of collusion with the state even as the regime silenced critical voices from the media. Censorship was rampant during this period as rumors ran wild that the government may have been responsible for some media workers' deaths.[2]

Mekbel had a higher profile than most journalists. Trained for the military in France, he started out in journalism in 1963 with the communist-leaning paper *Alger républicain*. At this famed outlet, the young writer (only twenty-three at the time) found himself under the tutelage of Henri Alleg. Alleg was the famous intellectual whose 1958 exposé on the French military's use of torture during the Algerian War of Independence (1954–1962), *La question*, sent shockwaves around metropolitan France and the world. Mekbel was forced to abandon his journalism career upon Algerian president Houari Boumediene's rise to power in 1965 and subsequent crackdown on his political opponents, including the communists who supported *Alger républicain* and lamented the military taking on a greater role in government with Boumediene's ascension.[3] Mekbel was one of the few journalists who, after being forced to abandon their careers at this time, later resumed writing. Upon the opening up of Algeria's print media field to nonstate publications in 1990, Mekbel returned to his pen. At this time, he participated in the relaunching of his former paper, where he composed editorial works under the title *El Ghoul*, "the ghoul" in Arabic.[4]

By the mid-1990s, Mekbel had become Algeria's "most famous editorialist" and one of its most vibrant journalists.[5] He had earned this reputation despite working mainly as a writer commenting on the news with a humorous slant, not as an investigative reporter. Mekbel had also served as editor of *Le Matin*, his paper after he left *Alger républicain* in 1991. But his work attracted the attention of individuals beyond his avid fans. Mekbel and his colleague, caricaturist Ali Dilem (whose humorous but poignant drawings appeared on the same page as Mekbel's pieces), were often featured at the top of armed groups' death lists, which intellectuals jokingly called "hit parades" after the Top of the Charts countdowns for popular songs in the 1950s and 1960s.[6] Partisans of the armed groups or their sympathizers passed around these declarations of people to be assassinated for purportedly supporting the state. Supposedly, the higher up on the list an individual was, the more the groups wanted them eliminated. Mekbel also reportedly garnered government attention for his weekly *Le Matin* column published under the name Mesmar J'ha, the "nail of Juḥā."[7] Juḥā is a central figure in Algerian and broader Muslim-world folklore, a trickster and troublemaker who serves as an "antihero."[8] As with Mekbel's column, Algerians often associated Juḥā tales with humor.[9] By "nail of Juḥā," Mekbel was referring to a specific story in the legend's canon in which Juḥā swindles a man out of his money through his persistent deft conniving. Juḥā sells his home on the condition that he can leave a nail in the wall that the new owner cannot remove. The perennial troublemaker proceeds to use the nail to hang up a rotting carcass. Disgusted by the smell, the new owner leaves, and Juḥā ends up with both the money from the sale and his house. By using this title, Mekbel thus positioned himself as an obstinate, sly challenger to the powers that be and one who would mobilize comedy toward this end.[10]

At least some rebels seem to have viewed humorists as a greater threat to their cause than journalists working on security, as reflected in their decision to privilege the satirical writer and his cartoonist protégé on death lists. This reality, compounded with Mekbel's high profile, made him far more likely than the average Algerian media worker to be targeted for murder. Before December 3, 1994, the writer had already escaped one assassination attempt. So, that fateful afternoon, Mekbel ate facing the restaurant's door. On this occasion, though, the gunman came up to his table from the rear of the establishment. He did not miss his mark. Mekbel's last editorial about journalists leaving homes never certain of a safe return appeared the next day in *Le Matin* as news of his death sent shockwaves around the world and loved ones mourned his death.[11]

The Nail of Juḥā had fallen, leaving a gaping hole in Algeria's cultural landscape. By the end of Algeria's civil conflict of the 1990s, an estimated one hundred thousand individuals had perished in the violence. Along with Mekbel, two other media workers who were known for producing comedy—journalist Mohamed Dorbane and cartoonist Brahim Guerroui—figured among the dead.

HUMOR AS A TOOL OF CHANGE AND TRACING HUMOR OVER TIME

Mekbel's murder reveals that humor could have grave results during Algeria's civil conflict of the 1990s. By any measurement, the war was no laughing matter. The Black Decade or Time of Terrorism lasted more than a decade, tore communities and families asunder, and left approximately one hundred thousand individuals dead.[12] Competing insurgent groups claiming to want to install a more Islamic regime or to embody the nation's true revolutionary principles battled the military-backed regime that had been in power since independence in 1962. All sides employed masked agents who inflicted violence on enemies and suspected enemies among the general population at sometimes-unexpected moments, leaving ordinary civilians uncertain at all times as to both their security and who precisely was carrying out horrendous attacks against them.

Yet, throughout the harrowing armed struggle, some Algerians laughed. They employed cartoons and jokes, the two major forms of humor that persisted into this period, to express powerful ideas concerning the war's major events and actors and to redefine their position in the conflict, their communities, the broader Algerian nation, and the world as a result of the unsettling bloodshed. This use of humor as a critical discourse for responding to political battles for authority at the national level was not a new phenomenon in Algeria. Historically, communities had expressed ideas about power through oral and visual cultures in atmospheres where they had limited freedom of expression. With its ambiguity and its propensity for being transmitted orally and visually as well as textually, different and sometimes ideologically conflicting populations in Algeria used humor to comment on politics in the twentieth and early twenty-first centuries. However, Algerians used humor differently at the height of this harrowing conflict. Changes in humorous practices from times of peace to times of civil conflict attested to the disruption and suffering that the war represented for many Algerians.

This book analyzes shifts in humorous discourse about national politics produced in Algeria both before and during a raging civil conflict. It demonstrates the globally informed and creative ways that Algerian civilians tried to make sense of the bloodletting and develop narratives to decipher an opaque set of situations and political intrigues. I argue that humor served as a critical site for political expression as well as identity and social memory formation throughout Algeria's postindependence history. Building on this earlier legacy, humor remained one of the few outlets still available for political expression as threats of violence and censorship from competing authoritarian powers curtailed language during the war, as evinced in Mekbel's assassination.

Indeed, in the hands of Algerian communities during these horrific circumstances, humor took on greater power precisely because the war's belligerents limited other discursive outlets and spaces for exchange and reflection. Narratives of Black Decade violence shaped the consequences of that same violence.[13] Perspectives on the bloodshed articulated through humor produced similar consequences, but humor's relationship to events becomes clear only when one considers changes in Algerian communities' uses of humor over time. The Black Decade and the preceding October 1988 Revolution and democratic opening created ruptures in how Algerian communities employed humor. Humorous narratives and products could also have consequences that the makers of comedy themselves did not anticipate. For example, jokes that seemed to undermine authority could in fact remind civilians of its contours and rules.[14]

This book is inspired by and informs debates in the fields of humor, Middle Eastern, and African studies as well as debates concerning humor, political culture, and authoritarianism. To begin with, humor studies specialists remain divided over whether comedy and humor, especially jokes, can result in concrete social or political change. Some scholars claim that jokes are too ambiguous to produce tangible outcomes or that they merely reflect popular opinion; jokes are "thermometers" for social unrest but can never be "thermostats."[15] Drawing on theories of language and power, opponents of this vision of humor as ineffective contend that jokes can have significant consequences for societies, especially when employed by persons on the margins of power.[16] In relation to humor's efficacy to upend authoritarian power, some scholars contend that jokes can have the opposite outcome from the one that the subaltern joke-teller mocking authority may desire by dissipating tension and resistance. Humor then proves a less effective outlet for political anger than more direct action (the "pressure valve" theory).[17]

This fiery discussion has spilled over into Middle East studies very recently, with analysts querying, concerning the fall of Hosni Mubarak in early 2011, whether symbolic humorous stripping of the Egyptian leader was "more than a joke" and resulted in his ouster.[18] Literature on cartoons, though, has long recognized the propensity of these images to exert authority over readers and the societies that produce and consume them. For instance, work on France's *Charlie Hebdo* magazine demonstrates the capacity of the review's cartoons to reinforce sexualized notions of the otherness of Jews and Muslims.[19] Academics from different fields have arrived at similar conclusions while looking at other instances of cartoons channeling vehement antisemitism, including in Nazi Germany.[20] In a more recent and salient example, Saba Mahmood argued that the 2005 Danish cartoons portraying the Prophet Muhammad existed as more than mere symbols. Muslims did not have to accept a vision of cartoons that was rooted in semiotics, a field linked to Western Protestantism. For Muslims, the cartoons instead represented an affront, a serious act of violence that inflicted real harm on them, as the anthropologist noted through ethnographic conversations with Egyptian communities around the time of the cartoons' publication.[21]

It may be impossible to determine precisely when and where a joke or cartoon can spur individual or collective action unless one looks at moments of mass uproar against a particular cartoon or series of cartoons. Yet research and critical theory surrounding power, discourse, and humor aver that humor can shape or strengthen memory, reinforce or spread ideas or messages, stress the ridiculousness of a leader, inculcate hatred against a particular group, and inflict violence.[22] In other words, humor, regardless and sometimes because of its ambiguity, can have significant social implications and may shape the outcomes of historical events. Most importantly, political powers in this critical world area, as elsewhere, have viewed humor as a threat to their authority.[23] One need only look to the case of Abdel Fattah el-Sisi's government investigating a puppet for potential terrorism or the Syrian Asad regime's breaking of lead cartoonist Ali Ferzat's fingers to see that political authorities take humor seriously. This pattern holds true for Africa as well. For instance, Somali radio presenter Marshale was assassinated in 2012 after mocking Al-Shabaab, who had previously threatened the comic.[24]

While not universal, divisions between perspectives of humor as ineffective when in the form of jokes and effective in the form of cartoons illustrate the need for a change in scholarly approaches to humor. The present work adds to these robust conversations in two ways. First, it advocates for methods that examine functions of humor across genres and recognize possible intertextuality and influence between humorous genres as well as between humor and other forms of discourse. Second, the work pushes scholars to consider communities' use of humor, its production, and its reception over time.

Scholars tend to focus on certain genres of humor in their work rather than considering connections across humorous genres as a launching point for fruitful lines of inquiry. For instance, in literature on humor in the Middle East and Africa, jokes are often considered separately from cartoons, despite the fact that cartoonists can take inspiration from jokes and joke-tellers can be influenced by cartoons.[25] While genres of humor vary greatly in terms of content and modes of delivery and require specific analytical methodologies, these genres can overlap and influence one another, as this volume stresses through the prism of Algerian humor. Their disentanglement is a thorny task laden with the risk of missing what clues can be found in the intertextuality of two or more forms of humor—for instance, between jokes and satirical songs.

This book demonstrates that individuals and communities in Algeria used humor in a variety of forms that shaped key ideas over time. Yet, this shaping becomes detectable only if one considers the cross-pollination of ideas between various types of humor as well as between humor and other kinds of political culture and discourse. In the chapters that follow, I look at how jokes, cartoons, satirical songs, and humorous folk tales intersected with rumor, conspiracy theories, and news to reinforce ideas surrounding critical actors engaged in maintaining or challenging authority in Algeria. Humor's functions, then, depend greatly on a context that includes other contemporary forms of discourse.[26] Humorous artifacts from one genre can also influence products belonging to another. In Algeria, as elsewhere, profound connections existed between oral and written cultures. In keeping with exciting recent scholarship on earlier periods of North Africa's past highlighting oral readings of newspapers, I am especially interested in uncovering where oral and written forms of humor and narratives, especially cartoons, jokes, songs, slogans, rumor, news, and text, overlapped and potentially increased the impact of a message or idea.[27] I stress here that print cultures in the region continued to have vibrant oral lives and implications into the late twentieth century.

Furthermore, while recognizing the capacity of humor in the employ of actors and societies to effect change, this book does not claim to put forth a universal theory of humor and its functions under repressive regimes or in times of violence or political crisis. Concerning cartoons, Achille Mbembe writes that "to judge the political efficacy of images, it is necessary beforehand to specify their anthropological status within the cultures that give birth to them."[28] Following this thought, I argue that measuring the power of humor in any given instance requires one to consider the particularities of humor and its relationship to events as well as its connections to broader, longer-standing trends and movements. I assert that looking at changes in communities' practices of humor and the contents of humor over time can illuminate shifts in attitudes and reveal important facets of society, such as the limits of the taboo, the licit, and the blasphemous. The deeply dark and morbid humor of the 1990s in Algeria appears to have had limited precedent in the country, and making sense of this humor requires a comprehension of deeper practices of different Algerian communities' uses of political humor over several moments of their past. While the comedy of Mekbel and Dilem was innovative, Mekbel linked his work through the choice of his *Le Matin* column's title to the region's earlier humorous traditions. The major study contemplating changes in humor over a longer period in the Middle East is Khalid Kishtainy's groundbreaking 1986 work, *Arab Political Humor*. The task that Kishtainy assigns himself is a vast one, however, looking at humor across the Arab world over several centuries.[29] A balance between temporal and geographic scope seems necessary to measure the influence that humorous products can have in the hands of particular communities over time.

Reconstructing how communities engage with humor in different ways at different moments can prove useful task for historians and other scholars. Because humor is deeply rooted in the society that constructs it and can often be ambiguous in meaning, to grasp what was funny in the past requires an equally deep understanding of the community at hand.[30] Thus, the process of wading through humorous material may also help contribute to the historian's comprehension of a community. Humor often pushes taboos, and in this manner it reflects what a society may have found tolerable or intolerable at the time. Backlash to a particular humorous product can similarly pinpoint where the line was for this challenge to locally held taboos or the boundaries of good taste.[31] Humor can be employed to create in- and out-groups or to serve as a key framing device for movements, helping show how these groups wanted themselves or their causes to be defined and understood.[32] Understanding who produced humor and why or how humor was shared and received can likewise reveal information about social statuses, available technologies and access to them, and when humor landed or failed to land and why. When used as historical sources, other cultural products can be similarly informative; but humor is tied to amusement and is therefore capable of revealing aspects of a society related to personal and social amusement that other cultural products may not be able to.³³ Humor as a historical source, then, can allow for a better vision of past events and societies, and tracking the way a community shifts its usage, form, or content of humor can be informative as well.

While I stress the value of considering humor over time, I also want to push back against overly simplistic approaches to humor that view it as mainly or solely a tool of resistance. Several scholars have highlighted how humor, even a single joke or product, can simultaneously perform a multitude of functions, including both upending and bolstering political authority.³⁴ Despite their writings, Mostafa Abedinifard has identified a general problem in the field of humor studies: students of humor seem to favor a view of humor as a means of resistance to the detriment of the other potential roles that humor can play in societies.³⁵ In works by historians on humor, especially scholarship deciphering humor and its meanings in instances of authoritarian rule, this pattern becomes starker. With some notable exceptions (such as literature on cartoons), historians and scholars looking at historical case studies have typically underscored humor's capacity as a tool of resistance, a Scottsian "weapon of the weak," while neglecting its other possible functions.³⁶ Humor's functionality, though, is often complex, with the same joke capable of multiple simultaneous implications.³⁷ This complexity must be considered since, as Chad Bryant warns us, populations and scholars can mobilize the humor-as-resistance trope to obscure realities that might be less palatable to them.³⁸ In this book, I consider the polyvalent potential functions of different types of humorous cultures as Algerians produced and consumed them in specific circumstances.

Studies of changes in cultures of humor over time are generally missing from the field of Middle Eastern and African studies. This absence is notable in the flurry of research that has appeared in recent years on humor and in the context of the 2010–2011 "Arab Spring" revolts that took place across many parts of the Middle East and North Africa.³⁹ What is more, for the most part, projects concerned with the political and popular cultures of the Middle East and Africa and how they can shape or comment on national-level political dynamics or history overwhelmingly focus on print cultures, cinema, music, theater, and art.⁴⁰ Film and literature especially take up the lion's share of attention in the Maghrib. Scholarship analyzing culture as a space for critical reflection on politics or political action in Algeria has looked at football discourse, music, novels, and poetry.⁴¹ For instance, Jill Jarvis's recent work demonstrates that the act of composing and consuming print literature in twentieth-century Algeria was deeply political in itself rather than merely reflective of political intrigues and attitudes.⁴² Humor also constituted a political act with serious political consequences, but one that a wider array of Algerians could use and access than literary forms such as novels and short stories, as humorous practices such as joke-telling may be more accessible to a broader population. An investigation of humor can therefore round out the breadth of testimonies captured in this record of popular understandings of politics, history, justice, and the nation. Unlike the genres most often analyzed (except folklore, poetry, music, and dance performed or recounted in neighborhoods and homes or graffiti etched or painted on walls), humor, especially in folk forms such as jokes, can be produced by individuals with little or no cost of distribution. It is flexible, can be whispered, can produce and intersect with wider discourse, and can cross geographical, ideological, and genre boundaries. Humor captures and even venerates dialects and vernacular languages.[43]

Shifts in Algerian humor cultures, particularly a disruption and rapid morphing of them with the advent of the Black Decade, offer an ideal case for grappling with these questions of changing functions of humor in a population over time. To begin with, the country possesses long-seated practices of humor connected to other parts of the Maghrib and Islamic world. Scholars both in and outside of Algeria have noted the richness and diversity of humor within the country.[44] Humor marks the political vocabulary of Algeria. To give one example, Algerians often refer derisively to their country as "*bled mickey*"/ "the country of Mickey Mouse" when something goes awry, particularly with their undemocratic political system.[45]

Algeria also holds an important status in regional and global history, with historical episodes reflective of events happening around the world. A Muslim-majority territory by the premodern period, Algeria forms a critical part of the Maghrib, the northwestern region of Africa that today spans from Tunisia in the east to Morocco and Mauritania in the west. By using this term, some medieval Islamic writers distinguished this area, once the most western part of the Islamic world, from the Mashriq or "east," their term for what now forms the central part of the Middle East (Egypt, Sudan, lands in the eastern Mediterranean, Mesopotamia, and the Arabian Peninsula).[46] The northern part of Algeria was transformed into a province of the powerful Ottoman Empire in 1525.

In seeking to establish a Mediterranean empire, France overthrew Ottoman control and began its colonization of Algeria in 1830, decades before the height of European colonization of the African continent. Unlike other parts of France's empire, a large section of Algeria became part of France. Like other areas of the African continent under the colonial yoke, it also became a settler colony, with non-French European settlers gradually becoming French citizens and European communities expropriating vast amounts of land from local populations. French authorities categorized the populations of Algeria by racialized definitions of religion.[47] They forced French citizenship on almost all of Algeria's Jewish community in 1870, placing the community in a difficult position as indigenous but now naturalized European citizens. Algerian Muslims faced harsh discriminatory laws, including ones that forbade free speech and freedom of movement. Muslims could also become citizens and attain equal political rights after 1865 only if they renounced central facets of their belonging to the Muslim community (called "personal status"—namely, the right to be judged in Muslim courts for mostly family issues), which few did. After Algerian communities' sacrifices in the First World War, more Algerian Muslim men were allowed to vote for limited offices while retaining their personal status.

The interwar period witnessed a flourishing of political and cultural activities along with the advancement of new nationalist movements. A key question that emerged and continued into the immediate post–World War II era was whether Algerian Muslims would be able to remain Muslim while gaining rights equal to those of naturalized European or French settlers. Reforms to this effect faltered under settler resistance. An armed nationalist revolt coalesced around the National Liberation Front (Front de libération nationale, or FLN). The resulting War of Independence from 1954 to 1962 represented a critical moment in twentieth-century world history and inspired global imaginations. It provoked and continues to provoke debates around the world concerning decolonization.[48] The event, known in Algeria most commonly as the *thawra* (Arabic for "revolution"), came to emblemize the struggles of millions across the world against colonial rule and for greater dignity.[49] Internal divisions among the population that remained in Algeria, which was majority Muslim, flared as the FLN morphed into a one-party, military-controlled state.

After a period of economic crisis in the 1980s accompanied by economic liberalization, crowds across Algeria's major urban areas took to the streets in what would become known as the October 1988 Revolution to express their disgust with the regime. Then-president Chadli Benjedid responded to this Arab Spring–like event by initiating a series of reforms that, under pressure from civic associations and opponents of the FLN, led to a democratic opening and the advent of a multiparty system. When an Islamist party, the Islamic Salvation Front (*al-Jabha al-islāmiyya lil inqādh* in Arabic, known as the FIS for its French translation, the Front islamique du salut), was poised to win the country's first free legislative elections, the military flexed its muscle once again and halted the democratic process, triggering a deep political crisis as armed organizations formed to challenge the state. Thus, a mere three decades after liberation, like a handful of other Middle Eastern and African states postindependence and due to divisions over questions of an Islamist party's place in government, Algerians experienced a horrific civil conflict. The events of that war were shrouded in mystery as multiple actors established and promoted competing "regimes of truth" similar to instances of authoritarianism in the middle and late twentieth century elsewhere.[50] Capable of suppressing or punishing free speech and action, competing authoritarian powers—the state and clashing armed rebel organizations—took hold in Algeria in the early to mid-1990s. A dark humor surfaced during this period that, I argue, provides insights into lived experiences during one of the deadliest conflicts of the 1990s. Peace was reestablished through a process that lasted from 1994 to 2005 yet failed to deliver justice in the eyes of some Algerians.

Beyond its role as a response to this civil conflict, Algerian humor also attests to a "global intertextuality" of political humor.[51] Humor in Algeria from the postindependence period through the 1990s sometimes borrowed or adapted jokes that then circulated among socialist countries during the Cold War.[52] There is a possibility that fake checkpoint jokes from Algeria likewise spread regionally, demonstrating that Algerian humor could impact humorous practices elsewhere.[53] While these jokes and cartoons spoke to specific circumstances in Algeria, they could be adapted to resonate in areas beyond the country's borders experiencing similar events. The circumstances investigated here, then, and the humorous rhetoric that they inspired may reveal larger trends in humor production and consumption. Algeria's story of two revolutions (the War of Independence and the October 1988 Revolution), the failed democratic opening of 1988 to 1992, and the subsequent conflict holds lessons for comparison with humor's role in other moments across the Middle East, North Africa, and Africa more broadly. These moments could include civil conflicts in other parts of the region, such as Lebanon, or the role of humor in uprisings in Turkey, Iran, Egypt, Bahrain, Sudan, and elsewhere.

Moving to the global level, at least one conflict studies researcher has recently called for more materials investigating the links between humor and war.[54] Once again, the armed struggle in Algeria further mirrors instances of unclear violence during civil wars and insurgency movements that increased in frequency toward the end of the twentieth century. Humor addressing the conflict also offers a case study that critically differs from the instances of single-power authoritarianism in Europe (Nazi-occupied territories and the Soviet Union) that most historians working on humor under authoritarianism have studied.[55] A study of Algerian humor from this period may be useful for scholars working on similar contexts of opaque violence or competition between many authoritarian powers. Finally, perhaps due to the historical importance of humor as a means of engaging populations politically in Algeria, Islamists in the country have also employed humor in their messaging. In relation to humor, Islamists are often only discussed, even by specialists of political culture in the region, as opposing it or seeking to repress it.[56] This volume, in contrast, highlights Islamist humor and comedy.

Previous literature on Algerian humor, but specifically during the 1990s war, offers many insights that this book seeks to build on.[57] Much of this work focuses on a single genre of humor—namely, either jokes or cartoons, the two major forms to persist into the 1990s as the violence curtailed activities in the public sphere such as theater. These earlier chapters and articles also look at jokes or cartoons at specific moments of the country's history and generally conceive of humor as a critical arm of resistance to either the state or the armed insurgents of the 1990s. Abderrahmane Moussaoui's chapter on jokes in his landmark anthropological study of the civil conflict in Algeria acknowledges humor as a space where Algerians rethought the social implications of the war, including the shifts in gender relations brought about by the bloodshed.[58] Aïssa Khelladi's article offers the broadest coverage of political humor and its changes over time. He most notably acknowledges the presence of humor among the partisans and leaders of the FIS, Algeria's once-largest Islamist party.[59] All of these works underscore the importance of humor as a key facet of political culture in Algeria as well as "a weapon of the weak."[60] A longer historical approach to humor from the 1990s and a consideration of humor's functionalities beyond the resistance paradigm will broaden the conversations initiated by these scholars.

Beyond advocating for a longer and more nuanced approach to the functionality of humor in its many forms, this project deepens understanding regarding a generally underexamined part of Algeria's past: how civilian populations lived through and viewed the 1990s conflict. Writings on the 1990s have discussed the motivations and actions of the war's belligerents or the import of the war for international relations or regional geopolitics.[61] Civilians' perspectives on the conflict, though, have overwhelmingly been relegated to the sidelines, unless scholars are considering responses of writers, artists, and intellectuals to the war.[62] This lacuna may stem from some of the methodological obstacles addressed further below. Foreign media reports from the era also failed to capture the voices of the civilian majority who did not directly fight in the conflict.[63]

Yet, civilians' perspectives and memories of the war are critical to comprehending changes and ongoing debates with deep international and regional implications, especially surrounding current events in Algeria.[64] The Algerian state has held the fear of a return to disorder or an uptick in insurgency over the population like a sword of Damocles from the 2000s onward.[65] Analysts have pointed, without much evidence from the ground, to a supposed lingering fear among Algerians as a driver behind their key political decisions—namely, a purported desire not to come out en masse to challenge their regime during the Arab Spring.[66] A better understanding of at least some civilians' responses, as reflected in humor, to the circumstances of Algeria's Black Decade could assist specialists seeking to comprehend the 1990s and its enduring legacies.

Moreover, recent events have highlighted a greater need for deeper knowledge surrounding Algeria's conflict of the 1990s and its afterlives for Algerians and the region. Memories of the 1990s conflict along with events linked to the broader political crisis that it grew from have been present in the ongoing 2019 Ḥirāk movement in Algeria.[67] The so-called Arab Spring has invited comparison, sometimes accurate, sometimes inaccurate, between Algeria's 1988 October uprising, democratic transition, and subsequent armed conflict and other cases of territories undergoing political change following the events of 2010–2011.[68] After four attacks in the Ile de France region in January 2015, popular columnist and commentator on the Middle East Robert Fisk wrongly attributed the motivations of the assailants, who were of Algerian origin, to "wounds" of the colonial past. In the piece, he read the violence of the 1990s as a sign of lingering radicalization of Algerians due to the brutality of French imperialism.[69] The present work shows instead that Algerian civilians could actively reject and dissociate themselves from bloodshed through humor. As such, it serves to correct misunderstandings about this important episode in the recent Maghribi past while illuminating a wider range of experiences and contemporary understandings of the war than previously available.

In addition to being a history of humor and its functions over time, this book argues for the importance of humor as a source for historical work. The challenges confronting scholars working on Algeria's postindependence historiography are similar to those faced by historians working on other postcolonial states around the region and elsewhere. In her pivotal article on the challenges of reconstructing Algeria's postindependence history, Malika Rahal has called for historians to seek out more diverse sources for this past.[70] Historians Jean Allman and Omnia El-Shakry concur that postindependence history in the Middle East, Africa, and other settings can be complicated to access because of the very deeply political nature and complexities of the postindependence state archive.[71] I propose that humor can provide an archive beyond official state records yielding varying perspectives into these complex and contested pasts. Humor comprises a generally underutilized archive for the consideration of popular forms of nation-building as well as nation-contending in the Maghrib, the Middle East, and Africa.[72]

Continued questions and sensitivities surrounding the Time of Terrorism make work on the 1990s particularly difficult to undertake. Some groups speak openly about the events. Yet, the conditions of the conflict's peace process, including bans on any critique of the state's actions, may have prevented the emergence of widespread, shared social memories surrounding the conflict.[73] Humor, as this book shows, comprises an understudied and often underutilized source for reconstructing these and other hard-to-access pasts.

Reconstructing a story of civilians during the Black Decade requires not only innovative sources but also a careful methodology for discussing events that continue to be mired in uncertainty. Multiple theories abound as to which actors carried out the war's worst atrocities. My approach to violence in Algeria in the 1990s breaks away from visions of the conflict as a repetition of past patterns of behavior; a direct result of past violence, particularly the colonial period that dominates Maghribi historiography; or practices from the past disrupting the then present.[74] I seek to retrace events as they unfolded and give detail as transparent as possible about conflicting accounts of the violence.[75] However, my concern revolves less around what took place in the 1990s and rests more with how narratives about the violence, whether accurate or inaccurate or truthful perhaps to the best knowledge of the individuals who crafted them, intersected with and possibly reinforced or redefined violence.

I further demonstrate that some civilians sought through humorous discourse to undercut the idea that the violence of the 1990s, often called "Algerian violence," was in any way Algerian. Some joke-tellers and cartoonists strove to disassociate the perpetrators of violence from a national community that they "invented."[76] The narratives that they crafted rejected the notion of the conflict as explicitly Algerian violence. Instead, they anchored the violence in actors outside of the national community as they defined it or ascribed it to foreign agents. Moussaoui asserts that newspaper cultures, which he linked to government rhetoric, pushed the notion of armed rebel groups as foreign actors. I find that jokes articulated the same idea, while the popularity of cartoonists who distanced rebels from the nation demonstrates that some Algerian communities agreed with this interpretation of events.[77] These results may not be surprising. "Nationalizing" humor and comedy already had deep roots in Algeria by the 1990s.[78] It is because of humor's role as a popular space for defining and redefining the nation that I have chosen the title *Humor and Power in Algeria* for this volume. The cover image, imagining Algeria as a man kicking a French figure (then–governor general Robert Lacoste), also demonstrates the centrality of humor to nationalist rhetoric and imagery, here in a pronationalist piece of propaganda from the revolution.[79]

I do not aim to use the case of violence in the 1990s to speak, as others have, to global trends in Islamism, beyond the ability of Islamists to harness humor; the violence grew out of circumstances particular to Algeria, although connections existed between armed rebel and state agents in Algeria and elsewhere.[80] I acknowledge these links when necessary. The armed conflict that broke out in the 1990s in Algeria seems to have been inspired by questions of the legitimacy of the state, especially after the 1992 military interruption of the electoral process, as well as the potential place of the FIS in society. Violence was connected to national and international politics but could also be locally motivated, as seen in the score-settling attacks that Luis Martinez describes in his ethnographic study of two Algiers suburbs in the early and mid-1990s, then hotbeds of armed group activity.[81] Jacob Mundy likewise envisions the violence as increasingly "disarticulated" from national politics after 1993.[82] Fighting between the armed groups or between the groups and civilian militias also appears to have been common. Economic factors certainly seem to have been at play as well.[83] Through humor, some Algerians put forth ideas concerning political actors' motivations as well as the nature of Black Decade violence.

METHODOLOGIES, TERMINOLOGY, AND PERIODIZATION

Humor is a complex subject for historical inquiry. Jokes and cartoons can hold multiple meanings, not all clear at first glance to historians deciphering them decades after their creation. To accomplish the tasks laid out above, I draw on a combination of archival sources collected in Algeria, France, and the United States as well as oral history testimonies with over fifty oral history narrators. I refer to these study participants as *narrators* to stress their agency in creating their own testimony and in line with the Oral History Association's conventions.[84]

The Time of Terrorism remains a sensitive topic in Algeria. Despite some public discourse surrounding the conflict (rhetoric that I examine when appropriate) and increasing interest in the events with the ongoing Ḥirāk protest movement in Algeria, it remains difficult to conduct interviews with ordinary citizens about the Black Decade due to the potential for negative government or community response.[85] As a result and to minimize risk, almost all of my Algerian narrators are public figures, mainly hailing from the country's northern regions, who have previously spoken out on the issues that I requested they address in our exchanges. A handful of those interviewed were foreign scholars or journalists present in Algeria during the Black Decade. The status of most of my Algerian narrators as northern city-dwelling intellectuals means that the humor that I collected from them or that they produced might have echoed the viewpoints of the educated circles that they frequented more than the attitudes of the general population. At the same time, this humor could have circulated beyond these social groups, as some of my narrators attested and as contemporary scandals surrounding humor show.[86] To try to evaluate whether the conflict's combatants used humor, I spoke with journalists and scholars who had contact with the military or armed groups, including rank-and-file soldiers. As with normal civilians, I had to refrain from holding oral history exchanges with individuals who fought in the war. Article Forty-Six of the Charter for Peace and National Reconciliation makes inquiry into the actions of the state during the war illegal and punishable by imprisonment or fine.[87] Former partisans of the armed groups, although sometimes known to the state or their communities, live in circumstances where their past or academic-led interviews surrounding it could incite state repression.[88] For this reason, to minimize risk to narrators and in consultation with the sponsoring agency for my Algerian visa and residency permit (the Center of Maghribi Studies [Centre d'études maghrébines en Algérie] in Oran), I did not include any combatants in my study. Despite the terms of Article Forty-Six, some Algerians have discussed the conflict openly.[89] These include militants belonging to groups for the remembrance of the conflict and its victims such as Al-Ajouad or SOS Disparus. I acknowledge this public discourse when appropriate in the pages that follow.

Some public figures to whom I spoke fit a profile similar to that of populations I refrained from trying to interview. Some intellectuals and cartoonists whose testimonies I include spent extensive time in more working-class areas of the country. They have also frequently attempted to address issues or reproduce the voices of underrepresented communities in their work. Cartoonists in particular could draw inspiration from orally transmitted jokes that crossed socioeconomic barriers and lines demarcating geographic regions.[90] Their words are not, therefore, only reflections of an elite intellectual community sundered from the rest of the population.

In addition to jokes and testimonies collected through oral histories and print sources, I analyze thousands of caricatures published in Algeria's main Arabophone and Francophone newspapers along with almost a hundred jokes in Arabic, French, and Tamazight. Jokes and caricatures proved among the most popular forms of humor from this era, especially the Black Decade of approximately 1992 to 2005, that are still available to historians, so I hone in on them for this project. I collected these resources from archives and narrators located in Algeria, France, and the United States. This archive cannot reveal all of the political humor and humorous exchanges that existed in Algerian circles in the postindependence period, specifically the 1990s; I did not uncover, for instance, a sense of how women particularly engaged with humor, but I do discuss gendered aspects of jokes and cartoons.[91] These limitations notwithstanding, the messages that emerge from these humorous archives reveal powerful and changing attitudes as the country moved through different eras of its contemporary past.

I have generally not included extensive quotes from narrators about their experiences. In part, this decision stemmed from my desire to produce a standalone piece allotting me the space to comprehensively address their testimonies and the conditions in which I collected them. I also wanted to avoid any confusion between my interpretation of humorous materials and their stories. Where possible, when citing a joke told to me through an oral history exchange, I have mentioned narrators' interpretations of the joke, if they offered them, but in such a way as to clearly differentiate their reading from my own. Narrators did not necessarily agree with, create, or circulate the anonymously produced jokes that they shared with me. Therefore, my citation of them as sources for jokes should not be considered a sign of such actions on their part. Narrators' participation in this project was voluntary, and I offered them the opportunity to remain anonymous. The inclusion of some narrators' names and testimonies does not indicate an endorsement on their part of the content of this manuscript or of my reading of the sources at hand.

Humor is by its nature ambiguous and open to multiple interpretations. So how to overcome the challenge of making sense of a joke or cartoon retrieved from the past that once had a perhaps ephemeral meaning? To arrive at the most probable intended meaning of a joke or cartoon, I contextualize humor in events underway at the time. I also draw on critical, gender, semiotic, and humor theory and critical discourse analysis to make sense of diverse humorous expressions. I further determine the popularity, chronology, and impact of jokes and printed caricatures through cross-verifying their contents with information obtained through written archives. Whenever possible, in an attempt not to rely heavily on theories and approaches to humor developed outside of Algeria for analyzing humor produced or circulated within it, I have tried to pull in Algerians' own perspectives on the place of political humor within Algerian societies. Some jokes were adapted to Algeria from other contexts, but then individuals from inside the country eventually came to consider these works thoroughly Algerian. Finally, jokes and other popularly shared forms of humor are not necessarily signs of a collective ethos. While significantly characterized at times by Algerian actors as "Algerian humor," these artifacts cannot speak for the attitudes and opinions of communities across the country per se. For this reason, I try whenever possible to calibrate and be transparent about how widely transmitted a joke or discourse surrounding a cartoon was and when and how they were advanced or consumed and by whom. By leaning into these uncertainties, I aim to offer approximate understandings of at least some Algerian communities' employment of humor (namely, Algerian humor) at certain moments of the territory's past. However, I do not propose that my interpretations of jokes or cartoons are the only ones possible. Chapter 3, for instance, argues that jokes intersected with rumors and conspiracy theories to bolster the power of the war's belligerents. At the same time, civilians always got the last word or laugh in these jokes, a testimony to how Algerians may have concurrently used jokes filled with irony to resist the military and armed groups. While I disclose when and where a narrator assisted me with understanding a work of humor, any mistakes in interpretation are my own.

The resulting study is informed as well as possible by an archive that, due to the political sensitivities and the natural loss of testimonies to time, is most certainly not complete. However, once again, comparing the content of oral histories with written material helped me fill in any potential gaps. I have included citations to all sources for the same or similar humorous material for the sake of transparency. With a focus mainly on cartoons and jokes, this book also does not purport to be an exhaustive study of Algerian humor but rather represents a contribution to a broader and very robust conversation surrounding the topic, amplified recently by the Ḥirāk movement (which I return to in the conclusion) and a conversation being led by many Algerian scholars.[92]

Regarding terminology, the Algerian War of Independence was known in France until 1999 as the *guerre sans nom* (the "war without a name"). In contrast, the conflict that engulfed many parts of Algeria from approximately 1992 to 2005 has collected varying monikers over the years. The 1990s armed struggle was and continues to be a war with many names. This list of appellations includes the Arabic terms *waqt al-irhāb* (the "time of terrorism") and *snīn al-irhāb* (the "years of terrorism") as well as the Dark or Black Decade, the "years of blood" (*les années du sang*), and the "red/bloody years" or "decade." During the reconciliation process and in the laws that it enacted toward the end of the conflict from 1999 to 2005, the government officially referred to the armed struggle as the "national tragedy." The use of the term *tragedy* worked with the government's aim of "turning the page" on the previous years of bloodshed; tragedies often take place without anyone being at fault. As Vish Sakthivel reminds us, Algerians' choice of which term to present to certain audiences can prove a highly political one.[93] Hugh Roberts argues that the term *civil war* does not accurately describe the fighting that took place, as the state and armed groups were not as ideologically divided as they may have seemed and the armed groups generally did not establish their authority over a set and sizeable territory. What is more, French observers labeled the conflict a civil war, while neither the government nor the armed groups welcomed the use of the term.[94] However, some Algerians do not hesitate to assign this term to the political crisis that tore Algeria's invented national community apart. For example, the late Malik Aït Aoudia, one of the producers behind the documentary on the war, *Algérie: Autopsie d'une tragédie*, believes that *civil war* accurately describes the events that took place in the country in the 1990s.[95] The term *guerre contre les civiles* / "a war against civilians" is also used in common parlance.

I purposefully use all of the phrases that Algerians themselves have used to designate the violence that took place in the 1990s in their country. Algerians' views of the war and what they prefer to call it reveal their interpretation of events, an important reality for historians to recognize.[96] The lack of a fixed term for the conflict among Algerians, including the narrators to whom I spoke for this study, echoes the great ambiguity and lack of unified discourse or social memories surrounding the conflict. The task of assigning an eventual official name to the conflict, I believe, should lie with individuals affected by this crisis, a further reason that I am interchangeably using all of the current terms.

The armed groups that rebelled against the state in the name of Islam and toward concrete political aims likewise accrued a number of names, and the usage of one instead of another could reveal a speaker's political leanings. For sympathizers, the mainly male insurgents were *maquisards* or *mudjahidin*, terms previously ascribed to nationalist fighters during the War of Independence. For the state and their opponents, they were simply "criminals."[97] Jokes and cartoons from the period only occasionally designated whether a person belonged to a particular armed group. Instead, they often referred to members of such groups as "terrorists," a moniker used by some in Algeria for the insurgents. In an attempt to adopt a more neutral stance, I refer to these groups either by name or as "insurgents" or "rebels."

"Civilians," "state," and "armed organization"—the categorization of Algerian populations during the conflict along these lines undergirds all readings of the war, yet the lines determining the boundaries of each group proved blurry and far from stable. Civilians could show empathy toward or actively support the conflicts' battling sides. The same family could have some members backing or being part of the state and military, and others backing or active in the rebel camp. Given that my conversations were with civilian actors and secondary accounts written by civilians corroborated some of the information that these interlocutors provided, the humor presented here circulated at least in noncombatant circles. It is possible, however, that these jokes and even caricatures were also consumed by military and rebel partisans; we know, for instance, that rebels paid attention to caricatures. While I focus on civilian patterns of humor as opposed to other types (military or insurgent), I did not find evidence in the admittedly limited published memoirs and interviews with partisans of these groups that they produced and consumed a humor of their own that they may have equally claimed to be Algerian.[98]

For a definition of *humor* as I use the term throughout this manuscript, I rely on Rachel V. Kutz-Flamenbaum's encompassing delineation of it as "comic efforts to stimulate joy or amusement in others or the product of those efforts."[99] I use *comedy* to refer to constructed products intended by their creators to produce joy or amusement in an audience, as opposed to humor, which can also occur spontaneously or be situational.[100] *Satire* I employ only in the sense of a mockery or exaggeration of discourse, actions, groups, or individuals. In oral history exchanges with narrators held in Modern Standard Arabic or *darja*, I asked them to discuss *ḍaḥik* (laughter), *fukāha* (humor), *sukhiriyya* (sarcasm), and *hijā'* (satire). When conversations occurred in French, I employed the terms *rire* (laughter), *humour* (humor), *sarcasme* (sarcasm), and *satire* (satire). I did not treat these terms as interchangeable during oral history exchanges, nor do I treat them as interchangeable here, but I mentioned these different terms connected to humor to the narrators to ensure that I captured a broader vision of the different kinds and consequences of humor through our exchanges. These translations are not perfect, and wherever possible I attempt to include the original language of the narrators for transparency, especially when it comes to the content of jokes.

Unlike with other moments of Algeria's past, no consensus appears to exist among scholars as to the beginning and end dates of the 1990s conflict. Scholars point to the military's interruption in January 1992 of the second round of legislative elections that the FIS was poised to win as the starting point of the armed struggle, but violence had broken out the year before and was different in 1992 from what the bloodshed would eventually become in the following years.[101] Press culture did change in early 1992, so I consider it the beginning of the war, although, once again, this project traces continuities between humor from the conflict and that from earlier periods. The year 2002 is often given in the secondary literature as the final point of the Black Decade, but generally with no justification. Data from the Uppsala Conflict Data Program, limited in terms of its scope to state violence, suggests that the numbers of dead from 2001 and

2003 remained steady. The end date of 2005 more accurately reflects a decline in violence by the mid-2000s, and that year witnessed then-president Abdelaziz Bouteflika's proposal of a second major peace legislation, the Charter for Peace and National Reconciliation, which prompted strong humorous responses.[102] It is for this reason that this book concludes with the early 2000s.

SUMMARY OF CHAPTERS

This volume's first chapter looks at humor as a tool for bringing populations into politicized conversations in the context of the late colonial period and the first decades of independence, from approximately 1920 through the 1980s. It argues that regimes, political movements, and ordinary individuals considered humor a tool for instilling sentiments of belonging within different communities. They were successful in some cases, as seen through the popularity of certain humorous products from this period. A particularly salient question throughout these shifts was what Algeria meant and who could claim to be Algerian. New and repurposed forms of humor assisted agents of varying backgrounds in articulating powerful expressions of Algerian identity in ways intended to bring some populations together but generally at the exclusion of others.

The second chapter, focusing on Algeria's October 1988 Revolution and brief democratic transition from 1989 to 1992, takes this assertion a step further by positing that humor can play a critical role in the building of social movements and non-movements, potentially convincing these groups to take certain political actions based on ideological affiliations and beliefs. Just as humor binds individuals together, through the same process of defining the boundaries of identity, the producers of humor can employ their craft to drive wedges between communal sectors, evincing humor's potential power as a tool of exclusion and conflict. Chapter 2 notes how new parties that formed in the wake of October 1988 along with old stalwarts of power vied for followers in ways that sometimes frustrated, frightened, or galvanized the citizens they sought to bring into their political fold.

The conflict of the 1990s witnessed a ratcheting up of this process. With many previously established genres for humorous expression curtailed as an atmosphere of uncertainty and horror took hold, joke-tellers and cartoonists persisted with their craft during the war. Chapter 3 contributes to theoretical debates about the capacity of jokes to work as tools of subversion or, conversely, as indirect bolsters to authoritarian power. It takes as its case study jokes about the violent war between the military and armed groups claiming to want to install a more Islamic form of government and to overthrow the state that had prevented the FIS's 1992 electoral victory. Some Algerians crafted and shared jokes in seemingly clandestine manners that emphasized the direness of civilians' lot and, conversely, the strength of their assailants: once again, both the warring armed rebel organizations and the official state. These jokes appear to have both simultaneously undermined and enhanced the power of these competing authoritarian camps. At the same time, they centered the invented Algerian national community through self-deprecation, a long-standing practice in the country, with the "civilian-victim" population. Joke-tellers and consumers thereby distanced themselves from the perpetrators of violence, de-Algerianizing it in the process. Once again, humor served as an important form of political discourse and one that became even more important as the circumstances of the conflict limited other outlets for expression. This humor differed while also building on earlier humorous practices in the region, testifying to the importance of examining humor over time.

Moving away from orally transmitted jokes most likely produced and shared by ordinary citizens to the work of professional humorists, chapter 4 turns to the cartoonists who continued to create scathing politicized interpretations of events in Algeria in rhythm with their unfolding. Caricatures persisted into the 1990s while the country's earlier *bandes dessinées* traditions fell away as violence swelled. Cartoonists worked under constraints and in tense environments where lives were on the line. For the most part and in light of these restrictions, it appears that those artists who maintained a presence in print used their pens to denounce the insurgents, sometimes fueling theories surrounding them put forth by the government. Their drawings were not without consequence; caricaturists drew some of the only contemporary in-the-moment visual representations of the conflict that, while subject to censorship, may have been less so than the photographs of violence that the government permitted to appear in local and foreign media.[103] Chapter 4 considers how cartoonists' interpretations and representations of violence intersected with other narratives surrounding the bloodshed and actors' different roles within them. Their illustrations potentially shaped or reinforced understandings of the war, how to best resolve it, and who was ultimately responsible for the bloodshed. Through these images, cartoonists separated the armed groups claiming to rebel in the name of Islam from a peaceful Muslim-majority nation. Once again, Algerians turned to humor as an outlet for advancing powerful ideas about the political circumstances in which they lived with potentially significant consequences.

Chapter 5 then analyzes how cartoonists used their art to break with government rhetoric during the reconciliation process, which began in 1994 but picked up in pace from 1997 through 2005. Their work comprises a key example of a group using humor to confront official policy and forgetting about the atrocities that Algerian communities had just witnessed. These artists appear to have sought justice in their own way for the crimes of the 1990s as the government arranged blanket amnesties for rebel groups and banned investigations into the actions of its own agents during the conflict. Toward this end, the country's major caricaturists developed a carnivalesque lowering of some of its most sacred symbols and prominent figures. They also encouraged the formation of specific social memories surrounding the conflict of the 1990s just as the government looked to move past the violence by casting a shroud over events.

Above all, this book tells the story of the creativity and resilience of some Algerian communities. It illuminates the ambiguous, multifaceted ways in which political humor can assist populations with making sense of, playing with, and staking out claims in atmospheres of civil strife, state repression, and limited freedom of speech. Humor's capacity as a tool of war or peace is investigated here. The work as a whole calls for scholars to seriously consider humorous cultures and how they change over time and can function in different, even contradictory, ways. Finally, I hope to pay homage to the humorists such as Mekbel lost to the Black Decade and to highlight the voices of civilian populations caught up in the prolonged political and military struggle.

NOTES

1. Saïd Mekbel, "Mesmar J'ha," *Le Matin*, December 3, 1994. All translations are my own unless otherwise noted.

2. See chap. 4.

3. James McDougall, *A History of Algeria* (Cambridge: Cambridge University Press, 2017), 253–255.

4. Lazhari Labter, *Journalistes algériens, 1988–1998* (Algiers: Chihab, 2005), 130.

5. "Killed for a Column," *Irish Times*, May 2, 1998, https://www.irishtimes.com/news/killed-for-a-column-1.148284.

6. Mekbel himself referred to the "death lists" circulated by insurgents as the "hit parade." See DzWikileaks, "Said Mekbel: Je suis 4eme au hit parade des journalistes à tuer," Facebook, December 3, 2012, https://www.facebook.com/watch/?v=474778652572354.

7. Sometimes written *Djeha* and most accurately transliterated from Modern Standard Arabic as *Jiḥā*.

8. Abderrahmane Lounes, *Djeha* (Algiers: Casbah, 2009), dedication.

9. Lounes, *Djeha*, dedication.

10. See the bulk of his work from *Le Matin*.

11. Fellow journalists around the world paid homage to Mekbel and reprinted some of his editorial pieces. See, for instance, "'I Really Feel as if I Have Vanished,'" trans. Marlé Hammond, *Los Angeles Times*, March 15, 1995, EVB13.

12. The exact number of deaths that resulted from the conflict is difficult to estimate. I use one hundred thousand based on higher-end estimates calculated by human rights groups and

international organizations. See Jacob Mundy, *Imaginative Geographies of Algerian Violence* (Palo Alto: Stanford University Press, 2015), 40–43.

13. Mundy, *Imaginative Geographies*; Paul Silverstein, "An Excess of Truth: Violence, Conspiracy Theorizing, and the Algerian Civil War," *Anthropological Quarterly* 75, no. 4 (2002): 643–674.

14. See, for instance, Chad Bryant, "The Language of Resistance? Czech Jokes and Joke Telling under Nazi Occupation, 1943–1945," *Journal of Contemporary History* 41, no. 1 (2006): 133–151.

15. Christie Davies has been the loudest proponent in the field for the notion that jokes cannot result in meaningful change. He has declared, "Jokes are a thermometer, not a thermostat." See Davies, "Reply to Abedinifard, Jokes Have No Consequences," *Humor* 30, no. 2 (2017): 239–246; Davies, "Humour and Protest: Jokes under Communism," *International Review of Social History* 52 (2007): 291–306, especially 300.

16. See, for instance, Antonin J. Obrdlik, "'Gallows Humor,' a Sociological Phenomenon," *American Journal of Sociology* 47, no. 5 (1942): 709–716; Mostafa Abedinifard, "Structural Functions of the Targeted Joke," *Humor* 29, no. 3 (2016): 337–357. Abedinifard and Davies debated this question in the journal *Humor*. See Abedinifard, "Reply to Davies," *Humor* 30, no. 2 (2017): 247–253; Davies, "Reply to Abedinifard."

17. For the view that humor can serve to dissipate oppositional pressure on a regime, see, for instance, Alexander Rose, "When Politics Is a Laughing Matter," *Policy Review* 110 (2001–2002): 59–72.

18. The question of humor's influence on the outcome of the January 2011 revolution became a subject of debate in Mohamed M. Helmy and Sabine Frerichs, "Stripping the Boss: The Powerful Role of Humor in the Egyptian Revolution 2011," *Integrative Psychological and Behavioral Science* 47, no. 4 (2013): 450–481; L. Laineste, "Can Stripping the Boss Be More Than a Joke?," *Integrative Psychological and Behavioral Science* 47 (2013): 482–491.

19. Sandrine Sanos, "The Sex and Race of Satire," *Jewish History* 32 (2018): 33–63.

20. See, for instance, Sanos, "Sex and Race"; Randall Bytwerk, *Julius Streicher: Nazi Editor of the Notorious Anti-Semitic Newspaper* Der Stürmer (New York: Copper Square Press, 2001).

21. Saba Mahmood, "Religious Reason and Secular Affect: An Incommensurable Divide?," *Critical Inquiry* 35 (2009): 836–862.

22. See, for instance, Achille Mbembe, "La 'chose' et ses doubles dans la caricature camerounaise," *Cahiers d'études africaines* 36, no. 141/142 (1996): 143–170; Hannah Summerfelt, Louis Lippman, and Ira E. Hyman Jr., "The Effect of Humor on Memory," *Journal of General Psychology* 137, no. 4 (2010): 376–394. For an overview of the different schools or theories of humor studies, see John Morreall, "Philosophy of Humor," in *Stanford Encyclopedia of Humor*, last modified November 12, 2012, http://plato.stanford.edu/entries/humor/#SupThe.

23. Charles Tripp, "Power and Ridicule: Political Mockery and Subversion in the Middle East and North Africa" (lecture, Centre d'Etudes Maghrébines à Tunis, February 14, 2019), https://www.themaghribpodcast.com/2019/03/power-and-ridicule-political-mockery.html.

24. Abdalle Ahmed and David Smith, "Somali Comic Received Death Threats before Murder," *Guardian*, August 2, 2012, https://www.theguardian.com/world/2012/aug/02/somali-comic-marshale-death-threat#maincontent; "Ali Ferzat," Cartooning for Peace, accessed July 18, 2018, https://www.cartooningforpeace.org/soutiens/ali-ferzat-syrie/.

25. For excellent works related to humor in the Middle East and Africa that consider humorous genres separately from one another, see, for instance, Aḥmad Muḥammad Hūfī, *al-Fukāha fī al-'adab* (Cairo: Dār Nahḍa Miṣr, 1967); 'Ādel Hamūda, *al-Nukta al-siyāsīya*

(Cairo: al-Firsān lil-Nashar, 1999); Samer Shehata, "The Politics of Laughter," *Folklore* 103, no. 1 (1992): 75–91; Palmira Brummett, *Image and Imperialism in the Ottoman Revolutionary Press, 1908–1911* (Binghamton: SUNY Press, 2000); Fatma Müge Göçek, ed., *Political Cartoons in the Middle East* (Princeton, NJ: Markus Wiener, 1998); Hammadi Tamimi, *al-Fukāha fī shiʻr al-Tūnisī* (Tunis: Dar Bou Salamah, 1986). Some notable exceptions to this rule of analysts looking at different genres of humor separately are Sandra Swart, "'The Terrible Laughter of the Afrikaner': Towards a Social History of Humor," *Journal of Social History* 42, no. 2 (2009): 889–917; Ebenezer Obadare, *Humor, Silence, and Civil Society in Nigeria* (Rochester, NY: University of Rochester Press, 2016).

26. See, for instance, Anastasiya Astapova, *Humor and Rumor in the Post-Soviet Authoritarian State* (London: Lexington Books, 2021).

27. These works include Ziad Fahmy, *Ordinary Egyptians: Creating the Nation through Popular Culture* (Palo Alto: Stanford University Press, 2011); Arthur Asseraf, *Electric News in Colonial Algeria* (Oxford: Oxford University Press, 2019).

28. Mbembe, "La ʻchose,'" 144.

29. Khalid Kishtainy, *Arab Political Humor* (London: Quartet Books, 1985).

30. For more on the inherently social nature of humor, see Henri Bergson, *Le Rire* (Paris: Félix Alcan, 1900).

31. See, for instance, V. I. Želvys, "Obscene Humor: What the Hell?," *Humor* 3, no. 3 (1990): 323–332.

32. See, for instance, Rachel V. Kutz-Flamenbaum, "Humor and Social Movements," *Sociology Compass* 8, no. 3 (2014): 294.

33. Kutz-Flamenbaum, "Humor and Social Movements," 294.

34. David M. Bozzini, "The Catch-22 of Resistance: Jokes and the Political Imagination of Eritrean Conscripts," *Africa Today* 60, no. 2 (2013): 38–64.

35. Mostafa Abedinifard, "Humor and Gender Hegemony: The Panoptical Role of Ridicule vis-à-vis Gender" (PhD diss., University of Alberta, 2015).

36. James C. Scott developed the idea of a "weapon of the weak," a tool of resistance for marginalized groups and actors, in *Weapons of the Weak: Everyday Forms of Peasant Resistance* (New Haven, CT: Yale University Press, 1985). For examples of work lauding humor as an arm for the disenfranchised or downtrodden without consideration of other possible functions, see Steve Lipman, *Laughter in Hell: The Use of Humor during the Holocaust* (Northvale, NJ: J. Aronson, 1991); Kathleen Stokker, *Folklore Fights the Nazis: Humor in Occupied Norway, 1940–1945* (Madison: University of Wisconsin Press, 1997); Emil Draitser, *Forbidden Laughter: Soviet Underground Jokes* (Los Angeles: Almanac, 1978). For excellent works that buck this trend and consider multiple simultaneous functions of humor, see Bryant, "Language of Resistance"; Christopher Rea, *The Age of Irreverence: A New History of Laughter in China* (Berkeley: University of California Press, 2015). Rea's work traces shifts in trends of laughter and comedy in China between the late nineteenth and mid-twentieth centuries.

37. See, for example, Bozzini, "Catch-22 of Resistance."

38. Bryant, "Language of Resistance."

39. One example of a work on comedy burgeoning in the wake of the Arab Spring that does not fully acknowledge earlier humorous practices is Jacob Høigilt, "Egyptian Comics and the Challenge to Patriarchal Authoritarianism," *International Journal of Middle East Studies* 49, no. 1 (2017): 111–131. He mistakenly asserts that "adult comics are a new medium in the Arab World." Some notable exceptions of work on Arab Spring humor that bring a more nuanced frame to humor and consider longer-held practices of humor prior to the

uprisings include Helmy and Frerichs, "Stripping the Boss"; Deepa Anagondahalli and Sahar Khamis, "Mubarak Framed! Humor and Political Activism before and during the Egyptian Revolution," *Arab Media and Society* 19 (2014): 1–16.

40. See, for instance, Walter Armbrust, *Mass Culture and Modernism in Egypt* (Cambridge: Cambridge University Press, 1996).

41. See, for instance, Phillip Dine's and Tony Langlois's essays in Patrick Crowley, ed., *Algeria: Nation, Culture, and Transnationalism, 1988–2015* (Liverpool: Liverpool University Press, 2017).

42. Jill Jarvis, *Decolonizing Memory: Algeria and the Politics of Testimony* (Durham, NC: Duke University Press, 2021).

43. See discussion of humor in Algeria's 2019 protests in this volume's conclusion.

44. Aïssa Khelladi, "Rire quand même: L'humour politique dans l'Algérie d'aujourd'hui," *Revue du monde musulman et de la Méditerranée* 77–78 (1996): 225–237; Allen Douglas and Fedwa Malti-Douglas, *Arab Comic Strips: Politics of an Emerging Mass Culture* (Bloomington: Indiana University Press, 1994), 174–197; Christiane Chaulet-Achour and Dalila Morsly, "Plus d'un siècle de rire en Algérie," in *2000 ans de rire* (Franc-Comtoises: Université de Franc-Comtoises, 2002), 55–65. Some Algerian students have begun producing master's and doctoral theses on Algerian political jokes, specifically those related to certain regions, but none of these works (to my knowledge) deal with jokes from the height of violence in the country in the 1990s. See, for example, Hamid Qarlifa, "al-Nukta al-siyāsiyya fī al-Jazā'ir: dirāsa al-muqārina bayna al-'ahadatayn al-ra'isiyyatayn, 1978–1992" (master's thesis, Université Abou Elkacem Saad Allah d'Alger 2, 2008). Interestingly, one of my narrators, Mustapha Benfodil, mentioned wanting to write a thesis on popular humor when he was a university student in the 1990s. He claimed that a professor discouraged him from doing so on the grounds that the topic was not academic enough. Interview with Mustapha Benfodil, August 31, 2014.

45. Humorist Mohand Fellag notes that the term hailed from a rumor at the time of Walt Disney's 1966 death that the famed animator and entrepreneur would be buried in Algeria. See Mohand Fellag, *Djurdjurassique Bled* (Paris: J. C. Lattès, 1996), 126.

46. For an overview of terms used to describe the Maghrib, see M'hamed Oualdi, *A Slave between Empires* (New York: Columbia University Press, 2020), 7–8.

47. For more on the racialization of religious categories, see Patricia Lorcin, "Imperialism, Colonial Identity, and Race," *History of Science Society* 90, no. 4 (1999): 653–679; Muriam Haleh Davis, *Markets of Civilization: Islam and Racial Capitalism in Algeria* (Durham, NC: Duke University Press, 2022).

48. Matthew Connolly, *A Diplomatic Revolution* (New York: Oxford University Press, 2002); Todd Shepard, *The Invention of Decolonization* (Ithaca, NY: Cornell University Press, 2006); Jeffrey James Byrne, *Mecca of the Revolution: Algeria, Decolonization, and the Third World Order* (Oxford: Oxford University Press, 2016).

49. For more on dignity as an emotion in the Algerian War of Independence, see Christiane Marie Abu-Sarah, "To Drink a Cup of Fire: Morality Tales and Moral Emotions in Anti-colonial Activism" (PhD diss., University of Maryland, 2019).

50. Michel Foucault, "Truth and Power," in *Power/Knowledge: Selected Interviews and Other Writings, 1972–1977*, ed. Colin Gordon (New York: Pantheon Books, 1980), 131–132. Silverstein first applied Foucault's concept to rumors and conspiracies surrounding the 1990s in Algeria. See Silverstein, "Excess of Truth," especially 664–665.

51. Mehdi Semati, "The Geopolitics of *Parazit*, the Iranian Televisual Sphere, and the Global Infrastructure of Political Humor," *Popular Communication* 10, no. 1–2 (2012): 119–130.

52. See the joke on neighbors and checkpoints derived from a Polish joke in chap. 2.

53. Observation based on the author's conversations with colleagues from Morocco and Somalia.

54. Craig Zelizer, "Laughing Our Way to Peace or War: Humour and Peacebuilding," *Journal of Conflictology* 1, no. 2 (2010): 1–9.

55. In addition to Lipman, Stokker, and Draitser, see Bruce Adams, *Tiny Revolutions in Russia: Twentieth-Century Soviet and Russian History in Anecdotes* (London: Routledge, 2005).

56. See, for example, Asef Bayat, *Life as Politics: How Ordinary People Change the Middle East*, 2nd ed. (Palo Alto: Stanford University Press, 2013).

57. These works include Khelladi, "Rire quand même"; Mark McKinney, "The Frontier and the Affrontier: French-Language Algerian Comics and Cartoons Confront the Nation," *European Comic Art* 1, no. 2 (2008): 175–200; Abderrahmane Moussaoui, *De la violence en Algérie* (Paris: Actes Sud, 2006), 358–388.

58. See Moussaoui, *De la violence*, 358–388.

59. Khelladi, "Rire quand même," 233.

60. Moussaoui especially stresses humor's role as a coping mechanism for civilians as well as a tool of resistance and simultaneous self-deprecation, a theme I return to in chap. 3. Moussaoui, *De la violence*, 358–388.

61. See, for instance, James D. Le Sueur, *Algeria since 1989: Between Terror and Democracy* (London: Zed Books, 2010).

62. One notable exception to this pattern is William Lawrence's dissertation on youth. William Lawrence, "Representing Algerian Youth" (PhD diss., Tufts University, 2005). There are a handful of Black Decade memoirs that come from non-elite circles. See Nadia and Baya Gacemi, *I, Nadia, Wife of a Terrorist*, trans. Paul Cote and Constantina Mitchell (Lincoln: University of Nebraska Press, 2006). For more on intellectuals', writers', and artists' perspectives, see, for instance, Tristan Leperlier, *Algérie, les écrivains et la décennie noire* (Paris: CRNS, 2018); Cynthia Becker, "Exile, Memory, and Healing in Algeria: Denis Martinez and La Fenêtre du Vent," *African Arts* 42, no. 2 (2009): 24–31.

63. In a conversation with historian of modern Algeria James McDougall, Judith Scheele lamented the foreign coverage of the country's Black Decade / Time of Terrorism / civil conflict / war of the 1990s that rendered the territory a site of horror that seemed devoid of people. McDougall, *History of Algeria*, 292n5.

64. Faouzia Zeraoulia, "The Memory of the Civil War in Algeria," *Contemporary Review of the Middle East* 7, no. 1 (2020): 25–53.

65. For more on this subject, see Thomas Serres, *L'Algérie face à la catastrophe suspendue* (Tunis: Karthala, 2019).

66. See, for instance, George Joffé, "The Arab Spring in North Africa," *Journal of North African Studies* 16, no. 4 (2011): 507–532.

67. See Zeraoulia, "Memory of the Civil War"; Elizabeth Perego, "Beyond Paralyzing Terror: The 'Black Decade' in the Algerian Hirak," *JadMag* 7, no. 3 (2019).

68. For more on this topic, see Edward McAllister, "Immunity to the Arab Spring?," *New Middle Eastern Studies* 3 (2013).

69. Robert Fisk, "The Postcolonial Wound That Still Bleeds France," *Independent*, January 10, 2015, 10. See a critique of this piece in Natalya Vince, "Dangerous Shortcuts: Paris Attacks and the War of Independence," *Textures du Temps / Ḥakabāt al-Zaman*, November 22, 2015, https://texturesdutemps.hypotheses.org/1754.

70. Malika Rahal, "Fused Together and Torn Apart: Stories and Violence in Contemporary Algeria," *History and Memory* 24, no. 1 (2012): 118–151.

71. Jean Allman, "Phantoms of the Archive," *American Historical Review* 118, no. 1 (2013): 104–129; Omnia El Shakry, "'History without Documents,'" *American Historical Review* 120, no. 3 (2015): 920–934.

72. Exceptions include Fahmy, *Ordinary Egyptians*.

73. See Edward McAllister, "Yesterday's Tomorrow Is Not Today" (PhD diss., Oxford University, 2015); Article Forty-Six, "La Charte pour la paix et la réconciliation nationale," *Journal officiel de la République Algérienne*, February 28, 2006, 7. Zeraoulia's work suggests that a "public narrative" is emerging after the start of the 2019 protests. Zeraoulia, "The Memory of the Civil War in Algeria."

74. Abdelmajid Hannoum views the 1990s as a consequence of earlier colonial violence—namely, the violence of modernity. Luis Martinez contends that the violence stemmed from a long-standing imaginary or worldview that encouraged Algerians to seek war booty. See Abdelmajid Hannoum, *Violent Modernity: France in Algeria* (Cambridge, MA: Harvard University Press, 2010); Luis Martinez, *The Algerian Civil War* (New York: Columbia University Press, 2000). For a critique and overview of problematic ideas of cyclical or endemic violence, in the "West" as well as the Middle East and North Africa, see James McDougall, "Savage Wars? Codes of Violence in Algeria, 1830s–1990s," *Third World Quarterly* 26, no. 1 (2008): 117–131. Moussaoui likewise contests accounts of the 1990s that claim the violence stemmed from earlier conflict or economic issues alone. See Moussaoui, *De la violence*.

75. In this effort, I build on a number of works on Black Decade violence. See Mundy, *Imaginative Geographies*; Abed Charef, *Algérie: Autopsie d'un massacre* (Paris: Editions de l'Aube, 1998); Stathis Kalyvas, "Wanton and Senseless? The Logic of Massacres in Algeria," *Rationality and Society* 11, no. 3 (1999): 243–285; Myriam Aït-Aoudia, *L'expérience démocratique en Algérie (1988–1992)* (Algiers: Koukou, 2016).

76. Anne McClintock expands on Benedict Anderson's critical concept of "imagined communities" (groups of individuals believing that they share commonalities and should form a nation) by stressing that they are invented. See Anne McClintock, "Family Feuds: Gender, Nationalism, and Family," *Feminist Review* 44 (1993): 61; Benedict Anderson, *Imagined Communities*, 2nd ed. (London: Verso, 1991).

77. Moussaoui, *De la violence*, 353–354.

78. See chapter 1.

79. Political tract from SHD 1 H 2588. I am grateful to Christiane Marie Abu-Sarah for sharing this material with me.

80. See, for instance, Le Sueur, *Between Terror and Democracy*.

81. Martinez, *Algerian Civil War*.

82. Mundy, *Imaginative Geographies*, 50, 61.

83. See, for instance, Martinez, *Algerian Civil War*.

84. See "Principles and Best Practices Glossary," Oral History Association, accessed February 12, 2021, https://www.oralhistory.org/best-practices-glossary/.

85. To my knowledge, only two Algerian scholars have undertaken the task, and both admitted there were risks to participants or anonymity had to be offered to them. Faouzia Zeraoulia conducted interviews with seventy Algerians about social memories of the conflict, including victims of armed group violence. She did not include the full names of her informants, however, and she found that victims of state violence would not speak with her or

her team of researchers. See Zeraoulia, "Memory of the Civil War." Dalia Ghanem-Yazbeck also conducted research with former members of the armed groups, survivors of the conflict in Bentalha (the site of one of the war's worst massacres), and military and medical personnel. She admits that her interviews may have posed a risk to the former rebels. Dalia Ghanem-Yazbeck, "Challenging Fieldwork," *Anthropology Matters Journal* 17, no. 2 (2017): 28–56; Dalia Ghanem, "Sociologie de la violence extrême en Algérie" (PhD diss., Versailles Saint-Quentin-en-Yvelines University, 2012).

86. See, for instance, the account of a 2004 Dilem cartoon on pilgrims in Mecca provoking outrage from imams in mosques in Mustapha Benfodil, *Dilem président: Biographie d'un émeutier* (INAS, 2008), http://www.argotheme.com/dilempres%5B1%5D.pdf, 129–130.

87. Article Forty-Six, "La Charte pour la paix et la réconciliation nationale," *Journal officiel de la République Algérienne*, February 28, 2006, 7.

88. Ghanem explains that the terms of rebel combatants' reintegration into civil society explicitly forbid them from talking to "journalists and researchers." See Ghanem, "Challenging Fieldwork," 39, n. 11.

89. For example, memoires of the war exist. See, for instance, Nadia and Gacemi, *I, Nadia*.

90. See chap. 4 for more detail regarding this point.

91. For information on this topic, see Dalila Morsly, "Humour d'Algériennes, Hanan-El-Maz'ouka et Daïffa," in "Armées d'humour: Rires au féminin," ed. J. Stora and E. Pillet, special issue, *Humoresques* 11 (2000): 187–208.

92. See, among other works, Hiyem Cheurfa, "The Laughter of Dignity," *Jadaliyya*, March 26, 2019, https://www.jadaliyya.com/Details/38495/The-Laughter-of-Dignity-Comedy-and-Dissent-in-the-Algerian-Popular-Protests.

93. See Vish Sakthivel, "The Movement for a Society of Peace" (PhD diss., Oxford University, 2019).

94. See Hugh Roberts, *The Battlefield: Algeria, 1988–2002, Studies in a Broken Polity* (New York: Verso, 2003), 257–259.

95. Interview with Malik Aït Aoudia, December 19, 2014.

96. See forthcoming work by Sakthivel.

97. See, for instance, media coverage from the early 1990s such as *L'Hebdo libéré*.

98. Some of these accounts include Habib Souaïdia, *La sale guerre* (Paris: Découverte, 2001); Nadia and Gacemi, *I, Nadia*; Mohamed Samraoui, *Chroniques des années de sang* (Paris: Denoël, 2003).

99. Kutz-Flamenbaum, "Humor and Social Movements," 294.

100. Brett Mills, *Television Sitcom* (London: British Film Institute, 2005), 17.

101. Mundy makes this argument and illustrates that 1992 only became a significant date a few years into the war. Mundy, *Imaginative Geographies*, 39–40.

102. This organization is one of two whose data Mundy used to approximate the number of possible dead from the conflict. Mundy, *Imaginative Geographies*, 41; "PRIO Armed Conflict Dataset for Algeria," Uppsala Conflict Data Program, accessed February 15, 2021, https://ucdp.uu.se/country/615.

103. I owe this observation of cartoons responding in real time to events to Sandra Rousseau. See also Sandra Rousseau, "Une Drôle de mémoire: relations franco-algériennes et mémoire comique, 1954–2012" (PhD diss., Pennsylvania State University, 2015).

ONE

SIDE-SPLITTING WHILE NATION-FORMING, 1914 TO THE 1980s

THE FOLLOWING JOKE APPEARS IN a recent publication on Algerian political humor:

> Until 1990, Algeria endured a state-controlled press that was not too dissimilar from the Muscovite *Pravda*.[1] Every morning, *El Moudjahid*, the sole newspaper of the government and Party, denounced columns of workers and students who had the audacity to organize or prepare strikes.[2] Every morning, *El Moudjahid* revealed or denounced a plot hatched by foreign enemy forces, jealous of the radiant tomorrow of a serene socialism. Every morning, *El Moudjahid* announced the upcoming inauguration of the largest steelworks in Africa. It was in this context that a garbage collector from Algiers buys a kilogram of sardines that the vendor wrapped for him in an old edition of *El Moudjahid* with, on the front page, President Boumediene in the middle of workers from Hassi Messaoud on that well-known date of February 24, 1971, when he announced the nationalization of oil and gas production.[3] Unfortunately, before the garbage collector gets home, the sardines fall through the paper and our garbage collector finds himself with all of his sardines on the ground. Crazy with anger, the garbage collector grabs his friend as a witness and asks him: "How do you explain that every morning this newspaper can hold tons of lies, but it's incapable of transporting one little kilo of sardines?"[4]

> *Jusqu'en 1990, les Algériens ont subi une presse unique qui n'avait pas grand-chose à envier à la* Pravda *moscovite des années soixante. Chaque matin, El Moudjahid, le quotidien unique du gouvernement et du Parti, diffamait à longueur de colonnes les ouvriers et les étudiants qui avaient eu l'audace de se réunir ou de se préparer à faire grève. Chaque matin, El Moudjahid révélait*

ou dénonçait un complot ourdi par les forces ennemies de l'extérieur, jalouses des lendemains radieux d'un socialisme serein. Chaque matin, El Moudjahid annonçait l'inauguration prochaine de la plus grande aciérie d'Afrique. C'est dans ce contexte qu'un éboueur d'Alger vient d'acheter un kilogramme de sardines que le vendeur lui a enveloppé dans un vieux numéro d'El Moudjahid avec en première page le Président Boumediene au milieu des ouvriers de Hassi Messaoud, ce fameux 24 février 1971 où il annonce la nationalisation des hydrocarbures. Malheureusement, bien avant d'arriver chez lui, les sardines ne tiennent pas dans le journal et notre éboueur se retrouve avec toutes ses sardines par terre. Fou de rage, l'éboueur prend son copain à témoin et lui dit: "Comment tu expliques que ce journal peut supporter chaque matin des tonnes de mensonges et de bêtises et qu'il soit incapable de transporter un petit kilo de sardines?"

With this joke, the teller and listener alike share in a moment of reflection about the collective hardship of life under a repressive political system. The man here has earned his daily fish, only to be disappointed when a common misfortune befalls him. Rather than blaming the fishmonger for wrapping his product in a weak material, the man pivots his reaction—and provides the punchline—by critiquing the propaganda and censorship characteristic of national politics in Algeria at the time. The man could be experiencing this ultimately misfortunate adventure in any part of Algeria per the joke-teller's setup, although he most likely lived in a coastal region given his proximity to fresh seafood.

While legal scholar Bachir Dahak prepared and framed this version of the joke for readers of today (hence the definition of *El Moudjahid* and explanation of the dates), the joke itself is one that Algerians routinely told one another during the height of socialism in the country in the 1970s.[5] The joke in its original context would have reminded listeners of some of the central problems that then plagued Algerian civilians regardless of language, location, or ethnicity. The mention of one of only a handful of then extant daily papers, *El Moudjahid*, evokes the power and omnipresence of a single-party state system that banned independent media outlets and pushed propaganda onto citizens daily. Most scathingly, the joke-teller forthrightly declares that this single-party-led government arrangement has not resulted in "serene socialism" for the fledgling republic's everyday citizens despite supposed advancements such as second Algerian president Boumediene's nationalization of oil. One could argue that by implementing nationwide policies the Algerian state was creating a sense of unification. The joke, however, takes Algeria as a given, and the experience of laughing together at common burdens caused by the political system may have more effectively united listeners as Algerians while reminding them of these issues. Those who heard this joke might have commiserated with the now fishless man. By highlighting some of the major everyday issues then endemic in the country (the lack of a free press, the inundation of state propaganda, and possibly the scarcity of food or high food expense under socialism given the man's frustration), the joke bound listeners to the nation through reference to these common sources of suffering that Algerians experienced.

This joke is one of dozens of examples of humorous cultural products that circulated in and beyond the physical limits of Algeria in the twentieth century. Many of them, whether in the form of satirical songs, radio or TV sketches, jokes, or cartoons, helped define and reinforce ideas surrounding Algeria as a political entity just as an independent Algerian nation surfaced. From the interwar period to the 1980s, the country morphed from one of the longest-standing European settler colonies in Africa and the Middle East, under French control and deemed a part of France, to an independent nation heralded as a leader in global decolonization. The present chapter argues that political humor from the interwar period through the first decades of independence, across the colonial/postcolonial divide, provided inhabitants of the territory with ways of expressing and crafting a perceived common belonging to that territory, sometimes called *jazā'iriyya/algerianité* or "Algerian-ness." Most significantly, this trend in the use of humor was the case whether Algeria was conceived of as a nation-state or as an integral part of the French Empire or the wider Maghrib.

Various actors, including the pre- and postindependence regimes, embraced humor as a means of communicating powerful ideas surrounding territorial identities, but both pre- and postindependence states also actively surveilled comedy that they considered subversive. Humor was understood, then, by multiple groups as a powerful cultural product for tying together (or ripping apart) large "invented national communities," to borrow from Anne McClintock's reading of Benedict Anderson. However, what these invented communities were, exactly, shifted over time. Humor played a central role in this continuous invention and reinvention of the Algerian nation.[6]

Emerging scholarship on the Middle East and North Africa moves away from a general focus on elites' roles in nationalist movements to look at subalterns' or civilians' contributions to the development of nationalist consciousness.[7] As Ziad Fahmy and Jonathan Wyrtzen lament, historians of the Middle East and North Africa have tended to reconstruct the histories of emerging nationalist movements through reference to written sources.[8] Oral cultures' primacy as a motor for spreading ideas to mostly illiterate non-elites across the region has been only partially illuminated.[9] Some oral jokes or commentary on print cultures in Algeria bypassed the state censorship to which publications such as *El Moudjahid*, as the above joke avers, were subjected. Orally circulated or performed comedy sometimes allowed populations in Algeria to discuss the nation, among other subjects, outside the state's purview. Along with less clandestine forms of comedy, this humor permitted communities to create or debate the nation and consume ideas surrounding it. A study of Algerian nationalizing humor and oral commentary surrounding it further elucidates non-elites' roles in influencing nationalisms within the Middle East and North Africa.

Debates surrounding the nation in colonial Algeria were complex because of its prevailing power structures. Before independence, colonial French policy strove to divide Algeria's population between European settler and Jewish minorities and a Muslim majority, with racialized concepts of religious affiliation determining an individual's legal status.[10] Under French colonization, Algerians were victims of violence and widespread, devastating land appropriation. The 1865 Sénatus-Consulte Law technically allowed Muslims and Jews willing to give up their "personal status," a sign of belonging to their religious communities, including the right to be judged according to Islamic or Mosaic law, to become naturalized French citizens. Few accepted. The French state then subjected Muslim communities to a series of brutal and sometimes arbitrary laws called the Code of the Indigenous (Code de l'Indigénat). Algerian Jewish populations formed a minority in the territory's communities upon colonization in 1830. In 1870, the Crémieux Decree imposed French citizenship on most Algerian Jews, placing them in a complex position of being indigenous but naturalized while Muslim communities remained subjects with more limited rights in a discriminatory settler-colonial system. Jews still faced antisemitism and discrimination.[11] Favored in the system, settlers were naturalized as French citizens if they hailed from other parts of Europe throughout the nineteenth century and into the twentieth. Despite these distinctions, societies in Algeria during the colonial period were composed of overlapping, intermingling communities and players who could deftly move across supposedly fixed barriers.[12] Humor could also cross the very boundaries it could be used to create in French-ruled Algeria.[13] Ostensibly nationalizing or other forms of humor might have also coalesced populations around different nodes of belonging beyond the nation. However, the question of *Algeria*'s meaning remained front and center for all three of these communities—Muslims, Jews, and Europeans—a question they explored through comedy.

The superiority theory of humor furnishes tools capable of deciphering the Arabic- and French-language materials assessed here and how they could have helped reinforce or create invented communities in historical contexts.

Philosophers in this school insist that the creators of a joke could sever the imagined ties of the targeted person to their group through collective laughter at the individual's expense. Humor can thus create in- and out-groups, an important function for nationalism.[14] Readings of Louis Althusser's concept of interpellation and hailing prove fruitful as well. Proponents of diverging political views employed humor as a means of interpellation, hailing fellow Algerians, however they were defined, and exposing them to ideologies concerning larger invented communities to transform these individuals into subjects.[15] At the same time, both these hailing authorities and their rivals paid careful attention to how subjects being called to perform belief in ideological works responded, what political scientist Lisa Wedeen sees as interpellation's third step.[16] Through humorous interpellation or hailing, engaged actors (states, humorists, popular singers, playwrights, etc.) positioned themselves as centers of authority on national characteristics. They did so despite the presence of different poles of culture, nationalism, and other types of imagined belonging (regional, religious, ethnic, etc.) both within Algeria and beyond, some Algerian communities having strong senses of affinity with populations across the Maghrib and the globe.[17]

This chapter first examines humor as a site for the exploration of Algerian identity beginning in the 1920s and 1930s. I also illuminate early traditions of comedy that Algerian humorists later built on or referenced in their own work. The interwar period witnessed active debates over the future of Algeria as many movements and actors thought about how to overcome the harsh inequalities in the territory that the settler-colonial system had created and upheld. I then discuss the role of humor as a solidifying agent during different stages of Algeria's nationalist movements, especially during the War of Independence. The final part of this chapter explores the challenges facing Algerian communities and the Algerian state in the postindependence period. Throughout these different episodes, states and civilians understood and employed humor as a tool for uniting populations around a common notion of a singular Algerian identity, attesting to the importance of humor as political discourse in this period of nation-building.

EARLIEST STIRRINGS OF ALGERIANIZING HUMOR: 1914 THROUGH THE SECOND WORLD WAR

The northern part of the territory now called Algeria had from 1525 been an Ottoman province. Beginning in 1830, the French military set out to conquer that province and the territories that lay to the south, a task that took until the late nineteenth century and into the twentieth. From the 1840s onward, populations of Europeans mainly from France, Spain, Malta, and the Italian peninsula arrived in the territory.

Colonial policies categorized the population of the territory (from 1848 considered three integral departments of France) according to religious background with no regard as to whether individuals actively practiced the faith of their communities. What Algeria was—and could be—shifted over time. For instance, the term *Algerians* initially indicated only the population under the authority of the Ottoman Empire's province of Algiers but later became a notion that European settlers wished to appropriate by the end of the nineteenth century to distinguish themselves from French metropolitan communities.[18] Indigenous communities were also not the only ones to claim to be Algerian and to use humor toward this end. Significantly, the European settlers who wanted to claim an Algerian identity did so partially through creating and following a racist, antisemitic cartoon character from 1895 through the 1940s.[19] Cartoonist Auguste Robinet's widely popular Cagayous was a working-class settler and hustler. When asked if he was French, Cagayous frequently retorted, "Algerians we are!"[20]

The territory's Muslim communities were diverse in terms of ethnicity, languages spoken, and the areas of the vast geographic areas that they inhabited. The authority of the Ottoman-era *dey*, or governor of Algiers, was not centralized, nor did it extend far into mountainous and desert regions. Even into the twentieth century, a consciousness of being possible Algerian nationals had not set in among many of the territory's Muslim communities. Algerian Muslim thinkers living abroad in exile contemplated their space of belonging in the world and the best possible fate for their homeland, including potentially a Tunisian-Algerian entity under the Ottomans.[21] Historians such as John Ruedy, Charles-Robert Ageron, and Rabah Aissaoui concur that a sense of a specifically Algerian nation or at least patriotism was present among some Algerian Muslims in the late nineteenth and early twentieth centuries.[22] As James McDougall elucidates, though, the construct of the nation was a highly contested field in Algeria, as in other areas of the world.[23]

Ageron links anticolonial patriotism before the First World War to poetry, songs, and satire. Humor may have furnished Muslim and Jewish populations living under colonialism with a means of critiquing French authorities.[24] Concerning the origins of what some writers in Algeria consider Algerian humor, limited work exists on Muslim or Jewish humor or literature during the Ottoman period or early French period. Hints of patterns of political humor emerge from archives and secondary sources, however.

By the early twentieth century, humor had long held an important place in oral traditions and cultures across the Maghrib, particularly in the form of storytelling by men and by women, although these were distinctive, as men's storytelling was public and women's was restricted to the domestic sphere.[25] The origins of the once-popular form of storytelling extend back to at least the seventh century. Storytellers were an integral part of festivals and events. Itinerant storytellers or bards known as *guwwāl* ("sayer"), *maddaḥ* ("praiser"), or *ḥakawātī* (a Middle Eastern term for "storyteller") performed dramatic renditions of stories, including about recent events, and were well respected.[26] They could perform alone or in groups, and men storytelling in public sometimes followed the *ḥalqa* ("circle") format by allowing listeners to encircle them as they told their tales.[27] Their stories often entailed some humor or comedy, particularly in the tenth and eleventh centuries.[28] Interactions between storytellers and listeners were also important to integrating stories in communities and could shape performances.[29] While practices surrounding oral traditions certainly changed over time, the influential role of the *guwwāl* or *maddaḥ* has persisted over centuries. Additionally, orally transmitted poetry called *malḥūn* could contain humor and was often memorable enough to be passed down from generation to generation. Satirical poems especially targeted powerful figures, including Ottoman authorities and French settlers.[30] Thus, humorous oral traditions had deep roots in Algeria. Some of these practices continued well into the twentieth century and were considered strong influences on other cultural genres that also showcased humor, such as theater.[31]

Certain archetypes appeared time and again in *guwwāl* or *maddaḥ* performances and in other forms of orally transmitted cultures. For example, trickster characters such as Juḥā have been common in many parts of the Islamic world and could be gendered as male or female.[32] Tales of the common trickster Juḥā included humorous scenes, often occurring when the perennial troublemaker revealed certain aspects of society by acting unconventionally. He often confronted buffoonish or tyrannical rulers and their equally problematic or corrupt entourage of courtiers, additional archetypes in Maghribi folklore. He could also engage with disengaged ordinary people to make them aware of an aspect of their lives.[33] As seen in the introduction with the case of Saïd Mekbel's *Le Matin* editorial column, this earlier oral folklore could influence later forms of humor.[34]

Additionally, a genre featuring a libidinous shadow puppet called *Karakouz* (*karagūz*, Turkish for "black eye") that originated in the administrative and cultural center of the Ottoman Empire was popular among Algerian Muslims. Karakouz plays had taken root in North Africa by the seventeenth century.

Karakouz puppeteers could slyly attack figures in power. The Karakouz genre that often incorporated humor caught the attention of European authorities and visitors to the territory's coastal region once France began its military conquest in 1830. In 1835, a European tourist wrote of a Karakouz performance that he had witnessed. To his shock, the titular character played a fertility god who wielded a penis-like stick to hit what appeared to be French soldiers.[35] While certainly not nationalistic in the sense that they supported the idea of a nation, such performances may have united viewers in a common delight at witnessing a debasement of the enforcers of colonial authority. The French administration by several accounts was so concerned about the ability of Karakouz plays to instill hostility toward the occupiers within the populations under their control that they outlawed the genre by the early 1840s.[36] Puppeteers continued to put on illicit Karakouz performances through the end of the nineteenth century, but the banning of a cultural icon so popular within communities residing in what was once part of a larger Muslim empire represents the violent cultural suppression that occurred with settler colonialism. What is more, settler favorite Cagayous may have been named after Karakouz, a testament to humor's transcendence of barriers between communities, even if Cagayous embraced very different ideas.[37]

At the beginning of the First World War, though, as France entered the conflict and its authorities began drafting Algerian subjects and French citizens in the territory, one of the most anticolonial and possibly nationalizing cultural products of this period took form. According to a French official, this oeuvre fell within the parameters of satire.[38] A rapprochement between the German and Ottoman Empires at the turn of the twentieth century incited rumors across Algeria and neighboring Tunisia that Kaiser Wilhelm II had converted to Islam. At the outbreak of the First World War, when France's Third Republic declared war on Germany, the French state turned to its colonies as sources of logistical and material support as well as for soldiers and laborers. During this mobilization, rumors about Wilhelm's conversion solidified into a song prophesying that Wilhelm's rise would spell the end of French imperial rule in Algeria.[39] And perhaps no humorous cultural material from Algeria's indigenous community in the early to mid-twentieth century better proves through its content that some of its authors, although unknown and plural, intended the work to undercut or question French authority than this satirical song, which Orientalist-academic-turned-French-propagandist Joseph Desparmet called "*la chanson de l'époque*" / "the song of the time."[40] Some versions, especially those performed in front of French observers or potentially by pro-French performers, contained messages supporting the French government's attitudes toward Germany, its enemy. Many takes on the song, though, declared that Algeria was soon to be free and France had no claim over the territory. At least some Muslim communities in Algeria as well as Tunisia appear to have expressed glee, among other emotions, at the prospect of France losing in the war.[41]

The song's creators and sharers produced many verses. Desparmet collected at least thirty-eight different versions (with some parts in French but most verses in Arabic dialects) through Muslim contacts and French and indigenous Jewish high school students.[42] Even if the motivations of the anonymous authors of the lyrics remain unknown, its singers and consumers in most reiterations imagined Hadj Guillaume as liberating Algeria from French control and trumpeted him as a sort of Mahdi-esque deliverer of the people.[43] Did the song reinforce or invent a kind of nationalist sentiment through the humor some versions contained? Historian Arthur Asseraf correctly warns against seeing the lack of clear authors behind the song and its many versions as evidence of its collective nature.[44]

The content of the song itself invited listeners and singers alike to consider themselves as part of a community. What that community was and who belonged in it depended on the version, but it was always located in a world of competing empires and nations. Some of the song's verses pushed singers and listeners to consider themselves as a collective "we."[45] Its bards, who spoke a multitude of languages and possessed different ethnic and religious backgrounds, connected with listeners to ask how they might respond to the war, albeit generally fatalistically and ostensibly without power. The refrain declared,

> Oh, French people what is in your head?
> Algeria is not yours
> Germany is coming to take her from you
> It must return to how it was before (earlier in time)
> Ayy, ayy, what am I to do with him (what can be done with him)? Al-Hadj Guillaume his fortune rises

> *Yā Fransīs wāsh fī bālak?*
> *Al-Jazā'ir māshī dyālak*
> *Yjī al-Almān yaddīhā lak*
> *Lā budda tarj'a kīf fī al-zmān*
> *Ayy ayy kī na'mal lu? Al-Ḥājj Giyūm yaṭla' sa'du*[46]

The song's performers begin by calling out the rulers of Algeria. "*Wāsh fī bālak?*" ("What is in your head?"), they ask, followed immediately by the line "*Al-Jazā'ir māshī dyālak*" ("Algeria is not yours"), pronouncing this statement as the most natural of things. The proclamation seems to ridicule the French for daring to attempt to hold Algeria in light of shifting fortunes in the concert of nations. Such musing would inevitably entail thoughts about what Algeria was. References to nations also pepper several turns of the song.[47]

The colonial official who collected and wrote about the song, Desparmet, connected it to the Maghribi genre of humor *m'ānī* (humorous epigrams) and classified it as satire, highlighting the work's capacity for evoking laughter.[48] Despite its at times very serious content and the range of emotions that it undoubtedly stirred in singers and listeners, verses did indeed satirize the countries involved in the conflict. One potentially humorous verse, given its use of incongruity, followed Italy's entrance into the war on the side of France and associated the country with a stereotypical food:

> The Italian is a crazy man. He fills up the cannons with pasta.[49]
>
> *Al-Ṭālyān rājal mahbūl 'ammar l-mdāfi' bi-l-maqqārūn.*

In the discussion of the meeting of nations on battlefields around Europe and the Mediterranean mentioned in the songs, Algeria stands poised as yet another geographic region from which soldiers hail. The perspectives of the composers and singers are significantly placed in the first person singular or plural in the songs.[50] Other versions pointed to a Muslim *umma*, or global community of believers, that could be reunited if the Turks were able to defeat France with the help of Wilhelm II, guided as he was, according to the song, by Allah. Desparmet considered these versions more prayer than satirical pieces.[51] In Algeria, European, Jewish, and Muslim communities alike shared the "Hadj Guillaume" piece, showing the work's popularity and flexibility as an anthem against or for French rule; some versions substituted a line about Hadj Guillaume failing instead of his "star rising."[52] The collective first person here signifies that some iterations of the song may have fostered a sense of collective opposition for the people who sang versions critical of French rule, translating to shared mirth at the foreshadowing of better times ahead in a French-less future. This future was perhaps envisioned as part of the Ottoman Empire once more or possibly alone; the lyrics do not say. Common sources of suffering likewise emerge throughout the different versions, with particular ire shown for forced conscription and the separation of soldiers from their loved ones, although a version apparently sung by Jewish soldiers decried discrimination against them as they crossed the sea en route to war.[53] As was the case with later forms of political satire, dark humor that acknowledged social groups' hardships may have helped give rise to a sense of belonging to a larger nation.

Other humorous songs circulated throughout the interwar period that may have similarly reinforced a sense of common Algerianness among different communities. Scholar Saadeddine Bencheneb published an article on the genre in 1933 remarking on the spiking frequency of satirical political songs during the interwar period. Lyrics for the songs that he collected, mainly from the pen of Rachid Ksentini, centered on changes in Algerian society brought on by new forms of communication and entertainment: for instance, sons engaging in novel sports such as football and boxing or the advent of the gramophone.[54] A Muslim, Ksentini came from a modest background. He was employed as a cabinetmaker and sailor in the 1910s and 1920s before joining the El Moutribia (The enchantress) musical troupe.[55] The songs Ksentini composed criticized shifting gender relationships and women's growing independence and dealt as well with themes of love.[56]

Political verses written by Ksentini centered on the supposed hypocrisy of Muslim elected officials, elites who would maintain their power as their ranks expanded in the interwar period. As a result of 173,000 Algerian Muslims' service in the French army during the First World War, the government passed the 1919 Jonnart Law. This legislation granted some Algerian Muslim men limited political rights and privileges—namely, franchise in local elections and a shield from the brutal Code of the Indigenous that subjected Muslims to discriminatory policies and legal procedures. This expansion of the number of Muslim men who could both vote and retain their personal status significantly increased political life among Muslims in the interwar period.[57] One song written by Ksentini, "Fāqū" (Wake up! / They have woken up), was critical of Muslim figures working with the colonial system. It fell in line with other songs that poked fun at these figures' supposed hypocrisy.[58] Its third verse goes as follows:

> The "misters" have increased in numbers
> Every day they lay traps
> marked in the corners of madness
> of new turbans and kissing hands
> Pouring out drinks and pouring out some more
> Get drunk and worship God
> (Les gens / "the people") have woken up

> *Kathrū al-sadāt bi-l-sūstiyyāt*
> *Kull yūm naṣbāt*
> *Mtā' al falāt*
> *'amāyim jdad*
> *w-būs al-yad*

Asqī wa-jdad
Askar wa-'bad
*Fāqū*⁵⁹

Ksentini and other singers of this tune may have wanted to express their lack of faith in some Muslim delegates who had integrated into the French political system to represent the wider community's interests. With references to alcohol, the singers of these verses criticized notables for dishonoring their religion. They did so in ways, moreover, that would have aligned with the growing nationalist discourse of the Association of Algerian Muslim Ulama (AUMA for its French acronym, with *ulama* being Islamic scholars), a religious association that grew out of eastern Algeria in the 1930s and took up the question of Algerian Muslims' liberation from the brutal settler-colonial system.⁶⁰ Furthermore, after criticizing the behavior of these Muslim notables, the song's chorus urges them or the audience, "*fāqū kabbarū al-'amāma*" ("wake up, fatten" / "grow your turban"). The notion of a visibly fattening turban standing in for the growth in notables' wealth through corruption seems intended to provoke laughter among listeners. While Bencheneb attributes the song to Ksentini (who later performed a revue with the same name), the pioneer par excellence of Algerian theater in the 1920s and 1930s, Mahieddine Bachtarzi, claims that he worked on a play of the same name, *Fāqū*, and intended it as a move toward theatrical sketches attacking individuals who were hurting the Algerian people.⁶¹ For Bachtarzi, this song and his integration of it into a play with the same title represented the moment that his work became more overtly political.⁶² The lyrics here reinforce this idea given that they hailed Muslim communities along with Jewish and French audience members to act as one in viewing corrupt elites as agents threatening the Islamic community. Ksentini also performed the sketch alongside comedian Dahmoun and Ksentini's Jewish Algerian girlfriend, Marie Soussan. One time, he incited such ardent laughter in his fellow players that he had to interrupt the bit.⁶³ The participation of a Jewish Algerian actor, known to her audiences as such, may have signaled an imagined coexistence of Algerian Arabic dialect–speaking communities across religions.

Inextricably connected to humorous and satirical songs, performances part and parcel of what Algerian and foreign writers from the 1960s onward called *Algerian theater* emerged in 1926 and grew in popularity through the rest of the colonial era. While European communities held theatrical performances, Muslim actors and playwrights did not take the stage until that year. Plays often attracted students and rising petit-bourgeois populations living in cities and major towns. Women and men from differing ethnic and religious backgrounds attended performances, which were reviewed in papers for Muslim and for settler communities.[64] According to Rachid Bencheneb, the Algerian Muslim theater that began as a cultural phenomenon in the 1920s and 1930s sought to preserve an "Algerian personality."[65] Some of these assertions may contain a postindependence desire to envision resistance as existent in preindependence cultural fields. Yet, a survey of songs and themes from plays dating to the interwar era reveals their authors' ostensible intentions to comment on politics and the state of colonialism in the country in ways that may have been nationalistic but were not in line with the nationalism and invented nation that ultimately triumphed in Algeria.

The most prominent Algerian theater was created in the 1920s and 1930s. It was situated firmly in the capital of Algiers and therefore reflected the customs, personalities, and language of that coastal city in the throes of rapid change. In its earliest iterations, Algerian theater was inspired by work produced around the Muslim world, specifically the eastern Mediterranean, along with earlier spectacles put on during holidays.[66] Theatrical authors and performers took their craft around Algeria, noting audience reactions and possibly making alterations to render Algiers-created material accessible to extra-Algiers audiences.[67] By the middle of the 1930s, however, an extension of the El Moutribia musical group founded by Algerian Jew Edmond Yafil in the first decade of the 1900s held performances around the country as well as in Morocco and across the sea in France and Belgium.[68]

Music and comedy were deeply embedded in plays produced mostly in Algerian Arabic with some French. Many early performers and writers—namely, Allalou's Zahia Troupe—found that humorous sketches and Algerian Arabic resonated best with audiences, a rule of thumb that would continue to be true until the end of the interwar period, demonstrating a popular appetite for this kind of work.[69] What is more, many plays showcased comedy.[70] Allalou himself played an everyday sort of fool in the streets in Bab El-Oued while growing up and into adulthood.[71] This ordinary, naive, buffoonish character perhaps grew out of the Juḥā tales popular across the Islamic world. Once again, Juḥā was a trickster who often slyly defied individuals in power and who has inspired several characters in the pantheon of Algerian humor.[72]

By the 1930s, Mahieddine Bachtarzi had surfaced as the country's major playwright. He worked with Muslim and Jewish actors along with a handful of female players and some individuals of European origin.[73] Bachtarzi's rise to the fore of theater accompanied a greater politicization of plays. Bachtarzi used terms never before pronounced on stage, such as *ḥuqūq* ("rights," referencing political ones), *waṭan* ("nation"), *ittiḥād* ("unity"), *bladnā* ("our country"), and *qahr* ("repression"). They appeared in song lyrics that the troupe printed and distributed through pamphlets.[74] The "nation" and "we" to which Bachtarzi refers in the songs recovered from some of his shows appear to be broad and to include Europeans and Jews alongside the Muslim communities that the works more overtly addressed. His plays further glossed over differences within the Muslim community (regional, ethnic, or otherwise) beyond those of class.[75] Comedy as expressed in theater and popular songs from performances put forth strong messages about the eventual fate of Algeria while inviting its consumers to view themselves as part of a larger Algerian community.

In the 1930s, after nationalist movements had begun to take root, visions diverged as to what an Algerian nation would look like if the territory's political structure were overhauled to allow more rights for the Muslim majority. Three major strands of nationalism took shape during this period. The first, represented by Ferhat Abbas, envisioned an Algeria in which Muslims would be able to gain equal rights to French citizens of the territory. It rejected full assimilation in favor of allowing Muslims to retain their culture and religion. The AUMA, representing the second strand, was founded by 'Abd Al-Hamid Ben Badis in the eastern Algerian city of Constantine in 1931. Their brand of nationalism underscored Islam as a central facet of Algerian identity and Arabic as the nation's language. Members of the AUMA embraced the Islamic modernist ideas propagated by thinkers such as Egyptian reformer Muhammad 'Abduh (1849–1905). The organization and its leaders shaped perspectives of Algerian culture and its history in ways that later nationalists would take up.[76] They arguably helped secure a central place for Islam in the struggles of the decades to come. The final group to formulate strong visions of an improved lot for Algerian Muslims in light of a brutal imperial system was the North African Star. Initially comprising Maghribi workers living in France after the First World War, with the charismatic Messali Hadj at its helm, the North African Star advocated for complete independence of Algeria from France. While these movements dialogued with each other and sometimes had tensions, it does not appear that their heads or the rank-and-file partisans used humor to denigrate one another.

Amid these exchanges, in 1936, a significant if still minor section of the Algerian Muslim community came close to gaining a greater status within the colonial system when the leftist Popular Front government in France put forth a bill in the national legislature to extend full political rights to more Algerian Muslim men. While a modest change, this law, the Blum-Viollette reform, would have reduced some of the glaring inequalities between the European, Jewish, and Algerian Muslim communities. Bachtarzi made the conscientious decision to express his fervent enthusiasm for an Algeria where European and indigenous communities would peacefully live together as equals.[77] In his play *An-nisā'* (The women), the family and friends of a European man and a Muslim woman grapple with the complicated circumstances that arise when the two decide to get married and start a family. Such "mixed" couples were rarities during the late colonial era. Things work out in the end for the couple living in the fictitious Violletteville, which Bachtarzi aptly named after the legislation that he so fully believed might result in a better future for the nation.[78] Bachtarzi openly and unapologetically employed his art in the service of political rights and equality for Muslim Algerians while supporting what he believed to be the advantageous coexistence of Europeans, Muslims, and Jews. This play was well received by audiences and contained comedy.[79] However, a contemporary police report indicates that audiences perhaps did not find the play to their taste. The document notes that one audience received Bachtarzi's depiction of an interfaith Algerian nation with ambivalence and suspicion, a possible sign that his attempted interpellation of audiences into his view of the Algerian nation failed.[80] Regardless of its ultimate success, to further convey this message of interreligious and interracial national belonging to audiences, Bachtarzi produced pamphlets with overviews of plays and songs (fig. 1.1) in French and Arabic script, which he circulated in 1937 in support of the Blum-Viollette bill.[81]

Another Bachtarzi play that used humor to spread a nationalist message was *Les Benis Oui Oui*, literally translated as "the tribe of yes-men." *Benis Oui Oui* were intermediaries between the Muslim community and French and settler authorities. The play revolves around an entourage of cheats. Two of them work within the French administration, thereby earning the moniker used by some Algerian Muslims to ridicule fellow Muslims who served in the colonial regime. The two Muslim elected officials are both in the *délégations financières* ("financial delegations"). The *délégations financières* oversaw budget allocations.[82] One of the men, Ali Lommi, is tempted by a hooligan to try to trick scores of Algerian Muslims out of their money. The following is the play's second song, perhaps performed by a chorus of the actors and speaking directly to Ali:

> She says to him, his wife, buy for me yes, yes, yes,
> He says to him, his brother-in-law, offer me [something] yes, yes, yes
> He says to him, his friend, give me; he says to him yes, yes, yes
>
> Come and gamble, O Sid Ali, yes, yes, yes
> Come and get drunk, O Sid Ali, yes, yes, yes
> Come and dance, O Sid Ali

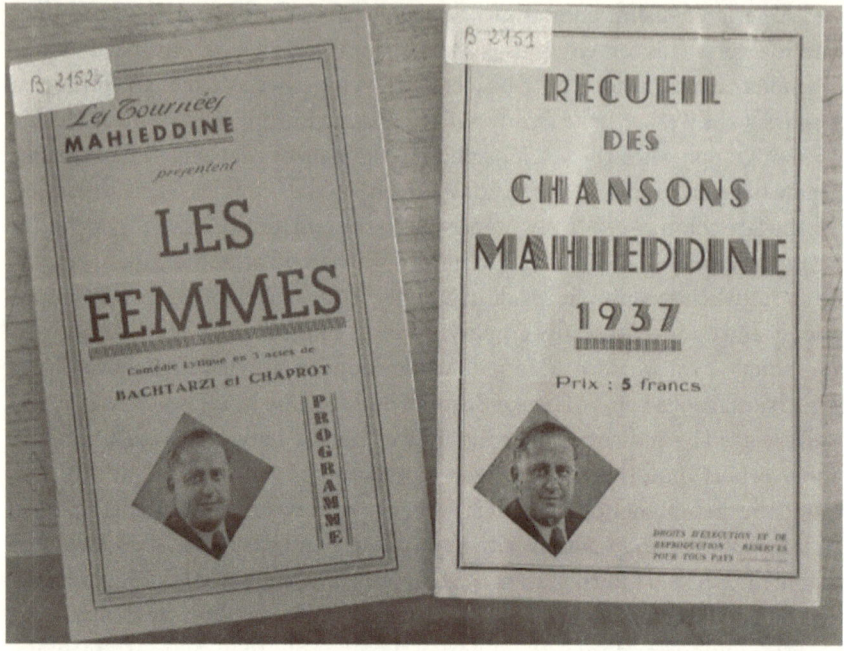

Figure 1.1. Playwright Mahieddine Bachtarzi circulated playbills/pamphlets in the 1930s to further spread play content, including humorous numbers, promoting the possibility of an inclusive Algerian-French nation. Pamphlets found in ANOM B 2151 and ANOM B 2152.

> He does not know anything in politics except "yes, yes, yes"
> Works for the people in his head with "yes, yes, yes"
> There is no word as exhausting as the word "yes, yes, yes"
>
> *Tqūl lu martu ishrī lī wīy wīy wīy*
> *Yqūl lu nsību ahdīlī wīy wīy wīy*
> *Yqūl lū ṣāḥbu taʻṭī lī yqūl lu wīy wīy wīy*
>
> *Tjī tgammar yā Sīd ʻAlī wīy wīy wīy*
> *Tjī taskar yā Sīd ʻAlī wīy wīy wīy*
> *Tjī tashṭaḥ yā Sīd ʻAlī wīy wīy wīy*
>
> *Ma yaʻraf fī al-sīyāsa ghīr wīy wīy wīy*
> *ʻāmil fī al-nās b-rāsu b-wīy wīy wīy*
> *Mā kānsh kalima makḥāsa ki-kalimat wīy wīy wīy*[83]

The repetition of the word *oui* here symbolizes Muslim officials' sycophantic working relationship with French administrators and corrupt Muslims to the supposed detriment of Muslim communities overall. By addressing Sid Ali in this way, the song paints him as a buffoonish hypocrite for using alcohol and engaging in gambling as a Muslim. Despite its scathing portrayal of some elected Muslim officials, though, the play did not oppose colonialism. Bachtarzi may even have used the piece to praise good French leaders.[84] A reading of the text, however, makes it appear that, as with Ksentini's "Fāqū" song examined above, Bachtarzi may have wanted to critique self-serving, corrupt officials within Muslim communities for betraying these groups and preventing their betterment and unification with other parts of society. Instead of outwardly challenging French control, something impossible given the strong hand of the censor or something he perhaps did not want to do, Bachtarzi lambasted Muslim agents working with colonial authorities who purportedly kept the population from progressing. He sought to change and empower Muslim audiences while depicting the complex, multifaceted societies that prevailed in Algeria during this period and exchanges across ethnic, religious, and national lines. His plays also questioned the Muslim-French binary that the territory's ambiguous colonial status entailed.[85]

Like Bachtarzi, the AUMA sought to unite Muslim populations around a common identity. They also recognized the importance of public performances for this goal and therefore encouraged the formation of theater troupes. Among these groups of players who advanced the association's ideas was the troupe Muḥibbī al-fann (Lovers of art). The AUMA leadership viewed theater, a cultural genre associated with humor in late colonial Algeria, as a forum for educating audiences about its messages of piety and the need to culturally preserve a unified Muslim community whose language (Arabic) and customs were under assault by colonial authorities.[86]

Print cultures were also important sources of comedy during the interwar period. Within urban spaces, a limited number of Algerian readers followed satirical reviews from Egypt and Tunisia, products of the cultural renaissance or *al-Nahdha* underway throughout the Middle East since the nineteenth century. Their consumption of these papers, especially Tunisian ones, might have comprised the first encounters that audiences within Algeria had with Arabic-language pictorial caricatures and newspaper humor.[87] Muslim Algerians' engagement with these works produced around the region shows connections between communities living in the three French departments of Algeria and other parts of the Mediterranean and Muslim worlds. Concerning works published closer to home to which Algerian Muslims may have been exposed, the settler publications available to the limited Algerian Muslim readership also used caricatures. The latter often rendered Algerian Muslims as well as Jews their subjects for ridicule, usually in violent and offensive ways. The most popular settler satirical paper, *Le Turco*, was named after a derogatory term for Algerian Muslim soldiers (*tirailleurs*) in the French army and contained Orientalist images of Algerian Muslims alongside antisemitic rhetoric. While not directed toward Algerian Muslim communities but often insultingly mocking them along with Jewish communities, these cartoons, their message that real Algerians were European settlers, and their style may have left a mark on these marginalized groups.[88]

Several other types of humor might have helped give rise to the development of an Algerian national belonging. Jokes told among local populations during the period of French rule tended to be autoderisive and may have helped foster a national identity or consciousness. While jokes by Algerian Muslims seemed to mock their own kind, Aïssa Khelladi believes these same stories actually targeted colonial administrators, settlers, or the Muslims who worked with them. Contemporary folk tales from Tunisia also elided mention of Europeans but may have subtly criticized them.[89] Jokes seemed to have escaped the attention of colonial surveillance, and oral history narrators were, for the most part, too young to recall the colonial era.

One joke follows this pattern of self-derision. It recounts the tale of a wealthy settler and estate owner commanding an Algerian Muslim employee to watch over his prized possession, a purebred dog, while he is away on business. The employee's task is to ensure that the female canine does not have any contact with "dirty native dogs." The ethnically European man returns to his lands, though, to find the animal heavily pregnant. When he confronts the employee, he responds, "Bah! What was I to do? She was pregnant before you left!" The overtones and allusions to the so-called peril of racial intermixing are clear.[90] In the end, though, the Muslim worker absorbs the joke's humor by accepting an impossible job while not mentioning that fact to his high-class employer, although the latter is caught off guard and does not get what he desires. The self-deprecating humor encapsulated by this joke, one that does not appear well known, may evince larger political and labor dynamics at play to which any number of Muslim workers in Algeria in similar positions could relate.[91] Overall, humor from this early part of the twentieth century assisted various communities in Algeria with experimenting with the idea of Algerian-ness and with contemplating power structures then in place.

FRENCH COLONIAL SURVEILLANCE AND APPROPRIATION OF MUSLIM-MAJORITY HUMOR

French authorities throughout the 132 years of colonization in Algeria approached local forms of humor with suspicion, fearful that the wrong kind of gag could foment dissent against their power. As indicated by the suppression of the territory's robust and popular Karakouz culture, surveillance of these politicized forms of comedy was a practice that states exercised throughout the colonial era and that the postcolonial regime maintained. These different regimes' interest in keeping tabs on humor demonstrates the potential power that they perceived humor and its wielders to have. Humor was recognized, then, as a possible subversive tool that had to be suppressed or could alternatively be harnessed to preserve the settler regime and French control over Algeria.

By 1917, police were arresting civilians found singing, chanting, or humming "Hadj Guillaume."[92] Beginning with Bachtarzi's politicized plays in 1934, French administrators began surveilling, censoring, and requiring authorizations for theatrical performances. Fear of police reprisal prompted Bachtarzi's group to put off performing Ksentini's/Bachtarzi's *Fāqū* review, with insults aimed at reportedly corrupt Muslim officials, in 1932, demonstrating that official pressure could lead to self-censorship.[93] *Les Benis Oui Oui* was outlawed on a number of occasions.[94] After mid-1935, Bachtarzi permitted plays to be surveilled and submitted their texts to administrators for approval in advance of performances.[95] For distributing collections of his songs that praised and spoke of an inclusive, harmonious Algerian nation (fig. 1.1), Bachtarzi witnessed the seizure of these works, was sentenced to an ultimately suspended term in prison, and subsequently saw local government subsidies for his plays withdrawn.[96]

After the Second World War, general surveillance units required that every new play go through them before hitting the stage, lest the plays contain anti-imperial messages.[97] Intelligence agents also attended showings and observed the responses of audiences, recording whether they witnessed any signs of politically driven disturbances. Any potential ties between players, authors, or directors and nationalist organizations such as the nationalist Movement for the Triumph of Democratic Liberties were likewise investigated.[98]

Humor as a tool of political persuasion could work in multidirectional ways to unite populations into an invented national community. Two separate powers representing France and the French government turned to humor to bolster their popularity among Algerian Muslim communities at a critical moment for the territory and the world. In the midst of the Second World War, Vichy and the Allied powers in control of French Algeria employed comedy in the form of plays performed by state-supported theatrical troupes to convince Muslim subjects to back their respective sides in the war at different times. The Vichy government harnessed theater, once again a genre generally steeped in humor in Algeria, to inculcate pro-Vichy views in the territory's Muslim residents. The Allies did likewise.[99]

Figure 1.2. France's Army of Africa commissions a magazine directed toward its Maghribi soldiers that tells the story of a pro-Ally Juḥā, a measure most likely intended to use North African humorous traditions in the service of the Allied cause. "Djeha n'est pas collaborationniste."

In terms of print culture, Free France's Armée d'Afrique (Army of Africa), a key portion of its ranks in the liberation of France and Europe from Nazi control, published *Al-Naṣr*, a magazine for soldiers from France's Maghribi territories of Morocco, Algeria, and Tunisia. The monthly review functioned primarily as propaganda to convince soldiers, all low ranking, of the righteousness of the Free French Army's struggle against the Axis powers. The writers of this magazine, whose authorship remains difficult to determine, appropriated touchstones of Maghribi humorous cultures to inculcate pro-Allied views in Arabic- and French-reading recruits.[100] In the first issue of the magazine, an imagined Juḥā tale has the trickster moving through the space of a liberated Maghrib village (fig. 1.2). Juḥā here is a North African soldier in the French military. Through his actions, he shows himself to be devoted to the cause of an independent Algeria. The trickster speaks in French with a North African accent, and the illustrator (or illustrators) assigns him larger lips. These characteristics were common tropes in portrayals of France's Black soldiers in the early to mid-twentieth century.[101] The character also comes off as a fool, thinking that a bottle of Vichy water in a store signaled that its purveyor was an Axis sympathizer.[102]

These humorous images and calls to earlier humorous traditions testify to the Free French Army's hopes that they could use humor to persuade colonized soldiers to fight valiantly for the Allied powers. The creators of this paper for the cause of Free France certainly attempted to use comedy to ideologically hail already-conscripted Maghribi soldiers into anti-Axis ideologies.

NATIONALIZING HUMOR DURING DECOLONIZATION

The period from the end of the Second World War through the early 1950s witnessed a burgeoning nationalism, particularly in the wake of the May 1945 massacres in Setif, Guelma, and Kherrata that left upward of tens of thousands of Algerian Muslims dead. At celebrations on May 8, 1945, of the Allied victory in Europe, some nationalist Algerian Muslims belonging to the Algerian People's Party (Parti du peuple algérien, or PPA) participated in a demonstration in the central-eastern town of Setif. The PPA was the inheritor of the North African Star's populist, anticolonial message when that group was outlawed in 1937. Clashes broke out between participants, bystanders, and local police, with the latter firing on crowds. In the days that followed, some Algerian Muslims attacked local farms and villages, killing 102 settlers. Settler groups and the army retaliated with uneven force, rounding up and summarily executing thousands of Muslim boys and men in an event that many later participants in the nationalist armed rebellion of 1954 to 1962 characterized as the moment that they decided that a continued relationship with France was no longer tenable.¹⁰³ Reforms to lessen the inequalities between Muslims and European settlers or Jews whose citizenship rights were reinstated after being stripped during the Second World War faltered in the late 1940s. More Algerian Muslims thus started to envision independence as a better option than continued existence under French authority.

In this period of mounting tension and building on earlier theatrical traditions, televised comedy sketches by Algerians, which appeared in the 1950s and included Bachtarzi and Touri, sneakily attacked French settlers through self-derision.¹⁰⁴ A similar pattern manifested in satirical songs of the same period, particularly those of Ksentini.¹⁰⁵ Through this covertly anticolonial humor, Algerian Muslims defined themselves in opposition to the European population.¹⁰⁶ As with theater and satirical songs of the interwar period, the contribution of these songs and televised routines to the formation of a shared national identity appears significant given the low literacy rates among Algerian Muslims at this time.¹⁰⁷ As with earlier songs and theater, most of the nationally produced television shows at the time were in local Arabic dialect instead of other languages spoken at the time in the country such as Kabylian Tamazight, Modern Standard Arabic, and French.¹⁰⁸

Print culture humor persisted into this era as well. At least two artists, Djamel Aït Djaffer (better known for his poetry) and Said Zanoun, drew cartoons for both papers and pamphlets shared locally. These artists' drawings have been notoriously difficult to track down, but they may have constituted the first caricatures drawn by Muslim Algerian artists. In the 1950s, small numbers of the Muslim populations began reading French-language *bandes dessinées*, a Belgian style of comics, from France and Belgium that settler communities were bringing into the country.¹⁰⁹

Throughout the years immediately following the Second World War, settler populations and the French state failed to reconstruct the rigidly nonegalitarian structures undergirding colonial society. An Algerian Assembly to draft laws for the territory was created, but settlers were allotted an equal amount of power to that of Algerian Muslims, who greatly outnumbered them. A century and more of colonial policies had resulted in a world where religious affiliations, ethnic backgrounds, and geographic origins determined racial categories according to which European settlers obtained far greater rights and privileges, including freedom of speech, than the majority of the communities in France's three Algerian departments.¹¹⁰ Seeking to mobilize the frustration of the disenfranchised Muslim majority and considering that pro-integration nationalists had failed to bend the will of the rigid French settler regime, a group of nationalists formed the National Liberation Front (FLN) to achieve independence through armed revolt.

On November 1, 1954, the FLN launched its first attack against European settlers. The assault set in motion a seven-year-long conflict in which the FLN emerged as the leading armed nationalist group against the settler order and later the full force of the French military. The FLN was far from a unified movement, and infighting occurred among leadership, with purges taking place occasionally throughout the revolt. Conflict also erupted between nationalist factions loyal to Messali Hadj, who launched their own armed uprising under the banner of the Algerian National Movement (MNA, Mouvement algérien national), and the FLN. Over time and as the major belligerents appealed to international communities for support, the Algerian War of Independence became a watershed moment for the postwar era as well as world history.[111]

With claims of over a million Algerian Muslims dead (although the actual lives lost were probably fewer), the war is remembered by specialists of Algerian humor today as a serious endeavor that did not entail much humor.[112] The texts that nationalist theater produced, whether from the official FLN theater group's repertoire or outside of it, reinforce this vision. The FLN established a troupe in 1958 that performed in exile from Tunisia and other countries friendly to the FLN's cause for an independent Algeria. Texts of plays were reprinted, though, in the newspaper *El Moudjahid*, which was transmitted clandestinely in Algeria.[113] In a wartime play set in Algiers's notorious prison, Serkadji (Barbarousse in French), a character recites a story. It follows the pattern of a joke, the only hint at humor in an otherwise starkly serious work. The tale centers on a group of French soldiers stumbling upon a corner of a house that they believe to be a secret hiding space for FLN combatants, only to discover that the nook is a bathroom.[114]

The FLN included cartoons in publications intended to rally Algerian communities to its cause of nationalist armed struggle.[115] Some of these sketches had serious messages about the nationalist movement, but others mocked French authorities and figures. While their authorship is anonymous, the creators of tracts and editors of the major FLN papers, *El Moudjahid* and *Résistance algérienne*, included these sketches alongside propaganda aimed at convincing readers of the righteousness of their fight and responding to the psychological warfare that the French army was simultaneously undertaking. French military services recovered this Arabic and French print material from around virtually all of Algeria, suggesting that comic pictures were considered by nationalists to be capable of speaking to individuals regardless of their region.[116] Pamphlets

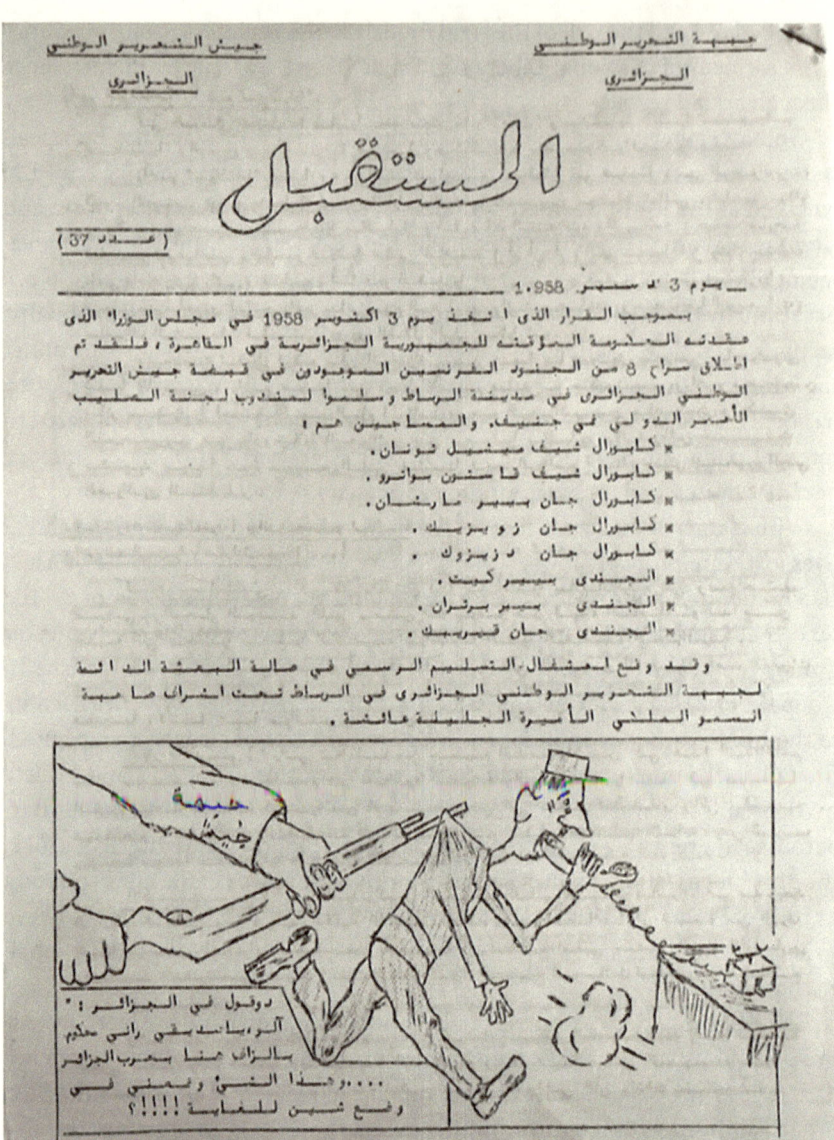

Figure 1.3. A December 1959 FLN publication includes a cartoon of President de Gaulle presumably calling someone outside of Algeria to let them know that he is very "tied up" with the war.

and clandestine organs formed a significant tool in the FLN's repertoire for building their popularity and instilling their ideas concerning the Algerian nation. The inclusion of humorous drawings in these pamphlets is telling.

These cartoons depicted a landscape in which the FLN and its army were strong, larger-than-life heroes overcoming buffoonish, diminutive French figures who acted in heinous ways toward Muslim civilians. Figure 1.3 offers a glimpse into the humor that nationalist leaders harnessed to convince the masses of the righteousness of their cause.[117] Like a few other caricatures of anonymous authorship, it satirizes a key French figure in the fight to suppress nationalist rebellion: President Charles de Gaulle. Other drawings attacked Governor-General Robert Lacoste, renamed Lahonte, "the shame." De Gaulle in other cartoons was depicted as "La Quille," the French word for a bowling pin, perhaps inviting readers to root for his fall.[118]

This cartoon depicts de Gaulle in a position of weakness, having been picked up by the rifle of a hulking arm labeled "FLN" and "ALN," the acronym for the FLN's armed wing (Armée de libération nationale, or National Liberation Army), as though the notoriously tall French leader was insect-like compared to the nationalists' strength.[119] The telephone here may bear multiple meanings as a signifier. French army officers could make the notorious *gégène*, a small taser-like tool used to torture suspected nationalists, with an instrument of modernity—electricity—in the form of telephones (then called *magnetos*). They could also use generators intended to power telephones as their energy source.[120] The place of the telephone within France's Geneva Accord–breaking torture sessions in Algeria was universally known by the December 3, 1958, publication date of Henri Alleg's *La question*.[121] In any event, the 1959 caricature belittles the French leader, cowering as he has to admit failure to the metropole through a device that French soldiers used to inflict pain on suspected nationalist supporters.[122] While bringing followers into a singular readership through text, subtexts, and codes, these FLN/ALN-produced works communicated images of what nationalist fighters were reportedly like and should be, stressing the unity of the Algerian Muslim population in its push for freedom from a ridicule-worthy, if deadly, colonial system.[123]

NATIONALIZING COMEDY IN THE WAKE OF INDEPENDENCE

The seven-year-long War of Independence left much of Algeria deeply damaged and populations scrambling to rebuild lives following an immensely brutal conflict while also uncertain as to the future of their nation. Throughout the war, the FLN had articulated its desire for naturalized Algerian Jews and European settlers to stay in the country, provided that they accept living in an independent Algeria. Yet, the territory's European population, later known as the *pieds-noirs* ("black feet"), fled the country en masse as a settler terrorist group, the Secret Armed Organization (OAS for its French acronym), destroyed some critical infrastructure and worsened tensions between Muslim and European communities as independence neared. Many members of the indigenous Jewish community left as well. With this destruction and loss of population, the postindependence rebuilding of state and society proved an arduous challenge.

In particular, the ultimate success of the FLN's liberation struggle and the end of French colonialism in 1962 opened up a violent power struggle among the movement's leadership that greatly and immediately impacted the population's sense of whether the revolution, the common term in Algeria for the independence, was going to be honored in the postindependence period. During the war, fighting between the FLN and the MNA along with FLN purges and reprisals against unsupportive civilians resulted in the deaths of thousands. In the lead-up to independence, the heads of the ALN and the overarching National Committee of the Algerian Revolution (CNRA, Comité national de la Revolution Algérienne) coalesced around two major factions seeking supremacy over the new state. The first group fell behind the National Liberation Army General Staff (EMG, Etat-major général), helmed by then-colonel Houari Boumediene and possessing bases on the Tunisian and Moroccan borders. This camp was supported by Ahmed Ben Bella, one of the historical FLN founders; internal *wilayas* (districts into which the ALN had divided Algeria and France) I and VI; and individuals aligned with the so-called Oujda Clan, which included the future president of Algeria Abdelaziz Bouteflika. Oujda was the eastern Moroccan border town in which key leaders of the EMG were stationed during the war. The second group backed the Provisional Government of the Algerian Republic or at least opposed the EMG. It counted among its partisans members of internal *wilayas* I, III, and IV along with Hocine Aït Ahmed, Mohamed Boudiaf, and Krim Belkacem.[124]

These clashes and the ultimate victory of the EMG, representing the part of the insurgent army situated outside of Algeria (the Army of the Exterior), immediately gave some Algerians the impression that the revolution had been stolen by "outsiders."[125] From the earliest stirrings of independence, some Algerians were further skeptical of individuals, some of whom had fought for the French army, who had joined the rebellion late in the game when an FLN victory was assured. These last-minute nationalists were called the *marsiens* for the month of March (*mars*) in French, the time of the 1962 Evian Accords outlining the end of the conflict.[126] The term also meant "Martians," potentially a humorous insult and a further way of marking them as foreign to the new nation.

Amid these events, the FLN remained uncertain and divided as to what the ideological and real framework of the postindependence state would be. At the May–June 1962 Tripoli Conference, various FLN leaders presented visions for the postindependence state. Some pushed for Marxist and socialist ideologies to prevail, while others wanted a government based on Islamism or one that would officially be secular. No consensus took hold. Plans for implementing the platform were also never hammered out.[127]

The country's postindependence leaders quickly moved to profit from its revolutionary legacy to further bind civilians to a sense of common Algerianness as marshaled by the FLN. For example, the postindependence government renamed streets after fallen anticolonial heroes, declared major dates of the War of Independence national holidays, and constructed monuments to major FLN figures and institutions. This worship of the conflict's martyrs and glorification of the revolution eventually became so intense that it alienated the generation born after independence.[128]

The above discussion does not intend to imply that only generational divisions existed in Algeria during this period; the population was at risk of splintering along other lines or over the question of whether the postindependence regime represented the true intent of the revolution. Doubts about the latter idea persisted despite the state's efforts to bolster national unity and unanimous support for the one-party, military-backed system. Wishing to challenge a regime that he viewed as unrepresentative of the country, Aït Ahmed spearheaded an armed rebellion against the national government from Kabylia through his organization, the Front of Socialist Forces (FFS, Front des forces socialistes). Located to the east of Algiers along the Mediterranean coast, Kabylia is an Imazighen (Berber)-majority territory where the majority of the population speaks Tamazight. The uprising lasted from September 1963 to June 1965. Infighting among political elites would continue at the highest echelons of power through the postindependence period, but with little input from the general population and usually (and purposefully) outside of its view.[129] The most visible and significant shuffling of power occurred with the June 1965 ouster of first president Ahmed Ben Bella by Houari Boumediene. The latter promoted socialism but also Arabization policies and a Cultural Revolution in the 1970s that created limited space for more conservative ideals when it came to Islam and the Arabic language as central aspects of the nation. His time as the head of state was fraught with risk for political opponents on the left such as communists as well as proponents of a greater place for Islam in the government, including the al-Qiyam al-islāmiyya (Islamic Values Society). Boumediene's government suppressed that organization on the national level from 1970 onward. This repression would not keep opposition movements down, though. Amazighism, a movement for the improvement of the rights of Imazighen, grew in strength in Algeria during this period as a response to state policies. Activists in Kabylia rose up for greater rights and against government repression in the 1980 "Berber Spring." The protests represented the greatest unarmed mass gathering and movement against central state authority since independence.[130]

Given the fault lines dividing the country's leadership postindependence, its lack of popular legitimacy, and its internal factionalism along with Algeria's broad geographical, linguistic, and ethnic diversity, the government had a strong interest in promoting a unified national identity. This notion of a national character also had to refrain from threatening or questioning the authority of the FLN and, by extension, the military, which generally had a large hand in controlling the organization. Among other measures and sites of possible unity formation, the government turned to comedy to overcome communal fissures within the population.[131] The sole legal political party, the FLN, coopted and cultivated humorous talent to spread its propaganda of national consciousness. Enthusiasm among the people for having gained independence may have similarly prompted an outburst of pride in the Algerian nation that sparked additional nationalizing forms of comedy. It also appears that, regardless of the government's strategies, some Algerians enjoyed the humor from state-owned media. At the same time, although working within state agencies, many of the professional humorists discussed hardships endured by ordinary Algerians, especially pervasive shortages and underdevelopment. In a twist of irony, the suffering of ordinary Algerians was itself depicted as particularly Algerian, a common denominator linking residents of the territory to one another.

Popular humor discussing national politics did not generally acknowledge splits between groups inside the state vying for power. Nor did comedy tailored outside of state-controlled venues (such as jokes that I recovered) attest to tensions between opposition groups forced to conduct their activism clandestinely. Instead, most popular political humor took as its target the government, the FLN, and the country's leaders.

Humor from first Algerian head of state Ahmed Ben Bella's brief rule (July 1962 to June 1965) seems scarce. For instance, the new government after independence initially feared that foreign comics could have a negative influence on the country's youth. Cartoons were similarly not produced during this period.[132] However, second president Houari Boumediene's government perceived laughter and fun as an important part of its political repertoire. In a quote to *Algérie-Actualité*, a state-run French-language weekly magazine, his minister of the interior, Bachir Boumaza, declared, "Revolution is serious, but not necessarily austere. It has to know how to smile and laugh at itself."[133] The regime adopted levity as part of its ideological arsenal.

Indeed, even the War of Independence, an event that was approached with the utmost reverence, could provide humorous fodder that Boumediene reportedly appreciated. In 1967, with approval and financial backing from the Ministry of the Interior and the National Office for Cinematographic Commerce and Industry, Mohamed Lakhdar-Hamina produced his second full-length feature, *Hassan terro*/(Hassan the terrorist). The film, based on an earlier play by comedy-sketch artist Rouiched, traces the story of a bourgeois simpleton and coward (Rouiched as "Hassan") who becomes a nationalist hero of the Battle of Algiers despite his best efforts to stay out of the conflict.[134] Rouiched himself held the nationalist clout necessary to mock a new genre of enemy of the Algerian people that had reportedly surfaced in the wake of independence.[135] The film was not well received by critics but had the highest attendance in Algiers's cinemas of any Algerian movie by the early 1970s, a sign of its popularity in the capital at least. The film went on to gather a cult following.[136] It perhaps did so by depicting a circumstance—Algerians being forced to choose a side during the war against France—through which many Algerians had lived. It thereby reinforced a sense of a common past and accompanying common future for members of the nascent nation. Boumediene was rumored to admire the film. He supposedly saw it as an effective jab at individuals in the government whom he considered *faux moudjahidine* ("fake *mujāhidīn*" in French), individuals claiming falsely to be War of Independence veterans to gain advantages in the new postindependence system.[137]

From the late 1960s to the early 1980s, Algerian bandes dessinées provide perhaps the clearest indication of how comedy and humor in the postindependence era helped foster a so-called national personality at the explicit behest of the state while still occasionally challenging the FLN. During these decades, Algeria's cartooning industry blossomed into one so robust that the country hosted its first comics festival in the eastern Algiers suburb of Borj El Kiffan in 1986 and the journalist Lazhari Labter could label it one of the most vibrant in the Middle East and Africa.[138] Bandes dessinées from this time tackled many issues and themes in an attempt to reinforce a sense of *algérianité* or singular nationalist and nationalizing identity among the population. Algerian cartoonists from this early period primarily looked to earlier European bandes dessinées (for example, *Spigo*) for models for their own work.[139] Regardless of this inspiration, whether appearing in stand-alone albums or as series in newspapers, these comic strips represented among the first occasions for Algerian Arabic to appear widely in print cultures. During this period, all cartoons or bandes dessinées passed through a state censor, since all the publishing outlets and editors were owned or controlled by the state.[140] Nonetheless, a few cartoons emerged that were critical in their assessments of Algerian society and government. Such cartoons often dealt with everyday issues that the cartoonists identified as unique to Algeria.[141]

This type of appraisal of Algerian culture and even, at times, politics was perhaps strongest in the works of Menouar Merabtene, better known by his penname Slim, as well as in the humorous revue *M'Quideche*, which combined the talents of several artists. Slim's series, inspired by the Battle of Algiers (both the event and the film by the same name) and entitled *Moustache et les frères Belgacem*, hit the scene in 1967 and came to be widely regarded as the country's second full bande dessinée. The album tells the story of a young, revolutionary Moustache who evades capture at the hands of the mean Belgacem brothers, local Algerians collaborating with the French authorities to suppress the FLN's campaign for independence, the hated *ḥarkīs*.[142] The bande dessinée's action is confined to Algiers's renowned Casbah neighborhood. Yet, as with the popular play that was later converted into the movie *Hassan terro*, *Moustache* confronted the darkly upsetting circumstances of the country's bitter War of Independence with laughter and by examining a specific set of events and characters, such as the *ḥarkīs*, that Algerians more than others could understand.[143] Slim stated in an interview that the album's subject, the Casbah, "wasn't my city . . . but in imagining a comic Casbah, I showed the Battle of Algiers from a different point of view." In other words, he did not know the Casbah very well but mainly wanted his work to depict one of the most important events in Algeria's War of Independence in a lighthearted way. The result was a story theoretically about Algiers that was nonetheless general enough to be accessible to all Algerian audiences.[144]

Figure 1.4 provides some clues to explain Slim's possible intention in crafting this cartoon. The cartoonist presents a general scene from the Casbah neighborhood. In the picture, though, individual figures are undertaking activities that Algerians performed in neighborhoods and towns throughout the country. A man is at a counter of a café, a pastime for men throughout Algeria. A man to the center right of the picture between the garage and the military post can be seen praying. Additionally, a minaret is rising in the background above one of the buildings. Both of these details could connect the predominantly Muslim Algerian readers from across the country to the characters involved in the bande dessinée, given their Islamic character. A woman is dressed

Figure 1.4. Slim's imagining of the Casbah during the Battle of Algiers in *Moustache et les frères Belgacem* (Mustache and the Belgacem brothers).

in a haik (*ḥāyak*), a garment worn both in Algiers and elsewhere in the country. Other than her apparel, though, there are no indications, such as street signs, that the action is taking place in the Casbah. The Arabization of French, a common facet of Algerian dialects of Arabic, is represented by the sign to the right of the image saying "Hotel Fichy" rather than "Hotel Vichy." Vichy is a place in France, the site of the Nazi-collaborationist government in World War II, whereas Fichy is not, and the letter *v* does not exist in Arabic, whereas *f* does (thus, Arabic speakers can use an *f* in lieu of a *v*). Consequently, Slim did not render the scenes and characters of *Moustache* so specific to the Casbah, a neighborhood that he admitted to hardly knowing, that Algerian readers more broadly could not feel a sense of affinity with the actions taking place in the album. Instead, *Moustache* appears to have represented an effort on the part of the cartoonist to celebrate Algerian-ness. Slim and his editors seemed to hope that the consumer would naturally gravitate toward the dashing Moustache and share in a common dislike of the odious *harkī* Belgacem brothers, traitors like those of Vichy France. Characteristics of Algerian heroism were thus defined by the artist from Sid Bel Abbas through sketches in the nationally distributed, state-owned press. What is more, before this comic strip, the cartoonist Aram had published a series of sequential cartoons featuring a character named Naar, meaning "fire," who, in Slim's words, was "an attempt to create an Algerian superhero."[145] From their earliest stirrings in the late 1960s, Algeria's *bédéistes* (bandes dessinées artists) strove through humorous sketches to promulgate a shared Algerian national identity in line with state agendas.

In February 1969, with the support of the FLN, Algeria's young aspiring cartoonists, including Slim, Haroun, Aram, and Maz, launched the country's first regularly printed collection of bandes dessinées—*M'Quidech*. As was the case with cartoonists who came after them in the late twentieth and early twenty-first centuries, these illustrators hailed from various socioeconomic backgrounds and regions in the country, although all possessed some level of education.[146] The artists named the revue after a popular Algerian folk character who often triumphed over larger, more powerful opponents, a sort of David-against-Goliath figure, a purposeful attempt at positioning the work as an extension of earlier comic folk traditions. Targeted at children, the magazine featured Algerian characters, Algerian storylines, and, for the dialogue, an Algerian dialect of Arabic. One serial cartoon, *Richa Causes a Scandal*, featured a local girl as she comically navigates her way around a local city filled with mosques and colonial-style buildings occupied exclusively by Algerians. By making an Algerian girl the protagonist of the piece and placing her in a local setting, the cartoonist created Algerian characters and situations with which children in the country could identify.[147]

The choice of *M'Quidech*'s editors and artists to focus on subjects particular to Algeria was not a coincidence. In a newspaper article commemorating the magazine, journalist Lazhari Labter cited a document shared between the "principal directors" of the magazine and FLN officials that outlined the publication's objectives. Labter quotes the internal FLN text as declaring that *M'Quidech* would result in the promulgation of "common heroes of an Algerian sort" and "Algerianize customs and environments," while making the physical attributes of characters far from those features overwhelmingly associated with European or American cartoon characters of the time; the document forbade the appearance of any "blonds with blue eyes" or "men with prominent chins." Labter notes that FLN officials supported the project because they saw the paper as a possible way to undermine similar European and North American cartoons that they believed heroicized Western culture. Like the other magazines and cartoons discussed above, the review reflected attempts to humorously foster a national identity immediately following independence from French colonial rule in harmony with the government's agenda of national consciousness building.[148]

Cartoonist Slim crafted an Algerian everyman town dweller named Bouzid whose adventures were closely followed by readers of *La République* and *El*

Moudjahid as well as stand-alone albums. With most action located in the real town of Oued Besbes in central-western Algeria, from the late 1960s through the 1980s *Zid ya Bouzid* (Go oh Bouzid!) was intended for national audiences and commented on nationwide policies such as the Agrarian Revolution. Algerian dialects of Arabic were prevalent through the technically French-language albums, making them unintelligible for non-Maghribi audiences. Bouzid comics depict the titular character thwarting actors threatening to undermine Algeria's revolution or the nation, mainly through intentional sabotage, hoarding materials, or putting bureaucratic obstacles in citizens' way.[149] Cultural writers and fellow cartoonists have remarked on the distinctive vision of Algeria that Slim drew through these comics.[150] The artist even entitled a review of his work *L'Algérie de Slim* / (Slim's Algeria).[151] Appearing in state-controlled outlets, *Zid ya Bouzid* critiqued the social circumstances in which many Algerians lived but did not attack government policies directly.[152]

During the 1970s and 1980s, bandes dessinées also more conspicuously supported the cause of national unity by depicting the valiant struggle of nationalist fighters during the War of Independence or earlier instances of conflict with French authorities. With this effort, they followed a plan laid out by a government-controlled publishing industry that sought to promote the interests of the state by instilling in readers a sense of national belonging. These works were not humorous; quite the opposite, they dealt with violent clashes and other serious topics. Nevertheless, their inclusion in a format typically associated with fun signifies that the state wanted to use cartoons and comedy as a means to bolster an unwavering belief in the existence of the nation. Some albums set during the original French conquest of the territory also insinuated that the nation had taken form long before the rise of Algerian nationalism in the interwar period.[153] Other laughter-inducing cartoons appeared in newspapers alongside articles, and these one-panel caricatures also reinforced a shared Algerian national identity. Slim created such works for the Francophone weekly magazine *Algérie-Actualité* in the 1980s. One cartoon (fig. 1.5) joked about how to "Algerianize" the nation's universities, suggesting that Algerian students eat Algerian rather than French food, consuming fillets of *ṭūmāṭīsh* (Algerian Arabic for "tomato") instead of French *steak-frites* (steak and French fries).[154]

Such national-consciousness-raising humor in the 1960s, 1970s, and 1980s surfaced even when and where the state was not behind its formal production. Popular jokes engaging with problems endemic to the country or national politics or comparing Algerians to citizens of other nations (e.g., beginning with "an Algerian, a French person, and an American") thrived during these three decades.[155] Like bandes dessinées and films from the three decades immediately

Figure 1.5. Slim cartoon from *Algérie-Actualité*, March 13–19, 1980, 5.

following independence, jokes from this time attest to the rise of a shared Algerian national consciousness and worked to buttress this consciousness.

Political jokes were told in both public and private spaces throughout this period. As in most societies, gatherings with families and friends either at home or in public spaces such as cafés, public baths, and on the sidewalk often provided opportunities to tell jokes that sought to entertain but also to mirror social realities of the time. Humorous jokes ranged from the mundane and innocuous to the ferociously sexual and could be recounted by men and women, young and old alike. Joke-telling could work in a circular fashion; one person tosses out a joke and then another tells a different one in what can quickly evolve into an hours-long joke-telling session.[156]

Jokes that ridiculed presidents and national politicians reminded Algerians of their status in a common nation and their unity, for better or for worse, under a shared set of leaders. Every person who told such a joke inevitably acted out or performed his or her membership in the national community; they were criticizing a common government official and the circumstances under which his rule caused them to live. Furthermore, these jokes would not be understood by those uninitiated in the specific struggles that these joke-tellers ideologically hailed listeners to associate with Algerian daily life, framed here as such although obviously present elsewhere. The *El Moudjahid* fish joke is an example of this humor that reminds listeners of Algerian circumstances while pushing a political message. The common citizen suffering or getting by under the system becomes, through self-deprecating humor, imagined as specifically Algerian, a replication of earlier practices of self-deprecating humor. The following joke portrays Algerians as Juḥā-esque in their ability to engage with authority in unexpected manners. It imagines an exchange between Boumediene and an unspecified town in the country during the second president's Agrarian Revolution:[157]

> After Boumediene had started the construction of socialist villages, he arrives in one to inaugurate it. He gets there and asks, "Where is the *shaykh* or leader of the tribe's council?" The villagers present the oldest patriarch to him. He tells him hello and that he is honored. He then tells the leader, "*Shaykh*, there is something I must tell you. We made houses with running water and electricity for you, we made a school for you, we made a mosque for you, we made a center for agricultural production, we brought tractors to you. Now the agricultural results are up to you." And supposedly the old man responded, "Oh Mr. President, now that you've given them everything, why would they work?"

> *Quand Boumediene a lancé la construction des villages socialistes, il inaugure un village socialiste. Yijī ū-il demande, "Wīn rāh shīkh tā' jamā'at al-qabīla," et on lui présente le patriarche le plus vieux. Donc, il lui dit, "Bonjour, je suis honoré." Il lui dit au cheikh, "Shīkh, il faut que je vous dise quelque chose, dirnā lkūm diyār bil mā' ū-bi-l'électricité, dirnā lkūm la-msīd, dirnā lkūm masjid, al-ḥammām, dirnā lkūm le local pour le matériel jibnā lkūm al-tractorāt. Durka 'alaykum al-intāj al-zirā'i." Et parait-il le vieux lui répond, "Yā sīd al-ra'īs, durka 'aṭītnā gā' al-shī, 'alāsh yakhdmū?"*[158]

According to this joke, Boumediene miscalculated how peasants would respond to the revolution. Simultaneously, though, as with other jokes in which Algerians emerge as silly or sly, self-deprecation permits joke-tellers and listeners to imagine themselves as separate from those in power. They are thereby fashioned as ordinary people, part of a public that often considered itself at odds with a government that did not understand them, a message with serious political implications.[159]

Other examples of political jokes further testify to this pattern of critiquing national policies and figures. Along with Boumediene, at least some Algerians turned to laugh at another powerful government official: Kaïd Ahmed, head of the FLN party from 1969 to 1974 and better known by his nom de guerre Commander Si Slimane. Kaïd Ahmed served as the butt of many humorous stories, popularly called *slimanaries*. There were reportedly so many of these moments where the party leader slipped up that Algerian residents are said to have compiled them into a clandestine book that then circulated around the country.[160] Algerians were also uncertain as to which stories were real or potentially fabricated by ordinary citizens for their amusement. Lines between humor and news were blurred.[161] Kaïd Ahmed's public gaffes in speaking, similar to American "Bushisms" of the 2000s, supposedly included a speech in which the FLN leader declared at the opening of a dam that Algeria's future was "in water," a statement that in French means "ruined."[162] As I explore more thoroughly in the next chapter, Boumediene's successor from 1979 to 1992, Chadli Benjedid (who was not widely anticipated to take the helm of state upon the second Algerian president's sudden death), inspired an entire subgenre of what is now defined as Algerian humor: the Chadli joke. These humorous stories centered on Chadli's lack of formal education and his purported inability to present a dignified view of Algeria on the international stage, both failings that Boumediene had effectively avoided; he spoke fluent Arabic and escaped the public-speaking blunders that befell Chadli. The earlier president also oversaw the state at the moment of its prestigious leadership of the Non-Aligned Movement. These jokes may have signaled how sections of the body politic viewed the president as buffoonish and failing in his duties to lead the state wisely and in ways that would inspire respect.[163] President-targeted humor under Chadli became much more personal and scathing than it had been under his predecessors. Finally, evidence of state surveillance of jokes throughout the early postindependence decades appears thin but at least one Chadli joke pointed to the state collecting jokes about the president.[164]

CONCLUSION

The building of Algerian nationalism was and remains a complicated and drawn-out process undertaken by actors from many levels of society. What is clear is that, by the 1920s and 1930s, a larger sense of being bound together had spread among Muslim Algerians who proffered differing views of what the nation could be. Humor often provided a binding agent that many actors used to invite listeners, consumers, and producers alike to perform belongingness to Algeria or to recognize or elaborate Algerian characteristics (Algerian-ness), continuously constructed as these ideas were. Such ideological hailing, part of Althusserian interpellations coming from elite and non-elite circles alike, appear to have been successful or were at least perceived to have been successful given archival and oral history testimonies revealing state surveillance of these measures.

With populations that suffered from high levels of illiteracy across the period in question, oral and visual forms of comedy especially assisted individuals as wide-ranging as French administrators, nationalist fighters, comic actors, and illustrators for children's cartoons with advancing ideas about Algerianness and the belonging of communities around the country to a greater political entity. New technologies such as film and television were adapted to allow broader audiences to experience earlier forms of comedy such as sketches and satirical songs. Events as serious as the War of Independence were not immune to parody. As most professional comedy producers in theater, TV, film, and cartoons worked from the capital city of Algiers, they fashioned themselves as conveyors of knowledge about the nation and this city as a center of its cultural production and power. Algerian Arabic, often mixed with some French and Tamazight, emerged as the language in which humorous efforts were undertaken in this center and the language in which cultural producers promoting Algerian-ness attempted to speak to communities across the country. Humor may have helped cement Algerian Arabic as a major language through which the invented people express ideas. On the whole, humor from the period was a critical site for Algerians to express their opinions on the highly political question of what the nation was and should be.

Indeed, these earlier forms of political humor inspired practices that continued into a moment of prolonged crisis that has lasted in Algeria from the late 1980s through the present day, illustrating the importance of studying humor and its changes over time.[165] A notion of a specially Algerian typology of humor also emerged by this period, as evinced in the writings of mainly Mediterranean urban-based intellectuals such as Abderrahmane Lounes.[166] References to humor, such as the popular appellation of Algeria by its citizens as *bled mickey* (the "country of mickey," for Micky Mouse, or any clown), became part and parcel of the country's political vocabulary by the time that economic, social, and cultural pressures, coupled with a corrupt, out-of-touch state, heralded first an era of popular revolution, then one of political opening, and then one of bloody civil struggle. This process began with an Arab Spring–like revolt, Algeria's October 1988 Revolution, and a brief democratic transition that the uprising helped put in motion. Humor's role during these events is the subject of the next chapter. Humor continued to prove a central space, albeit a less unifying one, throughout these seismic changes, as the stakes of national belonging transformed once more into questions of life and death.

NOTES

1. Founded in 1912, *Pravda* was the official newspaper of the Communist Party under the Soviet Union, just as Algeria's *El Moudjahid* (Arabic for "the fighter") paper was controlled by the North African nation's only political organization, the National Liberation Front. The annotations of this joke in notes 1 to 3 are my own. The joke in the original text appears above.

2. The National Liberation Front.

3. Hassi Messouad in Ouargala Province is the site of one of Algeria's largest oil fields. Houari Boumediene was the country's second postindependence president.

4. Bachir Dahak, *Les Algériens: Le rire et la politique de 1962 à nos jours* (Algiers: Frantz Fanon, 2018), 81–82. This joke may originally have been a Soviet one given that citizens within the Soviet Union could not transport fish in newspapers lest their scales sully the images of its leaders. Robert W. Thurston, "Social Dimensions of Stalinist Rule: Humor and Terror in the USSR, 1935–1941," *Journal of Social History* 42, no. 3 (1991): 544. All translations are my own unless otherwise noted.

5. Dahak, *Les Algériens*, 81–82.

6. McClintock views the process of individuals viewing themselves as part of larger collective "nations," Anderson's "imagined communities," less as "imagined" and more as "invented." See Anne McClintock, "Family Feuds: Gender, Nationalism, and Family," *Feminist Review* 44 (1993): 61; Benedict Anderson, *Imagined Communities*, 2nd ed. (London: Verso, 1991).

7. See Ziad Fahmy, *Ordinary Egyptians: Creating the Nation through Popular Culture* (Palo Alto: Stanford University Press, 2011); Adam Mestyan, *Arab Patriotism: The Ideology and Culture of Power in Late Ottoman Egypt* (Princeton, NJ: Princeton University Press, 2017); Jonathan Wyrtzen, "Performing the Nation in Anti-colonial Protest in Interwar Morocco," *Nations and Nationalism* 19, no. 4 (2013): 615–634.

8. See Fahmy, *Ordinary Egyptians*; Wyrtzen, "Performing the Nation."

9. See Fahmy, *Ordinary Egyptians*, for instance. Historians of Africa have better examined oral cultures' propensity for advancing nationalist ideologies and creating national identities. See Toyin Falola, *Nationalism and African Intellectuals* (Rochester, NY: University of Rochester Press, 2001); Susan Geiger, "Tanganyikan Nationalism as 'Women's Work': Life Histories, Collective Biography, and Changing Historiography," *Journal of African History* 37, no. 3 (1996): 456–478.

10. For more on the racialization of religious categories, see Patricia Lorcin, "Imperialism, Colonial Identity, and Race," *History of Science Society* 90, no. 4 (1999): 653–679; Muriam Haleh Davis, *Markets of Civilization: Islam and Racial Capitalism in Algeria* (Durham, NC: Duke University Press, 2022).

11. For more on Algeria's Jewish community, see Benjamin Stora, *Les trois exils: Juifs d'Algérie* (Paris: Stock, 2006); Rochdi Ali Younsi, "Caught in a Colonial Triangle: Competing Loyalties within the Jewish Community of Algeria, 1842–1943" (PhD diss., University of Chicago, 2003); among other numerous works.

12. See, for instance, Christopher Silver, *Recording History: Jews, Muslims, and Music across Twentieth-Century North Africa* (Palo Alto: Stanford University Press, 2022). I place

colonial here in quotation marks because not all subjects living under colonialism necessarily viewed themselves as "colonized," and continuities existed across so-called precolonial and colonial periods. Arthur Asseraf, "Khoualdia Salah and the Networks of Pan-Islamic News around 1900" (paper presented at the Middle East Studies Association's Annual Meeting, New Orleans, LA, November 15, 2019); M'hamed Oualdi, *A Slave between Empires* (New York: Columbia University Press, 2020).

13. European settlers participated in the humorous impromptu sketches for which some Muslim and Jewish performers became known in the interwar period. European actors also played in the troupes run by Muslim artists, coauthoring some of the works that reached out to and attempted to unite Algerian Muslims. See Christiane Chaulet-Achour and Dalila Morsly, "Plus d'un siècle de rire en Algérie," in *2000 ans de rire* (Franc-Comtoises: Université de Franc-Comtoises, 2002), 61; pamphlet on the play in ANOM Library B 400.

14. Giselinde Kuipers, "The Sociology of Humor," in *The Primer of Humor Research*, ed. Victor Raskin (Berlin: Mouton de Gruyter, 2008), 382–385. For an overview of the different schools or theories of humor studies, see John Morreall, "Philosophy of Humor," in *Stanford Encyclopedia of Humor*, last modified November 12, 2012, http://plato.stanford.edu/entries/humor/#SupThe.

15. Louis Althusser, "Ideology and Ideological State Apparatuses," in *Lenin and Philosophy and Other Essays*, trans. Frederic Jameson (New York: NYU Press, 2001), 115–120.

16. Lisa Wedeen, *Authoritarian Apprehensions* (Chicago: University of Chicago Press, 2019), 10.

17. See the section below on the Hadj Guillaume song.

18. Sylvie Thénault, "1881–1919: L'apogée de l'Algérie française et les débuts de l'Algérie algérienne," in *Histoire de l'Algérie à la période coloniale, 1830–1961*, ed. Abderrahmane Bouchène, Jean-Pierre Peyroulou, Ouanassa Siari Tengour, and Sylvie Thénault (Paris: La Découverte, 2012), 159–184.

19. See David Prochaska, "History as Literature, Literature as History," *American Historical Review* 101, no. 3 (1996): 670–711; Paul Siblot, "'Cagayous antijuifs': Un discours colonial en proie à la racisation," *Mots: Les langages du politique* 15 (1987): 59–75; James McDougall, *A History of Algeria* (Cambridge: Cambridge University Press, 2017), 361n70.

20. McDougall, *History of Algeria*, 112.

21. James McDougall, *History and the Culture of Nationalism in Algeria* (Cambridge: Cambridge University Press, 2006), 39–43.

22. John Ruedy, *Modern Algeria*, 2nd ed. (Bloomington: Indiana University Press, 2005); Charles-Robert Ageron, *Histoire de l'Algérie contemporaine* (Paris: Presses Universitaires de France, 1964), 181–182; Rabah Aissaoui, "Politics, Identity, and Temporality in Colonial Algeria in the Early Twentieth Century," *Journal of North African Studies* 22, no. 2 (2017): 182–204.

23. See McDougall, *History and Culture*.

24. Ageron, *Histoire de l'Algérie contemporaine*, 182.

25. Older women were storytellers as well but for audiences of other women within private spaces. Khalid Amine and Marvin Carlson, *The Theatres of Morocco, Algeria, and Tunisia: Performance Traditions of the Maghrib* (New York: Palgrave Macmillan, 2012), 18–19.

26. Amine and Carlson, *Theatres of Morocco*, 18–19. See also Arthur Asseraf, *Electric News in Colonial Algeria* (Oxford: Oxford University Press, 2019).

27. Amine and Carlson, *Theatres of Morocco*, 18.

28. Kamal Salhi, "Morocco, Algeria and Tunisia," in *A History of Theatre in Africa*, ed. Martin Banham (Cambridge: Cambridge University Press, 2004), 39.

29. Amine and Carlson, *Theatres of Morocco*, 18.
30. Aïssa Khelladi, "Rire quand même: L'humour politique dans l'Algérie d'aujourd'hui," *Revue des mondes musulmans et de la Méditerranée* 77–78 (1996): 226.
31. Amine and Carlson, *Theatres of Morocco*.
32. See, for instance, Christa Catherine Jones, "Female Tricksters," in *Women and Resistance in the Maghrib: Remembering Kahina*, ed. Nabil Boudraa and Joseph Ohmann Krause (New York: Routledge, 2022), 123.
33. Khelladi, "Rire quand même," 226.
34. See the discussion at the beginning of this volume's introduction.
35. Arlette Roth, *Le théâtre algérien de langue dialectale, 1926–1954* (Paris: François Maspero, 1967), 14–15, citing Puckler-Muskau, *Chroniques, Lettre, Journal de voyage*, tome 2 (Paris: Fournier, 1836–1837).
36. Roth, *Le théâtre algérien*, 15.
37. Prochaska, "History as Literature."
38. Joseph Desparmet, "La chanson d'Alger pendant la Grande Guerre," *Revue africaine* 73 (1932): 57.
39. See Asseraf, *Electric News*, 118–128; McDougall, *History and Culture*, 105–106.
40. Desparmet, "La chanson d'Alger," 60; Asseraf, *Electric News*, 119n55.
41. Desparmet lists different takes on the song's lyrics. Desparmet, "La chanson d'Alger," 62–83. This is Desparmet's interpretation of the work and its thirty-eight versions that he collected as flexible, one that Asseraf shares. See Desparmet, "La chanson d'Alger," 54–61, especially 58; Asseraf, *Electric News*, 118.
42. Desparmet, "La chanson d'Alger," 54–61.
43. In Islamic theology, the Mahdi will return before the end of days to bring justice to the world. McDougall (*History and Culture*, 105–106) sees the song as building off of Mahdist prophecies.
44. Asseraf, *Electric News*, 126.
45. Meaning "significations," *m'ānī* were comic idioms. Desparmet, "La chanson d'Alger," 62–83.
46. This is my translation. Desparmet translates *sa'duh* as "his happiness" or "his star." Desparmet, "La chanson d'Alger," 58, 62.
47. Desparmet, "La chanson d'Alger."
48. See Desparmet, "La chanson d'Alger," especially 60.
49. Desparmet, "La chanson d'Alger," 68, 79. Incongruity, in which objects or people are out of place or behave as they should not, is recognized by humor specialists as one of its key characteristics. Morreall, "Philosophy of Humor."
50. Desparmet, "La chanson d'Alger."
51. Desparmet, "La chanson d'Alger," 73–74.
52. Desparmet, "La chanson d'Alger," 58.
53. Desparmet, "La chanson d'Alger," 64–65.
54. Saaddedine Bencheneb, "Chansons satiriques d'Alger," *Revue Africaine* 74 (1933): 75–117, 296–352.
55. Roth, *Le théâtre algérien*, 64–65.
56. See S. Bencheneb, "Chansons satiriques d'Alger."
57. See Ruedy, *Modern Algeria*, 112–113; McDougall, *History of Algeria*, 152.
58. See, for instance, the lyrics of "The Counselor / *Le Conseiller*" in S. Bencheneb, "Chansons satiriques d'Alger."

59. S. Bencheneb, "Chansons satiriques d'Alger," 85, 109–110, 338–341.
60. S. Bencheneb, "Chansons satiriques d'Alger," 84–85. For an overview of this movement, see McDougall, *History and Culture*; Charlotte Courreye, "L'Association des oulémas musulmans algériens et la construction de l'Etat indépendant algérien" (PhD diss., Université Sorbonne Paris, 2016).
61. Mahieddine Bachtarzi, *Mémoires, 1919–1939*, vol. 1 (Algiers: SNED, 1968), 143–144.
62. Bachtarzi, *Mémoires*.
63. Bachtarzi, *Mémoires*, 143.
64. Roth, *Le théâtre algérien*, 49–53.
65. See Rachid Bencheneb, "Allalu et les origines du théâtre algérien," *Revue des mondes musulmans et de la Méditerranée* 24 (1977): 29–37. Ahmed Cheniki speaks more of a "theater of Algeria" during this initial period. Ahmed Cheniki, *Le théâtre en Algérie* (Paris: Edisud, 2002), 15.
66. Roth, *Le théâtre algérien*, 15–16, 21–23.
67. Bachtarzi, *Mémoires*. The author notes newspaper cultural critics' responses along with those of the theatergoers throughout the volume.
68. Bachtarzi, *Mémoires*.
69. Roth, *Le théâtre algérien*, 45.
70. R. Bencheneb, "Allalu"; Cheniki, *Le théâtre en Algérie*, 20–21.
71. R. Bencheneb, "Allalu," 29.
72. See the later part of this chapter on Slim's Algerian "everyman" character Bouzid. Prochaska draws a line between Cagayous, Juḥā, and Bouzid. Prochaska, "History as Literature," 702.
73. French settler Louis Chaprot worked with Bachtarzi on his plays. Pamphlet on play in ANOM Library B// 400.
74. Rachid Bencheneb, "Les mémoires de Mahiéddine Bachtarzi ou vingt ans de théâtre algérien," *Revue des mondes musulmans et de la Méditerranée* 9 (1971): 18; ANOM B 2152.
75. Observations based on lyrics in play pamphlets/bills/song collections. ANOM B 2152.
76. See McDougall, *History and Culture*.
77. It bears noting that Bachtarzi was not always so optimistic or positive about the ability of Europeans and Muslims to form one nation or community. He paints a much bleaker picture in an earlier play, *'Ala an-nīf*. ANOM 9H37.
78. Pamphlet, "Les femmes," found in ANOM B 2152.
79. Roth, *Le théâtre algérien*, 136; pamphlet, "Les femmes," found in ANOM B 2152.
80. Joshua Cole, "A chacun son public," trans. Stéphane Bouquet, *Sociétés et représentations* 38, no. 2 (2014): 45, citing ANOM Alger 2I/41, document "Rapport de la Sûreté départementale d'Alger, soirée organisée par 'El-Moutribia,' 6 décembre 1937."
81. Pamphlets found in ANOM B 2151 and ANOM B 2152.
82. McDougall, *History of Algeria*, 105–106.
83. ANOM B 3494.
84. Roth, *Le théâtre algérien*, 74, 124–125.
85. See Cole, "A chacun son public," especially 35.
86. See Courreye, "L'Association"; Jane E. Goodman, "Acting with One Voice: Producing Unanimism in Algerian Reformist Theater," *Comparative Studies in History and Society* 55, no. 1 (2013): 167–197. Bachtarzi knew and was friendly with key leaders of the AUMA from the 1930s onward. See, for example, Bachtarzi, *Mémoires*, 146; Goodman, "Acting with One Voice," 176.

87. S. Bencheneb, "Chansons satiriques d'Alger," 79; 'Abd al-Raḥman Bakr, *al-Ṣaḥāfa al-aākhiriyya fī miṣr* (Giza: Arab Press Agency, 2018). Satirical Italian and Valencian papers were also present in Algeria in the late nineteenth and early twentieth centuries. Asseraf, *Electric News*, 41–42, 45–46.

88. Prochaska, "History as Literature," 682–684; Siblot, "Cagayous antijuifs." Editions of *Le Turco* are available for review at https://gallica.bnf.fr/ark:/12148/cb328822628/date&rk=42918;4.

89. Khelladi, "Rire quand même," 225; Sabra Webber, *Romancing the Real* (Berkeley: University of California Press, 1991).

90. For more on contemporary fears of Europeans regarding "racial intermixing" in the colonies, see John McCulloch, *Black Peril, White Virtue: Sexual Crime in Southern Rhodesia, 1902–1935* (Bloomington: Indiana University Press, 2000).

91. Interview with anonymous. The interview was not recorded, so I am paraphrasing here. For more on Muslim laborers and fear of "interracial mixing" in colonial Algeria, see Sara Rahnama, *The Future Is Feminist* (Ithaca: Cornell University Press, forthcoming).

92. Desparmet, "La Chanson d'Alger," 59.

93. Bachtarzi, *Mémoires*, 143–144.

94. Roth, *Le théâtre algérien*, 41.

95. Bachtarzi, *Mémoires*, 254–255.

96. Roth, *Le théâtre algérien*, 42; Mahieddine Bachtarzi, *Recueil des chansons Mahiéddine*, ANOM B 2151.

97. Roth, *Le théâtre algérien*, 42–44.

98. See ANOM Département d'Alger 4I/183.

99. Roth, *Le théâtre algérien*, 29, 34.

100. See also Olivier Blazy, "La presse militaire française à destination des troupes indigènes," trans. Robert A. Doughty, *Revue historique des armées* 271 (2013): 51–59.

101. See Alison S. Fel and Nina Wardleworth, "The Colour of War Memory: Cultural Representations of *Tirailleurs Sénégalais*," *Journal of War and Culture Studies* 9, no. 4 (2016): 319–344.

102. "Djeha n'est pas collaborationniste," *An-Naṣr*, first issue, June 1943. Dossier entitled "An-Nasr" in ANOM 4I/182.

103. See, for instance, the testimonies of women nationalist combatants in Djamila Amrane, *Des femmes dans la guerre d'Algérie: Entretiens* (Paris: Karthala, 1994).

104. Khelladi, "Rire quand même," 226.

105. Khelladi, "Rire quand même," 226–227. The artist sang about the problems that the local population faced that stemmed from colonial policies. See Amnay Idir, "Rachid Ksentini: Le rire pour supporter la misère," *El Watan*, September 13, 2005.

106. Khelladi, "Rire quand même," 226–227.

107. Mohamed Benrabah, "Competition between Four World Languages in Algeria," *Journal of World Languages* 1, no. 1 (2014): 46. At independence, of a population of ten million Muslims, French-language readers numbered one million versus the three hundred thousand Algerians who could read Arabic at that time (Arabic has since surpassed French in terms of readership based on press numbers). Print materials were not produced in Tamazight at the time, and Benrabah does not address literacy in Judeo-Arabic.

108. See Idir, "Rachid Ksentini."

109. Ameziane Ferhani, *50 ans de bande dessinée algérienne et l'aventure continue* (Algiers: Dalimen, 2012), 20–21. For readers unfamiliar with the genre, *bande dessinée* is French for

"drawn strip" and constitutes a genre of comics and cartoons in and of itself. For more information, see Thierry Groensteen, "The Impossible Definition," in *A Comic Studies Reader*, ed. Jeet Heer and Kent Worcester (Jackson: University of Mississippi, 2009), 130. Cartoonist Slim gives an overview of the history of cartooning in a recorded presentation he gave at the University of California, Los Angeles, in 2008. See https://www.youtube.com/watch?v=5jCsKpxCfVQ, accessed July 8, 2013.

110. For Muslim Algerians' lack of free speech and censorship during this period, see Asseraf, *Electric News*.

111. Matthew Connolly, *A Diplomatic Revolution* (New York: Oxford University Press, 2002).

112. Several narrators intimated to me that laughter during or about these events was typically absent. For instance, interview with Ameziane Ferhani, March 15, 2015. See also Khelladi, "Rire quand même," 227. For an overview of the literature on war dead and casualty numbers, see McDougall, *History of Algeria*, 232–233, 378n162.

113. Julie Champrenault, "La transition culturelle en Algérie indépendante," in *Le Maghreb et l'indépendance Algérie*, ed. Amar Mohand-Amer and Belkacem Benzenine (Paris: Karthala, 2012), 96–98.

114. Hocine Bouzaher, *Des voix dans le Casbah: Théâtre algérien militant* (Paris: François Maspero, 1960), 103.

115. For instance, interview with Ameziane Ferhani, March 15, 2015.

116. See SHD 1 H 1715, 1 H 2588, 1 H 2589, 1 H 2590, and 1 H 4458. I am grateful to Christiane Marie Abu-Sarah for sharing this material with me.

117. SHD 1H2590.

118. SHD 1 H 1715, 1 H 2588, 1 H 2589, 1 H 2590, 1 H 4458, and tract 39 located in SHD 1 H 2588.

119. SHD 1H2590.

120. See Raphaëlle Branche, *La torture et l'armée pendant la Guerre d'Algérie, 1954–1962* (Paris: Gallimard, 2001); Kristin Ross, *Fast Cars, Clean Bodies* (Cambridge, MA: MIT Press, 1996).

121. Henri Alleg, *La question* (Paris: Editions de Minuit, 1958), 55.

122. SHD 1H2590.

123. For more on ideal, wartime portraits of FLN fighters, see Christiane Marie Abu-Sarah's forthcoming work.

124. For more on this split, see Amar Mohand Amer, "Les wilayas dans la crise du FLN de l'été," *Insaniyat* 65–66 (2014): 105–124.

125. See, for example, Natalya Vince, *Our Fighting Sisters: Nation, Memory and Gender in Algeria, 1954–2012* (Manchester: Manchester University Press, 2015), 102–139.

126. McDougall, *History of Algeria*, 232.

127. McDougall, *History of Algeria*, 240–242.

128. Martin Evans and John Phillips discuss this phenomenon. See Martin Evans and John Phillips, *Algeria: Anger of the Dispossessed* (New Haven, CT: Yale University Press, 2007), 107.

129. McDougall, *History of Algeria*, 237–238.

130. Bruce Maddy-Weitzman, "Contested Identities," *Journal of North African Studies* 6, no. 3 (2001): 38.

131. Khelladi, "Rire quand même," 227.

132. Slim gives an overview of the history of cartooning in a recorded presentation he gave at the University of California, Los Angeles, in 2008. See https://www.youtube.com/watch?v=5jCsKpxCfVQ, accessed July 8, 2013.

133. *Algérie-Actualité*, November 14–20, 1965, cited as well in McDougall, *History of Algeria*, 260.

134. *Hassan Terro*, dir. Mohammed Lakhdar-Hamina (Algiers: Office des Actualités Algériennes / Office of Algerian News, 1968).

135. He had run messages for the FLN during the revolution. Rachid Sahnine, *Mémoires de Rouiched* (Algiers: Editions el-Adib Chihab, 1993), 108–145.

136. See Lyle Pearson, "Four Years of North African Film," *Film Quarterly* 26, no. 4 (1973): 22.

137. Interview with Ameziane Ferhani, March 15, 2015.

138. Lazhari Labter, "L'Algérie renoue avec le neuvième art," *Takam Tikou* of the French National Library, March 10, 2011, https://takamtikou.bnf.fr/dossiers/dossier-2011-la-bande-dessinee/l-algerie-renoue-avec-le-neuvieme-art-l-occasion-du-festival-international-de-la-bande-dessinee-d-alger.

139. Interview with Redhouane Assari, June 4, 2013.

140. Slim gives an overview of the history of cartooning in a recorded presentation he gave at the University of California, Los Angeles, in 2008. See https://www.youtube.com/watch?v=5jCsKpxCfVQ, accessed July 8, 2013.

141. See, for instance, Slim, Réédition de *Zid ya Bouzid I et II* (Algiers: ENAL, 1986).

142. Ḥarkī was a particular Algerian term for local soldiers serving in the French army during the country's War of Independence, who were widely perceived as turncoats; thousands of them died in vengeance attacks following the FLN's victory in the war.

143. Slim, *Moustache et les frères Belgacem* [Mustache and the Belgacem brothers] (Slim via Lulu.com, 2011).

144. Omar Zelig, *Slim, le gatt, et moi* (Algiers: DALIMEN, 2009), 46.

145. Zelig, *Slim, le gatt, et moi*, 46.

146. See the cartoonist biographies in Lazhari Labter, *Panorama de la bande dessinée algérienne* (Algiers: Lazhari Labter, 2009).

147. "Richa fait scandale" [Richa causes a scandal], in *Le journal de M'Quidèch* (Algiers: ENAG, 2003).

148. See the documentary shown at Slim's May 8, 2008, University of California at Los Angeles lecture, published November 25, 2009, https://www.youtube.com/watch?v=qxPb2F69UCU. Lazhari Labter, "Qui se souvient de *M'Quidèch*?," *Liberté*, February 9, 1999, 11, citing a document between FLN officials and the "principal directors" of the paper for which he gives no reference in the article.

149. See Slim, *Une loubia pour un marsien naïf* (Slim via Lulu.com, 2011) (original strip from 1980); Slim, Réédition de *Zid ya Bouzid I et II*; Slim, *Zid ya Bouzid III* (Algiers: ENAL, 1986); Allen Douglas and Fedwa Malti-Douglas, *Arab Comic Strips: Politics of an Emerging Mass Culture* (Bloomington: Indiana University Press, 1994), 188–197.

150. Zelig, *Slim, le gatt, et moi*, 11, 57.

151. Slim, *L'Algérie de Slim* (Paris: Editions l'Harmattan, 2000).

152. Douglas and Malti-Douglas, *Arab Comic Strips*, 188–197; see also, for instance, Slim, *Zid ya Bouzid I*.

153. See, for instance, Mustapha Tenani, *Hommes du djebel* (Algiers: ENAL, 1985). Evans and Phillips discuss historic comics that were popular in the 1970s and 1980s. See the section "Bilingual Politics" in Douglas and Malti-Douglas, *Arab Comic Strips*, 180–188; Evans and Phillips, *Algeria*, 108.

154. Slim, *Algérie-Actualité*, March 20–26, 1980, 9; Slim, *Algérie-Actualité*, March 13–19, 1980, 5.

155. See Dahak, *Les Algériens*.

156. Interview with Zineb Sedira, March 29, 2015.

157. The Agrarian Revolution initiated in 1971 redistributed land and established socialist villages in the hope of ramping up production and improving the lives of rural farmers.

158. Interview with Ameziane Ferhani, March 15, 2015.

159. Natalya Vince and Walid Benkhaled contend that the people versus *"pouvoir"* (an Algerian term for the regime from the French word for "power") construct has an important history in Algeria. Vince and Benkhaled, "Afterword: Performing Algerianness," in *Algeria: Nation, Culture, and Transnationalism*, ed. Patrick Crowley (Liverpool: Liverpool University Press, 2017), 244–245.

160. Dahak, *Les Algériens*, 61–74.

161. Dahak, *Les Algériens*.

162. Dahak, *Les Algériens*, 67.

163. See, for instance, Dahak, *Les Algériens*; Evans and Phillips, *Algeria*, 101. Interview with Ali Silem, December 27, 2015. Regarding Chadli jokes, Ali Silem explained that they were intended to make Chadli seem inferior to Boumediene, or that they emerged because the later president was so much less popular than his predecessor. Interview with Ali Silem, December 27, 2015.

164. Interview with Hichem Baba Ahmed (Le Hic), June 25, 2013. The joke describes Chadli getting so fed up with jokes at his expense that he orders the secret police to collect all the jokes about him and place them in a bag. They do so, and he proceeds to throw the bag in the bay of Algiers to get rid of them for once and for all. A few seconds later, fish rise to the surface of the water, dead from laughter (*"morts de rire"* in French).

165. Thomas Serres recognizes this crisis as ongoing. See Thomas Serres, *L'Algérie face à la catastrophe suspendue* (Tunis: Karthala, 2019).

166. Abderrahmane Lounes, text, and Rachid Marai, drawings, *Histoires extra et ordinaires du cimetièr-monde* (Algiers: SNED, 1983); Khelladi, "Rire quand même."

TWO

HUMOR IN REBELLION AND UNCERTAIN TIMES, 1988 TO 1992

A guy goes to the doctor. He enters the office. "My head is exploding. When I sleep, the whole night I have a terrible headache, and when I turn over, I die." The doctor asks him, "What's wrong? Why?" "It's because of this democracy, doctor." The doctor says to him, "Democracy? How?" The man replies, "Oh yes ... before it was the dictatorship. People used to think for me [in my place]. I was left alone. And now, all day long, I have to manage at work, in the café, everywhere, at home, with neighbors, everywhere people are asking me for my opinion. All day long, I have to get by as best as possible and me, I don't have an opinion! I have only the tiniest of opinions." He then proceeds to ask the doctor for medicine, at which point the medical provider explains that he has only one choice: "The solution ... get 15 or 20 people together and form a party ... the party MGMD: the *mdīgūṭiyyīn* [disgusted] with democracy party!"

Wāḥid jā ʿand al-ṭbīb.... dkhal ʿand al-ṭbīb. "Rāsī rāh yṭarṭag. Mānīsh narqud, līl kāmil j'ai un mal de tête terrible, līl kāmil w-ānā natqallab rāḥ nmūt." Qāl lu wāsh bik waʿlāh? "C'est à cause de la démocratie hādiyya a-ṭbib" Qāl lu, "Kifāh la démocratie?" Qāl lu "Mais oui." Qāl lu, "Bikrī kānat la dictature. Kānū al-nās ykhammū [they thought] fī blāṣtī j'étais tranquille. W-durk al-nhār kāmil w-anā ngambaṣ fī al-khadma, fī al-qahwa, partout, fī dār al-jīrān, partout on me demande mon avis w-al-nhār kāmil w-anā-ngambaṣ w-anā j'ai pas d'avis ū-kī ykūn ʿandī un avis ṣghīwar hakda.... Wallāh la démocratie ghīr 'deathmocratie.'"... Qāl lu... "La solution ... lamm khamsṭāsh willā ʿashrīn kīmā antāya ū-dīr un parti, le parti MDGD le parti taʿ al-mdīgūṭiyyīn min la démocratie!"[1]

HIT COMEDIAN MOHAND FELLAG RECOUNTED this joke as part of his 1990 stand-up routine entitled *SOS Labess* (Save our ship—everything is fine). The joke hints at three patterns concerning the use of humor during Algeria's brief democratic experiment from 1989 to 1992. First and foremost, as opposed to earlier moments of the country's postindependence past, a freer humor flourished during this period of lighter censorship in forms never before seen in the country. While Rachid Ksentini had performed comedy routines in the 1920s and 1930s, these sketches were not nearly as overtly political as *SOS*. Comedy produced within print culture, especially cartoons and caricatures, demonstrated the more open atmosphere of the early 1990s, marking the inauguration of non-state-controlled press outlets. The number of print outlets multiplied, allowing for the emergence of new artists ready to push taboos in this new, freer atmosphere.

Second, comedians produced work revealing a range of emotive responses to political changes following Algeria's economic problems of the 1990s and a widespread anti-regime revolt in October 1988. Throughout Fellag's routine, he evokes skepticism regarding his country's ability to transition to democracy and a fear that the widening of the political field will give rise to Islamist hegemony. Only a moment after this joke, Fellag joshes that next year there may not be a March 8 on the calendar in Algeria. This comment references the rising influence of the nation's new and most popular Islamist party, the Islamic Salvation Front (FIS). Some Algerians thought the group stood against women's rights and therefore might oppose International Women's Day celebrations on March 8.[2]

Finally, this joke suggests that humor throughout this period reflected the presence of a more openly divided political sphere. Humorists such as joketellers and cartoonists crafted work seemingly intended to discredit political figures to the benefit of others, as evinced by Fellag's jab at the FIS. These artists also expressed their apprehension toward the political opening, a measure that they believed might not result in the Algerian people taking up the reins of power, as they often imagined. This disbelief is echoed in the doctor's suggestion of adding a party to an already crowded field as well as the patient's expressed distaste for the democratic opening.[3] Politics in Algeria at the time, Fellag suggests, could make one's head hurt. The next section of *SOS Labess* sees Fellag laughingly bemoan that democracy in his country, unlike in eastern Europe, where similar openings were taking place, would result in an implosion rather than an explosion, with Algeria collapsing in on itself.[4]

As opposed to the larger patterns of nationalizing political humor that reigned from the 1920s through the 1980s, humor makers from the October 1988 Revolution and the subsequent democratic transition appear not to have sought to bring citizens together into a larger Algerian community. Rather, as this chapter argues, this humor in various comic sources bore witness to and possibly worsened divisions in Algeria as roiling identity politics moved from the margins to the center, and the one-party regime made way for the inauguration of a multiparty system. Humor from 1988 to 1992 still helped foster communal belonging as Algerianizing humor from the interwar period through the 1980s had. This time, however, humor may also have played a yet stronger role in fostering divisions between different political camps.

Political humor flourished from the October 1988 Revolution through the government's interruption of the first open, multiparty parliamentary elections that the country had ever witnessed in January 1992. For five days in October 1988, scores of mainly young men in many of Algeria's urban centers took to the streets. They railed against corruption and the disdain that they believed the state and country's kleptocratic elite had shown them. In response to these events and as a way of revamping and reforming the long-standing single party—the National Liberation Front (FLN)—then-president Chadli Benjedid ended the FLN's monopoly over formal political power in the country, overseeing changes to the constitution in 1989. These amendments allowed political opponents to create a never-before-seen multiparty system in Algeria.[5]

The January 1992 action on the part of the military to keep the FIS out of the government ushered in a period of increasing political violence and uncertainty and the expansion of armed dissident ranks against the state. Jacob Mundy has argued against 1992 as the starting point for the conflict of the 1990s.[6] Yet, this moment witnessed the start of a stark constriction of spaces for free expression. Humor from the 1988 Revolution and democratic transition through January 1992 attested to the period's more open atmosphere, one still replete with mounting friction over who would control the system now that its rules had changed. Therefore, this period's humor generally worked differently from the humor that preceded as well as followed it once insurgents entered into open warfare against the state that had canceled elections to prevent a FIS victory.

Asef Bayat's concept of "social non-movements" illuminates how communities can come together and act in similar ways despite lacking preexisting connections, a useful notion for comprehending political humor's functionality as Algerians coalesced in more public ways to discuss national politics. Bayat defines social non-movements as groups of individuals working toward similar political goals in a decentralized, "quiet" manner.[7] In Algeria, political humor from 1988 to 1992 appears to have assisted in facilitating common actions on the part of citizens who may never have met but who through shared codes such as jokes came to adopt the same political stances. They could in turn use these symbols to demonstrate their political affiliations. The case of political humor in Algeria from October 1988 and the democratic opening illustrates that humor may be able to shape social non-movements in powerful ways that Bayat has briefly evoked.[8] What is more, formal movements from across Algeria's political spectrum also used comedy as part of their discursive repertoire for convincing fellow Algerians to support their camp, following an earlier practice of using humor in ideological messaging.

An analysis of this humor highlights the emotional responses of at least some Algerians to one of the most misunderstood but crucial periods in Algeria's past, one that some Algerians today view as their "Arab Spring" revolt and accompanying opening.[9] Post hoc accounts of this era mainly view it as a prelude to the later civil conflict.[10] A slower reconstruction of humor from different moments during these tense years demonstrates how communities emotionally lived events in real time.[11] For instance, anger at the FLN did not instantly translate to mass portions of the population turning to the FIS; instead, the latter party had to win followers over through language, the provision of services that the government failed to ensure, and appeals to emotion.[12] A reading of the texts produced by and about varying political groups shows where and among whom some messages landed and others were rejected. Humor could thus inspire individuals to join movements or social non-movements dedicated to effecting change.

The first section of this chapter looks at humor as a potentially mobilizing element during Algeria's five-day-long October 1988 revolt. I then examine how, in the wake of the opening of the one-party system to a multiparty one, humor assisted parties and their followers with defining their political stances and building up coalitions. I first look at popular jokes about contemporary politics, followed by the art of Algeria's cartoonists who were then increasing in number as the democratic transition also triggered an opening up of the media to new, semiprivate publications.

MOBILIZING LAUGHTER AND MIRTH IN OCTOBER 1988

When the voices of the youth and the fed-up rang out across many of Algeria's major cities for five days beginning on October 5, 1988, comic banter, mainly of a dark and bitter sort, did as well. Black October (as Algerians later dubbed ordinary-civilians-turned-protesters' clashes with police and the military) resulted in the deaths of an estimated five hundred individuals and was swiftly accompanied by a violent state crackdown on communities around the country. October 1988, alongside the ever-important War of Independence, was a defining national event that generated martyrs in whose name a myriad of actors have staked claims. As Algerians today frequently draw comparisons between this event and contemporary geopolitical happenings across the region—above all, the Arab Spring—a deeper grasp of this history is essential to contextualizing contemporary Algeria and the past lenses through which many residents of the country view their present.[13]

By all accounts, Houari Boumediene's socialist endeavors to modernize and increase agricultural and industrial production in the 1960s and 1970s had failed. The state-controlled sectors hired large portions of the population, but their projects typically did not yield expected results. Wealth from hydrocarbon exports permitted the government to stave off a crisis despite the dysfunctions of its economic planning. In the 1980s, though, the country's economy slid with the price of gas and oil. The liberalization of the economy during this period further exacerbated the financial struggles of households across the country. Demographically, the population had leaped in size without an accompanying augmentation in the number of jobs. Shortages of everyday goods and the foreign currency allocations from the state that allowed Algerians to travel abroad plagued the majority of the population. At the same time, politicians, military figures, and anyone with connections to higher-ups were able to display more ostentatious signs of wealth than they had been able to during the 1960s and 1970s, when socialism had been the state's overarching ideology.[14]

The economic situation in the country was especially dire for working-class populations and a generation of young men who lived in malaise as opportunities for them to achieve what they considered to be "the good life" (to employ Lauren Berlant's term) dried up.[15] Throngs of unemployed young men hung around the streets of Algeria's cities and villages, earning the nickname *hittiste* by the mid-1980s. This was a pun on the popular ending *-iste* used in French for professional titles (for example, *chimiste* for "chemist"). The term played on the knowledge that state socialism of the 1970s was supposed to ensure every individual in Algeria an occupation through which they could contribute to the postindependence socialist national community. Consequently, so the joke went, these young men did have jobs—to lean against walls (*ḥīṭ* in Arabic) and keep them propped up. This premise was a laughable notion but one that conveyed the youths' bitterness and the acute observation that the state had failed to deliver earlier promises made in the name of socialism.

President Chadli Benjedid had likewise failed to inspire the type of respect and admiration that many held for the stoic and silent but articulate (particularly in Modern Standard Arabic) Boumediene. Jokes lambasted Chadli's apparent stupidity and inability to represent the country on the international stage with dignity, themes that would be reproduced in October 1988. Jokes went so far as to imply that he was more stupid than a donkey, a deep insult in North African societies and evidence of distaste for his rule.[16]

The demonstrations against the country's lamentable and unequal political and economic affairs began on the morning of October 4, 1988, in Algiers. Tensions had already been growing in the country, with automobile workers in Rouiba undertaking strikes in late September, fueling rumors of a possible general strike by that fateful evening.[17] Young Algerians had also closely followed the resistance of their Palestinian counterparts, then engaged in a series of protests against Israeli control in the West Bank and Gaza Strip that had been going on for over a year. Interviews with William Lawrence reveal that what was eventually known as the First Intifada, another pre–Arab Spring case study of mainly civil resistance, inspired the protesters' choice to take to the streets and decry their regime.[18]

Theories exist accusing the pro-reform faction of the government, spearheaded by President Chadli, of inciting the protests. According to this version of events, Chadli's reform-minded backers in the government sought an excuse to move forward with plans to alter state structures despite hostility from certain parts of the FLN and the military. Some residents of the Bab El-Oued neighborhood where unrest initially broke out recalled a general absence of police on the streets on the morning of October 5, 1988, lending credence to this conspiracy theory. Concrete proof of state intervention in the events still eludes historians, though.[19] What is known is that beginning in the evening of October 4 and continuing into the next morning, students, some as young as ten, began looting storefronts and marching on different parts of the capital. Many demonstrators hailed from poorer neighborhoods, where residents widely believed that Algeria's rich upper class was siphoning off all of the country's wealth to fill their personal coffers and maintain ostentatious lifestyles. State forces initially showed restraint when dealing with the protesters who were decrying Chadli, but by October 6 they were openly firing on crowds. The unrest spread quickly to several other cities around the country, including Oran, Mostaganem, Tiaret, and Annaba. On October 7, Islamist partisans organized a march following Friday prayers in Algiers that remained mostly peaceful. The next day, however, the army, which Chadli had called in to restore order, fired broadly on protesters. On what would be the final day of the protests, October 10, preacher Ali Belhadj led a march in favor of the installation of rule based on Islam from the Algiers neighborhood of Belcourt. When the procession reached Bab El-Oued, shots rang out, leaving dozens dead and scores more seriously injured. Mere hours later, Chadli appeared on national television to announce his intention to implement "economic" and "educational" reforms. He also announced that he would stay in power.[20]

After Chadli's proclamation and amid the mounting bloodshed, the protests finally ceased. However, the Algerian People's National Army, the stalwart of the revolution that had liberated Algeria from France, had fired on its own people. Government agents tortured the protesters that they had rounded up during the events, acts of violence that these citizens could not quickly forget. Black October forever altered the population's relationship with the state. The country had just lived through its most intense internal violence since the War of Independence, and many Algerians blamed the state for this bloodletting.[21]

The swelling anger of the country's disenfranchised and economically marginalized youth sparked the October 1988 Revolution. As Hugh Roberts correctly points out, protesters, mainly young and male, took to the streets not out of rage inflamed by economic inequalities but due to their sense of a lack of regard the state showed them on a day-to-day basis. The protests were more than mere bread riots; frustration with the declining quality of life as well as a sense of being cheated out of what they felt was owed them by a government once saturated in oil money propelled the turn of events.[22] Young people particularly became enraged as party officials and generals lined their pockets with embezzled state money while ordinary civilians suffered from a lack of steady income and endured long lines to get even the most basic necessities. The government's active disinterest in and neglect of the livelihood of the average struggling Algerian was widely described using the term *ḥugra* (often written *hogra*), roughly translatable as "contempt" or "disdain."

Yet, despite the focus in the literature on anger as the driving emotion behind the October 1988 revolt, emotions linked to humor also appear to have played a critical role in mobilizing protesters. October 1988 participants used humor to express anger and some joy at taking the streets as well as to build affiliation with fellow rioters while effectively calling out the individuals and groups the crowds blamed for their grievances. Humor further permitted participants to viscerally involve their bodies in the emotion-charged movement against the country's kleptocratic elite. The act of slapping officials in the street to ridicule them; laughing at an image of the most powerful man in the country, then-president Chadli Benjedid, reimagined as a beast; or stomping on material symbols of corruption linked demonstrators through performances steeped in affect. And, more often than not, they were also steeped in humor. These actions additionally bound protesters together and created common symbols and codes that could be recognized across groups that had never communicated with one another and were not necessarily part of formal networks. In other words, humor helped protesters come together in a social non-movement some twenty years before the Arab Spring.[23] Moreover, as a source for reconstructing this past, the humor that October 1988 protesters produced reveals their concerns and the reasoning behind their decision to take to the streets to declare their disgust.

Indeed, in the lead-up to October 1988, jokes often contained references to the growing gap between the rich and the poor in the country. The *hittiste* subgroup of the disenfranchised working class possessed their own humor that targeted authorities perceived to be responsible for their plight (police, bureaucrats, politicians, industrialists, etc.).[24] What is more, children from more impoverished neighborhoods used allegories about animals to attack their wealthier counterparts from the chic areas of Algiers, nicknamed the *chi chis* or *tchés-tchés* because of their posh use of French, resulting in them frequently making the sound *chi* or *tché* in everyday speech.[25] Divisiveness along socioeconomic lines marked popular humor from this time, signaling a fragmentation of the Algerian national community that rapidly became more prominent and virulent once Algeria's political system (theoretically) opened up in 1989.

Humor contributed to the carnivalesque atmosphere of the riots and later assisted citizens with parsing out the constantly moving political situation following the revolts. As such, this humor provides historians with a critical source for understanding the formation of communal belonging in an important case study of political transition in the region. Some of the narrators to whom I spoke averred that the events of October 1988 were generally devoid of humor; confrontations between the army and protesters did leave hundreds dead and many more scarred.[26] These narrators' claims go hand in hand with the body of literature on this event emphasizing anger as the driving force behind the riots.[27] However, testimonies collected through oral history exchanges or by journalists attest that some protesters found mirth and humor in the events up until the moment when the forces of order fired on crowds. Indeed, instances of humor, if not lightheartedness, shone through amid all of the events of Black October, and this humor may have assisted in pushing the spontaneous movement forward.

Radio presenter Mohamed Ali Allalou, once again living in one of the epicenters of protest, Bab El-Oued, noted an outpouring of comedy during the events. As he stated to me in a 2015 oral history interview, protesters circulated jokes about the country's wealthy elite while exuding emotions that went beyond the anger and frustration scholars habitually associate with the conflict. Speaking of the motivations for protesters going into the street, he stated, "It was pride! Finally, things were exploding... There were tons of jokes about... people who lived in Hydra [a wealthy neighborhood in Algiers]... who got rich [from the population]... Chadli [then Algerian president], the Islamists..."[28] Journalist Abed Charef similarly remarked in his volume on October 1988 that on the first morning of the riots, Bab El-Oued youth gave "the impression of just wanting to *faire quelques blagues* / make or tell some jokes."[29]

Concerning the content of jokes, a major source of anger for protesters was the notion that the corrupt upper classes with connections to the state and military were taking all of the nation's wealth. Allalou depicted the day's major happenings from his vantage point of Bab El-Oued, one of the epicenters of the protests. He claimed that the area awoke on the morning of October 5 to find that the streets were silent and lacking the usual presence of the police. Young men jumped at the unprecedented absence of law and order to break local storefront windows and grab prized consumer items that had long lain beyond their reach. Of particular value were Stan Smiths, Adidas sneakers coveted by the poor but within the buying power of only the rich.[30]

Amid this turmoil, Allalou recalls that rioting Bab El-Oued youth joked that kids in the chic neighborhood of Hydra were buying their own buses to burn. The rich children were trying not to be outdone by working-class kids who were protesting in less advantaged neighborhoods.[31] Young men likewise jeered that spoiled rich kids in the affluent neighborhood of Hydra were revolting by trampling on an expensive French brand of cheese that they regularly ate. The cheese bore the name *Président*, French for "president." The joke implied that privileged kids were mistaking their prized high-quality imported cheese for the target of the broader Algerian youths' anger, a sign of how out of touch they were with the real concerns of the country's poverty-stricken majority.[32] Allalou connects these jokes to a sense of pride and elation in the October 1988 protests that often goes unremarked by scholars given the very serious state repression that followed these events.[33]

The revolt was anchored in working-class neighborhoods rather than the wealthy boroughs of the country's major urban areas. The protesters were advancing a habit popular among poorer youth in Algeria; the *hittiste* had a penchant for mocking the rich sons and daughters of corrupt officials for their extravagant, overprotected lifestyles.[34] In these jokes, then, the gag was that the chi chi youth, not to be outdone, would follow suit but in a painfully misguided and tone-deaf fashion.[35] By taking a jab at what they imagined to be the chi chis' pitiful attempt at participating in the riots, the youth of Bab El-Oued were rhetorically creating or reminding each other of a division between themselves and the richer members of their own generation. In the process, they demeaned rich kids by ridiculing them as stupid (what good would stomping on cheese do?). Such a use of humor to separate certain sectors of Algerian society from one another would be repeated time and again as the period between 1988 and 1992 progressed.

As with Allalou, cartoonist Ali Dilem notes that he at least felt festive with the rising momentum of the youth protests and looting. The artist, then an early-twentysomething student living in his home neighborhood of El-Harrach, latched onto the opportunity to let loose and indulge in playful banter. He joked with friends by placing a small cloth over his mouth, possibly to mimic older women's wearing of the *'ajār*, a face covering that hides the mouth. By his own confession, the young future celebrity likewise proclaimed to friends he encountered in his neighborhood who were rioting that he was part of the nonexistent Patrice Lumumba Terrorist Movement, named after the assassinated postindependence Congolese leader. This ludicrous spur-of-the-moment invention of a secretive group in charge of the protests may attest to how some youths met the openness of the day, the first time in their lives that they were able to say whatever they wanted in the streets, with enthusiasm and a touch of folly.[36] Indeed, in speaking of the atmosphere before the police and military fired on crowds, Dilem confided to Sid Ahmed Semiane that "there was an incredible effervescence in the neighborhood, an unusual tension."[37]

Keeping with this theme of humor reducing powerful figures amid scornful laughter, posters of Chadli, the president who had initiated the hated liberalization policies, and his wife were placed on fake donkeys that rioters then walked through the streets. Demonstrators forced the police chief of the working-class Belouizdad (Belcourt) neighborhood to sit in a public square and be slapped by passersby while sporting only a pair of underwear. Elsewhere, protesters donned judges' robes that they had stolen from rioter-ransacked court buildings and law offices to stage mock trials of powerful greedy officials, their verdicts easy to imagine. Through these performances, October 1988 participants mocked state authority while flaunting their ability to challenge it as they reshaped a public space so critical to the symbolic maintenance of power in the country.[38] They also drew on patterns and ideas (Chadli as a donkey) that existed in popular jokes of the time. Humor, therefore, and preexisting humorous practices helped bind the population together through common codes.

Slogans of the 1988 street revolution targeted Chadli and contained hints of humor. The protesters resorted to name-calling, heckling the president as a eunuch. According to Naget Khadda and Monique Gadant, they chanted rhyming poems in local Arabic that heaped scorn on the leader who they felt had betrayed them:

> We don't want butter or pepper, but we want a good leader
>
> Mā bghīnā lā zabda wa-lā falfal lākin bghīnā zaʿīm fḥal [Khadda and Gadant translate fḥal to French as "intelligent et fort," "intelligent and strong"]
>
> Boumediene come back to us, Halima has come to dominate us
>
> Boumediène, arjaʿ līnā, Ḥalīma wallāt taḥkum fīnā
>
> Two rooms and a kitchen are better than Chadli and Halima
>
> Zūj byūt ū kūzīna khīr min Chadli ū Ḥalīma
>
> Chadli, that's enough vice, tell your son to return the money
>
> Chadli barkanā min al vīs [French word vice], qūl li-waldak radd al-devises[39]

As evinced in these rhymes, the protesters singled out the prominent role that they believed the president's wife, Halima, was playing in the government, to the detriment of the country. By asserting that Chadli's wife was actually in charge, the chanters of these slogans insulted the president by suggesting that he did not hold the role of leader in his marriage. The choice of Chadli as the patsy for the protesters' mockery hardly seems surprising given the tradition of president-bashing among the Algerian population. Here, though, protesters resorted to a particularly scathing comedy to insult their head of state in line with how Chadli had already been perhaps the most mocked of all Algerian presidents. The significance of these jokes, as is the case of humorous products from earlier periods, thus becomes clear only if one compares how humor is used over time.

Local notions of proper versus improper gender roles and actions and sexuality were infused through much of the humor of the October 1988 Revolution, with figures such as the Bab El Oued police officers having to profess they were gay (with homosexuality a taboo in Algeria at the time) and Chadli mocked for supposedly being effeminate. One graffiti tag depicted Chadli baring breasts that he used to feed his wife Halima on the one side and his band of reportedly corrupt officials on the other. While he was called a eunuch elsewhere during the protests, as mentioned above, in this image Chadli was using his penis to pee on the Algerian people. The at least partial emasculation of the president here reveals how central it was in the eyes of at least some October 1988 demonstrators that the nation's leaders embody traits that they considered to be masculine.[40]

Immediately after this tumult, what narrator Sid Ahmed Semiane deemed the first joke of the later Black Decade came to light.[41] The tale evoked the surfacing of a newfound mistrust between state agents and the population. Some Algerians repeated this joke throughout the 1990s. In doing so, they shifted the context from October 1988 to the period of terrorism, but the joke's main content and message—that the police can inflict terror on the population with impunity—were the same.

> This story takes place on Didouche Mourad [the major thoroughfare in downtown Algiers] about forty-five minutes before the start of the curfew. A couple of police officers are standing around waiting until the curfew falls to penalize anyone breaking it. Suddenly, one of the cops, seeing a man across the street, fires at him, leaving him for dead. Shocked, his colleague yells at him, "What the hell are you doing? There are at least forty-five minutes left before the curfew starts!" The officer shrugs and says, "I know him. He lives in Bab Ezzouar [a suburb of Algiers located fifteen kilometers from Didouche Mourad]. He would have never made it in time."[42]

> *L'histoire se passe sur Didouche Mourad, quarante-cinq minutes environ avant le couvre-feu. Deux policiers sont plantés là à attendre de punir quiconque enfreindrait la loi. Soudain, l'un des policiers voit un homme de l'autre côté de la rue, lui tire dessus et le laisse pour mort. En état du choc, son collègue lui crie, "Mais qu'est-ce que tu as foutu? Il reste au moins quarante-cinq minutes avant le début du couvre-feu!" Haussant les épaules, l'autre policier répond, "Je le connais. Il habite à Bab Ezzouar. Il n'y serait jamais arrivé à temps."*

Abderrahmane Moussaoui insists that an almost identical version of this joke circulated in the 1990s, as the joke continued to be taken up and passed along throughout the later armed conflict. He believes that the narrative highlighted Algerians' disgust with the state's ability to do what it wanted without punishment. It also underscored the difficulties of the curfews. Moussaoui's conclusion is most likely accurate.[43] Yet, the officer's nonchalant response to having shot someone he knows stresses the extent of his impunity; he does not fear that his colleagues or superiors or international human rights organizations might find out about what he has done and punish him. He holds the position of a law enforcer who acts above and beyond the law with no negative consequences. By portraying the power of the officer this way, the joke tailors a powerful image of state agents. Once again, this joke could fall under the category of resistance humor since it denounces or bears witness to the Algerian police's use of excessive force. At the same time, though, it portrays government agents as above the law and civilians as unable to escape their abuses. This joke recalls the state's violent bringing to heel the protests in ways that might have encouraged its listeners to now view state authorities, who had historically claimed to act in the people's interest, with apprehension. Indeed, as historian Martin Evans and journalist John Phillips have noted, Algeria's security forces crushed a popular, imagined link of confidence between themselves and the people when they fired on the October 1988 crowds during the protests.[44] This joke emphasizes that process and the change in the relationship between state and civilian.

What is more, the gunshot that takes the man's life also shreds a bond between men who know each other (in the version collected by Moussaoui, they are neighbors).[45] The man fires on someone from his own community or circle of acquaintances, to the horror of his own colleague. The joke acknowledges that state agents were not completely separable from citizens—it is not a random soldier firing on the unsuspecting man, whose death does not result from a higher-up's orders. Unlike earlier political comedy, then, this piece and its author(s) and circulators stressed newfound fissures rather than unity. This joke remained one of the most widely told of Algeria's Black Decade, a testimony to its ability to leave an impression and its relevance into the 1990s as abuses on the part of the government continued into that period. Curfews also came back.[46] By sharing this joke, tellers and listeners would be united in shared disgust or shock at state brutality toward civilians and at how this brutality, along with the broader political crisis, had eroded previous sinews of trust.

Three of my narrators identified this joke as Algerian.[47] However, this humorous piece was not entirely developed in Algeria. Instead, the joke seems to hail from Poland; Slavoj Žižek cites it in his *The Sublime Object of Ideology* as originating when General Wojciech Jaruzelski placed the central-eastern European country under martial law in December 1981.[48] Then–US president Ronald Reagan also related a Soviet version of the joke to an American audience in the late 1980s, suggesting that it had already spread to other parts of communist Europe.[49] Algiers residents' localization of this joke, which seems to have happened quickly as narrators chronologically placed the joke within the timeframe of the revolution and the days that followed, indicated that relationships between the everyday citizenry and the state were forever altered by these new events and state violence.

However dark and desperate, humor was present in at least some of the events surrounding Black October 1988. The presence of this humor suggests the existence of a wider array of emotional responses to events as well as sentiments underlying protesters' actions than scholars have previously acknowledged. Jokes, humorous quips and slogans, and carnivalesque smearing of the president and his entourage through playful performances helped drum up anti-regime sentiment and drive throngs of mainly male young protesters to the streets in Algeria's major urban areas during October 1988.

JOKES AND CULTIVATING UNSPOKEN COMMUNITIES DURING THE DEMOCRATIC TRANSITION

Following the five bloody days of protest, attempts by the higher echelons of power in Algeria to broker Chadli's promised reforms resulted in what many scholars have considered the first democratic transition in the Arab world.[50] At the same time, the president's speech on October 10 that, along with the bullets of security forces, curtailed the riots, affirmed his position at the country's helm. Chadli's public refusal to step down directly rebutted protesters' critiques of his leadership. As political scientist Myriam Aït-Aoudia's careful study of government structural changes at this moment shows, no single actor held complete control over the development of a multiparty system in Algeria. Instead, it was shaped by political agents often adopting strategies quickly in response to unprecedented, ever-shifting circumstances.[51] By late 1988, Chadli and reform-minded individuals in the FLN sought to shore up power and craft an interpretation of the October protests as a sign that changes were necessary. They also appear to have wanted to get ahead of popular demands. The actual inauguration of a multiparty system resulted from opposition organizations interpreting top-down changes to the constitution as permitting the creation of political parties beyond the FLN.[52] Rather than being doomed from the beginning, these alterations to the country's political structures arguably might have succeeded in ushering in a peaceful democratic system. They opened the way for more vibrant debates in civil society surrounding politics but also for the population's increasing polarization over the question of the newly founded FIS.[53]

Jokes throughout the period from the riots until the military's move to halt the legislative elections in January 1992 reflected growing tensions between different Algerian groups pushing opposing political views in this new atmosphere of negotiated change. Unlike the jokes that most definitely surfaced in the middle of the Time of Terrorism, these stories retained a sense of lightness. Joke authors appear to have especially worked to castigate certain political parties, evidence of the Algerian national community becoming increasingly splintered across ideological lines.

Although the October 1988 Revolution was short-lived, it shook the country's major institutions of power to the core. After the unrest waned, prompted by the reform-inclined section of the FLN party, Chadli delivered on the promises he had made in his speech to the nation on October 10. In December, he was reelected as president. Then, on February 23, 1989, he pushed through a new constitution (approved by the public in a quick referendum) that officially ended socialism and opened the door to a multiparty system. The Islamic Salvation Front (FIS, the major Islamist party after its legalization in 1989) cemented its lead among the early political parties to challenge the FLN, winning control of the majority of Algeria's municipalities and *wilayas* (provinces after independence) in June 1990 local and regional elections. The government under Chadli proved unable to stop the FIS's momentum despite gerrymandering voting districts to favor the FLN. This action triggered the state's arrest of key members of the FIS leadership in mid-1991 after the FIS came out in force to protest against the gerrymandering from April to June of that year.

Until the post-1988 period, according to political scientist Hugh Roberts, Islamism "had been largely confined to the fringe of Algerian public life," proving "fluid and nebulous."[54] Boumediene's government had followed its suppression of al-Qiyam al-islāmiyya with measures that alienated some citizens who favored a more Islamist regime by accommodating more secular socialist policies in government. At the same time, Boumediene made some concessions to Islamists such as reaffirming Islam as the official state religion in the new 1976 constitution. Chadli followed suit, most obviously with the 1984 Family Code, a law that might have pleased Islamist partisans. Among other provisions, the Code rendered women veritable minors who needed to seek male family members' permission to get married and travel outside of the country. The Ministry of Religious Affairs promoted state-curated ideas concerning Islam in the 1970s and 1980s, but prayer groups arose that allowed Islamists to spread notions beyond the government's surveilling eye. Some Islamists had connections to the Association of Algerian Muslim Ulama (AUMA), while others, such as sociology professor Abassi Madani, had fought in the War of Independence. Islamism grew in popularity in the 1970s and 1980s due in part to Boumediene's Arabization efforts in the education sector as well as the ideology's blossoming in other parts of the Middle East and Africa during the same period.[55] Arabization involved making Modern Standard Arabic the key language of school and university curricula as well as the government. The Arabization policies of the 1970s left a generation of youth educated in Arabic who were then unable to find positions in the many economic sectors where knowledge of French was still necessary. Arabic teachers from countries such as Egypt, who were needed to teach Modern Standard Arabic, may have brought different Islamist ideas into the country. Thus, exposed to Islamist ideas and angered at following the government's direction only to discover upon graduation that many jobs required French, many of these individuals turned to political Islamist groups for solace and to advocate for their rights.[56]

By the 1980s, the Soviet invasion of Afghanistan inspired at least several hundred Algerians to leave the Maghrib to fight on the side of the Islamist Mujahideen.[57] A small rebellion against the regime took shape under the leadership of Mustapha Bouyali and the name the Armed Islamic Movement (MIA for its French name, Mouvement islamique armée). A veteran of the War of Independence, Bouyali believed that the government was not upholding Islamic principles. His insurgency began in 1982 and continued after he was killed by state security forces in 1987. The MIA persisted in its struggle after Bouyali's passing and was one of the key groups revolting against the state in the 1990s.[58]

The democratic opening allowed Islamism to become mainstream. While some FIS supporters were truly invigorated by its promise to ensure a greater place for Islam and Arabic speakers in society, others simply backed the new party as the one most likely to hand devastating electoral defeats to the now-discredited FLN.[59] The FIS's two leaders were the young incendiary preacher Ali Belhadj, imprisoned for his activism in the 1980s, and softer-toned university professor Madani. Through a grassroots network of mosques and associations, they crafted an ambiguous platform for the FIS that appealed to broad sections of the Algerian population.[60] The movement was inclusive and shifting in its messaging, allowing it to garner a wide coalition of followers.[61] Whether the FIS would uphold democratic processes (future elections, respect for other parties, etc.) if elected was particularly murky. Amid this vague messaging, in FIS pamphlets, newspapers, and declarations, the party called for governance and a rearrangement of society along Islamic principles. Important areas for reform were in the fields of education and women's rights, with the party advocating for women to focus on family life and for education to be in Arabic and teach Islamic principles.[62] Other Islamist parties such as Mahfoud Nahnah's Movement for the Islamic Society or Hamas (later renamed the Movement of Society for Peace) and Abdallah Djaballah's Islamic Renaissance (Ennahda) Party also took shape in the wake of the political opening. They proved incapable, though, of amassing the same numbers of supporters as the FIS. Some Algerian communities felt that the FIS's brand of Islamism would mean that their lifestyles would have to change if the FIS ruled or that they would fall under a theocratic regime similar to Iran's.[63] Liberal, ostensibly secular individuals (who could still be devout Muslims) expressed concern that the FIS would undermine so-called democratic principles and, for feminists especially, initiate policies that would threaten their liberties.[64]

More left-leaning, secular politicians and groups formed parties as well. These organizations included the Socialist Vanguard Party / Parti de l'avant-garde socialiste (PAGS), which traced its roots back to the colonial-era Algerian Communist Party and had generally operated underground throughout most of the postindependence period. The non-Islamist opposition was more splintered, though, than the Islamist movement, which the FIS dominated by their June 1990 landslide victories in local and regional elections.⁶⁵ Soon, parties like the PAGS and other proponents of a more liberal Algeria became torn over how to respond to the increasing prowess of the FIS.⁶⁶

Jokes flourished amid this change. According to a psychologist who lived in downtown Algiers, the opening up of Algeria's political system and proliferation of political parties stoked joke-tellers' creativity. Dozens of new parties popped up in the country seemingly overnight (sixty in total), an evolution that at least some Algerians found worthy of ridicule.⁶⁷ As the psychologist explained, jokes emerged playing on the names of political parties in ways that spoke to these competing groups' varying stances on issues and their ideological posturing. Individuals—FIS partisans, according to Martin Evans and John Phillips, who also heard the joke—called the Rally for Culture and Democracy, a fervently anti-Islamist and pro-Amazigh rights party, the Rassemblement contre dieu (Rally against God).⁶⁸ This moniker played on the group's French acronym, *RCD* (Rassemblement pour la culture et la démocratie). Perhaps not to be outdone by Islamists, although this narrator did not indicate which insult came from which corner of the political ring first, members of the more secular parties concocted a similarly acronym-inspired label for the FIS: the Femme interdite de sortir (French for "woman forbidden from going out") party.⁶⁹ The jab insinuated that the FIS would curb women's activities in the public sphere.

The Front of Socialist Forces (known by its French acronym FFS for Front des forces socialistes), a heavily Kabyle-supported party that also criticized Islamism, similarly garnered two nicknames, one of which appears to have been created by supporters and the other perhaps by detractors. The first was Femme faut sortir, meaning "woman must go out," a play on its French acronym and possibly a direct rebuttal of the FIS pun. The second was a phrase in Tamazight, *Faṭma tfettel seksu*.⁷⁰ It translates to "Fatma rolls couscous." The choice of Tamazight appears purposeful; many FFS adherents hailed from Berber-speaking regions of Algeria. *Fatma* is also a common name for Algerian women and a slur once used by colonial-era settlers to designate all Algerian Muslim female servants and then all Algerian Muslim women in general. For this reason and in all likelihood, the choice of *Fatma* constitutes an insult. Islamists or other individuals (maybe members of the rival RCD) possibly wanted to suggest through this quip that FFS adherents were not progressive on women's rights.[71] At the same time, however, especially given the tradition of self-deprecating satire in the country, supporters of the parties themselves may have created these humorous yet serious nicknames as ways of proudly embracing others' stereotypes about themselves. Above all, identified as humorous by a narrator I spoke to, this play on party acronyms revealed tension existing between the two major groups—the Islamist movements and the secular, self-proclaimed democrats—who stood to challenge the FLN's hegemony in national politics.[72]

Yet, as the same narrator explained, part of the gag with these mock names involved Algerians' frustration with the high number of parties that appeared with the political opening, a sign of activists' tangible failure to streamline their efforts.[73] For instance, the FFS's and RCD's rivalry over pro-Amazigh-rights voters split their base.[74] Civilians therefore turned to jokes to create social codes for expressing their lack of faith in the new political parties to overcome disunity. They may also have wanted an outlet for the extended tension and political exhaustion that they felt as elections dragged or were pushed back, an exhaustion Fellag seems to been signaling with his joke.[75] This exhaustion did not translate into voter abstention; turnout stood at 59 percent of registered voters for the first round of legislative elections in December 1991, only a small dip from the 65 percent who voted in mid-1990 municipal and regional elections.[76]

Many of the longer, more complex jokes that surfaced between October 1988 and January 1992 fell along similar party divides or spoke to Algerians' general wariness toward the political game. The rise of political Islamism and particularly the FIS's move to the center of Algerian politics sparked several humorous jokes either putting the major Islamist party's leaders in laughable situations or taking aim at its everyday supporters and their political ambitions. The FIS's assumption of power in many municipalities and *wilayas* after June 1990 triggered possibly overblown reports of the party radically altering local social and cultural life in the areas it controlled.[77] These reported changes included shuttering liquor stores, a practice potentially already underway before June 1990; policing clothing on beaches; and forcing female local government employees to wear a *ḥijāb* (a type of Islamic headscarf).[78] The common phrase that some of the narrators to whom I spoke associated with the FIS's policies during this time (whether correctly or incorrectly) was *lā yajūz*, a term reflected in contemporary caricatures.[79] This phrase is translatable to "it is not allowed," and a narrator alleged that it was used by FIS partisans to denounce everything from alcohol to Western television programs to the white beans present in many traditional Algerian dishes, reportedly because they prompted flatulence and FIS partisans considered the bodily function sinful.[80]

The following joke shows how joke-tellers could seriously, albeit through humorous means, insult supporters and heads of the country's major Islamist party:

> At the time of the FIS, there is someone with a phobia. He hears the word "FIS" he goes crazy. One day, his wife is pregnant ... she gives birth, the doctor comes to see him and tells him, "Congratulations, you have a son [in French *fils*, the same pronunciation as *FIS*]." "Ah! FIS?!!"
>
> *Au moment du FIS, il y a quelqu'un qui possède une phobie ... Dès qu'il entend le mot "FIS," il devient fou. Un jour, sa femme est enceinte, elle accouche, le docteur vient le voir et lui dit, "Félicitations, vous avez un fils." "Ah! FIS?!!"*[81]

This joke reminds listeners that the FIS's unparalleled successes between 1989 and 1992 and the fervor of the party's base frightened many Algerian citizens; it is not unthinkable here that the man could be suffering from a veritable phobia of the party. According to one of my narrators, the reference to the FIS as being the "son" of the FLN constituted a sign that the party of the old guard was co-opting the nascent one.[82] Consequently, the FIS's critics could use the imagined filial connection to disparage the Islamist organization. However, Roberts believes that the FIS purposefully chose their name so that the acronym in French, the one used in common parlance, would be a homonym in that same language of the word for "son." That way, the Islamist party could present itself as the inheritors of the original FLN that had vanquished French rule. Roberts asserts that in a culture with intricate oral cultures, where wordplay was common, Algerian publics would have made the connection between the party's French acronym and the French word for "son."[83] The organization's name in Arabic, *al-Jabha al-islāmiyya lil-inqādh* (Islamic Salvation Front), aligned with their claims to want to lead Algerian society to a more righteous path, to salvation, and also created a connection with the FLN with the use of the word "front," *al-jabha* in Arabic.[84] This term happened to translate directly in French as *Front islamique du salut*, with the acronym FIS. By the same token, many FIS followers would have been more Arabophone than Francophone and may not have perceived the party's French acronym, arguably its most widely used name, as a presentation of themselves as the sons of the FLN. In that case, the joke here would only be a simple pun. The linking of the FIS to a deep-seated fear so great that it could cause a parent to recoil from his own newborn child may have been an attempt to humorously undercut the assertion that the FIS represented the earlier FLN's revolutionary spirit or was simply a means to mock the party as frightful. Civilians wary of the FIS's rise may have felt a sense of community with others holding similar views upon hearing this joke.

Joke-tellers likewise seemed to have ridiculed the leaders of the FIS for presenting themselves as holy figures able to speak in the name of Islam. The following joke presents one such story, which most likely circulated between 1988 and 1992:

> This is a joke born in the same afternoon as the visit of Abassi Madani to Blida [a town that was also a FIS stronghold located to the southwest of Algiers] in 1991, during the full glory days of the FIS.[85] All of the city's notables want to invite him to lunch in their homes. A real dilemma. And how did they resolve the question? It appears that one of them proposed that they let the Abassi Madani's Mercedes go until it should break down. At the place where it stops, he will have dinner![86]

> *C'est une blague née l'après-midi même de la visite de Abassi Madani à Blida en 1991, en pleine gloire du FIS. Les notables de la ville voulaient tous l'inviter pour déjeuner. Un vrai dilemme. Et comment ont-ils résolu la question? Paraît que l'un d'eux a proposé qu'on lâche la Mercédès de Abassi Madani au point mort et là où elle s'arrêtera, il déjeunera!*

An understanding of early Islamic history is necessary to decipher this joke. In the Islamic *sīra* or biography of Muhammad, the Prophet issued an almost identical announcement upon his arrival in Medina during the hijra, the displacement of the early Islamic community from Mecca to the more northern city in 622 CE due to persecution. The Prophet Muhammad then let loose his she-camel, and where she stopped was where he built the first mosque in Medina.

The joke's creators and this narrator recounting it after the fact as an authentic event are potentially mocking Abassi Madani on two grounds. The first may be a dismissal of the suggestion that Madani was like the modest Prophet Muhammad, a jab at his claim to be holy and capable of dictating how Muslims should practice their faith. The heads of the FIS, including Madani, touted themselves as humble servants of the "dispossessed," supposedly leading lives that starkly differed from those of the excessively greedy, opulent military and FLN leaders of the 1980s with their extravagant villas and cars.[87] The joke may insinuate that Madani's possession of a Mercedes was contrary to his preaching of humility and his claims to work on behalf of Algeria's poor. Madani did indeed have a Mercedes.[88] Madani had a taste for Mercedes-Benz cars, and a rumor ran that he received them as gifts from the Saudi Arabian regime, a foreign state that financially backed the FIS.[89] It is possible, though, that Madani possessed a more modest version of the luxury car. Naysayers, then, were seeking an ersatz angle through which to attack the FIS leader's claim to humility. The joke could have intersected with or advanced the rumor about the Saudis purchasing the car while apprising the listener of a fact: Madani rolled around the country in a luxury-brand car. This example attests to how humor could convey information, real or slightly exaggerated, that might sway citizens toward or against a major political party. The narrative also stressed the difference between the lifestyles of the FIS leader and the Prophet while further linking the Islamist organization to an unpopular foreign actor, Saudi Arabia.

By the joke-teller's admission in this version, the joke likely surfaced after the 1990–1991 Gulf War, during which many Algerians criticized Saudi Arabia for supporting the US.[90] The joke's creator may have also wanted to undercut Islamist claims to abide by customs of the early Muslim community. This interpretation would be in line with another 1990s joke in which a taxi driver forces an Islamist out of his car after the latter preaches the importance of emulating the Prophet Muhammad's companions. Fed up with the lecture, the cabby exclaims that taxis did not exist during that period, so the man should step out of the ride.[91] The story and the Madani Mercedes joke reveal a supposed tension between the trappings of modernity and Islamists' messages. Through weaving and sharing these narratives, the jokes' tellers and consumers might have felt like a collective group in their opposition to Islamists.

Yet, FIS partisans appear to have given as good as they received when it came to jokes. One joke offers a rather favorable, if odd, depiction of Madani. It goes as follows:

> One day, a man made fun of Madani for wearing his white, loose-fitting *gandoura* [*kandūra*] by saying that the FIS leader looked like a big refrigerator. Madani, unfazed, opened up his *gandoura* robe to expose his penis, quipping, "If I am a fridge then here—grab a nice big coke!"[92]

This joke, like many told earlier about Boumediene, may have served to reinforce Madani's standing in the eyes of the listener rather than diminish it.[93] In Arabic, saying "my penis" is a way of saying "fuck" or "fuck this." In the Algerian context, Madani's actions and words constituted a powerful rebuttal to the heckler, a way of telling the person off. It is important to note that, despite the FIS's calls for modesty in relationships between men and women, individuals of the same sex could be nude around one another with no issue. Consequently, FIS partisans may have passed along this joke as a retort to criticisms of their dress or Madani.

Humor was an Algerian cultural tradition that the FIS also formally mobilized to fit their needs. Many scholars disassociate humor and fun from the political activities of Islamists, positing that they generally try to suppress comedy.[94] Beyond Islamism, writings on affairs such as the *Jyllands-Posten* and *Charlie Hebdo* controversies surrounding the publication of Prophet Muhammad cartoons portray Muslims as serious and purportedly incapable of following the spirit of a joke.[95] In the process, the authors of these works ignore a long tradition of humor and comedy in Islamic societies. In the case of Algeria's FIS party, ideas of their Islamist actors as anathema to fun or humor are false. For example, Madani referenced humorous folk trickster Juḥā in response to Chadli's April 1991 call for voting districts to be redrawn, an act that favored the FLN as the country moved toward legislative elections (this call initiated the May–June 1991 FIS strikes and protests). Madani called the then president a *"mismār* Juḥā," the nail of Juḥā, which had to be disposed of for the nation to thrive. Once again, in the tale this name references, the troublemaker sells his home to another man on the condition that Juḥā be allowed to keep one nail up in the structure. The buyer concedes, and Juḥā uses his nail to hang a rotting carcass on the wall, effectively driving out the new inhabitants. The trickster thereby recoups the premises with the cost of the sale still in his pocket. Around the same time, Madani also dismissed fellow political opponents who wanted to join forces with the FIS to challenge the FLN as "smurfs." While this assertion was not public, it was known to the parties involved.[96] The leader of the often-serious FIS was thus at least fluent in local and transnational forms of humor. Ali Belhadj also had a reputation for peppering his speeches with jokes.[97]

In sum, the jokes that emerged during the democratic opening in Algeria revealed deep political tensions pushing Algerians into opposing groups. At the heart of the conflict was the right to speak for Algeria and determine its future. Yet, contrary to jokes that circulated around the country during the height of terrorism, jokes recounted from this period critiqued opposing political sides in a more lighthearted manner and did not exclude whole groups from the invented Algerian national community. Channeling strong messages about the stances and practices of political parties, they may have also worked to convince swaths of the population to respond in similar ways to politicians' calls to vote in their favor.

Jokes from this period presented an image of a divided body politic frustrated and fatigued with political change or eager to shore up support for their side in political debates, often by attacking the other side. Of important note and except for the RCD being called "the Rally against God," no single joke from the transition was widespread enough or popular enough for me to find it in multiple sources. The latter included published joke collections, contemporary publications, and oral history exchanges with different narrators.[98] Therefore, unlike the curfew joke localized to an Algerian context immediately during or following October 1988 or the fake-checkpoint jokes from later in the 1990s, democratic transition jokes may have been so fragmented along ideological lines that none could emerge as emblematic of the period or representative of so-called Algerian humor. Such a shift, noticeable only if one follows patterns of humorous political cultures in a territory over time, potentially testifies to the ruptured nature of the body politic during this period.

THE PRESIDENT WEARS NO PANTS: THE BLOSSOMING OF ALGERIAN CARTOONING AND THE PRIVATE PRESS

An encounter took place in mid-December 1990 that forever changed the history of Algerian humor. The fateful meeting was between Ali Dilem, a young student in his second year of art school, and Saïd Mekbel, an already well-known communist activist and newspaper writer who would be assassinated, as recounted in the introduction, just four years later. Dilem hailed from El Harrach, a tough, working-class neighborhood in the country's capital, a hotbed for political Islamism of all sorts and brands. Dilem himself had once trained to become a muezzin and later was admitted to Algiers's Ecole des Beaux-Arts / School of Fine Arts, the nation's most prestigious art institute.[99] There, he crossed paths with the acclaimed artist Denis Martinez. Upon noticing his pupil's talent for doodling figures, Martinez arranged a meeting for the aspiring artist with Mekbel. The journalist was desperately looking for a fresh caricaturist to draw for his paper, *Alger républicain*. In seeking a new artist, Mekbel wanted someone untainted by the previous world of state-controlled media and therefore perhaps less likely to self-censor.

But the appointment that eventually launched the artist's career went catastrophically at first. Dilem had left his notebook inside Martinez's car when both went inside the *Alger républicain* headquarters to meet Mekbel. After realizing his mistake, the student went back to the vehicle only to discover that it had been stolen along with all of the sketches that he had carefully prepared the night before to impress Mekbel and secure the gig. After three hours of searching the neighborhood for the jacked automobile, Dilem gave up and returned dejected to Mekbel's office. At the older intellectual's insistence, he sketched a quick copy of one of the drawings that he had created the evening before. While the artist had not painstakingly labored over the work as he had the now-stolen version, the writer took one look at the drawing and nodded. He declared that the neophyte's picture would appear in the next day's edition of *Alger républicain*, one of the most widely known and well-respected periodicals in the country, a legacy of earlier Algerian intellectualism. As promised, the cartoon by the novice artist graced the last page of the journal. The picture showed Chadli Bendjedid, Algeria's infamously unpopular "cauliflower president" (mocked for his head supposedly resembling the vegetable), stripped down to his underwear while playing a tennis racket like a banjo (fig. 2.1).[100]

Before this moment and very much unlike joke-tellers, Algerian cartoonists had never dared to deride such a public, authoritative personality as the president. In 1991, when this caricature appeared, Algeria's cartooning industry had only just begun to let out a sigh of freedom after years of operating under strict censorship with all work subject to FLN/state approval. Artists such as Slim working from the late sixties until 1990 for state papers depicted aspects of the country's social life such as product shortages.[101] Political figures, however, were off-limits as objects of their trenchant derision, even if subjects like the scarcity of foodstuffs touched squarely on the political. For instance, in 1984 the state halted Slim's attempt at ridiculing Chadli in a caricature by seizing all copies of the newspaper set to be distributed.[102] This was not the case after 1990, however. With this three-by-two-inch doodle of Algeria's most powerful politician caught with his pants down for all of *Alger républicain*'s readership to see, a precedent in the history of the country's media was broken. The sacredness of a president was forever publicly discarded in print. Algerian cartooning would never be the same.

The democratic transition triggered an opening of the country's press industry to private entrepreneurs. With political change post–October 1988 afoot, Algerian media workers clamored for greater freedoms through groups such as the Movement of Algerian Journalists. Responding to this pressure, Mouloud Hamrouche's Media Code of 1990 ushered in a time of freer albeit still limited expression in the country.[103] The new law did not trigger a complete opening of the press to free and impartial interests, and newspapers were expensive to launch. For this reason, the private newspapers that appeared at this time were founded by journalists who had previously worked for government-owned papers who received state funds to establish completely new publications. These writers and artists had already supported the state, were accustomed to self-censorship, and continued to be state-funded.[104] Still, the removal of the state's monopoly over print media led to the proliferation of news-related publications (over 150) in a nation that had previously possessed only a handful of them.[105]

Figure 2.1. The Algerian president Chadli Bendjedid in his skivvies stating, "Sports: After the African Cup, the Performance of Morcelli [*sic*; Noureddine Morceli, an Algerian track star], Algerians were pleasantly surprised to discover that Chadli plays tennis."

The Media Code of 1990 that inaugurated these changes afforded pathways for new genres in which civilians could advance humor-tinged ideas with more liberty. In this larger political-cultural ecosystem, humorists like Fellag could thrive. As Dilem's picture of Chadli with his pants down illustrates, cartooning was one such field that flourished with freer discourse than had previously been possible. For example, a survey of newspapers from October 1988 reveals that Algerian cartoonists held back from commenting on the protests, an inevitability given state control over newspapers as well as the government's employment of harsh force against its own people during the events.[106]

During this blossoming of Algeria's press from approximately 1990 until 1992, Algeria's cartooning industry took off. Many of the dozens of newspapers that surfaced in the wake of the liberalization of the press in 1990 hired cartoonists. Editors' inclusion of these artists on newspaper payrolls that were often tight and in publications spanning the ideological gamut demonstrates their significance as contributors to papers' editorial lines as well as their ability to connect with audiences.[107] Toward the middle of this period, Algeria's seasoned *bédéistes* (authors of Belgian-style *bandes dessinées* comics), along with newcomers such as Dilem, also banded together to form satirical biweekly magazines. Moreover, Algeria's caricaturists sketched political subjects and figures without as much fear of legal retribution in the form of fines, endless trials, or imprisonments, a departure from what the situation was like before 1990 and would be only a few months after the canceled 1992 elections. This era therefore signaled a flourishing of political humor in Algerian media, which now encompassed Algerians embracing all different political and ideological persuasions. This moment constituted the apex of a vibrant, relatively free atmosphere in which cartoonists and humorists produced a great body of work—but with what implications?

As with joke-tellers, cartoonists expressed ideas that encapsulated and widened divisions in Algeria's political field while also echoing some of the frustrations and incertitude of the general population concerning the democratic transition. They united individuals and groups through the socially consumed products that they created and in ways that may have resulted in their mobilization for one political group or another. As with jokes, cartoons appear to have reflected the supposed split of society into pro- and anti-FIS camps. They also may have helped forge social non-movements surrounding the question of the place of the FIS in society and politics. This pattern is most clearly reflected in the work of some of the most eminent cartoonists during this period.

One publication that stood out among these hundred-plus periodicals was *Alger républicain*, a newspaper close to the PAGS. *Alger républicain*'s caricaturists often illustrated Islamists negatively, especially in the run-up to the December 1991 legislative elections. The theme of the Islamist movement as supposedly being detrimental or opposed to the well-being of women appeared time and again in the newspaper's depictions of the group's partisans, usually represented by men with beards and gandouras/kandūras.[108] One caricature by Fathy, printed on April 16, 1991 (only the fourth edition of the paper), reveals two bearded men with sharpened teeth, perhaps to signal their malicious character, on either side of a woman donning a haik (ḥāyak).[109] Each ostensible and identical "Islamist" tries to pull her to their side. Their attempt to seemingly possess or obtain this woman results in her being on the verge of being torn apart. The title of the cartoon is simple: "Intolerance." The physicality of the men's pulling on the woman and the shocked expression on her face illuminate a supposed propensity for violence on the men's part and, by extension, on that of the Islamist partisans.[110] The message rings clear: intolerant Islamists are harming Algerian women and are thus sinister (see fig. 2.2).

Fathy's interpretation of Islamists as potentially violent was not an isolated one in the pages of *Alger républicain*. The artist Djilali Beskri produced a caricature that appeared in the December 19, 1991, edition of the paper, mere days before the first round of nationwide legislative elections. This time was one of high anxiety for Algerians who disliked the FIS, as the party appeared poised for a landslide victory. In the drawing, the leaders of Algeria's major political parties are shown as mice telling each other to stay quiet so as not to wake up the sleeping cat toward the front of the image, who bears the likeness of Abdelhamid Mehri, then the secretary-general of the FLN, which controlled the national government. A bearded mouse in pious Islamic attire stands in the background of the picture where none of the leaders are looking, atop a throne composed of cheese. In his hand, the rodent holds a lit match, and the shadow that the flame casts reveals that he has a bomb with him. He is undoubtedly going to take the throne, most likely a symbol of the Algerian national parliament given the timing of the picture's appearance, with deadly results. Beskri's sketch conveys a sense that the major liberal political parties are collectively so distracted by not wanting to disturb the FLN or individually so preoccupied with trying to obtain power for themselves that they neglect to note the supposed danger that Islamists in general (the mouse shows no affiliation to any particular Islamist party) pose to the entire political system.[111] This drawing communicated a powerful message to readers, possibly binding them together through fear of a potential Islamist electoral victory.

Al-Ṣaḥḥ Āfa was a satirical journal that was first published in 1990 and was based in Algeria's second-largest city, Oran. *Al-Ṣaḥḥ Āfa* means "the truth is a

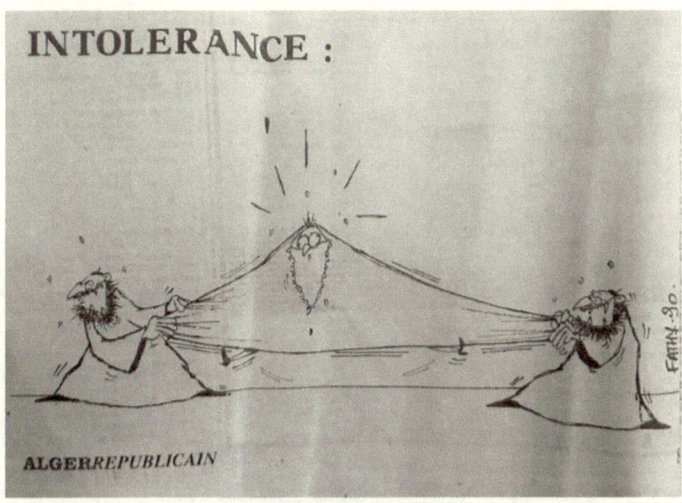

Figure 2.2. Two "Islamist" men violently pulling apart a Muslim woman wearing a haik (*ḥāyak*) in Fathy's April 1990 drawing for the "democratic" newspaper *Alger républicain*.

scourge" and is a play on the Arabic word for journalism, *al-ṣaḥāfa*. At times, it similarly portrayed Islamists as posing a pernicious threat to the country. At others, though, the paper recognized how widespread tension was between adherents of political Islam and the section of the population that purportedly espoused more democratic or open values.[112] Regarding unfavorable depictions of Islamist partisans, several cartoons from the paper's limited run in 1990 and 1991 displayed individuals in beards and gandouras/kandūras committing heinous acts. One particularly scathing *al-Ṣaḥḥ Āfa* cartoon from this period shows a man with a beard and in a typical Islamic male outfit for Algeria uncoiling the wire to a bomb. He seems to be in the middle of an urban area, and behind him are some cultural buildings, including one labeled *Museum of Cinema* and another labeled *Institute of Music*. The sketch implies that Islamists may attack cultural institutions.[113] Other examples of men in gandouras/kandūras wielding lit bombs abound in the newspaper.[114] After the May–June 1991 pro-FIS protests and during a wave of arrests against the FIS and its leadership, a certain Baraji depicted Ali Belhadj opening up his clothing to reveal a stash of weapons, everything from grenades to guns to a hatchet to a knife (fig. 2.3). The picture thereby implied that the FIS leader possessed lethal intentions.[115] It further insulted the figure by showing him, like Chadli above, in his underwear. Admittedly, *al-Ṣaḥḥ Āfa* sometimes attributed a violent nature to state agents in

Figure 2.3. A smurf, most likely standing in for the FLN, informs Abassi Madani, "Your importance is finished. Thank you for the work." A vulture over the tank responds, "That is the important thing." The other vulture adds, "The important thing is that the path to democracy continues."

images in which it did the same to ostensibly Islamist partisans. In the drawing just examined, a man (not visible) in a military tank sardonically wishes the FIS partisans whom the vehicle is crushing a "happy *'aid al-adḥa*," an important holiday in which Muslims sacrifice a sheep or other animals in remembrance of Ibrahim's near-sacrifice of his son Isḥāq. These well-wishes would most likely strike the readers as being perverse given that the man is about to bulldoze FIS partisans. To add insult to injury, these pro-Islamist partisans are depicted as the objects of sacrifice: sheep. In this way, the cartoonist implies that the state can prove just as brutish or prone to violence as the FIS supposedly can, while FIS followers are seen as literal sacrificial sheep.[116] *Al-Ṣaḥḥ Āfa* took aim at other groups beyond Islamists, such as the state. However, its pages still spoke to and possibly reinforced widening rifts in the nation through readerships coming together to consume powerful ideas about the country's lead political actors, especially the FIS, Islamists more generally, and the state.

El Manchar, a French-language satirical weekly paper whose title translates from Arabic as "the saw," became one of the most widely read and appreciated humorous endeavors of the democratic transition. The new initiative united an established generation of artists who had drawn for daily and weekly state-run periodicals with newcomers such as Dilem. Appearing first in late November 1990, the publication quickly garnered avid followers. Adlène Meddi, then a teenager in the working-class neighborhood of El Harrach, remarked how, unlike with other print media containing news that soon became old and dispensable, people collected and kept the editions of *El Manchar* that they purchased. There was, in his opinion, a sense of the importance for posterity of the publication along with the longevity of its content to inspire mirth.[117]

The satirical review's circulation numbers also attested to its popularity. They started at 44,000 and burgeoned to 160,000 per bimonthly issue by November 1991, a number that rivaled those of papers that conveyed the news seriously.[118] The publication's mix of articles and cartoons covered a range of subjects around the country, responding to some time-sensitive happenings along with general states of affairs. *El Manchar* cartoons could be single squares reminiscent of caricatures or whole-page sequential works similar to Slim's earlier *Zid ya Bouzid* strips. Cartoonists and authors alike wrote almost exclusively in French with some code-switching between Arabic and French.[119] Concerning its propensity for political critique, some readers bemoaned that the original "combatants" of Algerian *bandes dessinées* stuck to social issues rather than attacking politicians.[120] However, political content did shine through the paper, especially when it came to addressing the place of political Islam in the country.

The review published several drawings that ridiculed the FIS and alluded to the threat that the party supposedly posed to the nation. The paper mocked partisans and leaders from groups that fell all along the political spectrum, from the most liberal to the most conservative. Yet, a disproportionate number of its cartoons and pieces criticized the FIS or Islamists. Images like ones that the established artist Melouah produced associated the Islamic Salvation Front with violence. One of his cartoons portrayed a bearded man (a symbol for an Islamist partisan) as a diabolical Santa Claus, complete with a sack full of truncheons for beating people instead of the usual bag of presents. Other cartoons on the same page, also drawn by Melouah, display a series of whips and sticks and label them according to the region where they will be used against people celebrating the New Year. Melouah names many neighborhoods that were FIS strongholds, such as Kouba and Bab El-Oued, in the cartoon, declaring that revelers will be beaten there (see fig. 2.4).[121] Yet another caricature by Hankour has a bearded man walking proudly several paces in front of a woman, who is veiled and wearing modest clothing. The woman's eyes are closed as if she is sad, and she seems to be looking down, perhaps a sign that she is abused. The man's beard goes past his shoulders and back beyond his arms to extend to

Figure 2.4. Melouah's representations of "Islamist" partisans, complete with clubs.

the woman's hands, where it effectively binds them. Hankour suggests that political Islamism, here represented by the beard and the couple's clothing, suppresses women in a violent and highly unpleasant way.[122] Like artists from *Alger républicain* and *al-Ṣaḥḥ Āfa*, *El Manchar* illustrators put forward powerful ideas of political Islamists to readers.

In addition to the forthright depictions of the FIS and Islamists as violent, Algerian cartoons from the 1990–1991 Gulf War that laid into the American campaign against Saddam Hussein's regime subtly but efficiently attacked the FIS.[123] The Islamist party had ties to Saudi Arabia.[124] The FIS initially refrained from overtly criticizing the Saudi-supported US attack on Iraq due in part to its earlier condemnation of Saddam Hussein and his regime's August 1990 invasion of Kuwait. However, most Algerians viscerally decried American intervention in the region and viewed the attacks as a massacre by a superpower in international politics.[125] By mustering anger at Saudi Arabia and its Western allies for bombarding Iraq, some of Algeria's cartoonists strove to undermine the FIS from early 1991 onward. This period was an especially critical one for all Algerian parties; legislative elections were initially set for June and July of that year, although they would later be pushed back to December and January.

Furthermore, this pattern cut across linguistic lines; Algeria's satirical Arabophone newspaper *al-Ṣaḥḥ Āfa* derided the multinational coalition as sharply as Francophone newspapers did.[126]

In 1991, journalist Samy Abtroun and Dilem, both employed with *Le Matin*, put out an album that more explicitly linked the FIS to Saudi rulers and chastised the party for what they considered its hypocritical, changing stance on the Gulf War. It was entitled *La guerre des Boushés* or the War of the *Boushés*. The final word does not mean anything in French. Instead, it rendered George H. W. Bush's last name a homonym of *boucher*, the French word for "butcher," an obvious attack on the American leader for bombing Iraq. The whole collection harshly critiqued the campaign and Arab governments' response to it. In one image, a bearded man strokes his chin. The words "Algeria: the other war" and "the FIS call for jihad" lie at the top of the picture as the man, most likely a FIS supporter, ponders, "But one wonders against whom?" The artist and writer thereby underscore that the FIS wavered as to whom to back at this moment of the conflict.[127] Another picture features Abassi Madani saying two phrases with two different dates. The first date is November 16, at which time Madani cries, "Saddam Hussein is a tyrant!" The second, labeled January 16, the eve before the US-led coalition struck Iraq, has the FIS leader declaring, "It is necessary to support him!" Abtroun and Dilem excoriate the FIS's shifting position on Saudi Arabia and the war in ways that undermine the FIS while relaying reports of their ties to the Gulf nation.

The whole *Guerre des Boushés* album operates as a critique of the FIS's fluctuating stance toward Saudi Arabia and the international coalition's campaigns against Iraq. By associating the FIS with the disliked Saudi party in the conflict, Dilem and Abtroun appear to have wanted to eat away at the party's popularity and credibility for Algerian citizens, who overwhelmingly supported Iraq.

The FIS were also able to dish out critiques at their adversaries and seem to have responded directly to negative satirical portrayals of themselves. One of the most widely distributed FIS newspapers, *El Monquidh/al-Munqidh* (The savior), regularly employed a cartoonist who signed their drawings "FIB." FIB's sketches roasted Christians, alcohol imbibers, and newspapers that pushed a more liberal and democratic viewpoint on major issues of the day.[128] The artist made illustrations that responded to events that caricaturists working for those other papers addressed. For instance, amid the Gulf War, perhaps to counter criticism of the FIS for not doing enough to advocate against the multinational coalition, *El Monquidh* published an image critical of Saudi Arabia and the US. In the drawing, a Saudi man shakes the hand of an American man, identifiable as such because he sports a jacket with an American flag. The Saudi greets

Figure 2.5. Cartoon by FIB.

the American, "Welcome to your first [i.e., home] country." A bubble above the American's head shows an oil barrel, indicating that his interests in dealing with the Saudis revolve around petroleum. The cartoon seemingly knocks both the United States' intentions in the region and the willingness of the Saudis to accommodate their demands.[129] The work communicates the FIS's new desire to distance itself from the Middle Eastern power by the end of 1990 and thereby testifies to the importance of caricaturing for political branding by this moment of the transition, with cartoons a battleground between opposing sides.

Other FIB drawings attacked drinkers, Christianity, and movie theaters, a sign that the images were intended to convince readers of the righteousness of the FIS's views.[130] Furthermore, this art figured into the sort of cultural war that was underway over how Algerians should behave, particularly whether they should renounce or accept Western products and lifestyles. One especially denunciatory piece (fig. 2.5) depicts a cross engraved on a bomb that the cartoonist placed in front of a mosque. FIB appears to suggest here that Christianity poses a direct threat to the safety and well-being of Muslim communities. In this manner, the artist advances criticisms that the FIS had made of "Western" ways, here symbolized by Christianity, in a Muslim or Algerian context.[131]

All in all, cartoonists' work served as an important conduit for decrying opponents of all stripes in the lead-up to Algeria's first free legislative elections in 1991. In many ways, the divisions portrayed through this art reflected or possibly served to broaden the growing rift between backers of political Islam, specifically the FIS, and those citizens who were supporting parties that claimed to be more liberal. These cartoonists' work, taken with the jokes examined above, points to a practice of using humor as a way for at least some Algerians to shape ordinary citizens' perspectives of key agents in the political transition and build affiliation with like-minded individuals. Apprehension and fear also emerge from this archive of cartoons, whether drawn for the ostensible purpose of bolstering or thwarting political Islamism.

CONCLUSION

In the wake of Black October and the increased democratic liberties that followed those bloody events, Algeria's cartooning industry as well as day-to-day joke-tellers benefited from a previously unknown level of freedom in the types of products they could craft. This change only occurred due to the actions of October 1988 protesters, who significantly used humor as a tool for expressing their discontent with the regime and building affiliation with one another. From the opening up of the press in 1990 until the start of the war, new laws permitted a myriad of never-before-seen possibilities for Algeria's media workers.

The dynamics of the Arab world's first democratic transition—a negotiated, constantly moving process—also provided cartoonists as well as joke-tellers with ample fodder for their forms of political satire. In this atmosphere of newfound liberty and as opposed to earlier humor, humorists produced work that increasingly mirrored the division of the population along strong ideological and political lines, ruptures then threatening to tear the Algerian national community apart. This humor may have worsened the polarization of the population into pro- and anti-FIS camps.

During Black October and the transition, humor assisted political parties along with ordinary citizens in their attempts to drum up support for their positions, even when humor contained expressions of fatigue over enduring uncertainty or the democratic opening itself. Most importantly, all sides jockeying for power on the national stage, including Islamists generally considered to be anti-fun, recognized and used humor as a means of advancing political messages. These actors sought to forge coalitions and groups, social movements and non-movements, and to act together to support them, whether through votes or by adopting symbols displaying ideological or party affiliations. As with earlier forms of comedy that brought Algerians together under an idea of a nation, rhetoric such as jokes or cartoons could be such symbols. While the anti-regime humor of October 1988 had its roots in earlier *hittiste* humor, divisive, anxious humor from the transition had little precedent in humor from Algeria's past. Like earlier moments in the twentieth century, humor from October 1988 through January 1992 served as a critical space for Algerians to express opinions about systems of power in the country with very serious implications. It also intersected with other forms of discourse.

Although these years witnessed a flourishing of free expression, in what would later appear to be a strange twist of fate, the Black Decade that followed saw various political actors and the general crisis roll back these earlier advances. After the first round of the legislative elections in December 1991 showed the FIS ahead and about to take power, the military halted the second round. The state then outlawed the FIS and proceeded to arrest some of its partisans. War broke out as these actions prompted some proponents of political Islam to take up arms against a state that they considered illegitimate. During the conflict, attacks proliferated against Algerian intellectuals and anyone seen opposing either side of the conflict. Not all of the North African nation's caricaturists would survive the Time of Terrorism, and, although I was unable to uncover any cases of an individual being killed for telling a joke, the deteriorating security situation forced joke-tellers to indulge in their passion in secrecy. Many ordinary Algerians would seek refuge abroad from the indiscriminate assassinations that started taking lives daily. The citizens who stayed faced a mounting security crisis in which discourse became hazardous, information surrounding this very impasse difficult to obtain, and uncertainty as to what any day could bring the norm. Narratives, conspiracy theories, and rumors flared. Humor in this Black Decade featured centrally in civilians' attempts to grasp and make sense of the often unclear but nevertheless terrifying events unfolding around them.

NOTES

1. Mohand Fellag, *SOS Labess*, DailyMotion, performed March 8, 1990, published 2014, https://www.dailymotion.com/video/x1zvikv.
2. Fellag, *SOS Labess*.
3. Fellag, *SOS Labess*.
4. Fellag, *SOS Labess*.
5. For an overview of this process, especially how two opposition movements' actions ensured that the constitution was interpreted as allowing new parties, see Myriam Aït-Aoudia, *L'expérience démocratique en Algérie (1988–1992)* (Algiers: Koukou, 2016), 57–154. Hugh Roberts discusses the FLN's attempt to reform during this moment. See Roberts, *The Battlefield: Algeria, 1988–2002, Studies in a Broken Polity* (New York: Verso, 2003), 105–127.
6. Jacob Mundy, *Imaginative Geographies of Algerian Violence* (Palo Alto: Stanford University Press, 2015), 15, 39–40.
7. Asef Bayat, *Life as Politics: How Ordinary People Change the Middle East*, 2nd ed. (Palo Alto: Stanford University Press, 2013), 14–15.
8. Bayat, *Life as Politics*, especially 129–152.
9. See, for instance, Edward McAllister, "Immunity to the Arab Spring?," *New Middle Eastern Studies* 3 (2013).
10. This is also Aït-Aoudia's interpretation on this literature. See Aït-Aoudia, *L'expérience démocratique*, especially 12–15.
11. See Aït-Aoudia, *L'expérience démocratique*.
12. For more on the FIS and efforts to woo voters, see Aït-Aoudia, *L'expérience démocratique*, 155–184.
13. McAllister, "Immunity."
14. For an overview of this history, see James McDougall, *A History of Algeria* (Cambridge: Cambridge University Press, 2017), 278–281.
15. Lauren Berlant, *Cruel Optimism* (Durham, NC: Duke University Press, 2011), 13.
16. See, for instance, the joke about a woman substituting a picture of Chadli for that of an ass in an attempt to heal her sick son using folk medicine. Lounes Dahmani, *Blagues: Made in Algéria* (France: Dahmani, 2007).
17. Martin Stone, *The Agony of Algeria* (New York: Columbia University Press, 1997), 64.
18. See William Lawrence, "Representing Algerian Youth" (PhD diss., Tufts University, 2005).
19. Prominent politician and then Algerian ambassador to the European Economic Community in Belgium Sid Ahmed Ghozali claimed that he was in contact with the president and his advisors throughout the protests. He has asserted that Chadli and his

entourage provoked them. In an interview about October 1988, he stated, "The fuse was lit by the presidential residence." See Séverine Labat and Malik Aït Aoudia, *Algérie, 1988–2000: Autopsie d'une tragédie* (Paris: Compagnie des Phares et Balises, 2005). Interview with Mohamed Ali Allalou, December 17, 2014.

20. Aït-Aoudia, *L'expérience démocratique*, 59.

21. See Martin Evans and John Phillips, *Algeria: Anger of the Dispossessed* (New Haven, CT: Yale University Press, 2007). Evans reiterates this view in a more recent think piece. See Martin Evans, "Contextualising Contemporary Algeria: June 1965 and October 1988," *Open Democracy*, May 25, 2012, https://www.opendemocracy.net/martin-evans/contextualising-contemporary-algeria-june-1965-and-october-1988. Evans and Phillips also argue that the events altered Algerians' relationship to the state. See Evans and Phillips, *Algeria*, 105–106.

22. Roberts, *Battlefield*, 107; Evans and Phillips, *Algeria*, 103–104.

23. Bayat, *Life as Politics*, 14–15.

24. Evans and Phillips, *Algeria*, 110–111.

25. Interview with anonymous, January 13, 2015.

26. For instance, the journalist Chawki Amari informed me that, as a resident of Algiers, he did not hear any jokes during the tense days of the October 1988 revolt. Interview with Chawki Amari, July 3, 2013; interview with Gyps, September 24, 2014.

27. For example, Evans and Phillips describe some of the carnivalesque nature of the October 1988 protests, but they still pinpoint anger as the general motivation behind the events. Evans and Phillips, *Algeria*, 102–142.

28. Interview with Mohamed Ali Allalou, December 17, 2014.

29. Abed Charef, *Octobre*, 2nd ed. (Algiers: Laphomic, 1990), 85.

30. Interview with Mohamed Ali Allalou, December 17, 2014.

31. Interview with Mohamed Ali Allalou, December 17, 2014.

32. Interview with Mohamed Ali Allalou, December 17, 2014.

33. Interview with Mohamed Ali Allalou, December 17, 2014

34. Evans and Phillips, *Algeria*, 110–111.

35. Evans and Phillips, *Algeria*, 110–111. This interpretation is Allalou's as well. Interview with Mohamed Ali Allalou, December 17, 2014.

36. Interview with Mohamed Ali Allalou, December 17, 2014.

37. Sid Ahmed Semiane, *Octobre, ils parlent* (Algiers: Le Matin, 1998).

38. These events are described in Naget Khadda and Monique Gadant, "Mots et choses de la révolte," *Peuples méditerranéens* 52 (July–December 1990): 19–24.

39. Slogans from October 1988 as cited in Khadda and Gadant, "Mots et choses," 20. I am using the translation provided by Evans and Phillips with some minor alterations, in *Algeria*, 103.

40. Khadda and Gadant, "Mots et choses," 20, 22.

41. Joke told to me by journalist Sid Ahmed Semiane. Interview with Sid Ahmed Semiane, October 12, 2014.

42. Interview with Sid Ahmed Semiane, October 12, 2014.

43. Abderrahmane Moussaoui, *De la violence en Algérie* (Paris: Actes Sud, 2006), 363–365.

44. Evans and Phillips, *Algeria*, 105.

45. Moussaoui, *De la violence*, 363–365.

46. Moussaoui, *De la violence*, 363–365.

47. Interview with Chawki Amari, July 3, 2013; interview with Sid Ahmed Semiane, October 12, 2014; interview with Lounes Dahmani, August 11, 2013.

48. Slavoj Žižek, *The Sublime Object of Ideology*, 2nd ed. (London: Verso, 2008), xix–xxx. I thank Michael Behrent for informing me that this joke is cited in this source.

49. See Historical Speeches TV, "Reagan tells Soviet jokes," YouTube, April 7, 2016, https://www.youtube.com/watch?v=-wPKt5W8I5Y.

50. Aït-Aoudia, *L'expérience démocratique*, 12–15.

51. Aït-Aoudia, *L'expérience démocratique*, 12–15.

52. The constitution permitted "associations of a political character to form," but the FIS and the Rally for Culture and Democracy (RCD) interpreted that term to mean "party" and declared themselves parties in February 1989. See Aït-Aoudia, *L'expérience démocratique*, 80–134.

53. See Aït-Aoudia, *L'expérience démocratique*.

54. Roberts, *Battlefield*, 65.

55. For an overview of this history, see Michael Willis, *The Islamist Challenge in Algeria* (New York: New York University Press, 1996); Roberts, *Battlefield*, especially 3–33; Ahmed Rouadjia, *Les frères et la mosquée* (Paris: Karthala, 1990).

56. Roberts, *Battlefield*, 11–12; Bruno Etienne, *L'Islamisme radical* (Paris: Hatchett, 1987), 219.

57. Willis, *Islamist Challenge*, 92–93.

58. Roberts, *Battlefield*, especially 3–33.

59. The FLN's popularity had never been measured, but it seems to have declined in the 1980s and in the wake of October 1988, particularly among youth. The FLN still performed well in elections in 1990 and 1991, trailing behind only the FIS. See Lawrence, "Representing Algerian Youth."

60. Aït-Aoudia, *L'expérience démocratique*, 154–184.

61. See Evans and Phillips, *Algeria*, 132–134, 147–153.

62. See Willis, *Islamist Challenge*, 138–149, and the contents of *El Monquidh*.

63. Some cartoons from the satirical newspapers *El Manchar* and *Baroud* drew comparisons between Algerian Islamism and Iran in early and late 1992, suggesting that a pattern between Algerian Islamists and Iran had already been established among the population. See the numerous cartoons in the February 1992 editions of *El Manchar* insinuating that Iran was a puppet master controlling Algerian Islamists and the cartoon by Mustapha Tenani, *Baroud*, August 1992, 10. The government under the new High Council of State in early 1992 tried to connect the FIS to Iran by claiming that Iran had given three million dollars to the party's legislative electoral campaign. Willis, *Islamist Challenge*, 301–302. For more about possible unfounded fears that the FIS had forced changes in dress and lifestyle in the communes they controlled after June 1990, see Willis, *Islamist Challenge*, 158–159.

64. For one feminist account of this period, including fears, see Khalida Messaoudi, *Unbowed*, trans. Anne C. Vila (Philadelphia: University of Pennsylvania Press, 1998).

65. See Evans and Phillips, *Algeria*, 154, for information about the rivalry between the FFS and the RCD.

66. See, for instance, Malika Rahal, "1988–1992: Multipartism, Islamism, and the Descent into Civil War," in *Algeria: Nation, Culture, and Transnationalism, 1988–2005*, ed. Patrick Crowley (Liverpool: Liverpool University Press, 2017), 81–100.

67. Rahal, "1988–1992," 146.

68. Interview with anonymous, January 13, 2015; Evans and Phillips, *Algeria*, 156.

69. Interview with anonymous, January 13, 2015.

70. I am transliterating from Tamazight using the guide included in J. M. Dallet, *Dictionnaire français-kabyle*, vol. 2 (Paris: SELAF, 1985), xiii. Interview with anonymous, January 13, 2015.

71. Evans and Phillips, *Algeria*, 154.

72. Evans and Phillips, *Algeria*, 154.

73. Evans and Phillips, *Algeria*, 146.

74. Evans and Phillips, *Algeria*, 154.

75. The government pushed back elections for representatives for the People's National Assembly, Algeria's national parliament, after the First Gulf War to late 1991.

76. J. C. Brule and J. Fontaine, "Géographisme dans l'islamisme politique en Algérie," *Bulletin de l'association de géographes français* 74, no. 1 (1997): 85.

77. Drawing on notes from François Burgat, Michael Willis points out that these reports of the FIS policing beach clothing and shorts and shuttering movie theaters and bars were sometimes overstated or obscured how the FLN had already initiated these measures before the FIS took control of local governments. He identifies the French press and the Algerian government and press seizing on these stories and exaggerating them. See Willis, *Islamist Challenge*, 158–159; François Burgat and William Dowell, *The Islamic Movement in North Africa* (Austin: University of Texas Press, 1993), 284.

78. Willis, *Islamist Challenge*, 158–159; Gilles Kepel, *Jihad*, 2nd ed. (Paris: Gallimard, 2003), 269–270.

79. See, for instance, the cartoon by Mémèd entitled, "Layadjouzeries [sic]," *El Manchar*, March 1991, 6.

80. Interview with Mohamed Ali Allalou, December 17, 2014.

81. Interview with Zineb Sedira, March 29, 2015.

82. Interview with Ali Silem, December 27, 2015.

83. Roberts, *Battlefield*, 97.

84. Faouzia Zeraoulia, "The Memory of the Civil War in Algeria," *Contemporary Review of the Middle East* 7, no. 1 (2020): 32.

85. Blida was the home of many fervent FIS backers.

86. Interview with Zineb Sedira, March 29, 2015.

87. Aït-Aoudia, *L'expérience démocratique*, 170–178; Evans and Phillips, *Algeria*, 147–151. Madani wore what some consider Islamic attire that was supposed to stress the humility of the wearer.

88. Luis Martinez describes Madani entering a neighborhood in a Mercedes to visit a military entrepreneur with Saudi connections. Luis Martinez, *The Algerian Civil War, 1990–1998* (New York: Columbia University Press, 2000), 26. See also "Algerie: Le faux père tranquille de l'Islam," *Le Monde*, June 14, 1990, https://www.lemonde.fr/archives/article/1990/06/14/algerie-abassi-madani-le-faux-pere-tranquille-de-l-islam_3990439_1819218.html. A Saudi prince acknowledged the funding. Willis, *Islamist Challenge*, 202.

89. Kepel, *Jihad*, 267.

90. See the section on Gulf War cartoons below.

91. Interview with Zineb Sedira, March 29, 2015.

92. Joke related during an interview with cartoonist Saad, March 5, 2015. I am paraphrasing this joke.

93. Interview with Ali Silem, December 27, 2015. Silem discussed Boumediene jokes reinforcing his power.

94. See, for example, Bayat, *Life as Politics*, 137–158.

95. For coverage of these writings, see Giselinde Kuipers, "The Politics of Humour in the Public Sphere," *European Journal of Cultural Studies* 14, no. 1 (2011): 63–80; Sandrine Sanos, "The Sex and Race of Satire," *Jewish History* 32 (2018): 33–63. For humor in Islam, see Anīs Faraiḥa, *al-Fukāha 'and al-'arab* (Beirut: Maktaba Ra's Beirut, 1962); Georges Tamer, ed., *Humor in der arabischen Kultur* [Humor in Arabic culture] (Berlin: De Gruyter, 2009); Jeremy Farrell, "Comic Authority," in *Words That Tear the Flesh*, ed. Alan Baragona and Elizabeth L. Rambo (Berlin: De Gruyter, 2018), 85–117; Franz Rosenthal, *Humor in Early Islam* (Leiden: Brill, 2011).

96. McDougall, *History of Algeria*, 287, 384n134, citing an interview between the author and Abderrahmane Benamara.

97. Evans and Phillips, *Algeria*, 132.

98. Bachir Dahak, *Les Algériens: Le rire et la politique de 1962 à nos jours* (Algiers: Frantz Fanon, 2018); Dahmani, *Blagues*; jokes sometimes included in newspapers; interviews with specialists of humorous cultures in the country such as Ameziane Ferhani. Interview with Ameziane Ferhani, March 15, 2015.

99. Mustapha Benfodil, *Dilem président: Biographie d'un émeutier* (INAS, 2008), http://www.argotheme.com/dilempres%5B1%5D.pdf. The muezzin of a mosque is responsible for the call to prayer.

100. This story is told in Benfodil, *Dilem président*, 50–51. Drawing by Dilem in *Alger républicain*, December 20, 1990, 1. The "cauliflower" appellation was a joke recounted to Martin Evans in October 1989. See Evans and Phillips, *Algeria*, 115n19.

101. See, for example, Slim, Réédition de *Zid ya Bouzid I et II* (Algiers: ENAL, 1986).

102. Interview with Slim, August 20, 2014.

103. Lazhari Labter's private papers detail the late 1980s and early 1990s activities of this movement, known by its French acronym, MAJ, that pressured the government into embracing press reform.

104. For more on the limitations of the press liberty during this time, see Cherif Dris, "La nouvelle loi organique sur l'information de 2012 en Algérie," *L'Année du Maghreb* 8 (2012): 303–320. The press in Algeria published the amounts of government subsidies that each paper received in the early 1990s. See "Dossier presse," Library of the Algerian Cultural Center, Paris, France.

105. Susan Slyomovics attests that there were hundreds of newspapers founded at this time, whereas Evans and Phillips give the number of 150. Susan Slyomovics, "Sex, Lies, and Television: Algerian and Moroccan Caricatures of the Gulf War," in *Women and Power in the Middle East*, eds. Suad Joseph and Susan Slyomovics (Philadelphia: University of Pennsylvania Press, 2001), 74; Evans and Phillips, *Algeria*, 145. See also Hafid Gafaïti, "Power, Censorship, and the Press: The Case of Postcolonial Algeria," *Research in African Literatures* 30, no. 3 (1999): 51–61; Dris, "La nouvelle loi organique."

106. See, for instance, *Algérie-Actualité* from this period.

107. Interviews with Mahfoud Aïder, Mustapha Tenani, Mohamed Mazari, and Hicham Baba Ahmed, June 13, 2013.

108. Gandouras/kandūras are garments for men associated with the Islamic faith in this context.

109. A haik/ḥāyak is a white veil worn by women in certain regions of Algeria with a separate facial covering.

110. Drawing by Fathy, *Alger républicain*, April 16, 1990, 8.

111. Drawing by Djilali Beskri, *Alger républicain*, December 19, 1991, 4.

112. See, for example, drawing by Mokakem, *al-Ṣaḥḥ Āfa*, May 13 to 20, 1991, 7. This image had one man who ostensibly represented the liberal democrats being suspicious of an Islamist man and vice versa. Thus, the newspaper addressed the distrust both sides had for one another at this time.

113. Drawing by Baraji, *Alger républicain*, May 1 to 6, 1991, 6. So many illustrators worked for newspapers in Algeria after 1990 and used pseudonyms that it is not always possible to know their true identities.

114. See, for instance, drawing by anonymous (signature illegible), *al-Ṣaḥḥ Āfa*, June 12 to 18, 1991, 7; drawing by anonymous, *al-Ṣaḥḥ Āfa*, June 5 to 11, 1991, 7.

115. Because of the number of cartoonists working in papers during this period, I was not able to get real names for every artist whose work I uncovered through archives. Cartoon by Baraji, *al-Ṣaḥḥ Āfa*, June 25 to July 2, 1991, 5.

116. Cartoon by Baraji, *al-Ṣaḥḥ Āfa*, June 25 to July 2, 1991, 5.

117. Interview with Adlène Meddi, September 21, 2014.

118. Numbers from Lies Sahar, "Tempête sur la presse," *Algérie-Actualité*, July 23 to July 29, 1992, page number unknown, "Dossier presse," Algerian Cultural Center, Paris, France.

119. See El Manchar from this period.

120. Interview with anonymous, January 13, 2015; "Presse: Une année t'manchir," *El Watan*, October 27, 1991, 199, "Dossier presse," Algerian Cultural Center, Paris, France.

121. Drawing by Melouah, *El Manchar*, December 1990, 3.

122. Cartoon by Hankour, *El Manchar*, January 1991, 14.

123. Slyomovics, "Sex, Lies, and Television," 82.

124. Willis, *Islamist Challenge*, 202.

125. See Slyomovics, "Sex, Lies, and Television."

126. See, for instance, drawing by Kaba'ari, *al-Ṣaḥḥ āfa*, February 26 to March 6, 1991, 5. See also Slyomovics, "Sex, Lies, and Television."

127. Texts by Samy Abtroun, drawings by Ali Dilem, *Golfe: La guerre des Boushés* (Algiers: ENAG, 1991), 36.

128. I was not able to identify the real name of FIB, especially as the topic of having voted for the FIS or supported the FIS is still a taboo one in Algeria.

129. Drawing by FIB, *El Monquidh*, December 19, 1990, 8.

130. See, for instance, drawing by FIB, *El Monquidh*, October 4, 1990, 14.

131. Drawing by FIB, *El Monquidh*, October 4, 1990, 8. See the description of the FIS leaders' distaste for Western television in Evans and Phillips, *Algeria*, 133.

THREE

LAUGHING AT VICTIMS AND ASSAILANTS THROUGH POPULAR JOKES FROM THE BLACK DECADE

At the beginning of the Civil War and right after the cancellation of elections that resulted in a FIS victory and when the two major leaders of the party (Abassi Madani and Ali Belhadj) were declared outlaws, the poor uncle of Nassreddine died as the result of an incurable disease. He arrives at heaven's door and the Guardian asks him, "Who is your god?" Terrified, the man answers, "Madani." "Who is his prophet?" "Ali Belhadj..." Stunned, Heaven's Guardian loses his temper with the man and asks, "How dare you associate the name of the Almighty and His prophet with these vulgar individuals!" The uncle collects himself and then responds, "Well, there is no God but God and Muhammad is his prophet!" Reassured with this response, the Guardian asks him why he answered the way he did at first. The uncle replied, "I'm sorry but I thought it was another fake checkpoint!"

Kī bdāw al-tisʿīnāt ū-mūr mā ḥabsū al-intikhābāt lī rbaḥ fīhum al-Fīs (FIS, Islamic Salvation Front), *w-al-zūj lī shāddīn al-ḥizb* (Abassi Madani wa Ali Belhadj) *aʿlanūhum khārij al-qānūn fī waqt lī bārāj (faux barrage) kānū dāyrīn ḥāla. Waqthā māt ʿamm Naṣraddīn kān mrīḍ mraḍ mā yabrāsh ū-kī wṣal l-bāb al-janna saqsāhu al-ʿassās: shkūn rabbī? Al-rājal khāf, jāwbah: Madani! Shkūn al-Rasūl? Ali Belhadj. Al-ʿassās talfatlū, ū-bdā yʿayyaṭ: kīfāsh? Rabbī ū-rasūlū raddīthum aʿbād. ʿAmm Nassredinne rājaʿ rūḥū ū-qāl lu: Lā ilāha illā Allah wa Muḥammad Rasūl Allah. Al-ʿassās taṭman, saqsāhu w-al-jawāb tāʿ muqbīl ʿalāsh? Jāwbah: sāmaḥlī ḥsabtha fū bārāj (faux barrage)!*[1]

JOKES WERE SOURCES OF AMUSEMENT that could trigger unamusing consequences in the context of Algeria's Time of Terrorism; the wrong joke told to the wrong person could result in death.[2] How and why, then, did Algerians persist in sharing jokes? What purposes did joke-telling serve in a conflict that threatened to rip a national society apart and left an estimated one hundred thousand dead? Were jokes bastions of resistance as some scholars have asserted jokes tend to be in instances of authoritarianism, or did they perform a much more nuanced role in the case of Algeria's Black Decade?[3]

The joke above is typical of a multitude of jokes that Algerians across socioeconomic groups told during the height of the civil conflict in the country, which lasted from approximately 1991/1992 to 2005. The target of laughter proves in the end not to be the FIS leaders it mentions, Ali Belhadj and Abassi Madani, the individuals one may have expected civilians to lambast as professional humorists of the era did.[4] Instead, although the joke insults the two FIS leaders by having Heaven's Guardian call them vulgar, the narrative primarily mocks Nasreddine's uncle, perhaps a stand-in for Algeria's civilian population, for incorrectly believing that the Gates of Heaven are a fake checkpoint.[5] The uncle-as-citizen's lamentable position and laughable error serve as the joke's patsy. Conversely, listeners of the joke's punchline would walk away with an amplified sense that rebel action was widespread; the uncle's use of the phrase *another fake checkpoint* insinuates that he had previously stumbled upon these tools employed by rebels to inflict terror and seize wealth. Thus, the joke avers, these armed insurgents were everywhere.

Jokes like the one told above emerged after the military stepped in to halt the second round of legislative elections in January 1992. It was far from a funny period; state violence also grew apace after the interruption of the elections. After the military intervened to cancel the second round of votes on January 11, 1992, government forces proceeded to arrest some Islamist partisans. The new regime swiftly outlawed the FIS. The state placed detainees from these efforts in several prisons, including harsh concentration camps in the desert South.[6] The creation of these centers might have prompted individuals at risk of being caught by the state's dragnet to join preestablished and new rebel groups to avoid capture.[7] In a possible example of humor informing political vocabulary and the imagined landscape of the war, a fifteen-thousand-strong new antiterrorist group created in early 1993 earned the nickname *ninjas* because the balaclavas they sported made them look like Teenage Mutant Ninja Turtles.[8] Like the armed rebels at times, ninjas were difficult to identify precisely because they wore masks. From the end of 1994, local militias equipped by the government, called *patriots* by sides favorable to them, also entered the fray. The government later admitted that some of its soldiers abused their force, accepting responsibility for 6,146 cases of forcefully disappeared persons (individuals arrested and never seen again).[9]

The months that followed the halting of elections witnessed greater acts of violence on the part of the Armed Islamic Movement (MIA), a preexisting organization that had been fighting against the state since 1982, and Takfīr wa al-hijra (Excommunication and exodus), formed in late 1991. When the MIA proved recalcitrant and unwilling to accept wider portions of the population who wanted to take up arms in the wake of the electoral interruption in 1992, other groups promulgating armed jihad against the military/state as well as civilians began to coalesce. No fewer than seven surfaced throughout the 1990s and into the 2000s.[10] Some groups took up arms against the state because it had prevented the FIS's electoral victory. Most of the FIS's leadership was arrested and subsequently sought to negotiate the party's relegalization with the state.

The 1992–1994 period witnessed possibly the greatest surge in the number of militant groups as well as their supporters. The two central rebel organizations were the Armed Islamic Group (GIA) and the Islamic Salvation Army (AIS). They warred with each other, as well as the state, and diverged in both their policies on violence toward civilians and their political goals. The GIA was a more decentralized organization that leveraged violence against the state, civilians, and foreigners whom it deemed opposed to its cause. It advocated for the total overthrow of the regime instead of a wider place for Islamism within it. The AIS was formed in 1994 by FIS elements that remained after the 1992 electoral interruption (a narrower, less-encompassing FIS than that of the earlier 1990s), and it took up arms with a concrete goal of bringing the government to hold negotiations for the relegalization of the FIS.[11] All of the armed groups, though, differed from each other in terms of motivations, tactics, messages, ultimate political goals, attitudes toward international actors and groups as potential allies or enemies, and positions vis-à-vis potential negotiation and reintegration into an Algerian society that had not been radically altered. They were also not static; the GIA changed over time with different leaders at the helm and had an offshoot, the Salafist Group for Combat and Preaching (founded in 1998), that went on to become Al Qaeda's branch in the Maghrib (Al Qaeda of the Islamic Maghrib). Individual members of the groups, especially the more loosely organized GIA, could also have acted in ways that contradicted the organization's official policy or line.

Caught between the government and warring rebels, civilian communities became split over key questions, including whether the state should relegalize the FIS and which side to back during the war. Civilians also engaged in fierce debates over whether the state should seek a resolution to the conflict through negotiation or the annihilation of the insurgent movements. Civilian and military supporters of dialogue became known as *conciliators* and individuals favoring military suppression of the rebellions as *eradicators*. Amid this uncertainty, acts of terror took place across the country, mainly in the form of assassinations, public bombings, kidnappings, village-wide massacres, and fake roadblocks where insurgents could exhort money from or punish unsuspecting victims. The June 1992 assassination of the fourth Algerian president, Mohamed Boudiaf, the War of Independence hero who had returned after a political exile to lead the state earlier that year, emphasized for many that no one was safe.[12]

While during this period the nation's major editorial cartoonists generally took a stance on the question of negotiations with rebel groups and who was to blame for the war, jokes reveal no such bias for or against the conflict's armed side.[13] Few of the dozens of jokes that I collected directly ridiculed the war's main belligerents. In his ethnographic work on the Algiers suburbs of Eucalyptus and Baraki, Luis Martinez noted that some of his interlocutors mocked the police and state agents.[14] Yet, a narrator who told me one of the very few jokes that I found that could be interpreted as antipolice explained that the joke expressed sympathy for the dire straits in which police found themselves because of the war (the jokes is analyzed below).[15] On the contrary, rather than mocking the Islamist or state actors who were rumored to be behind (and, in the case of some rebel groups, claimed to be responsible for) violent attacks, civilians themselves served as the butt of most jokes, following a long-held tradition in Algeria of self-derision.

Who told jokes? It is difficult to know whether state soldiers or rebels passed along jokes related to the ongoing struggle. The jokes presented here appeared in compilations created by civilians or were ones I gathered through oral histories with researchers or with Algerian journalists or intellectuals who were in the country during the conflict. They hail, most likely, from civilian circles. But jokes can cross boundaries. Journalist Aïssa Khelladi recounts that tracts distributed by rebel organizations contained humorous rhetoric, although the dozen or so armed-group tracts that I recovered did not.[16] It is possible, then, that insurgents or state agents told the humorous stories that became known as terrorism jokes.[17] The jokes analyzed here, though, were most likely told by civilians. I read them, then, as markers of civilian humor rather than the humor of the combatants. Through poking fun at themselves, Algerians sought to alleviate stress, fear, and the alienation that was associated with the conflict by reverting to earlier patterns of self-deprecating humor. By taking a jab at the boozer, the young, macho tough guy, or the overly zealous pervert, these jokes provided Algerians relief by discussing familiar targets for humor in an unsettling new era characterized by fear and bloodshed. It also allowed them to critique the armed groups and state in indirect, discreet ways.

Of course, by its nature humor is ambiguous, and a joke can be open to multiple interpretations. The joke about Nassreddine's uncle could also be ridiculing the FIS leaders for issuing strong statements regarding religion and society on which some Algerians believed that they had no right to speak. Yet, consistently, jokes from this period painted civilians as unable to escape when confronted with the major armed actors in the war. These jokes could be read as bitter commentaries on daily life during the Time of Terrorism and thus subtle jabs at the government or armed rebel organizations. At the same time, though, they often exclusively mocked the victims of violence, emphasizing their vulnerable position in the conflict. Take, for instance, the following joke: "What has the same lifespan as a fruit fly? An Algerian journalist." The teller of this joke, himself a once-threatened journalist, would not necessarily want to mock members of the country's media industry for being targeted for assassination by extremist groups. However, the joke still highlights their vulnerability as a population.[18]

Furthermore, the reality that Algerian jokes did not directly target insurgents or state agents does not mean that they were devoid of any political significance.[19] As these funny short tales poked fun at Algerian civilians, they portrayed rebels and military actors as fearsome, powerful figures capable of heinous crimes. These jokes also represented the conflicts' belligerents as so well entrenched in the country that they were virtually inescapable. In doing so, they attributed power to these agents that, while real in many circumstances, at times exceeded the authority that they possessed. This stereotyping of the war's major actors was not without consequence. Like conspiracy theories, jokes conveyed critical ideas surrounding those individuals, institutions, and events that the jokes targeted or even simply mentioned.[20] Although most jokes likely could not have successfully spread messages without working in tandem with rumors, they still painted images of the conflicts' major actors as powerful while implying the helplessness of civilians who tragically found themselves in their crossfires. By portraying armed Islamist factions and the military on the whole as fearsome, many civilians may have simply reiterated what they felt was the reality of the situation. However, as this chapter argues, in doing so they may have augmented the imagined strength of both groups, thereby shaping the political imagination of at least some Algerians during the conflict.[21]

By themselves, jokes worked as touchstones of resistance to the terror, significant elements that permitted Algerians to survive during an unprecedented period of carnage, a sign of how banal death had become.[22] It is crucial, though, to compare jokes to other cultural elements that influenced Algerians' political imagination and understanding of events during the conflict. A close reading of jokes and their intersections with other discourse demonstrates that they may have indirectly assisted the armed Islamist rebels and the military by consistently testifying to the strength of these actors as both groups were scrambling for hegemony. Yet, jokes also allowed citizen-victims to have the last word, deliver punchlines, and express ideas surrounding the violence. As the present piece avers, subaltern humor in a circumstance of competing authoritarian powers can simultaneously work to uphold and thwart these same powers. Determining when humor functions as resistance or not requires a longer understanding of the humorous practices of the populations employing the humor.

This chapter begins with an overview of theories surrounding power and humor under authoritarian rule. Next, I provide an overview of the parameters of joke-telling during the civil conflict in Algeria. Then, I look at jokes that aggrandized the presence and power of the war's belligerents while also showcasing civilian resistance, demonstrating that subaltern humor can simultaneously uphold and thwart authoritarian power. Throughout, I show that jokes performed complex functions during Algeria's civil conflict of the 1990s.

JOKES AND POWER

"But why are you so secretive?" then French president Nicolas Sarkozy asked an Algerian minister. "Because it is precisely our secrecy that gives us our power," the minister replied, with a smile.[23]

Scholars have sought to elucidate the complex relationship between power and humor, especially during times of war and severe state repression. Many have asserted that individuals and groups bereft of power have employed humor against those who wield it. In their view, humor then constitutes an important means of subaltern resistance.[24] These theorists along with others have insisted, moreover, that jokes have the power to shape societies as well as historical events.[25] Other humor experts have countered these claims by contending that humor can actually assist these governments in maintaining power. It can do so most notably by providing critics of oppressive regimes with a merely discursive and indirect—rather than a more active—form of dissent.[26] Christie Davies asserts that these two strands of thought attribute far too much agency to jokes. He claims that humor does not possess enough power to shape events.[27]

Measuring the efficacy of jokes to trigger change is a difficult task. For instance, Egyptians shared puns about President Hosni Mubarak in the days preceding his departure from power, but does this reality mean that Egyptians laughed him out of office?²⁸ Amid a popular movement, humor can be pervasive, but, short of creating a situation where the presence and absence of humor could be controlled in the context of the revolt, scholars may never resolve the question of whether humor can stoke rebellion or merely reflect the existence of revolutionary fever.

Deeply connected with the popular notion of subaltern culture as generally rebellious, many theorists have assumed that the existence of overt political humor inevitably signals the presence of democracy or at least a desire for it.²⁹ Much less attention, especially among historians, has been paid to political satire beyond its propensity for use as resistance, the consensus being that ridicule helps the disenfranchised lambast their oppressors.³⁰

Pinpointing causation over correlation proves elusive when it comes to humor. Fortunately, critical theory concerning the interplay between discourse and power offers solutions to questions of humor's capacity for influencing events. For instance, Achille Mbembe notes that caricatures serve as language and consequently act as language does in the sociopolitical sphere, meaning that these illustrations can entail violence: "The pictographic sign does not belong only to the field of 'vision.' It also reveals that of speaking. It is, in itself, a figure of speech . . . This language expresses itself not only for its own sake or as a way of describing, narrating, or representing the real, but also a particular strategy of persuasion, in fact, violence."³¹ Like caricatures, jokes can serve as a form of violence. As David Bozzini has pointed out, no matter how incendiary, speech that attributes a subordinate role to a population living under systematic persecution reinforces the power of the tyrannical state in question.³² Lisa Wedeen reiterates the capacity of humor to both resist and buttress state power. She stresses that humor can simultaneously create a space for opposition voices to express themselves while reinforcing the neoliberal and autocratic state systems that these voices are challenging.³³ Algerian jokes worked in similarly complex and ambiguous fashions. On the whole, however, George Orwell's quip, "Every joke is a tiny revolution," runs up against a limit in the case of Algeria's Time of Terrorism.³⁴

Occlusion of events drove the Time of Terrorism. Anthropologist Paul Silverstein has contended that conspiracy theories regarding which side of the conflict committed its worst atrocities served the purposes of both the military and the armed organizations by further obfuscating an already opaque situation.³⁵ By presenting a multitude of possible truths, these theories added extra depth to the mystery surrounding some of the war's most heinous crimes, insinuating that both the military and armed organizations were capable of tremendous force.³⁶ It appeared as if death could come at any moment at the hands of any agent, an idea that Silverstein maintains supported the causes of the war's different belligerents. By asserting that foreign powers were manipulating the rebel groups (a declaration hard to disprove), the state insisted that it was facing a cruel enemy and needed to bypass normal rules for handling violence, such as refusing to hold trials that met international standards for fairness.[37] AIS militants mobilized rumors that the then emir or leader of the GIA, Djamel Zitouni, was an undercover state agent, in order to discredit their rival.[38] Assuredly, rumors that questioned which belligerent was behind which attack or exaggerated the pervasiveness and power of the insurgents provided a sense of legitimacy to the state's claims that it was combatting a fearsome enemy and that the fight necessitated extreme measures. Furthermore, as the more recent exchange between Sarkozy and the unnamed Algerian minister cited at the beginning of this section attests, such opacity regarding the Algerian state continued to bolster its power.

Both the rebel groups and the state profited from stories, even comical ones, that painted either belligerent as super powerful or omnipresent.[39] The GIA may have wanted publicity. Operating near the nation's capital, as the organization did, meant greater press coverage and a boost to the organization's reputation.[40] Some jokes from this period, with their attribution of terror and power to the conflict's major belligerents and their propensity for obscuring the distinctions between them, functioned much as conspiracy theories did. Of course, jokes differ most greatly from conspiracy theories in that they are not meant to offer truths to listeners. However, these jokes consistently poked fun at the victims of violence rather than its perpetrators. By producing such a discourse, even one intended for humorous aims, Black Decade jokes reinforced the power of insurgents as well as the military at a time when they were engaged in a fierce struggle for supremacy. Yet, once again, civilians still spoke through and in jokes and, by making the punchline of jokes about themselves and in light of broader patterns of self-derision, centered the invented nation in ordinary Algerians—an act of resistance.

JOKE-TELLING IN ALGERIA DURING THE PERIOD OF TERROR

As the ranks of the rebel groups and frequency of attacks and fighting with state forces grew after early 1992, fear engulfed everyday life. Individuals who could be assassinated initially included anyone who worked directly for the state. In the months following the cancelation of elections, armed insurgents took over whole sections of towns in the countryside and the suburbs of Algiers, and assassinations of public servants and police officers began to take place. According to some sources, the army let a number of areas in which the populations supposedly helped the rebel groups "bleed"; in other words, as punishment for backing their adversaries, state security agents refused to intervene when fighting broke out between rival groups in specific areas where many civilians supported the armed groups.[41] Insurgents later expanded the ranks of individuals they considered worthy of execution to anyone they believed was supporting the state—that is, not only intellectuals such as writers, doctors, and professors but also anyone who worked in the education, medical, or media sectors. Individuals whom the armed group had selected for assassination could receive death threats in the form of mysterious phone calls or bullets placed in an envelope and left on their doorstep. Other members of the country's intelligentsia had their names written on death lists that circulated around the capital or were put up on mosque walls. Yet other intellectuals and artists, especially those from more working-class, conservative neighborhoods, had friends (who knew insurgents) warn them to move from a particular area or stop their cultural activities.[42] These threats ratcheted up the level of fear pervading many parts of the country.[43] Quite understandably, the terror provoked psychological and health problems for some Algerians.[44]

Death became common currency from 1992 into the 2000s, with individuals in some parts of the country waking up at times to find neighbors' remains in the streets or to hear of recent nearby killings. Certain regions of Algeria witnessed more frequent atrocities and fighting than others. Some working-class neighborhoods and suburbs of Algiers saw assassinations and public bombings. The Mitidja Plain to the southeast of Algiers saw horrific bloodshed as well. Anonymous Algerian joke-tellers spread the following joke during the latter part of the 1990s that speaks to how frightful realities were impacting the nation as a whole. It breaks down the history of the country by postindependent president, finishing during sixth Algerian president Liamine Zeroual's tenure from 1994 to 1999, arguably the worst years of the bloodshed:

> If you didn't find housing during the time of Ben Bella, you will never find housing.
> If you didn't study during the time of Boumediene, you will never study.
> If you didn't make money during the time of Chadli, you will never make money.
> If you didn't make love during the time of Boudiaf, you will never make love.
> If you didn't die during the time of Zeroual, you will never die.[45]

Thus, at the height of the Black Decade, some Algerian joke-tellers communicated the belief that anyone could find themselves caught up in the war and lose their lives.

How did joke-telling unfold amid these horrific conditions? As narrators and newspapers from the period attest, everyday life persisted in the 1990s, yet the period of terrorism ushered in constraints on social interactions. During this time, as Abderrahmane Moussaoui explains, people tended to rely on each other rather than on official news outlets to determine what was going on in the country. I did have a narrator explain, though, that inhabitants of Algiers bought and read newspapers more faithfully during the period to track events.[46]

In some parts of the country, neighborhoods, once tight-knit communities where most residents knew and trusted one another, lost their sense of home and security.[47] Conversely, once attacks against police officers and then civilians began taking place every few hours across the country, community life became very limited. Curfews also impacted the café and street culture. Unlike bars, cafés tended to merge their interiors with the street through the institution of the *terrasse*, or outdoor patio, where Algerians could sit for hours sipping beverages. During the 1990s, the cafés' openness most likely made them dangerous places for Algerians to tell jokes. Streets also became zones where individuals had to pay attention to what they said. Indeed, street corners, areas in front of buildings where people had been able to joke with friends about politics in the democratic opening with less fear, were now sites of concern regarding who was listening and for whom these listeners could be working. Exposing the wrong word, symbol, or clothing at the wrong place at the wrong time could bring death. Any sign of being too "Occidental" or "French-like" (not veiling, wearing Western-style clothes, drinking alcohol, or selling or reading French-language publications) could prompt an attack against a person or their family. Armed militants employed gruesome tactics to subdue the population into doing exactly what they wanted. In certain parts of the country, selling alcohol or Francophone newspapers became impossible.[48]

Given these circumstances, members of the armed groups or state forces may have attacked individuals for telling a joke that they deemed to be blasphemous or contrary to their cause, as the Nazi Gestapo and the Soviet NKVD had done in territories under their surveillance.[49] However, I was unable to uncover any specific cases of Algerians being harmed for having told a joke.

Moussaoui related a popular rumor from the height of the Black Decade that demonstrates the sense of paranoia that became ever present and reflected the reality that the violent struggle split many families right down the middle.[50] There was at least one case of a relative joining an armed organization to later return and murder a member of his own family as a sign of his loyalty to the group.[51] According to the rumor (as told by the anthropologist),

> The GIA was cracking down in the region (supposedly in Western Algeria) and condemned one of their adversaries (the poor victim of this tale). A letter was sent to him announcing the date and hour of his execution. Warned that he was destined to die exactly at midnight, he decides not to run and leave his home but to surround himself with friends and family. Everyone is watching out over the areas surrounding the house, listening for any suspicious noises. Shut away in his room, the man waits nervously, one eye fixed on the door and the other scrutinizing the hands of the clock. When the hands on the clock line up to mark the fatal hour, his nephew brandishes a weapon that he had hidden up until this time. "Your time has come," the nephew says to his uncle with a calm voice, before killing him in cold blood.[52]

In light of the reality that members of the same family sometimes found themselves split into different camps, this rumor appears as a testament to the internecine violence that ripped communities and homes apart during the war.[53] The rumor signals that death could still strike even in the purported security of one's home—no one could be trusted, not even close family.

A few spaces did offer safe environments for Algerians to swap jokes. Some intellectuals whom I interviewed stayed in bars or at friends' homes all night during the curfew not only to enjoy drinks, the general ambiance of the cabarets or a pal's apartment, and, of course, sharing a few jokes but also for security reasons. By switching up the establishments and homes they frequented every night, they could avoid potential attacks in the middle of the night by armed militants. The atmosphere at these parties and clubs was jovial and ripe for ribaldry.[54] In particular, researcher Séverine Labat told me that jokes abounded at the soirées she attended while in Algiers in the early 1990s.[55]

Furthermore, some Algerian media workers noted that joke-telling among this particularly imperiled sector of the population grew in frequency. Dark humor especially peppered everyday personal encounters. At least some media workers joshed over how funny it was that they spent part of their time expressing their desire to be killed by bullets rather than by having their throat cut with a knife.[56] The chief editor of *El Watan* (Algeria's most widely read Francophone newspaper), Omar Belhouchet, commented on the atmosphere in the military-protected coastal residences in which they lived during the worst of the violence against media workers. He noted that colleagues persisted in joking despite the pain of being separated from their families and communities.[57]

The main subjects of jokes concerning the civil war dealt with travel around the country, particularly at night, as this once-banal activity became a perilous undertaking with the onset of terrorism.[58] Perhaps the context surrounding the false checkpoints—the reality that anyone could come across one by accident and find themselves interrogated by insurgents—allowed Algerian joke-tellers to imagine how various subsections of their country would respond to such terrifying circumstances. In any event, the butt of the jokes almost always turned out to be the unsuspecting civilian.

TERRORISM JOKES AND VICTIM TARGETING

> An Algerian man driving at night ... encounters a checkpoint and he can't tell whether the armed men now frighteningly surrounding his car belong to the military or a terrorist group. They ask him, "Who do you like better? Us or them?" Not knowing which side (military or "Islamist") the men are on, the citizen, scared to death, responds, "I think you're both fine. I'm the idiot who decided to take this road."[59]

On the surface, this joke does not appear humorous. A citizen may suffer any of the terrible fates (death, mutilation, rape, extortion, etc.) awaiting unfortunate souls who fell into fake checkpoints. Rather than the joke searing the Islamist or government soldiers, however, it ends abruptly with the man cowering and seemingly admitting his fault in his own victimization. Quite simply, the punchline implies that the joke is on him.

Jokes like this one peppered the sociocultural landscape of Algeria during the height of terrorism in the 1990s and early 2000s. Rather than using their sharp wit to cut at the Islamist or state soldiers who carried out the major operations of the war and whom some foreign and local observers viewed as the forces behind the conflict's major tragedies, some Algerians turned the knives of mockery on themselves. These highly gendered jokes often made civilians, almost always male, the butt of jokes that highlighted men's ability to overtly display masculine forms of courage (although through speaking back alone they were displaying masculine bravery).[60] Not only did these types of jokes give rise to dark self-derision, but they may have played into the hands of the war's major actors while also simultaneously working against soldiers and their leaders. Indeed, several popular jokes described the armed groups and military not as laughable buffoons or lascivious beasts, as cartoons did, but instead as powerful figures in control and able to strike anywhere and at any time (even if civilians in the jokes could speak back to these authorities, often in ironic ways). Of course, seven of the sixty-eight jokes that I collected scorned either the state or armed rebels. On the whole, far from undermining the legitimacy or strength of the military or armed Islamist rebels, terrorism-era jokes may have helped bolster their power. Twenty-eight of the sixty-eight jokes I uncovered that were recounted by civilians, excluding politicians, at least somewhat highlighted the power of the Islamist or state soldiers.

In the joke provided above, for instance, whichever group of deadly, armed men, Islamist or military, the man has had the misfortune of coming across, his ultimate fate lies in their hands. They hardly speak, and they do not need to be described, since listeners of such a joke would already know that rebel and government soldiers both donned military apparel at checkpoints. The teller of the joke makes it clear that all of the power lies with the armed agents. What is more, it does not matter for the punchline and the joke's overall effect whether the men holding the Kalashnikovs are state or insurgent soldiers; in the voice of the teller and the ears of the listeners, they hold the same level of danger. This same joke also bears witness to a sense of hopelessness that many Algerians felt throughout the conflict. For instance, the man in this story does not attempt to connive his way out of the situation; he is resigned to his fate. For their part, the armed militants seem to represent an ever-present danger for individuals who oppose them or get caught in their traps, and their presence in the joke translates to the man's possible demise.

Consequently, rather than disparaging rebels or government soldiers, such jokes highlighted how far-reaching state and rebel authority was. They also insinuate that the state and armed rebels alike engaged in atrocities. Admittedly, on the whole, jokes did not attribute mass civilian massacres or assassinations to military agents. However, placing the military's and the armed groups' purported brutality on par with one another, as some jokes do, conflates the two agents in the minds of the joke-tellers and their audiences. The joke at the beginning of this section implies that the military agents were as capable of harming civilians as the rebels were; if not, the man could answer that he supported the insurgents, and even if he was in the hands of state soldiers he would emerge from the checkpoint unscathed.

Algerians' conscious or unconscious decision to construct the state as the rebel fighters' equal in terror created an image of soldiers as powerful and, again like the armed insurgents, above control by any other authority. Jokes rarely accused government agents directly of committing the sort of horrors that some rebel groups claimed responsibility for; at the same time, though, they could imply that soldiers or police officers violated the rights of and harmed civilians in ways similar to the rebel groups.⁶¹ Take the following joke:

> A man is caught in a false checkpoint. Without knowing whether the checkpoint is manned by terrorists or state agents, when the man who looks like a soldier asks him, "Are you with the army or with the Islamist organizations?" "With the army, of course," he replies. To his chagrin, the soldier turns out to be an Islamist and drags him out of the car to beat him up. Before letting him leave, they make a large cut across his left cheek. The man then continues on his way. After a while, he comes up to a second checkpoint. Once again, the armed man there asks him whose side he's on. Thinking back to what had just happened to him, he responds, "I'm with the Islamists." The soldier turns out to be with the state military so he pulls the driver out of the car, beats him up, and then cuts his other cheek. When he goes to the hospital, the surgeon who's going to stitch up the wounds asks him which one he would like to start with. "My mouth," he replies, "Start by sewing up my mouth so I can no longer speak."⁶²

Soldiers mete out the same punishment to the helpless citizen as the members of the rebel groups do with no fear of punishment. Both the state and armed groups act with impunity and to the detriment of civilians, a sign of their power. This joke presents the possibility of a man being harmed by both groups on the same night. Violence was ambiguous, being carried out by all sides, and almost ensured.

The ambiguity of who exactly was manning a checkpoint may have incited jokes such as this one, just as some civilian testimonies contradicted or cast doubt on the state's official take on certain events—namely, that it protected rather than harmed civilians. These testimonies also inspired conspiracy theories.⁶³ At the same time, though, jokes occasionally placed the military and the armed groups on par, an assertion that may have further clouded the mystery surrounding the infamous question from the war: *"Qui tue qui?"* / "Who is killing whom?"

Another joke directly implicates the ninjas, the counterterrorist special forces that the government created in 1992, in a massacre of unarmed men:

> In February 1998, in a mosque located in the Glacière neighborhood of Algiers, faithful men, especially men who tend to have a radical view of Islam, are getting ready to finish their last prayer of the day. The Imam is at the front of the congregation and the practitioners are still sitting on their prayer rugs when, suddenly, a dozen heavily armed hooded soldiers (the famous "ninjas") burst into the room. The soldiers place themselves in the four corners of the

room and their leader puts himself at the front, just beside the Imam. "Who among you knows Abassi Madani?"

Even though this mosque was known for its support of Islamists . . . no one wants to respond to the soldiers' question. The leader of the group is enraged by the silence of those listening and he insists that they answer by acting like he is getting ready to fire on them.

Scared like the others, one gentleman dares to stand up and declare that he knows Abassi Madani perfectly well. "We have always followed the FIS and its head Abassi Madani, we mobilized ourselves for him, our families, our savings, we are still ready to sacrifice our lives for him." Seeming satisfied, the leader of the "ninjas" asks those who share the man's opinions to go line themselves up along the wall to the right of the room. He then orders his men to kill them. . . .

The room is gripped with indescribable fear and the survivors really don't understand what is going to happen. Again, the head Ninja addresses his listeners: "Who among you knows God?"

Shock takes hold of all of the practitioners. . . . The head Ninja gets annoyed once more and seems ready to make use of his Kalashnikov. "Since no one among you knows God, we're going to decide what to do given this circumstance." It's then that from the back of the room a man begins to speak: "Us, it's true that we don't know God but the gentleman who is standing next to you (the Imam) must very certainly know him. It must be his neighbor or brother-in-law, he tells us about him every day!"

En février 1998, dans une mosquée de la Glacière à Alger, les fidèles, particulièrement radicaux, s'apprêtent à accomplir la dernière prière de la journée. L'imam est devant et les usagers sont encore assis sur leur tapis de prière lorsque, brusquement, une dizaine de militaires cagoulés (les fameux "ninjas") lourdement armés, font irruption dans la salle. Les militaires se positionnent aux quatre coins de la salle et leur chef se met en face, juste à côté de l'imam: "Qui d'entre vous, ici, connaît Abassi Madani?"

Bien que cette mosquée soit très connue pour son soutien à tous les islamistes . . . personne ne veut répondre à cette question des militaires. Le chef du groupe des "ninjas" est énervé par le silence de son auditoire et il insiste tout en faisant mine de se préparer à tirer. Apeuré comme les autres, un monsieur ose se lever et déclare connaître parfaitement Abassi Madani: "Nous avons toujours accompagné le FIS et son chef Abassi Madani, nous avons mobilisé pour lui nos familles, nos fortunes, nos maisons, nos voitures, nous sommes encore prêts à sacrifier nos vies pour lui." Apparemment satisfait, le chef des "ninjas" demande à ceux qui sont du même avis d'aller se mettre le long du mur à droite de la salle. Il ordonne alors à ses hommes de les abattre.

> *Alors que la salle est au comble de la peur, le même chef Ninja s'adresse aux autres fidèles et leur dit: "Qui d'entre vous connaît Liamine Zeroual?" De nouveau, c'est le silence et les gens échangent entre eux des regards inquiets. Comprenant très vite que le militaire allait encore s'énerver, un homme se lève et dit avec beaucoup d'assurance qu'il connaît bien Liamine Zeroual, qu'il a adhéré à son parti dès le départ, qu'il a mobilisé toute sa famille et tous ses proches pour le succès de son parti politique le RND. Le militaire demande alors à ceux qui sont du même avis que ce monsieur d'aller se mettre le long du mur à gauche de la salle. Il ordonne à ses hommes de les abattre....*
>
> *La salle est saisie d'une peur indescriptible et les survivants ne comprennent décidément rien à ce qui vient de se passer. De nouveau le chef Ninja s'adresse à son auditoire: "Qui d'entre vous connaît Dieu?"*
>
> *C'est la stupeur qui s'empare des fidèles.... Le chef Ninja s'énerve encore une fois et semble prêt à faire usage de sa kalachnikov. "Puisque personne d'entre vous ne connaît Dieu, nous allons prendre les décisions qui s'imposent," crie-t-il en demandant à ses hommes de se mettre en position. C'est alors que du fond de la salle, un homme se met à parler: "Nous, c'est vrai que nous ne connaissons pas Dieu mais par contre le monsieur qui est à côté de vous (l'Imam) doit très certainement le connaître. C'est sûrement son voisin ou son beau-frère, il nous en parle tous les jours!"*[64]

Another version of this joke has an emir (a leader of an insurgent group) and armed rebels entering the mosque. When the emir asks the assembly who knows God and a man signals the imam, the imam quips that he does not know God but instead knows the emir's mother, using sexual innuendo in a rare moment when a joke narrative directly ridicules an insurgent.[65] The interchangeability of the ninjas for the armed groups highlights the purported similarities between the two, most notably their supposed propensity for cold-blooded killings as well as their power to disrupt ordinary Algerians' lives.

The practice of swapping one antagonist for the other in different versions of the same joke and jokes presenting the armed groups and military on par with one another in terms of power reveal perspectives that could contribute to a wider scholarly debate on whether the Black Decade constituted a civil conflict. The question itself emerged as the violence unfolded, as the Algerian state rejected the term and preferred to speak of the violence as the act of bands of aberrant "terrorists," while the French government favored "civil war." According to Hugh Roberts, drawing on literature delineating a universal definition of *civil war*, for a conflict to be considered civil the warring sides must establish authority over specific territories or be ideologically opposed with large followings, criteria that the fighting in Algeria did not meet by his evaluation.[66]

By showing the armed groups inflicting the same level of violence on hapless civilians as the state, these jokes indicate that some individuals may have seen both as equally formidable, suggesting that they had more equal control of territory and therefore making the term *civil war* applicable. Indeed, jokes portray the armed groups as organized and prevalent enough to terrorize civilians in any place and at any time. It should be noted, though, that Algerians today use the term *civil war* less often than *Time of Terrorism* and *Black Decade*, which could also be the result of the state's eventual victory. Nonetheless, jokes offer insight here into how some individuals in Algeria viewed the war's belligerents as well as the nature of the conflict itself.

Predating 1998, when it appeared in a volume, the following joke represents a missed occasion for Algerian joke-tellers to roast one of the war's most notorious belligerents: "Antar Zouabri, the bloody GIA emir, was just killed by security forces and finds himself now in heaven waiting in line for his judgment. The angel at the front of the room is calling out final decisions as each recently deceased person moves up to the front of the room. 'You—you go to heaven, right door! You, hell, the door to your left.' Finally, it's Zouabri's turn. 'What's your name?' asks the angel. 'Antar Zouabri.' 'Zouabri, Zouabri . . .' says the Angel looking, 'Ah, here it is! Deliveries are made through the back door.'"[67] Caricaturists ridiculed the armed rebels, sketching them as devilish, bloodthirsty animals.[68] This joke refrains, however, from such a scathing treatment of Zouabri. At the most, the joke lightly pokes fun at him for perhaps assuming that he, someone responsible in the eyes of many Algerians for innumerable civilian deaths, would be placed in either heaven or hell according to the same procedure as everyone else. Yet, this very exceptionalism allots him a high level of power; even in the afterlife, his reputation precedes him, although the angel does instruct him to enter through the back door, a passage reserved for servants. He is also denied access to heaven, although the joke does not say whether he corrects the angel and where he ultimately ends up. In a war in which the GIA declared themselves responsible for deaths, one could surmise that such a joke may have taken on a resistance tone, perhaps ridiculing a GIA leader for being stupid. Yet, the tellers of this joke stress that Zouabri's actions on Earth have yielded very deadly results.

Of course, not every joke needs a butt. However, Algerian jokes from the period depicted civilians as laughable, if brave enough to speak, while giving a great amount of clout to the war's belligerents. Jokes told by oppressed persons in other circumstances belittled the formidable entities that they encountered. These authoritarian jokes from elsewhere draw a strong contrast to Algerian terrorism-era jokes. Indeed, subaltern resistance jokes from other contexts such as Jewish humor in the Holocaust tend to outright denounce oppressors as idiots, savages, or any other variety of negative attributes.[69] In contrast, the following joke once again has a civilian, a man pursued by GIA members, filling the role of the jester. The narrative does arguably stress the absurdity and the danger of the situation he is in but fails to assign negative characteristics to the armed insurgents, who end up appearing as nobody's fool:

> A prisoner of the GIA escapes from the camp where they were holding him but his absence doesn't go unnoticed for long. The terrorists begin tracking him and, realizing that they're hot on his trail, the man flees to a local farm looking for shelter and a good hiding spot. Seeing that the farm is empty, he exclaims his relief and then decides to try hiding from the terrorists in a well next to the barn. He climbs down into the well using the bucket and rope located next to it and lowers himself down. After a few minutes, he hears the band of Islamists talking next to the well. "My God!" he exclaims "They've found me! At least they don't know I'm in the well." Then an idea dawns on him "Yes, that's it! I will echo whatever they say so they believe the well to be empty." "We've lost him," he hears one of them say, "He must have headed towards the village." "*Towards the village . . .,*" the escaped prisoner repeats. "That is," adds another, "if he's not still hiding in the forest." "*Hiding in the forest.*" "And me," states another terrorist starting to grimace and raising his knife, "I say he's hiding in this well." "*In the forest!!! In the forest!!!*"[70]

The last terrorist who correctly guesses the hiding spot of the poor man proves that the terrorists are not easily duped. Their power is thereby reinforced.

Not only did civilians serve as the butts of several Algerian terrorism-era jokes, but many jokes disparaged victims, who also possessed certain foibles and characteristics deemed worthy of ridicule. This story takes aim at lustful gentlemen:

> A real pervert is out after the curfew driving around Belcourt. . . .[71] He sees a woman in a *niqāb* and thinks to himself, "All right! Maybe I can score with her!" So he stops and asks the woman if she wants a ride. She silently hops into the car. He starts chatting with her, but she's not really talking. At one point, thinking he can take advantage of the situation to get lucky, he asks her if she would want to go out to the forest to speak a bit more "intimately." The woman doesn't say anything, so the pervert takes this as consent and starts to get really excited that she's willing to sleep with him. He drives them out to a pretty isolated spot, stops the car, and hops out. He opens the door for his silent companion and then goes to the trunk of the car to pull out a piece of cardboard so they'll have something to lie on while they're getting

busy. As he's putting the cardboard on the ground, he turns around to see that the woman has lifted her niqāb and has a Kalashnikov that was hidden underneath her garment. He then looks at her beseechingly and asks, "Well, don't you want to pray?"[72]

Once again, the teller of this joke emphasizes the strength of armed Islamists while subverting any notion of the civilian's power. After all, it is his penchant for women that leads to the ambiguous scenario from which he probably will not emerge alive. The narrative of the joke targets the pervert for incorrectly assuming that he could pick up a lady on the street at night, a generally taboo act in some Maghribi societies, without facing negative consequences. This joke also underscores the omnipresence of rebel militants; a seemingly harmless woman in a *niqāb* can be an armed insurgent. Death can peek out from any corner and crevice, even a sexy woman's veil. Of course, one could argue that the joke seeks to relieve the tension surrounding the violence by poking fun at a man hitting on a strange woman with the hope of having extramarital sex, an act viewed as abnormal by some social norms. Additionally, incongruity arises when the horny victim attempts to convince his deadly companion to pray; he tries to transform the place where he believed coitus was going to occur into a place of religious practice. Yet, the joke ends with a threat emerging from an unexpected place, thereby highlighting the omnipresence of death at the hands of rebels and their sympathizers.

"Sexual degenerates" were not the only ones whom Algerians made the butts of jokes. Nineties joke-tellers also derided alcohol drinkers for imbibing too much, sometimes to the point of being completely clueless as to what was going on around them: "A drunk guy pulls up to a false checkpoint. The terrorists manning the post can tell right off the bat that the guy is totally wasted. One of them sticks his Kalashnikov in the man's face and sneers, 'What are you doing brother?! You, who are supposed to be a Muslim, drinking alcohol?' The boozer snaps, 'Stop with the questioning already! Just slit my throat and let me be on my way!'"[73] This joke pokes fun at the drinker for being intoxicated while the terrorists appear once again to be dark and totally in control of the situation. Quite possibly, those individuals sympathetic to the cause of Islamist rebels could have recounted this joke to mock supposedly secular individuals who flaunted their unbelief according to some interpretations of the Quran as banning alcohol by unabashedly appearing drunk. In the joke, the intoxicated man has lost his senses to the point that he asks the terrorists to kill him, not realizing that if that comes to pass, he will not be able to get away from the self-righteous militants because he will be dead. At the same time, jokes that evoke individual citizens acting in ways condemnable in the eyes of Islamist rebels could be perceived as defying the latter's ideology and therefore their supposed struggle to restructure Algerian societies along more Islamic lines. Thus, such a joke could be perceived as an affront to the insurgents, who supposedly viewed alcohol drinking as a sinful undertaking and one of Westernized heathens.[74]

In addition to the tales above that reproached drunks and perverts, the following joke about an old woman proved perhaps the most enduring of the terrorism period:

> A bus falls in a fake checkpoint. The head of the terrorists orders his soldiers to kill all of the men and rape all of the women. A young woman sitting next to an old one bravely stands up and says, "At least let this old woman go. You're not going to rape her!" The old lady then stands up and says, "Hey they said they're going to rape all the women, so it's all the women!"

> *Kār ṭāḥ fī fū bārāj (faux barrage). Al-amīr qāl lhum aqtlū gā' al-rijāl wa nīkū gā' al-nisā'. Wāḥid al-mra qā'ida quddām 'ajūza waqfat w-qālat: "Yā sīdī khallū hādī al-'ajūza trūḥ, mā tnīkūhāsh!" Waqfat al-'ajūza w-qālat: "Qāl nīkūhum gā' ya'nī gā'."*[75]

The narrative recenters laughter at the expense of the old woman, who seeks sex or equality by strange means. Once again, civilians cannot escape the violence of the war, even if they are able to express themselves in the face of certain death.

Jokes that seemingly intended to insult state agents more often than not underlined the latter's power. The Didouche Mourad-Bab Ezzouar joke was initially told following the implementation of the curfew during the October 1988 Revolution, as recounted in chapter 2. It later became viewed as a joke on the curfew in effect in various cities from late 1992 through 1995.[76] Moussaoui insists that an almost identical version of this joke, one in which the firing officer is a neighbor of the man he shoots, highlights Algerians' disgust with the state's ability to do what they wanted to without punishment. He also believes that it testifies to the difficulties of the curfews, and this conclusion is most likely accurate.[77] Yet, the officer's nonchalant response to having shot his neighbor stresses the extent of his power to murder with impunity; he does not fear that his colleagues or superiors or international human rights organizations might find out about what he has done and punish him. He holds the position of a law enforcer who acts above and beyond the law with no negative consequences. By portraying the power of the officer this way, the joke paints a powerful image of state agents and likewise shows civilians as unable to escape their grasp.

Once again, this joke could fall under the category of resistance humor, since it denounces or bears witness to the use of excessive force by Algerian police and military. At the same time, though, it portrays the state's forces of order as all-powerful and the neighbor/victim as bereft of any rights. The state here is supreme, above ever having to face justice or questioning vis-à-vis its actions.

Relating to the powerlessness of Algerians in jokes, Moussaoui claims that these narratives sought to underscore the silencing of citizens' voices during the war—normally, the listener would expect the neighbor to treat the other neighbor kindly.[78] Here, to the contrary, we see that mutual respect between neighbors and a sense of community have been replaced by blind violence. Yet, even jokes like the one about the man getting shot preemptively for being out after curfew evinces the perceived power of the state.

RESISTANCE JOKES AND JOKES AS TENSION RELIEF

As discussed above, 1990s Algeria was a period and place in which entrenched armed combatants sought through acts of intense and often highly symbolic violence to hold swaths of the population in terror and thereby control their actions. Given this tense atmosphere, any method of reducing the high levels of stress, fear, and strain constituted a feat of opposition. Consequently, joke-telling that both distracted listeners from the war's events and derided the armed groups, state, or political figures that the people believed were orchestrating the bloodshed meets the criteria for resistance jokes as they have been defined by scholars in humor studies literature. Furthermore, certain jokes provided respite from the terror by lambasting politicians and groups purportedly responsible for the chaos.

To begin with, joke-tellers resisted the effects of such horror in an unusual fashion by ridiculing through terrorism-related humor different sectors of Algerian society who may have served as the butts of jokes before the 1990s, particularly if one thinks of the country's longer tradition of self-deprecating humor. Insurgent organizations employed terror as a means to check potential support for the government as well as to control civilians' actions, and vice versa. Joke-tellers were admitting that certain sectors of Algerian society such as more secular-minded individuals lay beyond the influence of the armed groups' ideology. In this way, these spinners of humorous tales acknowledged limits to the latter's ability to reconstruct society according to their will. The joke about the man three sheets to the wind reminds the listener that civilians were continuing to defy the armed insurgents' supposed goal, at least in theory, of creating a more Islamic regime across the land. The following joke, which displays the limits of some Algerians' religious knowledge, similarly fits into this category of jokes told during the war that resisted the armed groups:

> A bus is stopped by a terrorists' checkpoint. The armed man who gets onto the bus announces to the passengers, "All those whose first name does not end in '*dine*' [*dīn*] will be executed."⁷⁹ The interrogation begins:
>
> "What is your name?"
> "Nourredine [light of religion]."
> "And you?"
> "Azzedine [glory of religion]."
> "And you?"
> "Nasrdine [victory of religion]."
>
> The terrorist reaches the back of the bus and the poor fellow sitting there can't think of any more names that end in "*dīn*." But the terrorist approaches and asks, "So what's your name?" The man responds, "James Dean."⁸⁰

By asserting that some Algerians did not know very much about Islam, joke-tellers implied that Islamist plans for constructing a faithful national community were not coming to fruition or were perhaps impossible.

Jokes also never describe citizens succumbing to violence. Moreover, civilians were able to speak directly through these narratives to power brokers in the country. After his 1993 assassination, fans of Tahar Djaout attributed the following words to the slain author: "Silence is death. And if you speak, you die. If you stay silent, you die. So speak and die."⁸¹ The words referenced the situation of endangered Algerians during the early part of the Black Decade (Djaout had written about the rise of political Islamism).⁸² Many Algerians considered the act of speaking throughout the conflict a combat or emblem of resistance against fear.⁸³ Through their ability to speak in the direst of circumstances, civilian jokes manage to articulate their truths in the face of oppressive power.⁸⁴

Humor that targeted various sections of the civilian population echoed self-deriding humor from earlier periods of Algeria's history. By following earlier patterns, perhaps jokes, even those evoking details of a frightening present, allowed Algerians to communicate that the Black Decade had not displaced all cultural practices or vestiges of more normal times. The troubling events unfolding around them could not undercut earlier practices of joke-telling.⁸⁵ As journalist Adlène Meddi explained, in his view, for the majority of the population the most traumatizing aspect of the war was the loss of a sense of community, of a shared "brotherhood" among Algerians.⁸⁶ Jokes that stereotyped certain social groups or figures perhaps allowed the population to have a collective chuckle even at the height of madness in the country.

Furthermore, the jokes recounted above about drinkers, lascivious philanderers, and secular-minded individuals generally ignorant about Islam demonstrate that these civilians could be forgiven for their weaknesses, whereas rebels or state agents believed to be guilty of excessive force could not. The act of excluding members of the armed groups from derision may have in effect intentionally excluded these individuals from Algerian society by depriving them of being subject to the collective auto-derision that had characterized the country's humor from earlier periods. Joke-tellers aimed their wit at the civilian population rather than members of the armed groups to stress that these terrorists were no longer part of the national community.

Even a joke circulating in secret about the (semi)suppression of Algerian voices could represent an act of resistance. This was the case of the widespread joke recounted above about the man having his face cut up on both sides by an armed organization as well as by military soldiers. Here, civilians who belong to the same group of victims of / bystanders in the violence as the protagonist of the tale expressed their outrage or despair at being silenced by the armed political opponents. Jokes could allow repressed individuals to comment on their lot during the conflict, thereby representing another subtle way this popular form of humor could contest powerful individuals in indirect ways.

Algerian jokes did occasionally ridicule the armed rebels and state agents, though, in ways similar to those told by oppressed persons in other situations. Yet these jokes were the exception rather than the rule. The following is one such joke:

> A young guy from Algiers gets fed up one day with the system and the lack of justice and decides to become a terrorist. So he goes into the mountains where Islamist groups are located. When he comes across a group he wants to join, he introduces himself, and then the group, thinking he's not a double agent, decides to take him on. He starts to do all of the training sessions with them, he sleeps in tents as they do. After two weeks, though, he starts to flip out a bit, "How do you all go without women? I mean, I come from Algiers!" One of the rebels tells him, "Here's what you do—you go to the second mountain up there see and you'll find a barrel that you can, you know, use instead of a woman." The next day he goes up the second mountain and, sure enough, there's a barrel with a hole in it. He puts his dick into the hole and boom, he finishes, and then heads back down the hill to rejoin the camp. A couple of days later the chief of the group approaches him and says, "I'm really sorry but this is going to be a couple of difficult days for

you." Bewildered, the man replies "What? Is the military coming? Are they launching an offensive against us?" "No," the chief answers, "From tomorrow until Friday it's your turn to be in the barrel."[87]

C'est un jeune d'Alger qui en a marre, il décide aussi de devenir terroriste. Il y en a marre de la justice donc il monte dans la montagne au maquis. Et voilà ils le respectent ils le regardent c'est pas un gars infiltré bienvenue etc... Il fait des entraînements avec eux et tout. Ils dorment dans les tentes et... lui c'est un jeune d'Alger donc au bout de deux semaines il commence à leur demander "Mais comment vous faites... les femmes... moi je viens d'Alger..." "Ah c'est pas un problème," ils lui disent. "Tu prends la deuxième montagne tu vas trouver un grand bidon." Il monte la montagne, il trouve le bidon, et il comprend, il trouve le trou dedans il, tak tak tak tak il redescend dans le camp. Une semaine plus tard il dort et puis le chef vient (pour) le réveiller. Il dit, "Qu'est-ce que c'est? C'est une opération militaire...?" Il lui dit "Non, une semaine est passée. De demain jusqu'au vendredi c'est ton tour de rentrer dans le bidon."

The theme that Algerian Islamist armed agents engaged in homosexual activities with one another dominated humorous stories that lambasted the terrorists. Some Algerian communities at the time viewed homosexuality as inappropriate sexual behavior, and it is currently illegal to engage in homosexual sex.[88] By attributing anal sex between men to the rebel groups, the recounters telling this joke perhaps sought to portray the men as effeminate by some societal standards.[89] Perhaps some Algerian joke-tellers wished to explain the decision of so many men (and some women) to engage in armed rebellion supposedly under the banner of Islam by declaring that these individuals suffered from frustrated sexual desires.

ABSURDITY

In his article analyzing Czechoslovakian occupation-era humor, Chad Bryant questions whether satire in that context represented a collective effort to challenge Nazi authorities. He concludes overall that resistance humor was not as widespread as scholars previously assumed. According to Bryant, an alternative function of the gags was to allow the occupied Czechoslovakian population to express their emotions when confronted with the different absurdities of Nazi rule.[90]

Similarly, Algerian humor from this period was infused with cynicism, and certain jokes appear to have strictly served as a pressure valve for the bitter sentiments and hopelessness that plagued the population at the time. The placement of civilians in ludicrously bad situations, the depictions of stark violence, and the mocking of populations especially susceptible to being targeted for death all point to this desire for release as a major factor behind Algerians' joke-telling during the height of terrorism.

This joke demonstrates Algerian joke-tellers' capacity in the 1990s to exploit the absurd with the goal of getting a laugh:

> A bus falls into a fake checkpoint. The terrorists make everyone get off and, deciding that they're all infidels, start to behead the whole lot. One small old lady hides under the body of a passenger who has been killed. Before long, believing everyone to be dead, the terrorists depart and the military shows up a few hours later after someone discovers the massacre. When the soldiers arrive, they see the old lady, the only escapee from the massacre, going around and turning each head over so that the faces of the dead are looking up. A soldier approaches her to ask her what the hell she's doing. The woman replies, "I'm looking for the bus driver. He owes me change."

> *Kār yṭīḥ fī fū bārāj (faux barrage). Al-irhābiyyūn yhabbṭū al-ghāshī gāʻ. Qāl lak hadhū gāʻ kuffār w-bdāw yaqtlū fīhum. Wāḥid al-ʻajūza tkhabbāt taḥt jism wāḥid mīt. Shāfū shāfū qāl lak khlāṣ mātū, ū-rāḥū. Shī swāyiʻ min baʻd, al-jaysh yījū bash yashūfū al-madhbaḥa. Yṣībū al-ʻajūza al-waḥīda lī salkat, qāʻida tqallab fī rīsān al-mūta w-tshūf fīhum. Jundī qāl lhā wāsh rākī tdīr. Jāwabāthum: "Rānī nḥawwas ʻalā al-shūfūr (le chauffeur). Mā radd līsh al-ṣarf."* [91]

In this joke, a woman engages in the highly disturbing act of touching multiple decapitated heads over the question of a few cents. The narrator places her, like so many other protagonist victims of Algerian terrorism jokes, in a remarkably frightening situation—in the middle of a field where all of the passengers on the bus she was riding were slaughtered. Instead of acting devastated as one would expect the survivor of such a harrowing massacre to do, she stays focused on getting her change back. Jokes like this one and the one above about the drunk man requesting that his throat be slit and he be allowed to go about his business display civilians becoming used to violence or not willing to be deterred from their activities by it. These civilians also come off as unaffected or unfazed by the horror unfolding around them. While acknowledging the power of the armed groups, then, these jokes still demonstrate the power of civilians not to succumb to terrorization, another way these jokes can be similar to more overt forms of resistance humor.

Journalists served as the subjects of many a joke in the days when they were under constant threat. A popular editorial cartoon that might have been inspired by an already circulating joke queried, "How do you recognize an

Algerian journalist? He's the one with a pen in hand, two dinars in his pocket, and three bullets in the head."[92] Joke-tellers also poked fun at police officers being killed by the terrorists as often as every few hours beginning in the summer of 1993:[93] "What is blue all over and dies quickly? An Algerian police officer." The narrator who told me this joke insisted that he was not a supporter of the rebel Islamist groups, nor were the others who passed the joke around. Instead, he maintained that he and the other narrators were stressing the appalling turn that events took after the 1992 military intervention when some angry members of the armed organizations started assassinating state security agents. Humor pointed out the absurd in the conflict's everyday violence and assisted joke-tellers and their listeners in making it through the worst of the bloodshed. Once again, humor stresses the power of Black Decade belligerents while also indirectly working as a tool of resistance for civilians caught between them.[94]

Ameziane Ferhani, a cultural journalist and writer with *El Watan*, explains that, in addition to helping individuals express their frustration with and testify to frightening, absurd realities, popular jokes at the height of the horror allowed people to process what was happening. By imagining fictive circumstances that involved terrible events but ending the narrative with a satirical punch, joke-tellers processed reality but promptly removed themselves from it.[95]

CONCLUSION

While jokes that could be qualified as types of resistance humor did exist in Algeria during the height of terrorism, for the most part, these jokes made fun of the victims rather than the perpetrators of violence. At some moments, this dark humor proved harmless, with street humorists poking fun at civilians' pitiful situations for the sake of tension relief. At others, Algerian joke-tellers of the era took aim at figures and groups that they considered responsible for or culpable in the conflict (namely, the armed groups) and provided incisive comments regarding the current events in the country. Most notably, though, jokes highlighted the power of the state and the insurgent groups. Jokes about massacres, fake checkpoints, or state agents firing on civilians with impunity reminded listeners that a deadly war was underway and that belligerents could strike at any time and in sometimes unexpected places, messages that helped the state's and armed groups' causes. By underscoring the inability of everyday Algerians to escape the state and insurgents, jokes, even ones that showed civilian victims having the last word, augmented the imagined power of the combatants. The jokes reviewed in this work generally painted an image of the state and the armed groups posing as counterstates as all-powerful and implied their hand in all sorts of devious, violent activities that had widespread consequences. Yet, by poking fun at themselves, some Algerians may have sought to bring forward earlier patterns of self-deprecating humor (see chap. 1) to anchor the nation in the civilian pacifist majority just as belligerents were claiming to speak and act in its name. Such an act inevitably entails resistance. This revelation becomes possible, furthermore, only if one views these jokes in comparison with humor from earlier periods of Algeria's history. In particular, in this case, a variety of actors from the interwar period through the 1980s used humor, especially self-deprecating humor, as a way of imagining what Algeria was and should be, a legacy that joke-tellers in the 1990s may have advanced.

Algerian popular humor from the height of the Black Decade does not follow the pattern of subaltern jokes attacking the powerful for the benefit of the powerless that some theorists attribute to humor under authoritarianism. Instead, humor could support the powerful (in this case, the state and insurgents) by acting similarly to conspiracy theories and rumors in emphasizing their power. Civilians, though, appeared as ultimately unable to avoid the conflict's belligerents but still able to speak back to them and speak truth about the war in the face of deadly actors. Humor in the form of popular jokes thus performed multiple, simultaneous, and powerful functions during Algeria's Time of Terrorism. Jokes could both emphasize and uphold the power of the military and armed groups while also offering a way for civilians to speak back to these authorities and anchor the nation in ordinary, nonbelligerent Algerian communities. Thus, how humor in the hands of repressed populations works, whether as resistance or as a way of strengthening authoritarian rule, depends on context and circumstances. Algeria's lead caricaturists during the height of the civil conflict sought for their part to exclude agents of one side of the conflict from the nation as they offered strong theories on who was carrying out the violence and why. Their work and its impact form the subject of the next chapter.

NOTES

1. Interview with Zineb Sedira, March 29, 2015. I am including original scripts of jokes not otherwise attainable in other published work. I acknowledge, however, that jokes changed over time and that the precise wordings that interlocutors provided to me are not the definitive versions of the jokes. This joke appears to be a reiteration of an early joke that appeared at least in Iraq by the mid-1980s. The protagonist of this joke arrives in the afterlife and fervently professes his belief in the Ba'athist Party and its leaders and ideologues. See Khalid Kishtainy, *Arab Political Humor* (London: Quartet Books, 1985), 176.

2. I did not discover an instance in which someone had been killed for telling a joke. However, given that individuals in several communities during the conflict had to be careful about what they wore and said in public, it is conceivable that someone may have been killed

for telling a joke. Pinpointing the exact reason for which an individual who was targeted for assassination was killed is also a difficult task.

3. See, for instance, Oriol Pi-Sunyer, "Political Humor in a Dictatorial State: The Case of Spain," *Ethnohistory* 24, no. 2 (1977): 179–190.

4. Ali Belhadj and Abassi Madani were coleaders of the Islamist party the FIS. See chaps. 2 and 4.

5. To increase security during the Black Decade, the Algerian police and military established checkpoints where they would stop cars to look for suspicious activity. Members of the armed groups set up fake checkpoints, *faux barrage* in French and Algerian Arabic, where they terrorized certain citizens by robbing, raping, or murdering them.

6. For stories (some of which cannot be verified) regarding the concentration camps in the desert, called the "camps of the South," see Algeria Watch's website, especially the articles included in the dossier "Le Drame des ex-internés des camps du Sud" [The drama of the ex-prisoners from the camps of the South], http://www.algeria-watch.org/fr/mrv/internes/ex_internes/ex_internes.htm. See also Saphia Arezki, "Les camps d'internement du sud en Algérie (1991–1995): Contextualisation et enjeux," *L'Année du Maghreb* 20 (2019): 225–239.

7. Abed Charef, *Algérie: Le grand dérapage* (Paris: Editions de l'Aube, 1994), 392.

8. Martin Evans and John Phillips claim that the title *Ninja* stemmed from the cartoon show. Martin Evans and John Phillips, *Algeria: Anger of the Dispossessed* (New Haven, CT: Yale University Press, 2007), 188.

9. George Joffé, "National Reconciliation and General Amnesty in Algeria," *Mediterranean Politics* 13, no. 2 (2008): 217.

10. Here, I am including the MEI (Movement for the Islamic State), Takfîr wa al-hijra (*sic*; Excommunication and Religious Migration), the GIA (Armed Islamic Group), the AIS (Army of Islamic Salvation), the FIDA (Islamic Front of Armed Jihad), LIDD for the Islamic League for the Da'awa (*sic*; religious call or invitation to Islam) and Jihad, and GSPC (the Salafist Group for Preaching and Combat). For more background and a discussion of the genesis of some of these groups, see, for instance, Luis Martinez, *The Algerian Civil War, 1990–1998* (New York: Columbia University Press, 2000), 197–219.

11. Martinez, *Algerian Civil War*.

12. Cartoonist Slim cited Boudiaf's assassination as a turning point for him. He left the country shortly afterward for Morocco. Interview with Slim, August 20, 2014.

13. See chap. 4.

14. Martinez, *Algerian Civil War*, 80.

15. Interview with anonymous, a resident of working-class Kouba (an Algiers neighborhood), December 8, 2015.

16. Aïssa Khelladi, "Rire quand même: L'humour politique dans l'Algérie d'aujourd'hui," *Revue du monde musulman et de la Méditerranée* 77–78 (1996): 233. Tracts were collected through an exchange with a journalist who wished to remain anonymous.

17. Lounis Dahmani, *Algérie: L'humor au temps du terrorisme* (Paris: Bethy, 1998).

18. Joke told to me by anonymous, July 31, 2009.

19. For instance, I struggled to find a single humorous joke on Liamine Zéroual, president of Algeria from 1995 to 1999.

20. See Paul A. Silverstein, "An Excess of Truth: Violence, Conspiracy Theorizing, and the Algerian Civil War," *Anthropological Quarterly* 75, no. 4 (2002): 643–674.

21. I collected jokes mainly through conversations with journalists and public figures. While some of these individuals hailed from more most modest socioeconomic milieus,

they were intellectuals, and the jokes that I have compiled may therefore particularly reflect those that circulated among this subsection of society. The written collections of jokes that I uncovered were likewise composed by intellectuals. They did identify this humor, though, as Algerian or typical of humor that existed during the 1990s in Algeria. See, for example, Dahmani, *Algérie*.

22. Abderrahmane Moussaoui, *De la violence en Algérie* (Paris: Actes Sud, 2006), 358–388. Generally, scholars in Algeria and outside of the country have written about jokes from the Black Decade in French or English rather than Arabic. This may be due to the sensitive content of the jokes, which would preclude Algerian academics and journalists from publishing works about them openly in the country.

23. Marwane Ben Yahmed, "Présidentielle algérienne: Bouteflika devant un théâtre d'ombres," *Jeune Afrique*, March 19, 2014, http://www.jeuneafrique.com/Article/JA2774p022.xmlo/.

24. See, for instance, Ziad Fahmy, *Ordinary Egyptians: Creating the Nation through Popular Culture* (Palo Alto: Stanford University Press, 2011).

25. See, for instance, Pi-Sunyer, "Political Humor"; Fahmy, *Ordinary Egyptians*. Mostafa Abedinifard has asserted that jokes can play an important role in shaping societies with concrete outcomes. Mostafa Abedinifard, "Structural Functions of the Targeted Joke: Iranian Modernity and the Qazvini Man as Predatory Homosexual," *Humor* 29, no. 3 (2016): 337–357; Mostafa Abedinifard, "Reply to Davies," *Humor* 30, no. 2 (2017): 247–253. When I refer here to "subaltern resistance," I am thinking of James C. Scott's concept of "weapons of the weak." This theory posits that disenfranchised groups can sometimes mount opposition to states and those in power through cultural and indirect means rather than outright rebellion. James C. Scott, *Weapons of the Weak: Everyday Forms of Peasant Resistance* (New Haven, CT: Yale University Press, 1985). The question of humor's influence on the outcome of the January 2011 revolution became a subject of debate in Mohamed M. Helmy and Sabine Frerichs, "Stripping the Boss: The Powerful Role of Humor in the Egyptian Revolution 2011," *Integrative Psychological and Behavioral Science* 47, no. 4 (2013): 450–481; L. Laineste, "Can Stripping the Boss Be More Than a Joke?," *Integrative Psychological and Behavioral Science* 47 (2013): 482–491. Helmy and Frerichs argue that humor helped dispel fear amid the 2011 Egyptian Revolution, ultimately contributing to its success.

26. See, for example, Emil Draitser, "Soviet Underground Jokes as a Means of Entertainment," *Journal of Popular Culture* 23 (1989): 118; Alexander Rose, "When Politics Is a Laughing Matter," *Policy Review* 110 (2001–2002): 59–72; Hans Speier, "Wit and Politics: An Essay on Laughter and Power," *American Journal of Sociology* 103, no. 5 (1998): 1395. Once again, Davies identified these works as opposing the theory of humor as resistance. Christie Davies, "Humor and Protest: Jokes under Communism," *International Review of Social History* 52 (2007): 300n40.

27. Davies, "Humor and Protest," 300.

28. Helmy and Frerichs, "Stripping the Boss"; Laineste, "Can Stripping the Boss."

29. See, for instance, Joseph Boskin, "American Political Humor: Touchables and Taboos," *International Political Science Review* 11, no. 4 (1990): 474.

30. Several academics have questioned the power of jokes and political humor for resistance, and not merely by pointing out how engaging in joke-telling could detract from more open forms of revolt (see n. 11). Chad Bryant, "The Language of Resistance? Czech Jokes and Joke-Telling under Nazi Occupation, 1943–1945," *Journal of Contemporary History* 41, no. 1 (2006): 133–151, especially 133–139; David M. Bozzini, "The Catch-22 of Resistance: Jokes and

the Political Imagination of Eritrean Conscripts," *Africa Today* 60, no. 2 (2013): 38–64. Much historical work, in particular, has lauded political humor as a means of resistance, and most historians' recent writings on the role of political humor approach political mockery this way. See, for example, Kathleen Stokker, *Folklore Fights the Nazis: Humor in Occupied Norway, 1940–1945* (Madison: University of Wisconsin Press, 1997); Steve Lipman, *Laughter in Hell: The Use of Humor during the Holocaust* (Northvale, NJ: J. Aronson, 1991). Cartoonist Mahfoud Aïder claims that government officials occasionally used the Algerian satirical bimonthly paper El Manchar (for which Aïder drew) in this way during the early 1990s. Interview with Mahfoud Aïder, June 18, 2013.

31. Achille Mbembe, "La 'chose' et ses doubles dans la caricature camerounaise," *Cahiers d'études africaines* 36, no. 141/142 (1996): 143–170, citing W. J. T. Mitchell, ed., *The Language of Images* (Chicago, University of Chicago Press, 1980).

32. It should be noted that for this argument Bozzini relies on theories by Michel Foucault, Timothy Mitchell, and François Bayart. Bozzini, "Catch-22 of Resistance," 42–43, citing Timothy Mitchell, "The Limits of the State: Beyond Statist Approaches and Their Critics," *American Political Science Review* 85, no. 1 (1991): 77–96; Michel Foucault, *Discipline and Punish: The Birth of the Prison*, trans. Alan Sheridan (New York: Vintage Books, 1979); Jean-François Bayart, *The Illusion of Cultural Identity*, 2nd ed., trans. Steven Rendall, Janet Roitman, Cynthia Schoch, and Jonathan Derrick (Chicago: Chicago University Press, 2005).

33. Lisa Wedeen, "Ideology and Humor in Dark Times: Notes from Syria," *Critical Inquiry* 39, no. 4 (2013): 841–873.

34. From George Orwell, "Funny but Not Vulgar," in George Orwell, *Funny, but Not Vulgar and Other Selected Essays and Journalism* (London: Folio Society, 1968).

35. Silverstein, "Excess of Truth," 643–674.

36. Silverstein, "Excess of Truth," 643–674.

37. Silverstein, "Excess of Truth," 694. See also Evans and Phillips, *Algeria*, 188.

38. Gilles Kepel, *Jihad*, 2nd ed. (Paris: Gallimard, 2003), 406–407.

39. See Silverstein, "Excess of Truth."

40. Martinez, *Algerian Civil War*, 209.

41. Evans and Phillips, *Algeria*, 188.

42. This was the case with Mohamed Ali Allalou. Interview with Mohamed Ali Allalou, December 17, 2014; Mustapha Benfodil, *Dilem président: Biographie d'un émeutier* (INAS, 2008), http://www.argotheme.com/dilempres%5B1%5D.pdf, 59.

43. See Evans and Phillips, *Algeria*, 191.

44. Interview with Mohamed Mazari, June 13, 2013; interview with Sid Ahmed Semiane, July 9, 2013; interview with Omar Belhouchet, July 20, 2013.

45. The joke that I am presenting here is a composite of two versions of the same joke. Moussaoui, *De la violence*, 377. Evans and Phillips date the joke to circa 1998. Evans and Phillips, *Algeria*, 215. Here, I am translating the part of the joke from Moussaoui from French to English and have changed the formula of both versions of the joke for clarity.

46. Moussaoui, *De la violence*, 335–336; interview with anonymous, September 17, 2014.

47. See Edward McAllister, "Yesterday's Tomorrow Is Not Today: Memory and Place in an Algiers Neighbourhood" (PhD diss., Oxford University, 2015).

48. See Phil Rees and Philip Tibenham, *Algeria's Hidden War* (London: BBC Worldwide, 1994); Evans and Phillips, *Algeria*, 185–188, 201–206.

49. In his work on Holocaust humor, John Morreall notes that a Catholic priest, Josef Müller, was arrested and executed in Nazi Germany for repeating a joke. See John Morreall,

"Humor in the Holocaust: Its Critical, Cohesive, and Coping Functions," Holocaust Teacher Resource Center, November 22, 2001, http://www.holocaust-trc.org/humor-in-the-holocaust/. The documentary *Laughing with Hitler* also notes other cases in which German citizens, as well as civilians in Nazi-occupied territories, were executed for telling jokes. Rudolph Herzog, *Laughing with Hitler* ([S.l.]: Brummer und Herzog Filmproduktion / BBC, 2007). It is widely known that the Soviet secret police under Stalin arrested and severely punished individuals. See Peter Deriabin and Frank Gibney, *The Secret World* (Garden City, NY: Doubleday, 1959), appendix, for records of KGB files on joke-tellers.

50. Martinez discusses brothers of the same family falling on opposite sides of the war. Martinez, *Algerian Civil War*, 80.

51. Moussaoui, *De la violence*, 347.

52. Moussaoui, *De la violence*, 347.

53. Martinez, *Algerian Civil War*, 80.

54. For instance, interview with Sid Ahmed Semiane, July 9, 2013.

55. Interview with Séverine Labat, December 16, 2014.

56. Interview with Omar Belhouchet, July 20, 2013.

57. Interview with Omar Belhouchet, July 20, 2013.

58. Moussaoui, *De la violence*, 364–365.

59. Interview with anonymous, Algiers. I am paraphrasing this joke here because the narrator who recounted it to me preferred that I not take notes during our exchange. An anonymous narrator from the working-class neighborhood of Kouba told me a different version of this joke where the terrorist queries, "Who are you with? Us motherfuckers or those motherfuckers?" Interview with anonymous, Algiers. Moussaoui, *De la violence*, 368, offers another take on the joke that has the armed agent stick his gun in the driver's face and ask, "Who is the real man? Me or you?" to which the poor individual replies, "Neither of us. It [the gun] is the real man."

60. I discuss the place of gender and masculinity in "Algerian humor" from this period in depth in Elizabeth M. Perego, "Emasculating Humor from Algeria's 'Dark Decade,' 1991–2002," *International Journal of Middle East Studies* 52, no. 1 (2020): 67–86. See also Moussaoui, *De la violence*, 367–370.

61. Pamphlet from the Islamic Front of Armed Jihad, known as FIDA, collected from a journalist who wishes not to be named for this book (the group claimed to want to assassinate intellectuals). Communiqué 51 by GIA was also believed to be the organization claiming responsibility for major massacres of early fall 1997. Jacob Mundy, *Imaginative Geographies of Algerian Violence* (Palo Alto: Stanford University Press, 2015), 79.

62. Joke dating to "circa 1994" from Evans and Phillips (their translation), *Algeria*, 201–202. Zineb Sedira also told me that she heard this joke in France among Algerians she spoke to for a project on Algerian humor, and it has appeared elsewhere. Interview with Zineb Sedira, March 29, 2015; Moussaoui, *De la violence*, 366. Moussaoui's version is a French one that may have used the original language (if the joke was initially told in French).

63. Jacob Mundy recognizes the sites as ones of masculine control. See Jacob Mundy, "Visualising National Reconciliation after the Algerian Civil War: Violence, Gender and 'Virtual Justice' in Film," in *Spectacles of Blood: A Study of Masculinity and Violence in Postcolonial Films*, ed. Swaralipi Nandi and Esha Chatterjee (Chicago: University of Chicago Press, 2012), 41.

64. Joke included in Bachir Dahak, *Les Algériens: Le rire et la politique de 1962 à nos jours* (Algiers: Frantz Fanon, 2018), 156–157.

65. Moussaoui, *De la violence*, 387.

66. Hugh Roberts, *The Battlefield: Algeria, 1988–2002, Studies in a Broken Polity* (London: Verso, 2003), 257–259.
67. Dahmani, *Algérie*, 36. In the album, Dahmani designates this joke as an "authentic" one that Algerians shared during the Black Decade.
68. See chap. 4.
69. See Morreall, "Humour in the Holocaust."
70. Lounis Dahmani, *Blagues: Made in Algéria*. Paris: Dahmani, 2007.
71. Belcourt is a working-class neighborhood in Algiers.
72. Joke told to me by Adlène Meddi, a journalist who grew up in the working-class Algiers neighborhood of El-Harrach. Interview with Adlène Meddi, September 21, 2014. I am paraphrasing another version of the joke that was recounted to me by a previous resident of the working-class Algiers neighborhood of Belouizdad. Interview with anonymous, September 15, 2014.
73. Interview with anonymous, September 26, 2014. A version of this joke was also included in Moussaoui, *De la violence*, 367. I am equally paraphrasing this take on the joke.
74. The FIS, in whose name the AIS fought, denounced alcohol. See chap. 2.
75. This was one of the most widely known jokes from the 1990s and was recounted to me by a number of narrators. Zineb Sedira also heard this joke as she collected "terrorism"-related jokes from the 1990s for a project. Interview with Zineb Sedira, March 29, 2015. Cartoonist Dilem further published a caricature that visualized the joke and the exchange between the elderly woman and the arms-bearing men. Dilem, *Le Matin*, March 7, 1996.
76. Joke told to me by journalist Sid Ahmed Semiane, who explained the joke's adaptation in the later period. Once again, it was originally a Polish joke. Interview with Sid Ahmed Semaine, October 12, 2014.
77. Moussaoui, *De la violence*, 363–365.
78. Moussaoui, *De la violence*, 363–365.
79. Presumably because *dīn* in Arabic means "religion" and individuals who bear a name with that term are more religious. Many popular first names in Algeria end in *dīn*; for instance, Nourredine translates as "light of religion."
80. Dahmani illustrated a take on this joke in *Blagues*. The joke is also available on the website http://www.yabiladi.com/forum/blagues-arabes-droles-7-3553203.html as well as in Dahak, *Les Algériens*, 158.
81. These words were attributed to Djaout by 1997. See Julija Sukys, *Silence Is Death: The Life and Work of Tahar Djaout* (Lincoln: University of Nebraska Press, 2007), 119.
82. Tahar Djaout, *Le dernier été de la raison* (Paris: Editions du Seuil, 1999).
83. This was the case for Algerian cartoonists during the 1990s. See chap. 4.
84. See also Perego, "Emasculating Humor."
85. See chap. 1. Also, in terms of jokes targeting philandering men or individuals who drink, while it is difficult to find collections of jokes that dealt more with social than political issues, earlier jokes speculated on politicians' alcohol consumption and sex lives, among other topics. See, for instance, Dahak, *Les Algériens*.
86. Interview with Adlène Meddi, September 21, 2014.
87. Chawki Amari revealed this joke to me in an interview. Interview with Chawki Amari, July 3, 2013.
88. See "Algérie: Condamnations collectives pour homosexualité," Human Rights Watch, October 15, 2020, https://www.hrw.org/fr/news/2020/10/15/algerie-condamnations-collectives-pour-homosexualite#.

89. Moussaoui came to the same conclusion in his work on Algerian humor during this period. Moussaoui, *De la violence*, 369–370.

90. Bryant, "Language of Resistance," 151.

91. Interview with Saad, March 5, 2015.

92. This joke is taken from a famous editorial cartoon by Ali Dilem. "Dilem du jour," *Le Matin*, March 2, 1994, 24. Some of Dilem's cartoons appear to have been based on popular jokes. See chap. 4.

93. Evans and Phillips, *Algeria*, 187.

94. Interview with anonymous, Algiers; interview with Omar Belhouchet, July 20, 2013.

95. Interview with Ameziane Ferhani, March 15, 2015. Writer Y.B. expressed that he turned to humor in the 1990s to distance himself from the horrors taking place across his country. See Thierry Oberlé, "Like He Said: A Vitriolic Chronicle of Algeria," *Grand Street* 65 (Summer 1998): 51.

FOUR

DRAWING LINES THROUGH THE AMBIGUITY OF TERROR, 1992 TO 1997

LIKE JOKE-TELLERS, ALGERIA'S CARTOON ARTISTS working for the country's press industry continued their work through the beginning of the Black Decade violence. Their work was constrained, however, by conditions imposed by the war. Indeed, the life of a newspaper at the height of Algeria's conflict of the 1990s was a complicated if ephemeral one. The paths of circulation that a single copy of any day's publication could follow were highly restricted and dependent on local politics against the background of the raging armed struggle. Papers were printed in the morning; delivered to *tabacs* (small convenience stores, tobacco shops) in towns, villages, and cities across the country; and then purchased individually by patrons throughout the day for a cost of seven to ten dinars, affordable for even minimum-wage earners.[1] Yet readership was not strictly limited to direct purchasers of a paper. Patrons of coffee shops could leave a paper that they had bought for the next sipper of sugary coffee to peruse at their leisure. Purveyors of the news could share copies of publications they bought with friends or family at work, home, or school or talk about what they had read.

Furthermore, the media that the state either directly controlled or condoned, including the private press, were not the only conveyors of information about current events available to Algerians. Clandestine publications bearing news and messages from insurgent organizations were common in some areas but were passed along only in secret in regions under tighter government control. In zones with heavier rebel influence, kiosk owners were unable to sell staples of the private and government-controlled press since, according to documents that may have hailed from their circles, insurgent groups viewed licit papers' content as anathema to their existence.[2]

News, and the presentation of it, became highly charged in the atmosphere of uncertainty and division endemic during the Black Decade. Journalists and editorial boards working for outlets, especially printed newspapers and magazines, were drawn into fierce debates dividing the population over the legitimacy of rebel actions against the state, whether the government should negotiate with the armed groups, with which groups the dialogue could be held, what the political future of the FIS and political Islamism more generally could be, and what power should look like in the country. The years 1992 to 1997 witnessed the emergence of several insurgent organizations fighting the state and each other for supremacy. Two major groups formed during this period: the Islamic Salvation Army (AIS), linked to members of the FIS, and the Armed Islamic Group (GIA). The AIS sought to force the government to the negotiating table through attacks limited to state apparatuses and actors, at least according to the organization's official rhetoric. In contrast, the GIA earned a reputation for carrying out atrocities against civilians and wanted to completely overthrow the regime.[3]

Editorial boards of publications tolerated by the state sometimes splashed photos of atrocities reportedly committed by rebels across front pages. On other days, licit newspapers such as *El Watan*, *Le Matin*, and *El Khabar* displayed the eviscerated remains of insurgents. Occasionally, victims' bodies could also be showcased, a marker of the cruelty produced, according to the editorial line of the vast majority of papers, by "terrorists" and "barbarians."[4] The publication of these harrowing images of carnage may have resulted from the military supplying such images directly to the outlets in which they appeared.[5] In most major papers, usually opposite photographs of the conflict's victims on the last page of the newspaper but occasionally on the front alongside the gruesome visuals, sat the creative fruit of the country's dwindling but persistent cartooning community.

Readers sitting in a café, at a bus stop or train station, or at home consumed the news. However, the proliferation of conspiracy theories during the Black Decade and the longer-standing oral means of sharing and commenting on information that existed in Algeria, as elsewhere, meant that print papers constituted only part of the larger tapestry of the country's news production.[6] Newspaper editors were keenly aware of the importance of orally circulated information. Many papers established sections where unsubstantiated information could be presented as rumors. The titles of these sections referenced oral practices of circulating news (one example was *El Watan's* "On vous le dit" / "We are the ones telling you," a reassuring phrase used to shore up faith in the listener that the information was accurate).[7] This signaling to oral cultures shows that journalists could benefit from the fervent oral rumor-swapping happening around the country and move into the market. State-owned television channels also presented the news, but Algerians were able to consume foreign coverage of events in the country as well via satellite dishes.[8] Access to outside information was important, as domestic news was tightly controlled and could be misleading. In anthropologist Abderrahmane Moussaoui's view, the Algerian media, including the private press, could fuel purposeful misinformation or rumor.[9] Cartoons entered into this socially constructed landscape of exchanges surrounding current events at a time of shifting circumstances that made information more tightly controlled but also more critical than ever.

As with other sections of periodicals, the impact of caricatures was not restricted to direct buyers or readers of the papers in which they were printed. Malik Aït Aoudia, a resident of a downtown Algiers neighborhood, noted the rich oral life of Dilem's *Le Matin* and *Liberté* editorial sketches in particular. He insisted that individuals often queried to one another, "Have you seen today's Dilem?"[10] Such conversations could prompt verbal relaying of a cartoon's contents. The scandals that the artist's work was able to incite by the end of the 1990s point to his large following and capacity for stoking admiration or, conversely, rage.[11] Dilem had garnered the moniker "the voice of youth" in his country. The nickname was a nod to the caricaturist's positioning as a member of the generation born in the years following independence who came of age amid the country's growing political, economic, and security crisis of the late 1980s and 1990s.[12] Dilem seemed to have supplanted earlier artists drawing the Algerian nation by the middle of the Black Decade, particularly as the production of *bandes dessinées* slowed and many illustrators from the industry's earlier generation fled abroad.[13]

Perhaps the strongest indication of the impact of cartoonists in the country during the height of Black Decade violence can be found in the vituperative language that insurgent organizations appear to have lobbed at this voice of youth and his ilk. In an interview with a French news program alongside Saïd Mekbel, Dilem claimed that his name occupied one of the highest places on a list of intellectuals to be killed. In a later interview, the artist revealed that a neighbor had warned him at one point that he would be the next public figure to be assassinated.[14]

Through an exchange with an Algerian journalist, I obtained a supposed death list from the AIS. Bitterly and laughingly called "hit parades" by the threatened intellectuals themselves, this document and others like it gave the names of journalists whose "poisons" needed to be "cleansed from the country" for being part of a "treacherous and apostate journalism engaged in a violent struggle against Muslims."[15] Whether a real order of the AIS (possibility A) or a piece of propaganda composed by a rival armed group, the state, or some other element (possibility B), this document demonstrates the important position that humorists, of all media workers, held as either critics of the armed organizations (possibility A) or pundits who someone wanted to intimidate through chicanery (possibility B). Three individuals—Brahim Guerroui, Mohamed Dorbane, and Saïd Mekbel—who had produced cartoons at one point in their careers or were working primarily as cartoonists were killed during the Black Decade. These threats and assassinations suggest that cartooning was taken by the armed groups as a serious challenge to their cause.[16]

Algerian cartoons from the height of so-called Algerian violence (1992–1997) offer a view into how at least some communities perceived the violence and how caricaturists and editors themselves wanted to present events to readers. While not meant to always be taken seriously or at face value, caricatures worked along with the rest of a newspaper and in tandem with other cultural outlets to influence or spread perspectives on what was happening in Algeria at a moment in which the identities of actors and agents became blurred and the only certainty was at least some Algerian civilians' suffering. These cartoon renderings of war take on greater significance given how theories about the notoriously opaque conflict and its actors informed individuals' decisions.[17]

Jokes played with the ambiguities of violence during the 1990s. They stressed how previously accepted and legible meanings ("soldier," "state," "Algerian," "rebel," etc.) had been disconnected from symbols, with masks potentially covering the faces of assailants or agents supposedly charged with protecting the national community.[18] Someone manning a checkpoint could prove to be an agent either of the state or of the armed groups, and both were capable of inflicting harm on civilians.[19] In other words, jokes could encapsulate the *"qui tue qui"* ("who is killing whom") theory surrounding the war. This idea, first proposed in the early 1990s, described Algeria's violence in that decade as so mired in mystery that no one was sure who was carrying out which atrocity and against whom.[20] These three words, crucially presented in French, have come to represent for many the ambiguous nature of the 1990s violence. However, cartoons almost exclusively framed "Islamists/rebels," a category obscuring differences between many Islamists and the armed groups, as the drivers of civilian-directed carnage. They further painted violence as stemming from national macro- rather than micro-level intrigues despite evidence to the contrary.[21]

I argue here that Algeria's cartoonists used their unique and widely followed platforms to visualize events in a *guerre sans visage* ("war without a face") and voice a complex array of opinions—most likely their own and perhaps those of their communities—concerning Algeria's unfolding security crisis and political situation.[22] The majority of cartoonists, composing in French and Arabic with plentiful inclusions of *darja* (Algerian Arabic dialect) and some Tamazight, presented their viewpoint that the conflict stemmed from national as well as transnational intrigues. They pinpointed political Islamism, as embodied in politicians' and civilians' advocacy for a stronger place for Islam in Algerian politics, as the major force compelling the violence and insisted that violent strands of political Islam did not represent Algeria. They drew both the first and last words of the infamous theory that contemporaneously detailed Black Decade bloodshed—who was being killed and by whom—within a vacuum of visual content and verifiable information surrounding these events.[23] They also sought to draw boundaries between who was and was not Algerian and what practices were and were not Algerian in light of the violence.

Quite significantly, while no evidence connects Algeria's cartoonists to any particular government agency or can prove that they composed their work under the direct control of state actors, their perspectives on the violence often echoed official ones even at moments when cartoonists were ridiculing government policies or leaders in other ways. This is not to say, however, that caricaturists purposefully adopted government rhetoric; instead, these shared narratives of the Black Decade may have emerged organically from their viewpoints or the those of the communities in which they lived surrounding the heightening crisis. More than being mere observers of the war, cartoonists were its interpreters and targets.

These findings indicate a greater need for scholars to consider how sectors of the civilian population may have held attitudes similar to those of the government without necessarily making these sectors pro-regime. For their part, cartoonists may have conscientiously chosen to direct their "combat" toward Islamists versus state actors when responding to the continuing bloodshed.[24] The potential for humorous art to intersect with and potentially reinforce or shape views concerning violence remains an unexplored but critical question given the endemic scarcity of facts and the place of the country's increasingly curtailed cultural field as one of the only locations for debating politics at a time of stark tension. This section identifies points where it appears that humor—here in the form of cartoons—may have weighed on or reflected popular opinions as to which side of the conflict should be held responsible for it.

On the whole, Algeria's cartoonists drew portraits of the violence as stemming from political Islamism but not Islamized. Cartoonists adopted tropes that may at first glance appear to repurpose Islamophobic, Orientalist stereotypes to apply them to members of the GIA and other rebel groups along with political Islamists, whom they sometimes purposefully conflated with the armed agents. At the same time, they appear to have striven to de-Algerianize the agents of violence while depicting the bloodshed as a loss for the true national community, comprising, as they conceived it, the conflict's civilian victims, survivors, and agents of collective mourning and resistance. Moussaoui reports that media from this period, which he links to state rhetoric, advanced rumors of the armed groups as foreign to Algeria.[25] Cartoonists did push this notion of rebels as existing beyond the parameters of the nation, although they may have done so independently of government pressure. In the process, as with the tellers of jokes, these artists reworked critical notions of who belonged to the national community in light of the violence. Their drawings may also reinforce that such a reworking was underway across several communities. In particular, concepts surrounding Algerian Islam versus non-Algerian forms of Islam were deeply embedded in their messages. Their ability to keep the attention of readers, as their popularity evinces, suggests that part of the public did not necessarily disagree with these visions of affairs and of *algérianité* (Algerian national character), ones that jokes supported as well.[26]

Yet, while not breaking with the state's vision of insurgent elements committing all massacres, caricaturists underscored the government's supposed failures to protect the body politic from harm while excoriating officials' decisions to challenge the freedom of the private press. Assertions from armed organizations that they were acting in the name of a purer form of Islam or that they represented the will of Muslims also faced censure from these artists, who portrayed purportedly authentic local forms of Islam and being Muslim and anchored proper Algerian Muslimness in the pacifist civilian majority.[27]

There were upward of hundreds of thousands of cartoons published in a variety of newspapers during the Time of Terrorism in Algeria. Because of this vast volume of material, this chapter focuses on a handful of artists (Ayoub, Slim, Dilem, and *El Manchar*'s creators) who drew consistently during the 1990s and whose illustrations garnered significant followings. Most cartoonists from other papers created oeuvres with messages similar to the ones these artists produced.[28] Material supposedly from the armed groups that I was able to recover did not contain illustrations, nor did any widely followed newspapers promote Islamism. State newspapers did not provoke much discourse when it came to their cartooning sections, and cartoons from state papers did not deal with the violence as explicitly as the illustrations from private papers.[29] Given the oral life of cartoons examined here, the absence of any mention of cartoonists working for state papers in the press or in oral history narratives that I collected insinuates that they did not have much of an influence.

The chapter begins with an examination of the conditions in which Algerian cartoonists produced their art during the 1990s conflict. I then analyze cartoons that dealt directly with the violence and advanced powerful ideas surrounding it. As with jokes, cartoons took on greater significance during this period and became a space for civilians to contemplate what precisely was happening around them with important consequences. Here, cartoons may have worked to reinforce government visions of the war by depicting the bloodshed as a result of the efforts of political Islamists or armed groups. Furthermore, as with earlier types of humor in Algeria and contemporary jokes, this artwork associated Algerian-ness with pacifist civilians.

THE PRESS AND THE CONSTRICTION OF INFORMATION FLOW DURING THE HEIGHT OF TERROR

Algeria's brief experiment with even limited press freedom came to a definitive end before the cancellation of the 1991–1992 legislative elections and the accompanying rise to power of the High Committee of State in January 1992. The government, through varying efforts, censored the media throughout the 1990s, mainly in the name of protecting the army's fight against the armed insurgents. Repression began in the six months leading up to the eventually canceled legislative elections once Mouloud Hamrouche was replaced as prime minister by Sid Ahmed Ghozali in mid-1991. The state then reestablished a Ministry of Communication and started cracking down on papers for publishing material deemed to be too pro-FIS as early as that summer.[30] This pattern of the regime restricting or halting publications increased in frequency after the suspension of the second round of legislative elections in January 1992. Satirical works were not immune. In August 1992, the state halted the Arabic-language paper *al-Ṣaḥḥ Āfa* for challenging the government through such actions as publishing detainee letters from the *camps du sud* ("camps of the south," detention centers around the country where, beginning in 1991, the state placed individuals suspected of subversive, pro-FIS activities).[31] Satirical papers could tackle serious political matters and earn the ire of the *pouvoir*, "power" in French, a common name in Algeria for the state.

Regardless of this reining in of greater press liberty, it is difficult to overstate the importance of the domestic press as a conveyer of information just as news had become a highly prized and sought-after but elusive commodity. The Black Decade produced population displacements based in part on civilians' conceptions of which areas might prove to be safe. Individuals determined their personal plans for moving around the country according to available information. Government-imposed restrictions on the media reduced the number of formal news outlets that were able to maintain even the slightest margin of independence from government control. State-imposed limitations on domestic and foreign journalists alike heightened the crucial position of the domestic press, however threatened and severely hampered in its capacity for accessing, processing, interpreting, and presenting details about what was unfolding in the country.[32] The flight abroad of the country's major novelists and literary figures in the early 1990s meant that Algeria's journalists took on the role of the country's leading intellectuals.[33]

However, communities did not believe that papers, whether private or public, were neutral repositories of fact-based information. The rhetoric of armed groups treated journalists as state agents and therefore apostates dedicated to spewing government lies.[34] Rumors abounded regarding potential connections between Algerian state authorities and journalists. Generals' ownership of or connections to a handful of newspapers toward the mid-1990s sparked whispers of artists sketching satirical work at the command of military higher-ups.[35] At least one media worker suggested that some of his journalist colleagues had government "handlers" who fed them information.[36] Indeed, Mohamed Samraoui, a former leader of the Department of Intelligence and Security (Département du renseignement et de la sécurité or DRS), Algeria's military intelligence agency, asserted that the DRS had established a "Press Service" charged with "manipulating public opinion." The service reportedly placed members on editorial boards of the country's major newspapers.[37] To at least partially corroborate this claim of direct government control over domestic newspaper content, an *El Watan* archivist disclosed that officials directed newspapers to display photographs of victims' remains at certain times to discredit rebels.[38] A 1997 Human Rights Watch report related that the government had established "reading committees" to scour each daily or weekly issue and suppress security-related information that came from the state's Algerian Press Service.[39] Finally, beyond accusations of the military's direct manipulation of information through the employment of undercover agents or by orders, Samraoui accused the DRS of orchestrating some of the threats that journalists had received in the early 1990s. These threats included physical letters with menacing words, pieces of soap to ostensibly wash corpses, and funeral shrouds sent to the media workers' residences.[40]

In addition to direct state censorship, possible infiltration and intimidation, and actions such as seizing all printed editions of paper containing "incendiary" information, the government could censor media through its ownership of the country's major printing presses. Throughout the 1990s, papers struggled to keep up with the debts they owed this national enterprise. The presses could and did stop printing works even if the money owed was eventually paid.[41] Finally, the private press was not truly and entirely private. It received subsidies and advertisement funding from the government, although these financial sources did not necessarily mean that the papers were under the thumb of the state.[42]

Beyond these possible and sometimes confirmed mechanisms of state interference, papers needed to sell copies by producing work that appealed to Algerian communities. Cultivating a broad, paying readership provided publications with a source of revenue to supplement that coming from state corporations' advertisements and subsidies. Consequently, editorial committees might have faced financially driven constraints on what they could publish based on a desire to bring readers on board and get papers to fly off newsstands.

Pressure on journalists also came from colleagues. While frequently uniting to mourn slain or missing colleagues or denounce repression, journalists clashed when it came to seeing colleagues as potentially pushing a political agenda or working for the state as "mercenaries of the pen."[43] The pro-reconciliation reporter Ghania Mouffouk endured an insult from the pages of *El Watan* that called her an "Islamist in a miniskirt."[44] Youcef Zirem claimed that the arrest of Fayçal Metaoui, an *El Watan* journalist who dared to tackle such controversial topics as forced disappearances, for noncompletion of his obligatory military service was co-orchestrated through a cabal of DRS-backed *El Watan* employees. The very need, though, to curtail Metaoui's work signals some level of autonomy that journalists were able to maintain in this atmosphere of censorship and speculated retaliation and infiltration.[45]

Civilians, as well as high-ranking military leaders, were divided over the best solution to the conflict. Some advocated for negotiations with armed groups and the FIS ("conciliators"), while others preferred that the military defeat and suppress one or both groups ("eradicators"). Some private newspapers covered events in such a way as to indicate that their editorial boards were organizing newspaper content at the orders of the government, thus leaning toward the eradicator stance, or that these papers' leaders independently supported this viewpoint, which favored armed suppression of the rebel groups over dialogue.[46]

Press headlines that seem to betray a pro-eradicator position declared the armed insurgents to be "barbarians" or "terrorists" (*irhābiyyīn*) promoting barbarity (*wahashiyya*) in the country, although, according to pro-reconciliation journalist Salima Ghezali, the government enforced the use of those terms for the armed groups.[47] The cover of one edition of the antinegotiation hardline paper, *L'Hebdo libéré*, touted Algeria as the "final resting place of fundamentalism." An accompanying drawing showed the arm of a police officer firing on a band of hyenas, a direct transmogrification of insurgents and an effort to dehumanize them.[48] This front page was explicit in its message but not much more radical than other presentations of insurgents in the pages of the country's most widely read papers. Journalists could describe rebel groups as the country's new ḥarkīs or sons of "ḥarkīs, Algerian Muslims who had served in France's army during the War of Independence and were widely looked down on in Algeria.[49] To be connected to these traitors meant one was a terrible individual, supposedly suffering from repressed anger over the treason of one's father or oneself. In this view, the government represented the bastion of the earlier Algerian Revolution, and insurgents' claims were invalid because they were descendants of national traitors. Similarly, on at least one occasion, the "eradicator" press labeled the armed groups "the new settlers," referencing the European population who had occupied the country under colonialism.[50] On another occasion, a paper referred to rebels as "the [Islamist] fundamentalist *Organisation armée secrète* (Secret Armed Organization, or OAS)." Pro–French Algeria military officers and European settlers had formed the OAS in 1961 to terrorize communities and undermine Algerian independence.[51] *Alger républicain* declared the FIS a ḥizb Faransā, "the party of France," an accusation since the Boumediene regime to imply that a politician in Algeria was acting for France and therefore against Algeria.[52] This rhetoric collectively demonstrates that papers could effectively seek to denigrate rebels as either traitors or outsiders to the nation. Despite their extremity (not all papers were this antirebel or anti-Islamist), these depictions offer a pathway for comprehending the general political atmosphere in which caricaturists produced their work as well as the type of discourse appearing alongside their drawings.

Unlike their counterparts in the newsroom working on security matters, caricaturists were only occasionally accused of collusion with the government over newspaper content. Lounis Dahmani was considered one artist to have created at the orders of a government figure, here General Mohamed Betchine, whose relative ran Dahmani's paper.[53] Despite the rifts between the so-called eradicator and conciliator press, journalists and cartoonists rallied around the shared mission of promoting free speech. Cartoonists from eradicator newspapers coordinated a campaign to liberate pro-reconciliation artist Chawki Amari after his July 1996 arrest and detention for a caricature insinuating that the regime had sullied the national flag.[54]

Caricaturing and other forms of journalistic work entailed dangers beyond running afoul of state censors. One hundred and five media workers were killed or forcefully disappeared between 1993 and 1996, when the murder of media workers decreased.[55] Assassinations of journalists appeared to cut across political leanings and stances on the question of dialogue. Journalists mentioned concerns that the government had orchestrated some of the attacks on their colleagues, with rebels carrying out others.[56] These collective threats, regardless of their origin and nature, meant that caricaturists produced their art in an atmosphere of fear and repression.

While caricaturists may not have been under the hand of the government, many artists' antirebel positioning hewed closely to pro-eradicator government viewpoints. It may have also earned them greater freedom to draw as they pleased. By the early 2000s, journalists Amine Kadi, Denise Ammoun, and Benjamin Barthe believed that by advertently or inadvertently toeing the state line when it came to Black Decade violence, Algerian caricaturists had "safe passage" when it came to pushing the limits of taboos in the country. They even penned these words after the state targeted Dilem with a series of judicial proceedings resulting in heavy sentences against the artist in the early 2000s.[57] By that period, the only cartoonists still composing were precisely those caricaturists who had adopted what could be regarded as eradicator positions toward the insurgency and its members. One of the two major pro-reconciliation newspapers, *La Nation*, did not survive the conflict, being outlawed in November 1996.[58]

Questions of cartoonists' agency, then, remain complex. Mark McKinney's article on cartoonists drawing the nation during the civil conflict of the 1990s alludes to pressure—ostensibly from the government or publications' editorial boards—for cartoonists to represent the nation. These questions of caricaturists' portrayals of Algeria and "the people" prove central to how they depicted the conflict and the significance of their work during a moment of uncertain violence. While there may have been some desire from paper leaders or the military (McKinney does not delve into their methods of influence) to draw the nation, in interviews artists insisted to the contrary that their content reflected their own will and vision of things despite the abundance of pressure imposed on them.[59] However, a sizeable portion of Algeria's population agreed and continues to agree with visions of the violence that external observers or the government wove; the linking of the bloodshed to armed insurgents hailed from below as well as above. Many cartoonists may thus have supported the government or expressed ire toward the insurgents of their own volition. I was able to identify only two instances of censorship of cartoons. The first was the arrest and imprisonment of Chawki Amari for a 1996 sketch in which he suggested that the state had "soiled" the Algerian flag. The second was Dilem's February 1994 forced visit to President Liamine Zeroual's residency, Palais d'El Mouradia, for depicting the head of state as Zorro in a series of cartoons. According to Dilem's account of the event, a man at the presidency explained that the president found the comparison to Zorro offensive. The cartoonist insisted that the depiction was actually favorable and left. When a member of the state's security forces visited the office of *Le Matin* the next day to continue the conversation, editor Mekbel suggested that Dilem leave the country for France, which he did.[60] These two cases were exceptional but demonstrated officials' power to intervene in cartoon production. It is probable, then, that government authorities found most of the cartoons that appeared in papers at least palatable. Censorship could bring dire punishment, though, as seen with Amari's detention. The cartoons in question here that received opprobrium attacked the state, not rebels.

Regardless of the forces behind their content, papers from this period achieved sizable readerships. Most periodicals sold between tens of thousands and two hundred thousand copies in the early 1990s, at least if one equates the volume of papers printed to total papers bought. Satirical papers *al-Ṣaḥḥ Āfa* and *El Manchar* figured among the most popular private weekly publications in the nation. In December 1991, *al-Ṣaḥḥ Āfa* was the most highly printed and, one can assume, purchased private weekly Arabic-language paper, with 88,400 copies printed for each edition. It was a remarkable feat for a satirical paper to outsell more serious conveyors of news about events at a time of intense political uncertainty.[61] *El Manchar* contributors, along with fans and cultural observers, confirm the paper's success and popularity in the first two years of its existence. Statistics corroborate that claim; *El Manchar* sold steadily in 1991 and 1992.[62] *Le Matin* and *El Khabar*, with Dilem and Ayoub at the helm of these papers' cartooning needs, proved the most popular private Francophone and Arabophone daily papers, respectively.[63] Along with other evidence such as claims that newspaper readers often skipped to caricatures when first picking up a freshly printed edition, these numbers and initiatives attest to the well-followed status of this humorous genre during the early 1990s.

Statistics must have varied throughout the later 1990s and into the 2000s. *El Khabar*'s daily copies printed reached 400,000 by the end of the 1990s, while *El Watan*'s numbers attained a more modest 150,000.[64] Yet, regarding the potential impact of caricatures among the Algerian population, even with these higher estimates, the number of newspaper copies printed per issue suggests that readerships of both private and public press remained low. Algeria's population in the mid-1990s stood around 26 million and grew to almost 35 million by what some analysts consider the end of the Black Decade era in 2005.[65] Furthermore, illiteracy affected an estimated 43 percent of Algeria's population in 1996.[66] Yet, Algerians orally discussed newspaper content and could grasp some cartoons' gist by sight even if illiterate. The oral discourse prompted by their content could be widespread and passionate, bringing more communities under their potential influence.[67] For instance, imams widely denounced a caricature in which Dilem made a joke about pilgrims to Mecca perishing in a human stampede in 2004.[68] Scandals like this one and the supposed fears of armed groups that newspapers would influence the population into practices of apostasy indicate that print periodicals made an impact, however small the numbers sold compared to the total population.

Determining whether these cartoons shaped beliefs about Black Decade violence or other highly politicized questions from this period remains difficult. Rumors and other narratives of what was happening in Algeria wielded actual power.[69] A handful of Algerian actors themselves weighed in on the potential power of press cartoons to effect change in the middle of the Black Decade. In a later part of the war and when in court for a cartoon, Dilem, the sole Algerian cartoonist to persist in his work uninterrupted throughout the 1990s conflict, rejected claims of influencing or shaping public opinion through his work.[70] It appeared, however, that other individuals disagreed with the artist. A military figure reportedly told Ayoub that his interpretations of Black Decade occurrences featured in a larger "*guerre psychologique*" / "psychological war" for Algerians' hearts and minds. The cartoonist related that a high-ranking military officer revealed to him, "We, the Ministry of the Defense, we didn't attack terrorists like you did with your drawings."[71] At least this military figure believed that Algerian cartoonists' work could undermine the rebel groups. Ayoub also mentioned that he felt his work had an element of "psychological warfare."[72] Like Dilem, Ayoub had avid fans, mostly individuals from the working-class, Arabophone populations that he spent much of his time depicting.[73] Such efforts on his part or on the parts of other influential cartoonists could have proved critical in a war when public support was at play. Instances of censorship by the state and the assassination or targeting of cartoonists suggested that the conflict's belligerents thought caricatures held sway over the population.

Artists (Dilem, Le Hic, Mustapha Tenani, Mohamed Mazari, and Mahfoud Aïder) and editors of private papers (Aïder and Abrous Outoudert) renowned for their caricature culture have mentioned the impact of caricatures with pride.[74] The cartoonists also stated the independence of their work from outside influence, including that of their editor. Exceptions to this rule included

Mahfoud Aïder advocating for constricting the appearance of certain antiterrorist messages at riskier moments and Chawki Amari and Dilem encountering some issues with directors and editorial boards.[75] Aïder saw himself and the *El Manchar* team, along with the rest of Algeria, as caught between two camps and noted that the *El Manchar* group placed themselves on the side of the state, the lesser of two evils.[76] Dilem claims to have quit *Le Matin* over a drawing that criticized the state's detention of journalists, a recourse against restrictions that Amari claims to equally have employed, including at the *Tribune*.[77] Again and again, though, the notion that cartoonists waged combat of their own volition during this period, mostly against "Islamic fundamentalism" and terrorism, emerged through discussions with them.[78]

Cartoonists also did not produce their work in a humorous vacuum; they could derive inspiration for their drawings from orally circulating popular jokes. At least one Dilem cartoon directly referenced a contemporary popular joke and could be understood only by readers familiar with the joke.[79] In an interview with me, Le Hic stated that cartoonists' pieces could borrow from other forms of popular humor to get their puns across.[80] There were thus intertextual connections between at least some cartoons and contemporary popular jokes.

The importance of the domestic press as one of the few organs of information beyond rumor compounded with the notoriously shrouded nature of the Black Decade to increase the possibility that cartoonists' perspectives on events shaped opinions.[81] Conflicting narratives about which actors were responsible for civilian bloodshed along with their motives persisted throughout the 1990s. These discussions reached a critical stage during the larger community massacres between 1996 and 1998. This moment witnessed an increase in the war's death count and international attention surrounding the conflict. The government's severe curtailing of reporters' access to rural sites of mass death and its refusal of calls for independent investigations into the bloodshed fueled rumors and uncertainty. For instance, a set of rumors averred that the government-equipped "patriot" civilian auto-defense groups had participated in score-settling against supporters of the armed groups. In this case, the violence may have stemmed more from local intrigues than purely from the stakes of national-level politics and struggles. The proximity of military and police stations to some of these areas (i.e., Bentalha) where dozens and hundreds of civilians were killed in a single night also stoked visions of the state having a hand in the bloodshed or refusing to intervene to stop it for political reasons, perhaps because Bentalha residents had overwhelmingly supported the FIS. In late 1997, voices across the world's diplomatic and nonprofit human rights circles began to clamor for possible investigations or intervention into the seemingly collapsing security situation in the country, calls firmly rejected by the regime. Some survivors of massacres claimed that their attackers wore fake beards and therefore may have been military actors or otherwise. In contrast, groups of Algerians and foreign observers affirmed with confidence that the armed groups were the ones attacking villages, while others raised questions and spun alternative narratives.[82] Confusion reigned as caricaturists offered their perspectives on the unfolding situation.

CARICATURISTS' PORTRAYALS OF (FOREIGN) INSURGENTS/ISLAMISTS AS THE DRIVERS OF VIOLENCE

Caricatures captured a general sense of desperation as Black Decade violence grew, to the point where a 1997 Dilem cartoon depicted a citizen unable to tell whether a paper covering atrocities was from that day or the one before.[83] Throughout the conflict, caricaturists waded into debates and engaged with theories over the nature of violence, who was responsible for the unfolding havoc, and the most appropriate possible resolutions to it. They did so through sketches depicting scenes or supposed agents of violence and import of the bloodletting for local communities as well as the invented national community.[84] All in all, Algeria's leading newspaper illustrators pinpointed Islamists, a category that they purposefully construed in broad terms, as the party responsible for the war and much of its violence. In the process, they may have contributed to a phenomenon similar to but not the same as what Jacob Mundy has called the "Islamization" of "Algerian violence." International organizations framed the war within broader conversations of Islam and violence. This concept further exonerated the government of any possible responsibility for the bloodshed and imposed metanarratives of the violence that had little bearing on reality.[85] Yet, many Algerian cartoonists linked the violence to political Islamism while separating Muslims and Algerian Muslimness from parties and advocates for a greater place for Islam in politics. In the worlds that they carefully scaffolded through daily or weekly work, cartoonists mainly obscured the potential hand of any specific agent beyond vague Islamists, the group they were admittedly freer to criticize, in violence against civilians.

Cartoonists' general depictions of Islamists and armed groups are key to deciphering the artists' work from this period. Were their demands legitimate, or were their partisans merely destroying the country in the name of Islam and Algeria? What was their relationship with the FIS? Who exactly joined organizations such as the MIA, GIA, and AIS, according to the artists? In general, cartoonists drew the armed militant rebels with characteristics typical of "Orientals" in Orientalist literature, art, and scholarship. Cartoonists' armed group or Islamist figures were backward, ignorant, violent, sexualized, and dirty.[86] They also come off as figures ripe for ridicule who did not possess a sense of humor, potentially making their skewering through laughter-inducing caricatures all the more stinging. Concerning Islamist/rebel activities, more often than not caricaturists depicted members of the armed groups inflicting harm on civilians. This is not to say, though, that these artists are Orientalists or Islamophobic. Instead, cartoonists distinguished between what they believed to be a foreign, radical Islam and indigenous forms of Islam.

Furthermore, most of the country's caricaturists drew pacifist Islamist partisans or members of the FIS, a broad movement, as identical in appearance and behavior to the armed insurgents. For example, consistently throughout the 1990s, Dilem ascribed terror, bloodshed, and other symbols of evil such as circling bats to anyone who supported Islamist camps.[87] Slim and Dilem both played with the popular FIS slogan "For her [the party] we live and for her we will die" to draw a line between the earlier FIS party and armed rebels.[88] Another mid-1990s Dilem cartoon envisioned the sundry ministries that would exist under an Islamist government. These included "Ministries of Mines and Sabotage, of the Burning of Schools, of Rapes, of Hold-Ups, of Assassinations of Foreigners."[89] Dilem associated Islamism with horrific acts. Slim referred in cartoons to the insurgents as the "bearded ones"/"*barbus*," a term that reduced legitimate distinctions between men who sported facial hair out of pious Islamic practice and rebels seeking to upend the state.[90] Cartoonists could occasionally break with this pattern and acknowledge that moderate Islamists comprised a category distinct from rebels.[91] Nonetheless, several of their works blurred the lines between more moderate proponents of political Islam and the very small minority (John Ruedy estimates no more than twenty-five thousand at their height) of millions of FIS voters and supporters who took up arms against the state.[92] Any differences between members of the various armed organizations (AIS, GIA, MIA, etc.) were also generally ignored, as in government discourse.[93]

Finally, unlike civilians or state agents, cartoonists caricatured all members of the armed groups as identical with no variation in appearance or action. By nature of their work, caricaturists can create characters or symbols to stand in for broader populations, and most Algerian cartoonists employed this liberty with panache in the 1990s when drawing rebels/Islamists. Algeria's lead artists gendered Islamists as male, with little to no exception, based on a survey of thousands of cartoons dating from 1992 to 2005. Beards and long, loose garments called *gandouras/kandūras* featured prominently among the physical traits of the armed groups as illustrated by Algeria's lead caricaturists. To mark these figures as thoroughly bloodthirsty and the major agents pushing committing violent acts, rebels/Islamists were sketched bearing bloodied knives and smoking guns, with flies floating around them. All of these symbols pointed to grisly undertakings.[94] To possibly dehumanize armed insurgents, after the mid-1990s Ayoub gave them cloven hooves, while Slim shrouded the eyes of his bewhiskered rebels/Islamists.[95]

Figure 4.1 illustrates this pattern of caricatures binding all varieties of political Islamists together. The work by Dilem poses as the popular newspaper game "identify the differences" between two almost interchangeable drawings. The cartoon is labeled "the game of seven errors" and challenges readers to identify the subtle distinctions between the two figures in the picture. To the right and the left stand two of Dilem's irate-looking Islamist characters. They seem to glare at the reader. Both bear an identical appearance and pack an arsenal of weapons ranging from grenades and guns to knives and bayonets. The only dissimilitude between the two figures is that the words *hardcore Islamist* are written above the one to the left, while those over the character on the right read *moderate Islamist*. Through this image, Dilem expresses a clear conviction that all Islamists, even moderate ones, are able and ready to perform violence.[96] The cartoon likewise exemplifies the artist's pattern of showing Islamists as all alike; the two men here are veritable carbon copies of one another, a point that the punchline of the cartoon rests on: they are short, violent, dirty, and irate given the tenseness of their faces. Detritus floats around the identical men as it often does in Dilem's portraits of rebels/Islamists, a possible sign of their supposed dirtiness. The men further sport attire that the cartoonist associates with the so-called Afghans, Algerians who had fought for the Mujahidin in Afghanistan in the 1980s against the Soviet invasion. The GIA wore this garb but not the then-newly-formed AIS and certainly not members of legal moderate Islamist parties such as Hamas (later Movement of Society for Peace).[97] The editorial team of *Le Matin* decided to include this image not once but twice in the newspaper in August 1994, once without the heading.[98]

Even Chawki Amari, one of the few Algerian cartoonists to draw for a firmly pro-reconciliation/dialogue paper, *La Tribune*, placed a knife in the hand of a person he labeled a FIS militant. The image, printed at the time of the 1995 Sant'Egidio peace talks between the FIS and some opposition parties, depicted the FIS figure saying that he had gone to Rome with the purpose of "finding foreigners." This discourse ties attacks on foreign nationals in Algeria, a regular feature of the 1990s violence, to the FIS, rather than separating this broader

Figure 4.1. "The Game of Seven Errors." "Hardcore Islamist." "Moderate Islamist." Dilem, "Dilem du jour," *Le Matin*, August 15, 1994, 24.

movement from the actions of the GIA, the armed group that supposedly attacked foreigners.[99] Given the pro-dialogue inclination of his paper, though, the cartoon may have slyly criticized eradicator stereotypes about the conference participants. Either way, the work attests to the existence of such ideas and could have been consumed by readers at face value.[100]

Ayoub did not associate violence or the tactics of the armed rebels with pacifist Islamists. The artist conscientiously refrained from employing the same essentializing tropes as his Francophone colleagues did in their art on rebels/Islamists. In an interview with Mustapha Benfodil, Ayoub explained,

> Some of my readers, when I castigate the "bearded ones," conflate [these representations] with religion and say that I am against Islam. Therefore, I arrived at a point where I exercised self-censorship on my drawings.
>
> *Certains de mes lecteurs, quand je fustige les barbus, font l'amalgame avec la religion et disent que je suis contre l'Islam. Donc, j'en suis venu à exercer une autocensure sur mes dessins.*[101]

Ayoub's decision not to criticize Islamists or conflate them with insurgents stemmed from readers' reception of his drawings rather than his own conviction. Still, in the same series of exchanges with Benfodil, the illustrator claimed that his message to the FIS had been, "My Islam is not your Islam."[102]

What is more, if cartoonists drew the Algerian nation, armed groups and Islamists were not fully part of it. Many caricaturists depicted the armed rebels as foreigners or working under the auspices of foreign elements. Like the later Dilem cartoon in figure 4.1, earlier 1990s caricatures from *El Manchar* sketched Islamists wearing garb generally associated with Iran or Afghanistan.[103] While Algerian fighters had participated in the Mujahidin's resistance against Soviet forces, references to the Shia-majority country more likely echoed some communities' concerns that the rise of the FIS would result in a post-1979-Iran-type theocracy rather than better-substantiated ties between Iran and Algerian Islamists.[104] Then, in early 1992, cartoonists for *El Manchar* advanced dubious government rhetoric that Iran had supported and was supporting the FIS. Their relaying of this rumor came at a critical moment in the state's crackdown on Islamists when such a trumped-up allegation would have harmed FIS claims to represent the popular will, which they did per early legislative election results.[105] Several cartoons displayed Algerian Islamists as puppets of Iran. One illustration even showed a mullah with an Islamist puppet stabbing a woman with symbols of the Algerian flag on her clothing.[106]

While the government ultimately shut down the paper for its criticism of the state, *al-Ṣaḥḥ Āfa* cartoonists had painted the party and "bearded ones" as many of their Francophone counterparts had. During the democratic transition, the newspaper depicted Islamists toting lit bombs.[107] Artists for the satirical biweekly sustained this pattern after the military intervened in the 1991/1992 legislative elections. Figure 4.2 features a man with a black turban and beard, presumably an Iranian mullah or an Afghan Mujahid, eyes full of rage. He is located to the right of the picture, indicating that he hails from the "East." The man's beard emerges like a snake from his chin and wraps itself around Algeria, preparing to squeeze the country or pull it into his shadowy whiskers. Algeria seems ready, though, to stand up to its aggressor coming from the East. An arm juts out from Algeria bearing a large gun with a bayonet that the country uses to hack away at the beard. The arm's sleeve sports a star, which appears on Algerian military and police insignias. Most likely, the image was intended to attest to the capacity of Algeria's forces of order, represented by the arm, to respond to Islamist insurgents.[108] The cutting of the beard plays on a register popular among cartoonists: facial hair featured centrally in many caricatures that made Islamists or the armed insurgents out to be violent or stupid.[109] This

Figure 4.2. Algeria is depicted here as a police officer heroically fending off an attack from a bearded man coming from the "East."

drawing further conjures up visions of an "East" meddling in internal Algerian affairs, a popular trope from at least Algeria's brief period of democratic transition through the present, a rhetorical tool for separating imported forms of Islam from local, authentic ones.[110] Most critically, Algeria is embodied as a military or police officer.

Dilem similarly published a cartoon about foreign fighters in response to the question of the Black Decade's internationalization that United Nations secretary-general Kofi Annan had raised amid the autumn 1997 massacres.[111] Internationalizing measures would have entailed international investigation and intervention into the ongoing bloodshed in Algeria. The image displays a general discussing his disapproval of the conflict's "internationalism" under the title, "Afghans, Tunisians, Moroccans, Libyans among the Terrorists." Jumping on information published early in the week in his paper about how foreigners had joined the rebel ranks, Dilem distanced the fighters from the Algerian population while refuting the idea that the war necessitated foreign intervention. Internationalization, in Dilem's conception of it, extended only to the armed groups, because the idea of international actors beyond Afghans taking control of the conflict was unthinkable.[112]

Cartoonists who obscured the lines between pacifist Islamists and armed militants also questioned Islamist/rebel religiosity. In doing so, artists subverted the central logic supposedly undergirding the insurgents' revolt: that they would usher in a more Islamic future for Algerians. A slew of caricatures produced by Ayoub later on in the 1990s pointed to greed rather than religious conviction as the driving factor behind rebel attacks on civilians.[113] In an especially pointed cartoon from March 1994, Dilem's armed Islamist insurgents raise their hands in celebration. One of them shouts, "Once we are in power, we will all have cards of former Muslims."[114] This cartoon contains a stratified set of messages surrounding the then-present moment within Algeria as well as its past. Dilem is most likely drawing parallels between these armed insurgents and the so-called fake *moudjahidines*.[115] The issue with the "former *mujāhidīn*" card, though, is that many Algerian communities believed that the postindependence state had corruptly offered veterans' benefits to fake War of Independence fighters, including tax reductions and lucrative job opportunities, among other advantages.[116] The cartoonist insinuates that the rebels will quickly shed their religious identity upon coming to power, a sign of the faultiness and opportunism of their proclaimed connection to faith. With this multilayered criticism of the armed groups and drawing on symbols of Algeria's past, Dilem subverted their discursive claims to stand for a truer form of Islam. He decried them as impostors.

In these ways, some cartoonists emphasized the transnational connections that existed between Algerian Islamists/rebels and outsider groups while questioning their belonging to Algeria or real Muslimness. At the same time, these artists also tailored authentic national civilian counterpoints to supposedly foreign rebels. These counterpoints, embodying the Algerian nation, were made up of ordinary citizens who never supported or mingled with the armed groups. With these recurring characters, cartoonists rhetorically separated the Algerian people from rebels.

Indeed, Algeria's major caricaturists subtly depicted the nation as Muslim by drawing these citizen characters and the spaces that they inhabited with Islamic markers. In the case of Dilem, he chose to portray the Algerian nation as his Madame Algeria figure, complete with a type of Islamic veiling particular to North Africa (the haik or *ḥāyak*) and especially associated with the capital, Algiers. The garment consisted of a long white cloth draped over the head and body, sometimes accompanied by a white facial covering. By 1997 and 1998, Ayoub employed similar-looking members of a family throughout his cartoons to perhaps represent the Algerian civilian population and even developed his own ostensibly female embodiment of the nation out of this mother figure, who appeared right when the massacres of the 1990s were reaching their crescendo. She also wore a veil, signaling that she was most likely Muslim.[117] The arrival of Ramadan each year prompted cartoonists to pen sketches commenting on food associated with the rich fast-breaking meal (*ifṭār*), the fast itself, and other religious practices.[118] Mosques also featured in the backgrounds of some urban or rural scenes.[119] For instance, Dilem showcased mosques at times in his work.[120] Beyond recognizing Islam, cartoonists also never questioned its general place in Algerian politics, such as Islam being the official religion of the state per the constitutions of 1989 and 1996.[121] In terms of exploring Algerian-ness and its links to Islam, caricaturists could also acknowledge that civilians broke with behaviors considered ideal for pious Muslims—namely, alcohol consumption. But cartoons that mentioned drinking did not exclude individuals partaking in the practice as non-Algerians or non-Muslims. They were not vilified, for instance, or rendered foreign actors or given attributes that would mark them as such but appeared as part of a wider array of Algerian characters.[122]

The choice to depict Algerians as Muslim and Islam as having a prominent place in everyday life is not surprising. After all, the majority of the Algerian population identifies with Islam or can claim descent from communities categorized as Muslim during the colonial period. Yet, in light of cartoons' broader content at this time, by showing the general population as Muslim and embracing more Algerian forms of Islam (*ḥāyak*), most cartoonists appeared to want to describe Islamic fundamentalism as hailing from foreign contexts and thus distinct from the faith of Algerian populations. These assertions undermined rhetoric from some of the armed groups that stated they wanted to implement an Algerian nationalist Islamist regime through their armed struggle against the state. All in all, cartoonists portrayed Islamists as all alike and the same as the armed groups, whose Muslimness was connected to foreign contexts and who were thus distinctive from the Algerian people, who embraced pacifist and sometimes hypocritical ways (drinking), in the eyes of some, of being Muslim.

CARTOONISTS' ENGAGEMENT WITH THEORIES SURROUNDING THE BLOODSHED

Cartoonists overwhelmingly used their work to either support or rebut widespread theories about which machinations and actors were at play as violence raged in many parts of Algeria by the mid-1990s. The killings of 1996 to 1998 included higher numbers of victims and prompted more widespread international coverage and outcry and, concurrently, satirical commentary from the country's leading editorial cartoonists about what exactly was underway in Algeria. As questions of the conflict's nature and possible internationalization became more prominent and fear among the population worsened, cartoons may have reached the apex of their influence over Black Decade narratives.

Algeria's most active and well-followed cartoonists generally dismissed the qui-tue-qui postulation as naive and misguided, another way that their drawings directly or indirectly supported the government's allegations that the armed groups were the major force behind mass violence. Defected secret service agent Samraoui claimed that the government developed the qui-tue-qui question as a means of painting foreign actors as wrongfully critical of the state and woefully ignorant of the conflict's parameters. That way, by portraying foreign critics as out of touch with what was happening in the country and as forwarding unfounded claims, the Algerian government could present its own voice as more trustworthy and in turn disseminate distrust of these foreign sources. While the state refuted the qui-tue-qui discourse as Samraoui contends, local and foreign observers had asked questions about government agents' hands in possible killings since the early 1990s.[123] Either way, on the whole, caricaturists' rhetoric surrounding qui tue qui matched the government's.

Concerning the country's most well-followed Arabophone caricaturist, throughout 1997, Ayoub moved from assigning violence to unknown or shadowy figures to laying the blame for bloodshed on the GIA and other individuals he drew as his armed rebel characters. In figure 4.3, Ayoub ridicules the qui-tue-qui discourse. The artist further identifies the theory as coming from France, a way of swiftly dismissing it and placing its origins and popularity beyond the national community. In the image, a heftier man toward the front appears to represent the group's chief. All three men sport beards and *gandouras/kandūras* and have bloodied blades in their hands. To possibly add to the filth often allotted to Islamist/armed groups by cartoonists, a dog is peeing on one of the armed men's legs. The man most likely to be their leader, given his different dress and appearance (the two men to the left have simpler attire and are not as corpulent), states, "France says that it doesn't know who is killing ... I hope [*j'espère* in French, code-switching, perhaps on purpose, from Algerian *darja*] this doesn't discourage their [his militants'] determination." The presumable *this* may be the killing alluded to in the picture's heading, "21 slaughtered is the toll from Wednesday's massacre." The tree behind the man has "GIA" etched on it and has a burrow near the bottom of the trunk labeled "Room of Operations," in line with Ayoub's habit of having smaller animals in his drawings mimic the behavior of humans. The tree leaves little room for debate concerning what

Figure 4.3. Ayoub seems to dismiss any question of "who is killing whom" / "*qui tue qui.*" Ayoub, *El Khabar*, November 30, 1997, 24.

forces are behind the massacre alluded to in the heading, while the drawing overall maintains the foreign nature of the qui-tue-qui question.[124]

Produced at the peak of mass killings, a cartoon by Dilem (fig. 4.4) shows a man saying to another holding a paper, "They say that they don't know who is killing [*qui tue*] in Algeria." His seemingly enraged friend replies, from behind a newspaper, "In any event, there is one thing that doesn't carry any risk of killing in France . . . ridicule." The man undercuts theories surrounding the ambiguity of agents of violence as laughable by drawing on a common French phrase. Like Ayoub, Dilem evokes the qui-tue-qui question to firmly place it in a foreign and, importantly, French framework; associating an idea with the nation's former colonizer could immediately make the idea suspect or susceptible to dismissal.[125] Algerians such as the ones drawn in the cartoon, the artist seems to imply, would not be duped. For Dilem, the agents of bloodshed were clear and anyone questioning the armed groups' guilt nonsensical.

Even when not evoking qui tue qui directly, many caricaturists ascribed assaults against civilians to the armed groups alone. Dilem generally asserted a view that the armed rebels were the singular actors engaging in civilian

Figure 4.4. Algeria's "voice of youth" makes fun of the *qui tue qui* inquiry. Dilem, *Liberté*, November 11, 1997.

bloodshed throughout the Black Decade. Figure 4.5 exemplifies this habit. Here, death arrives at an Algerian market. Dilem does not situate the scene in any particular part of the country, suggesting the ghoul could strike anywhere. The caption, "Death everywhere," reiterates this message. With finger raised, Death approaches a desk behind which one of Dilem's armed rebels/Islamists suspends his usual irate appearance to smile at this particular customer. The collector of souls says, "Some civilians to go, please." With this image, Dilem conveys the impression that the violence striking parts of the country applies to Algeria as a whole and can take place anytime and anywhere. Civilian deaths are so common that they can be ordered to go. The caricaturist from El-Harrach also links attacks on civilians to the group represented by the merchant figure here: the armed Islamist/rebels.[126]

In terms of the power of caricatures to intersect with and advance rather than dismiss rumors, Dilem produced a telling cartoon at a moment of mounting hysteria and outrage in the country as massacres grew in strength and frequency at the end of summer 1997. The piece featured one of the artist's typical armed Islamist characters speaking to readers. The cartoon's headline announces, "A new terrorist group: *el-ghadiboun ala lah* [al-Ghādhibūn 'ala Āllāh]," literally translated to "those angry against God." The man in this image seems disheartened and has a bat circling his head and what seems to be

Figure 4.5. Dilem's death figure orders civilians "to go" as one would a meal from a restaurant worker with an "Islamist" behind the counter. Dilem, *Liberté*, January 23, 1997, 24.

dirt coming off of him. He also holds the knife that Dilem habitually put into the hands of his Islamist/rebel figures. Viewers of the cartoon see that his hand is missing a finger as he raises it up. The irate, bearded figure states, "I have an index finger cut off like them [meaning the rumored new organization] . . . but me, it was a work accident."[127] The existence of this supposedly fringe, ultraradical group al-ghādhibūn was first reported in a paper that Jacob Mundy characterizes as staunchly "anti-Islamist," *Le Matin*. According to their coverage, this organization was rebelling against Islam.[128] Allegations of this group carrying out some of the bloodiest massacres of late summer 1997 emerged at the moment of these killings. Newspapers asserted that the group distinguished themselves through an incredibly blasphemous act purportedly meant to mark their turn away from religion. Accounts of their mayhem held that the group's members had sliced off their index fingers so that they could no longer point while reciting the *shahāda*, the Islamic pronunciation of faith and one of the religion's five pillars. Other sources for the group's existence beyond left-leaning papers appear sparse, and coverage of the group within Francophone papers may have been linguistically misleading, with the phrase *ala Allah* meaning "alongside God" in some circles.[129]

The joke in this drawing plays on incongruity by comparing the group to normal workers who could suffer occupational hazards. The knife-wielding man has inflicted self-damage, a source of humor in the drawing. With this cartoon, Dilem acknowledges and advances a rumor that might have been intended to sketch a more harrowing portrait of the insurgents that newspapers advanced alongside other accounts attributing violence to the armed groups. The artist then offers his rendition of the story, assigning blame for civilian deaths to a seemingly unholy organization in the prominent place that his daily drawing held on *Liberté*'s back page. Dilem distinguished the killers from the Muslim population, to whom, once again, he ascribed different levels of piety, possibly encouraging readers to do the same.

Theories surrounding so-called Algerian violence fed into questions of how international observers should respond to horrific incidents such as the murder in one night of hundreds of civilians at Bentalha. If the UN believed the government's assertions of its innocence and the guilt of the armed organizations, then an actual investigation of state conduct would be less likely and necessary. Cartoonists waded into these murky waters, generally to denounce international criticism of the Algerian government by foreignizing qui tue qui and questions of state involvement in massacres. For instance, in a cartoon from early 1998, Ayoub depicted the initiatives of international human rights organizations as potentially dangerous for the country, further eating away at the credibility of their reports on the unfolding humanitarian crisis in Algeria. A man stands next to an oversized tin can similar to one that would contain sardines. Instead of fish, snakes emerge from the receptacle and appear to lurch menacingly at Ayoub's cat and mouse. These animals personify the armed groups (felines) and Algerian civilians (mice). The term *munazammāt ḥuqūq al-insān*, "human rights organizations," appears on the can, but the first letter for the Arabic word for "rights" appears to read *'aqūq*, or human "wantonness" or "disobedience" organization. This potential play on the Arab word for "rights" may be intended to communicate that international organizations are not what they seem and may be inflicting pain on the country.[130]

Along with other *Liberté* journalists, Dilem appears to have perceived accusations against the military, along with calls for an external investigation of the massacres, as unjust and wrong. In a series of cartoons and articles in 1997, *Liberté* questioned a late-1996 Amnesty International report that implicated government armed forces and government-supported militias in the terrorization of civilian communities.[131] Later, Dilem reversed this certainty as to who was carrying out attacks. This switch arrived, though, at a moment when the cartoonist was frequently criticizing Bouteflika's peace measures, during which time Dilem seems to have criticized the now-noneradicator state more forcefully than before.[132]

If cartoonists blamed rebels for massacres, how did these artists portray other groups considered by civilians and organizations in and outside of Algeria to be possibly involved in the killing of civilians? A survey of the thousands of cartoons produced during the 1990s before this turn reveals that Dilem seems to have crafted only one drawing that directly implicated an agent of the state in civilian deaths. This drawing featured a low-ranking soldier, a group that Dilem hardly ever ridiculed or portrayed. The man lurks over the body of an ostensibly dead civilian under the title, "If all of the authors of excesses [*dépassements*] are judged, it will be the judges who will be overwhelmed [*dépassés*]." The English translation inadequately captures the French play on words, but the illustration indicates that state soldiers have exacted a large toll from the civilian population. The drawing represented a rare break (one of two drawings out of thousands) in Dilem's pattern of depicting Black Decade violence as the result of rebel agency.[133]

"Patriots," government-armed civilian militias, constituted the last group that rumors folded into the list of possible perpetrators of bloodshed against other civilian groups. These narratives attested that these organizations could inflict abuses on other civilians suspected of sympathy for or working with rebels. The name *patriot* positively linked these groups back to the proliberation struggles of the 1950s through the 1970s, when Algerian nationalists and postindependence papers praised worldwide anticolonial resistors as the nation's "patriots."[134] At their height, Black Decade patriots were estimated to comprise upward of eighty thousand men, three times the approximate number that joined the armed groups.[135] Unlike their Islamist foes, Ayoub and Dilem both depicted patriots as weak, embattled, and battered figures who valiantly struggled to take up the weapons that the state provided. For instance, Ayoub showed them in one cartoon as seemingly helpless, hapless, and ill-prepared civilians. A man, most likely a government employee, in a suit with an open, weapons-filled briefcase by his side sardonically quips, "This way . . . you'll die standing." The civilian figures hardly seem capable of inflicting harm on any group, especially as the man's words predict their impending demise. Ayoub thereby perhaps indirectly sought to dismiss any claims of patriot groups participating in the bloodshed even as he skewered the government for leaving civilians mainly to their own devices.[136] Dilem's drawings generally followed a similar pattern.[137] However, Slim appeared to celebrate the patriots, or at least those individuals opting to stave off attacks themselves. In one drawing from 1997, he showed a modestly attired man discussing how he took out a "terrorist" with a bottle of wine.[138] In addition to feting the patriots, the caricature implied that wine drinking was not incompatible with Algerian-ness, as it countered the Islamists/rebels he pinpointed as violent agents. In all, then, cartoons did not attribute excessive force or bloodshed to civilian self-defense groups.

CRITIQUES OF STATE RESPONSE TO VIOLENCE

Cartoonists' perspectives on the violence fit the state's narratives of the bloodshed in many ways. The artists filled in the unknown faces of masked assailants with Islamist/rebel features and linked the violence to national intrigues, effectively "Islamist-izing it" rather than "Islamicizing" to stress that the violence had to do with politically driven groups rather than Islam as a religion. However, artists simultaneously challenged government rhetoric that the military had a handle on the conflict. The main caption in one especially biting Dilem cartoon from September 1997 (fig. 4.6) reads, "Where is the state?" A man knocks frantically on a closed door as he tries to escape one of Dilem's Islamists/rebels. The imperiled citizen cries out, "Help!" The response from behind the door and inside the structure is "Come back tomorrow... We are closed!" In this image, as in many others, Dilem assigns sole responsibility for the bloodshed to Islamists/insurgents. The civilian man seeks help from authorities. The only government responsibility regarding civilian massacres as presented here was its inability, willful or otherwise, to protect citizens. The artist depicts a state derelict in its duty to protect, but not one guilty of excesses or of committing massacres. In this and other cartoons, focus on the state's negligence in preventing massacres relieved it from accusations of actively participating in them.[139]

One image that critiqued the state for its inefficacy vis-à-vis the conflict also offers the clearest evidence of a dialogue-wary cartoonist undermining regime policy. The drawing evinces that artists may have had some room to maneuver past official censors, a testament to their agency. In January 1997, the government advertisement agency pulled out of an agreement with Dilem's newspaper, *Liberté*. Then-president Liamine Zeroual gave a speech around this time claiming to have control of the country's security situation. The next day, the minister of the interior upbraided the press for putting forth "pro-terrorist propaganda" by extensively covering civilian massacres in their pages. Fearful of state reprisals, the private press suspended its emphasis on the horrific status of the security situation in the country. They then resumed coverage of the conflict and civilian murders, the results of rebel "barbarism" in the accounts they published, in April.[140]

Figure 4.6. The state, boarded up, leaves civilians to fend for themselves amid the savage attacks that Dilem ascribes to his "Islamist/rebel" characters. Dilem, *Liberté*, September 7, 1997, 24.

Ever the rebel, Dilem attacked Zeroual's promises to eradicate the armed groups and restore safety just after the minister of the interior's excoriation of journalists, likely as a direct rebuke of this action. Indeed, Dilem appears not to have heeded the official's call to refrain from mentioning assaults on civilians; the artist unflinchingly persisted in designing bloodied landscapes in contradiction of the interior minister's wishes. On February 2, 1997, only a few weeks following this announcement and Zeroual's address, Dilem produced a cartoon seemingly intended to show the hollowness of the president's reassurances that the state had the situation in hand. The drawing has a TV announcer's voice coming from the appliance proclaiming, "And now the president will address the live forces of the nation" (i.e., its citizens). Instead of a mass of curious listeners gathered around the set, decapitated heads lie scattered across the floor. The drawing's message flew directly in the face of the minister of the interior's warning to journalists.[141] It may thereby evince a level of freedom and an effort on Dilem's part to undermine state control over press content while also stressing the regime's failures to get the conflict in check.

Beyond pointing to the limitations of the state's power and its dereliction in its duty to protect citizens, though, like Ayoub and Slim, Dilem produced work that dovetailed with the state's version of events regarding who was carrying out the violence and why.

CARTOONISTS CRITIQUING NEGOTIATIONS

Algeria's caricaturists employed their pens to oppose reconciliation measures and denounce anyone supporting dialogue with the armed organization as flirting with dangerous politics. This point of view was shared by the eradicator military figures such as Khaled Nezzar, who stood at the helm of state power under Zeroual despite the president's overtures toward the AIS. Once again, it is impossible to conclude that caricaturists worked at the explicit orders of anyone within the government, but the majority of these artists appeared to have agreed with some of the politics of the so-called eradicator camp.

El Manchar cartoons from the early to mid-1990s posited negotiations and peace efforts as unfeasible at best or measures that might spell doom for the everyday citizens of the country at worst. Tenani painted a piece (fig. 4.7) in which a civilian approaches a carnival stand manned by Death. According to the "Wheel of Misfortune" situated behind the Grim Reaper, of the possible ways that the man has to die, "Sant'Egidio" is mentioned alongside famine and cholera. The 1994–1995 Sant'Egidio peace summit in Rome gathered members of the FIS and other pro-reconciliation parties. They hammered out a platform for an end to the crisis in Algeria, in which all signatories agreed to forego violence as a means of achieving political aims and to respect democratic processes in the country. By placing the peace agreement alongside horrific ways of passing on, Tenani suggested that relegalizing the FIS or going softer on rebels would result in further civilian demise.[142] A 1995 *El Manchar* work by "Mus" and "Hussam" (fig. 4.8) depicted a mass grave separating civilians from armed rebels. The sinister faces of the Islamists/rebels and their brandishing of arms suggest that civilians crossing the trench will meet the corpses' fate. One of the weapons-bearing insurgents announces, "The gap is widening between us but it is never too late to fill it in!" Since the collapsing of the distance between them would involve civilians meeting the ends of the rebels' weapons, the cartoon implies that the proverbial olive branch is a false one. After all, the "gap" is full of civilian victims. Peace with insurgents will entail peril. Of the dozen or so major caricaturists that published cartoons during the 1990s, the majority seem to have opposed negotiations with the armed groups, an unsurprising stance given their broader depictions of Algerian violence and its agents. Cartoonists likewise pinned pro-reconciliation activists as inadvertently promoting violence by promoting peace with actors supposedly incapable of being peaceful.[143]

Figure 4.7. "Algeria and the Wheel of Misfortune." The "Sant'Egidio" meeting to develop a peace agreement to end violence through dialogue is listed alongside "cholera" and "famine" as an unhappy potential outcome for participants in this "game."

Figure 4.8. Armed groups appear menacing as they propose peace literally over the bodies of dead civilians.

For one of the only cartoonists creating work that ostensibly favored peace talks, life became increasingly difficult. Chawki Amari spent a month in prison in July 1996 for a caricature insinuating that the forces of order in charge in the country, a state backed by pro-eradicator generals, had sullied Algeria's national flag. Amari drew at the time for *La Tribune*, which was forced to shut down for six months after Amari's arrest.[144]

CONCLUSION

In 2000, Ali Dilem, arguably the biggest star of Algeria's cartooning industry, won the International Prize of Newspaper Caricatures. To commemorate his victory, fellow Algerian cartoonist Mohamed Mazari ("Maz") sketched a drawing of the artist that appeared in Maz's newspaper *El Watan*. In it, he shows the spritely young caricaturist wielding a pencil to duel with a man dressed in *gandoura/kandūra* and holding a knife.[145] Given that Maz drew this cartoon after nearly a decade of armed combat between the state and armed groups, he most likely intended to glorify the supposed battle that Dilem, like Algeria's leading cartoonists, had waged during these years against Islamists/rebels. And wage a battle against individuals of this political and ideological leaning, Dilem and many other caricaturists had.

Throughout the Black Decade of the 1990s, as rumors ran wild and Algerian communities struggled to make sense of violence committed by masked agents, the country's beleaguered caricaturists assigned faces and attempted to fill in scenes left otherwise to the imaginations of an equally embattled population. Artists worked as "combatants" toward the goal of disassociating Muslimness in Algeria and Algerian national character from political Islamism, which many cartoonists centered as the motor behind violence against civilians. In the worlds carefully constructed by these artists, the qui-tue-qui question is as unworthy of serious discussion as it is a query ripe for ridicule. Their works went further, placing questioning of who was killing in Algeria in a foreign (French) and, ergo, misinformed context.

Among professional comedians, cartoonists were the only ones to keep up their craft into the 1990s as radio took on a more stoic tone and theatrical comedies and stand-up ceased. They produced work highly critical of the state, rebels, and international community alike but for different reasons and toward different ends. In the process and on the whole, they simultaneously but perhaps unintentionally supported state endeavors to pinpoint Islamists/rebels, a category blurring lines between moderate Islamists and rebels, as the sole party responsible for the armed conflict. Information about the conflict grew in importance just as the state constrained foreign and domestic journalists' access to sources. In this vacuum of verifiable news, cartoons provided communities with interpretations of events that reinforced or could have inspired critical ideas surrounding the violence. Cartoonists' popularity and the criticism they sometimes drew suggest that they held serious sway over their readerships.

Cartoons presented a vision of the conflict as one in which civilians were innately separate from the armed rebel organizations. Groups such as the AIS and GIA failed to amass widespread support, at least beyond a tacit or inactive type of backing, and lost popularity as the conflict wore on.[146] As reflected in jokes and cartoons of the time, humorous views of the armed insurgents as distinctive from and noxious to the nation could have eaten away at the organizations' popularity and popular legitimacy.[147] The general who conversed with caricaturist Ayoub above and may have had access to intelligence reports seems to have believed that cartoonists ultimately accomplished precisely this task. Cartoons as well as their creators and supporters appear to have worked to de-Algerianize the violence, especially for the actions that seemed most likely attributable to the armed rebels. They did so by making the armed insurgents out to be foreigners and by distinguishing between peaceful, supposedly more authentic Algerian forms of Islam from the faith in whose name rebels supposedly acted. Once again, as seen in the second chapter of this volume, humor could help reinforce in-groups and out-groups and worked as a space for thinking through the bounds of the nation in light of the harrowing violence.

Finally, cartoonists often marshaled seemingly Orientalist tropes of backwardness—sexual perversion, dirt, innate violence, and so on—to effectively "other" these Islamists/rebels and remove them from the Algerian national community as the artists conceived it. Yet, it would be a mistake to associate their labor with Orientalist projects; cartoonists spoke as members of a Muslim-majority society to other members of that society. What remains outside the purview of the research here is whether discourse reducing differences between insurgents and Islamists triggered an alienation or stigmatization of Muslim civilians who wore beards or supported licit Islamist parties. The stories of the harrowing military crackdown on moderate FIS militants on a granular level and discrimination experienced by overtly pious Muslims who did not necessarily embed politics in their faith or vice versa have yet to be explored thoroughly, most likely due to the military's ultimate victory in the conflict. Nevertheless, Algerian cartoonists used their critical space to distance violent Islamists, but not Muslims or Islam, from the invented national community, powerful messages about who was responsible for the violence and who was truly Algerian.

What is more, beyond rendering Islamists/rebels outsiders to the nation, cartoonists presented, advanced, or inflected narratives of violence that marked it as stemming from national politics. They thereby dismissed theories that local dynamics were at play in the bloodshed. Indeed, all cartoonists, regardless of their attitudes toward negotiations with rebels, attempted to make sense of the events going on around them from a national standpoint. Humor could still be used as an Algerianizing element, to the favor of some and the exclusion of others. Above all, though, political humor had important consequences in Algeria as many agents—here cartoonists—employed humor to express ideas about the nation and power. These artists would continue to use their craft during the period of reconciliation that resolved the conflict, lasting from approximately 1994 to 2005 but picking up speed in the late 1990s. The next chapter explores their responses to a state-brokered peace that ended the Black Decade but at the cost of justice.

NOTES

1. The minimum monthly wage in Algeria during the 1990s was five thousand dinars a month. These numbers, along with the price listed for daily papers, comes from François Gèze and Sahra Kettab, *Dossier 7: Les violations de la liberté de la presse*, Comité Justice pour l'Algérie, accessed August 17, 2015, http://www.algerie-tpp.org/tpp/pdf/dossier_7_presse.pdf, 13, n. 35. Newspapers that I saw from the early 1990s through the late 1990s ranged in price from 2.5 to 10 dinars.

2. Séverine Labat and Malik Aït Aoudia, *Algérie, 1988–2000: Autopsie d'une tragédie* (Paris: Compagnie des Phares et Balises, 2005); list signed by the AIS that was given to me by an Algerian journalist who had worked on security issues in the country during the 1990s and wished to remain anonymous for this book.

3. See, for example, descriptions of differences between the two groups presented in Luis Martinez, *The Algerian Civil War* (New York: Columbia University Press, 2000), 203–205.

4. See, for instance, the content of *Liberté* from this period, which generally referred to militants of the armed groups as "terrorists."

5. Jacob Mundy, *Imaginative Geographies of Algerian Violence* (Palo Alto: Stanford University Press, 2015), 155–156, n. 98.

6. For a work discussing how news spread historically in colonial Algeria, see Arthur Asseraf, *Electric News in Colonial Algeria* (Oxford: Oxford University Press, 2019).

7. Aberrahmane Moussaoui, *De la violence en Algérie* (Paris: Actes Sud, 2006), 357.

8. See Moussaoui, *De la violence*, 353–357.

9. Moussaoui, *De la violence*, 353–357.

10. Interview with Malik Aït-Aoudia, December 19, 2014.

11. Even outside of his disputes with the military and state in the early to mid-2000s, Dilem's drawings could provoke a wave of outrage on the part of readers or the political figures whom he mocked. See some of the incidents evoked in Farid Alilat, "Ali Dilem: Dessinateur iconoclaste," *Jeune Afrique*, February 28, 2000, https://www.jeuneafrique.com/67699/archives-thematique/ali-dilem-dessinateur-iconoclaste/.

12. William Lawrence notes that Dilem had earned this moniker among followers in the 1990s. See William Lawrence, "Representing Algerian Youth" (PhD diss., Tufts University, 2004), 116.

13. For more on "drawing the nation" in Algeria during this time, see Mark McKinney, "The Frontier and the Affrontier: French-Language Algerian Comics and Cartoons Confront the Nation," *European Comic Art* 1, no. 2 (2008): 175–200. *Bandes dessinées* are Belgian-style comics.

14. This video, produced between 1993 and 1994, was placed on YouTube and available around 2015 but has since been removed. See also Mustapha Benfodil, *Dilem président:*

Biographie d'un émeutier (INAS, 2008), http://www.argotheme.com/dilempres%5B1%5D.pdf, 59.

15. List signed by the AIS that was given to me by an Algerian journalist who had worked on security issues in the country during the 1990s and wished to remain anonymous for this book.

16. No evidence exists, though, to suggest that the armed groups' dislike of cartoonists stemmed from aniconism, which was historically common in some Muslim communities.

17. See Paul A. Silverstein, "An Excess of Truth: Violence, Conspiracy Theorizing, and the Algerian Civil War," *Anthropological Quarterly* 75, no. 4 (2002): 643–674; Mundy, *Imaginative Geographies*.

18. See chap. 3.

19. Mundy noted the gendered, masculine nature of checkpoints in Jacob Mundy, "Visualising National Reconciliation after the Algerian Civil War: Violence, Gender and 'Virtual Justice' in Film," in *Spectacles of Blood: A Study of Masculinity and Violence in Postcolonial Films*, ed. Swaralipi Nandi and Esha Chatterjee (Chicago: University of Chicago Press, 2012), 41.

20. Mundy, *Imaginative Geographies*, 67; Silverstein, "Excess of Truth."

21. Mundy, *Imaginative Geographies*.

22. The term *guerre sans visage* is Benjamin Stora's. See Benjamin Stora, *La guerre invisible* (Paris: Presses des Sciences Po, 2001), 46.

23. Jennifer Howell, "Investigating the Enforced Disappearances of Algeria's 'Dark Decade,'" *Journal of North African Studies* 21, no. 2 (2016): 213–234.

24. Interview with Mahfoud Aïder, June 13, 2013.

25. Moussaoui, *De la violence*, 353–354.

26. See chap. 3.

27. Vish Sakthivel also writes about differing ideas of Muslimness, piety, and authentic Islam within Algeria. See Vish Sakthivel, "The Movement for a Society of Peace" (PhD diss., Oxford University, 2019).

28. I looked at cartoons from more than a dozen periodicals dating to the conflict, including *L'Authentique*, *L'Hebdo libéré*, *Alger républicain*, and *Echa'ab* (French transliteration for *al-Cha'ab*). See the bibliography for the full list. Once again, I collected some rebel propaganda materials that were supposedly found by the army during raids on insurgents through a journalist who wishes to remain anonymous.

29. See, for instance, *Echa'ab* from this period.

30. Gèze and Kettab, *Dossier 7*, 7–9. Cherif Dris also acknowledges this shift with the rise of Ghozali and the restoration of the Ministry of Communication. See Cherif Dris, "La Nouvelle Loi organique sur l'information de 2012 en Algérie," *L'Année du Maghreb* 8 (2012): 303–320.

31. See *al-Ṣaḥḥ Āfa* from 1991 and Aïssa Khelladi, "Rire quand même: L'humour politique dans l'Algérie d'aujourd'hui," *Revue des mondes musulmans et de la Méditerranée* 77–78 (1996): 233. For more on the camps, see Saphia Arezki, "Les camps d'internement du sud en Algérie (1991–1995): Contextualisation et enjeux," *L'Année du Maghreb* 20 (2019): 225–239.

32. Mundy, *Imaginative Geographies*, 74–75.

33. Tristan Leperlier, *Algérie, les écrivains et la décennie noire* (Paris: CRNS, 2018).

34. List signed by the AIS that was given to me by an Algerian journalist who had worked on security issues in the country during the 1990s and wished to remain anonymous for this study; Martinez, *Algerian Civil War*, 159–161.

35. This was the case with Dahmani and his drawings for *L'Authentique*. Dahmani was accused by the generally antidialogue paper *L'Hebdo libéré* of possessing more freedom in his art due to his employment in the former paper controlled by a relative of Major General Mohammed Betchine. See McKinney, "Frontier and the Affrontier," 179–181.

36. Thierry Oberlé, "Like He Said: A Vitriolic Chronicle of Algeria," *Grand Street* 65 (Summer 1998): 51.

37. Mohamed Samraoui, *Chroniques des années de sang* (Paris: Denoël, 2003).

38. Mundy, *Imaginative Geographies*, 155–156, n. 98.

39. Human Rights Watch, *Algeria: Elections in the Shadow of Violence and Repression*, June 1, 1997, https://www.refworld.org/docid/3ae6a7d1c.html.

40. Samraoui, *Chroniques des années*, 118–119.

41. Human Rights Watch, *Algeria*.

42. See Dris, "La Nouvelle Loi"; Lies Sahar, "Tempête sur la presse," *Algérie-Actualité*, July 23–29, 1992.

43. Dris, "La Nouvelle Loi."

44. Ghania Mouffouk confirmed this information in Monique Durand, "Le combat des Algériennes," *Gazette des femmes*, last modified March 5, 2005, https://www.gazettedesfemmes.ca/2853/le-combat-des-algeriennes/.

45. Youcef Zirem, *Algérie la guerre des ombres* (Brussels: Complexe, 2002), 74.

46. "Eradicator" voices within the military and civilian population adopted a hardline stance against insurgents, opting to forego negotiations and put down rebel groups through sheer force, as opposed to "conciliators," who sought dialogue. See chap. 3.

47. Salima Ghezali, "De la presse bâillonée à la presse schizophrène," Algeria Watch, December 13, 2009, https://algeria-watch.org/?p=66935.

48. *L'Hebdo libéré*, March 30–April 5, 1994, 1.

49. See, for instance, "Sayah Attiah, un harki sanguinaire à la tête du Gia [sic]" [Sayah Attia, a bloody harki at the head of the Gia], *Alger républicain*, March 8, 1994, 24, as well as the cover of the November 30, 1993, edition of *Alger républicain*. This cover calls the members of the armed groups "harki killers" in that they are both harki and killers.

50. Some journalists actively reject the *eradicator* and *conciliator* labels. Interview with Omar Belhouchet, July 20, 2013. "Les Nouveaux Colons: Mitidja, marécage de l'intégrisme" [The New Settlers: Mitidja, fundamentalism's swamp], *Alger républicain*, November 3, 1993, 2. The Mitidja was a fertile plain south of Algiers that, along with the rest of the area between Blida, Médéa, and Aïn Defla, became known as the "triangle of death" during the armed struggle.

51. "L'O.A.S. intégriste localisée" [The fundamentalist O.A.S. located], *Alger républicain*, April 11, 1993, 5.

52. "Le FIS, grand hizb frança" [The FIS, the big party of France], *Alger républicain*, January 15, 1992, 3. See also Martin Evans and John Phillips, *Algeria: Anger of the Dispossessed* (New Haven, CT: Yale University Press, 2007), 100.

53. McKinney, "Frontier and the Affrontier," 179–181.

54. For instance, Maz and Slim both drew cartoons criticizing the government's decision to persecute their fellow artist. The drawing by Slim was printed in *Liberté* on a special page dedicated to calling for Chawki Amari's release and for the continuation of *La Tribune* on July 13, 1996. A drawing by Maz likewise demanding that the charges against Amari be dropped took up most of the cover of *El Watan*'s July 29, 1996, edition.

55. For a full list and account of missing and murdered media workers, see Lazhari Labter, *Journalistes algériens, 1988–1998* (Algiers: Chihab, 2005).

56. Human Rights Watch, *Algeria*.

57. Amine Kadi, Denise Ammoun, and Benjamin Barthe, "Dossier: Dérision et religion," *La Croix*, February 2, 2006, 5.

58. The other major pro-reconciliation paper was *La Tribune*, which is discussed further below. Gèze and Kettab, *Dossier 7*.

59. See McKinney, "Frontier and the Affrontier."

60. Both events are detailed in Benfodil, *Dilem président*, 59–60, 92–108. Campaigns for Amari's liberation appeared across the private press and displayed solidarity between cartoonists working for papers that opposed and supported negotiations with the armed groups. See, for instance, a drawing that cartoonist Maz crafted for the cover of the July 29, 1996, edition of *El Watan* demanding that Amari be freed. Maz, "Libérez Amari," *El Watan*, July 29, 1996, 1.

61. See, for instance, interviews and coverage included in Amel Hamidou, "Une Année de 't'manchir,'" *El Watan*, October 27, 1991.

62. Sahar, "Tempête sur la presse."

63. Sahar, "Tempête sur la presse."

64. Fatima Zohra Taiebi Moussaoui, "Le développement de la presse électronique en Algérie: Des dispositifs aux pratiques journalistiques," *L'Année du Maghreb* 15 (2016): 61–76.

65. See the statistic published by the Algerian National Office of Statistics, a government agency, in *Demography*, http://www.ons.dz/IMG/pdf/CH1-DEMOGRAPHIE.pdf, tables 32 and 33.

66. Human Rights Watch, *Algeria*.

67. Interview with Malik Aït Aoudia, December 19, 2014.

68. Alilat, "Ali Dilem."

69. Silverstein, "Excess of Truth," 643–674; Mundy, *Imaginative Geographies*.

70. Benfodil, *Dilem président*, 143–144.

71. Benfodil, *Dilem président*, 111.

72. Benfodil, *Dilem président*, 111.

73. Interview with Saad, March 5, 2015.

74. Interviews with Mahfoud Aïder, Mustapha Tenani, Mohamed Mazari, and Hichem Baba Ahmed, June 13, 2013; interview with Mahfoud Aïder, June 18, 2013; interview with Abrous Outoudert, January 19, 2014.

75. Interview with Mahfoud Aïder, June 18, 2013.

76. Interview with Mahfoud Aïder, June 18, 2013.

77. Interview with Chawki Arami, June 23, 2013; Benfodil, *Dilem président*, 76.

78. In a conversation with *El Watan* journalist and writer Mustapha Benfodil, Dilem rejects the term *combat*. Instead, he viewed his tenacity in the face of threats against his life as a carrying out of an internal *conviction*. Benfodil, *Dilem président*, 158. Four cartoonists agreed with the use of the term in an exchange with me. Interviews with Mahfoud Aïder, Mustapha Tenani, Mohamed Mazari, and Hichem Baba Ahmed, June 13, 2013.

79. Dilem, *Le Matin*, March 7, 1996, 6. The cartoon references a joke in which an older woman declares her desire to be sexually assaulted by rebels. This joke was included in Zineb Sedira's project on Algerian humor from the 1990s. She indicates that at least two individuals recounted it to her. Interview with Zineb Sedira, March 29, 2015. The joke also appears in chap. 3.

80. Interview with Hichem Baba Ahmed, June 25, 2013.

81. Mundy, *Imaginative Geographies*, 74–75.

82. For an overview of these competing narratives of the macro- and microscale killings occurring in Algeria during the period, see Mundy, *Imaginative Geographies*, 65–83, chart on 90.

83. Dilem, *Liberté*, January 7, 1997, 24.

84. See Anne McClintock, "Family Feuds: Gender, Nationalism, and Family," *Feminist Review* 44 (1993): 61; Benedict Anderson, *Imagined Communities*, 2nd ed. (London: Verso, 1991).

85. Mundy, *Imaginative Geographies*, 65–84.

86. See Edward W. Saïd, *Orientalism* (New York: Pantheon Books, 1978).

87. See his cartoons from the 1990s in *Le Matin* and *Liberté*.

88. Slim, "Slim ce matin," *Le Matin*, December 24, 1996, 24; Dilem, *Liberté*, October 16, 1997.

89. Dilem, "Dilem du jour," *Le Matin*, August 28, 1994, 24.

90. See, for instance, Slim's cartoons in *Le Matin* from 1996 to 1998.

91. See, for instance, *El Manchar* artists' depictions of Mahfoud Nahnah in the mid-1990s.

92. John Ruedy, *Modern Algeria*, 2nd ed. (Bloomington: Indiana University Press, 2005), 257.

93. Mundy, *Imaginative Geographies*, 77.

94. See examples of cartoons below.

95. See Ayoub's art in *El Khabar* after 1996 and Slim's drawings from *Le Matin* from 1996 to 1998.

96. Dilem, "Dilem du jour," *Le Matin*, August 15, 1994, 24.

97. Martinez, *Algerian Civil War*, 248.

98. Martinez, *Algerian Civil War*; Dilem, "Dilem du jour," *Le Matin*, August 21, 1994, 3.

99. Martinez, *Algerian Civil War*, 209; Hugh Roberts, *The Battlefield: Algeria, 1988–2002, Studies in a Broken Polity* (New York: Verso, 2003).

100. Chawki Amari, *La Tribune*, November 26, 1994, 6.

101. Benfodil, *Dilem président*, 110.

102. Benfodil, *Dilem président*, 107.

103. See *El Manchar* from 1991 and 1992.

104. See, for instance, Mémèd, *El Manchar*, April 1993, 1. This cartoon showed an enraged "mullah," distinguishable by his black attire, armed to the teeth and nibbling like a rat on a piece of cheese shaped like Algeria. He also carried a grenade launcher topped with an Israeli flag. The caption above the caricature read, "Iran, Iran Petits Mollah Sont . . ." The only armed group that likely had ties to Iran was Takfir wa al-hijra. See Michael Willis, *The Islamist Challenge in Algeria* (New York: New York University Press, 1996), 202–203, 301–302.

105. Willis, *Islamist Challenge in Algeria*, 301–302.

106. See numerous cartoons, including two with the puppet theme in *El Manchar*, February 1992, nos. 32 and 33. See especially the cartoon by Loxman, *El Manchar*, February 1992, 13.

107. See chap. 2.

108. Nad, pseudonym of Nadjib Berber, *al-Ṣaḥḥ Āfa*, January 21–27, 1992, 4.

109. See, for instance, the cartoon by Hankour, *El Manchar*, January 1991, 14, discussed in chap. 2.

110. Vish Sakthivel describes how moderate Islamists in Algeria have distanced themselves from more "Eastern"/radicalized strands of Islam. Sakthivel, "Society of Peace."

111. Mundy, *Imaginative Geographies*.

112. Dilem, *Liberté*, October 10–11, 1997, 24, appearing to comment directly on an article published days before. NS. L., "Ces terroristes venus d'ailleurs" [These terrorists from elsewhere], *Liberté*, October 9, 1997, 4.

113. See, for instance, Ayoub, *El Khabar*, August 4, 1999, 24.

114. Dilem, "Dilem du jour," *Le Matin*, March 29, 1994.

115. Natalya Vince and Walid Benkhaled discuss the proliferation of ideas about the fake *mujāhidīn* and their importance for tales of the revolution betrayed within Algeria. See Natalya Vince and Walid Benkhaled, "Afterword: Performing Algerianness," in *Algeria: Nation, Culture, and Transnationalism*, ed. Patrick Crowley (Liverpool: Liverpool University Press, 2017), 243–244.

116. Vince and Benkhaled, "Afterword," 243–244.

117. This woman sports a headscarf, perhaps signaling her belonging to the Islamic faith. Ayoub, *El Khabar*, March 8, 1998, 24.

118. See, for instance, Slim, "Slim, Ce Matin," *Le Matin*, January 26, 1997.

119. See, for instance, the work of Dilem from this period in *Liberté*.

120. See, for instance, portrayals of Madame Algeria from *Le Matin* from 1992 until 1996.

121. Copies of Algeria's 1989 and 1996 constitutions located at Digithèque MJP, accessed January 10, 2018, https://mjp.univ-perp.fr/mjp.htm.

122. See, for example, Ayoub's cartoons depicting men in bars such as Ayoub, *El Khabar*, October 13, 1997.

123. Samraoui, *Chroniques des années*, 19–22; Mundy, *Imaginative Geographies*, 67–70.

124. Ayoub, *El Khabar*, November 30, 1997, 24.

125. Ayoub, *El Khabar*, November 30, 1997, 24.

126. Dilem, *Liberté*, November 11, 1997.

127. Dilem, *Liberté*, September 15, 1997, 24.

128. Mundy, *Imaginative Geographies*, 79n104.

129. Mundy, *Imaginative Geographies*, 79n104.

130. Ayoub, *El Khabar*, April 5, 1998, 24.

131. The report in question is Amnesty International, *Algeria: Fear and Silence—a Hidden Human Rights Crisis*, November 28, 1996, https://www.amnesty.org/download/Documents/172000/mde280111996en.pdf.

132. One of his cartoons that appeared in the 2000 *Boutef président* album (published before in *Liberté*) showed a civilian squished between a soldier and an "Islamist" insurgent. The words "Who is killing whom" / "Qui tue qui" stand above their heads as the man caught in the middle quivers, "I am really badly positioned to say." This cartoon is also one of the very few in which Dilem implicates lower ranks of the army in the violence of the 1990s toward civilians. See Ali Dilem, *Boutef président* (Algiers: self-published, 2000).

133. Dilem, *Liberté*, March 12, 1997, 24. See also Dilem, *Liberté*, December 4, 1997, 24.

134. See *El Moudjahid* from the late 1960s, for instance.

135. The number of civilians that the government armed and formalized by paying wages to them remains difficult to determine. See Salah-Ed-dine Sidhoum and Algeria Watch, *Les milices dans la nouvelle guerre d'Algérie*, December 13, 2009, updated June 3, 2018, https://algeria-watch.org/?p=48532.

136. Ayoub, *El Khabar*, January 14, 1998, 24.

137. See, for example, Dilem, *Liberté*, January 8, 1998, 24. One of his cartoons addressed a citizen unable to tell whom to call during an attack. Referencing rumors implicating all sides in civilian slaughter, the drawing included patriots as one group that the citizen felt may have been assaulting his home. Dilem, *Liberté*, April 15, 1998.

138. Slim, *Le Matin*, September 11, 1997, 24.

139. Dilem, *Liberté*, September 7, 1997, 24.

140. Account as presented in Human Rights Watch, *Algeria*.

141. Dilem, "Dilem," *Liberté*, February 2, 1997.

142. Tenani, *El Manchar*, February 12–25, 1995, 7.

143. See, for instance, a portrayal of reconciliatory politician Louiza Hannoune with a gun in Mémèd, *El Manchar*, December 1993, 3.

144. Chawki Amari, *La Tribune*, July 2, 1996, 6; interview with Chawki Amari, July 3, 2013. See also Benfodil, *Dilem président*, 92–107.

145. Caricature by Maz in an article by Tahar Hani, "Avec le dessin, j'exorcise mon chagrin," *El Watan*, December 23, 1999, from the dossier on Dilem and the dossier on the press from this period, Library of the Algerian Cultural Center, Paris, France.

146. The reasons for this failure included FIS voters being more in favor of political solutions to the crisis or not willing to risk lives in the pursuit of establishing a more "Islamic" government and distaste with the violence that the organizations inflicted or the MEI in particular not seeking to increase its popularity. See Martinez, *Algerian Civil War*, 57–58, 111–118; Roberts, *Battlefield*, 258; James D. Le Sueur, *Algeria since 1989: Between Terror and Democracy* (London: Zed Books, 2010), 54, 57–58; Mundy, *Imaginative Geographies*.

147. See chap. 3.

FIVE

CARTOONS "DANCING ON COFFINS" AND DRUMMING UP MEMORY DURING RECONCILIATION, 1997 TO 2005

ON JANUARY 13, 2000, ONE of Algeria's most famous cartoonists, Ali Dilem, published a caricature exemplifying many of the satirical pieces he and other major cartoonists in the country were producing at the time. This was the period when the government started finalizing peace talks with certain sectors of the armed insurgent groups, notably the Islamic Salvation Army (AIS). The artist, by this point much beloved by readers and a renowned figure in Algeria's decimated intellectual community, did not hold back his disgust with the peace agreements brokered by then-president Abdelaziz Bouteflika's government. And disgust is what this particular cartoon conveyed.

In the drawing, the reader sees two simple curved lines forming an upside-down V. From the top of the image, where the lines meet, a mass of bodies descends, indiscriminate until they reach the bottom of what appears to be a mountain. They are coming down as if in a horde, small like ants but then eventually occupying the front of the drawing to unveil their true form: that of Dilem's typical "Islamist"/"rebel" character, complete with large, phallic-like noses, Islamic *gandouras/kandūras* (long white garments), and clueless looks on their faces.[1] Unlike the earlier rebel characters Dilem had drawn, the ones in this cartoon do not wield smoking Kalashnikovs or bloodied knives, symbols of doom and destruction in the context of an armed struggle that eventually left an estimated one hundred thousand Algerians dead. Similar to the artist's earlier renditions of the insurgents, though, flies circle around their heads, a testament to their supposedly filthy demeanor. The absence of weapons in their hands along with the title of the drawing, "The Terrorists Come Down from the Mountains," signals that these men represent the newest and then largest wave to date of *repentis*, the French word for "repentant ones" and a term that

Algerians employed to designate insurgents who laid down their arms under the late 1990s and 2000s amnesty agreements.²

But an entirely different, much more scathing, and vulgar reading of the cartoon is possible. Like many famed optical illusions, the drawing can be interpreted in one of two ways. In the first, the viewer could see the area below the concave V shape as being solid and the space above the line empty. From this perspective, the two lines delineate two sides of the mountain that rise to form a peak, as the title of the picture suggests. According to this way of viewing the cartoon, the area below the line would consist of a solid mountain with the sky above. Yet, if the reader imagines that the space above the line is filled in, then the mountain is suddenly inversed, and the area above the lines makes two large hanging masses. From this perspective, the curved lines seem to form two ample buttocks. In this reading, then, the "bearded ones" are streaming down from the exact point where the giant buttocks meet, its apparent anus. Thus, through this image (fig. 5.1), Dilem explicitly communicates that he considers the repentant ones to be no better than the basest and arguably most repulsive form of worldly material: human feces.³

At least one cartoonist in Algeria supported reconciliation efforts between the state and militant insurgents in the middle of the 1990s. By the latter part of this decade, though, Algeria's perhaps singular prodialogue cartoonist, Chawki Amari, had ceased drawing. For many remaining artists like Dilem who had spent years in hiding or abroad and lost many colleagues to the violence, agreements with the armed groups were not acceptable.

The overwhelming majority of Algeria's cartoonists who had toed the antidialogue line throughout the conflict's earlier phases viewed reconciliation efforts in the late 1990s through the mid-2000s with outrage. These measures de facto permitted suspected murderers and rapists to reenter society without facing punishment for their crimes. At the same time, major state-controlled press organs included caricatures in their pages that lauded the "sensible" path to peace that President Bouteflika had laid out through negotiations and proposed legislation. These government-commissioned pro-reconciliation sketches illustrate that the regime viewed cartoons as effective propaganda for convincing the population to support peace initiatives. Thus, as this chapter argues, caricatures communicated strong ideas about the *repentis*, the terms of the laws that eventually allowed thousands of former rebels to reenter civil society, and the state's attempts to conceal any responsibility that it may have held for the then-ongoing bloodshed. They seemingly did so to seek an alternative justice for the conflict's victims and survivors, a goal unattainable in reality due to government policies.

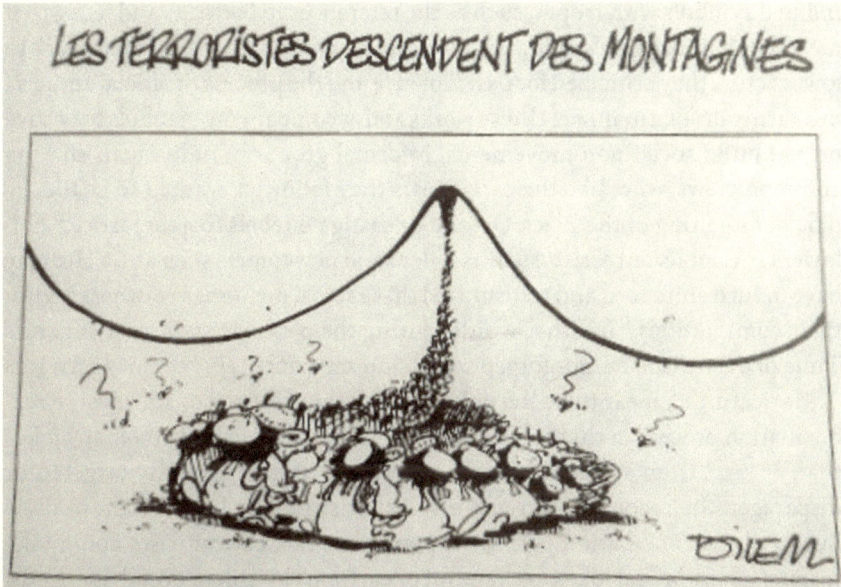

Figure 5.1. "The terrorists come down from the mountains."

Indeed, outside of *El Manchar* and these official papers, Algeria's cartoonists used their work to denounce and rally followers against peace initiatives.[4] In the process, they crafted an alternative and subversive world wherein perpetrators of atrocities, identified as the armed Islamist/rebels, would face justice in the court of public opinion. Cartoonists seem to have wanted to mark insurgents and partisans of reconciliation as ridiculous to obtain a justice otherwise impossible in the face of the government's move to amnesty armed militants in exchange for the militants laying down their arms.

A large component of the state's official reconciliation process involved drawing a cloak over the armed struggle. The state's aims in insisting on turning the page lay inevitably in incentivizing insurgents' return to civil society and to preclude any questioning of state agents' actions during the war beyond what the government was willing to admit. However, many cartoonists sought to keep the flame of the 1990s memory alive through their daily sketches. They also continued their practice of offering specific takes on who was responsible for the conflict that was only then beginning to wane. What is more, cartoons yielded communally recognizable and decipherable symbols for interpreting the recent violence, reconciliation measures, and official amnesia of certain aspects of the conflict to readers around the country. Very often, caricaturists imbued symbols with tropes, such as the references to buttocks and feces, that meet Mikhail Bakhtin's definition of *carnival*. Cartoonists used their work to lower actors they criticized for past violence and the process of official amnesia in a carnivalesque manner.[5] These works and accompanying symbols may have helped build social non-movements, informal groups of individuals sharing common views, who, like the cartoonists they followed, wanted to challenge official forgetting of the Black Decade or castigate rebels to gain justice.[6] Followers of established artists such as Dilem and newcomers such as Le Hic may have in turn embraced and transmitted these social memories to others within their communities.[7] In other words, during the peace process after Algeria's Time of Terrorism, humor forged social non-movements of memory activists.

Caricatures appear to be the only extant form of humor to address the reconciliation process in rhythm with its unfolding.[8] I failed to disinter any jokes that, at least from a textual analysis and their context, directly targeted or disparaged the reconciliation process. As artist Le Hic (who began to draw during the reconciliation period) explained to me, caricaturists could take inspiration from oral jokes.[9] A handful of cartoons by Dilem posed questions, as some jokes do. In one, the headline queries, "What will the repentant ones do after reconciliation?" The illustration shows an armed militant bargaining with a military general for a mistress, oil profits, and embezzled state money as part of his surrender conditions. The general replies positively to these demands but warns that the repentant one will have to go back to 1962, Algeria's independence, to get a shot at petroleum revenues or the state coffers, implying that he and fellow members of the military clique had already pilfered the nation's wealth.[10] This imagined exchange may have been Dilem's creation, it but hews closely to the formula of a joke.[11] Consequently, it may be that some cartoons from this era commenting on reconciliation did echo popular jokes circulating around the country.[12]

I open this chapter with an overview of state-initiated peace measures that were intended beginning in 1994 to convince rebels to abandon the armed struggle and return to Algerian civil society. I then shift to looking at how three of Algeria's most popular cartoonists from this time responded to these efforts, often by depicting them as potentially catastrophic for the nation given the violent attributes the cartoonists allotted their Islamist/armed group figures. State repression of this art is also considered, while the last section of this work examines how cartoonists working for official state newspapers appeared to respond directly to popular cartoonists' messaging about the peace measures. Above all, the present chapter demonstrates that humor, here in the form of cartoons, continued to serve as a critical space for Algerians as they imagined the potential implications of a peace process that seemed to deprive ordinary Algerians of justice. Cartoonists used their art to seek it.

ALGERIA'S RECONCILIATION PROCESS, 1994–2005

Algeria's fifth president, Liamine Zeroual, was elected in 1994 on a platform of bringing peace to the arguably beleaguered country. His government embarked on secret negotiations with former FIS leaders early on in his presidency. However, this dialogue ultimately broke down. The government then passed a law on amnesty, Law 95-12 of February 25, 1995, that provided a framework for permitting members of the armed groups to lay down their weapons and reintegrate into society under the condition that they had not carried out major crimes, a condition not investigated. This legislation set the precedent for peace measures that future president Abdelaziz Bouteflika would put into place.[13] Reconciliation over eradication became a more politically beneficial policy for both presidents to pursue as violence continued throughout the 1990s and might have flourished in part due to state negotiations with the AIS.[14] The AIS likewise sought a resolution to distinguish itself from the GIA and cut its losses.[15]

In theory, if surrendering rebels had committed grievous crimes under Algeria's penal code, they could not receive reduced sentences in exchange for laying down their arms. However, the law did nothing about state responsibility for any of the violence committed against civilians during the conflict. It particularly ignored the question of forced disappearances of civilians at the hands of military or police, an issue that began to gain broader attention in 1997.[16]

The Law of Civil Concord of 1999 succeeded the 1995 measure. According to the Civil Concord, anyone who had engaged in rape, murder, public massacres, or bombings would not be allowed to be reintegrated into society without punishment. Instead, in a continued attempt to convince these rebels to surrender, the Civil Concord decreed that they would be allotted more lenient sentences in light of their willingness to abandon the revolt. The actual enforcement of this portion of the law, though, proved elusive, if not completely absent. The law charged probation committees to accept the surrender of armed insurgents and determine whether capitulating individuals were eligible for amnesty according to the law—that is, they had not committed the exempted crimes. Human Rights Watch later called for the proceedings conducted by these committees to be made open to the public. The organization thought the move would permit Algerians and international observers to evaluate whether and how the Algerian state was investigating each dossier to ensure that former members of the armed groups who were amnestied had not, in fact, participated in rape or other forms of violent or deadly crimes, as the law stipulated.[17] Their calls for transparent hearings went unanswered. The public was thus left in the dark as to whether those terrorists who had placed bombs or killed or raped individuals had received adequate punishment under the law. What is more, the government had not put the infrastructure in place to investigate and rule whether a surrendering individual had indeed committed one of these infractions. Throughout the campaign that Bouteflika had spearheaded in support of the Civil Concord, the president also repeated that "those with blood on their hands" would be ineligible to benefit from the full terms of amnesty; the meaning of this phrase was left ambiguous. What exactly qualified as murder or rape, moreover, was left undefined in the text of the law as well as in the Algerian leader's public statements.[18] Consequently, the 1995 law and the Law of Civil Concord may have pardoned murderers and rapists that their own articles had rendered ineligible for such clemency.

Regardless of these concerns, Algeria's lower division of parliament, the People's National Assembly, passed the Law of Civil Concord. It was subsequently approved by 98.63 percent of the electorate who participated in an ambiguous national referendum vote on the measure, which took place on September 16, 1999; 85.03 percent of the nation's registered voters allegedly cast a ballot. The referendum queried whether civilians trusted Bouteflika's management of the peace process instead of having them weigh in directly on the Civil Concord.[19] Although the Concord technically expired in January 2000, it remained in place until the August 2005 advent of the Charter for Peace and National Reconciliation. This extrajudicial application of the law also attracted the criticism of several local and international human rights organizations and other opponents, but over time it went unchecked.[20]

Looking at numbers that Algerian military General Abdelkader Maïza released but that the government never officially confirmed, 386 individuals took advantage of the clemency offered by the Civil Concord. In contrast, 6,000 insurgents had gained readmission into civil society through the earlier 1995 law.[21] Thus, the Concord did not entice many rebels but symbolically boosted Bouteflika's clout as president and remains a controversial subject in Algeria to this day.[22]

The Charter for Peace and National Reconciliation that was announced in August 2005 provided a multipronged approach to bringing the more-than-decade-long violent crisis to a close. It renewed many of the major tenets of the Civil Concord. Yet, unlike the earlier legislation, the Charter tackled the question of the state's responsibility for extrajudicial killings. It indemnified families of "the disappeared," individuals whom the state claimed were victims of overzealous soldiers acting when dealing with civilians suspected of engagement with the armed groups. Indeed, the text of the Charter exculpates the government and military of any responsibility for these events. It asserted that the military had made no systemic effort to torture or harm individuals suspected of assisting the rebels. By this time, families of the disappeared had spent years pushing the government to know exactly what happened earlier in the 1990s when masked men presenting themselves as state agents came to their homes and took family members who were never seen or heard from again. The Charter refused to give in to their demands by renouncing any sort of inquiry into what happened in these instances. The same held true for the series of massacres of village populations that took place mainly from 1996 to 1998. Some international organizations and local figures believe that these collective killings were organized by the military or that state agents permitted them to take place to advance their own political agendas.[23] With the Charter, the state and military absolved themselves of any wrongdoing during the conflict. At the same time, the legislation made it a crime in Algeria for anyone to "use to their advantage the wounds of the 'national tragedy' [the government's term for the conflict] to attack the institutions of the Algerian Democratic and Popular Republic, to weaken the state, damage the reputation of the state, or harm the image of Algeria internationally."[24] The state's use of the term *national tragedy* to designate the armed struggle is particularly revealing. The choice implied that a series of unfortunate events had taken place, rather than an armed struggle fueled by different political agents' intrigues and actions.

In addition to allowing amnesty for rebels willing to submit to the state and allotting money to relatives of the disappeared, under the Charter Algerians had to agree to never again question the measures that government security agents had adopted during the conflict. Article Forty-Six of this legislation explicitly stated that no judicial actions could ever be taken against state agents who had been purportedly working at the time to ensure the nation's security.[25] Human Rights Watch concluded that it "offers more to perpetrators of human rights violations than it does to victims."[26]

For some observers and Algerians, the price of amnesty and peace under the auspices of the government (Bouteflika's regime in particular) was collective "amnesia."[27] In other instances of conflict resolution such as postapartheid South Africa, international courts or special impartial tribunals have overseen the implementation of peace and reconciliation efforts. Such was not the case in Algeria. The government, a party suspected of engaging in questionable activities, served as the sole arbiter of justice in the situation.[28]

Algerians voted in a September 29, 2005, referendum on the Charter. It passed with 97 percent of the vote with 79 percent turnout.[29] Yet, in its criticism of the Charter, Human Rights Watch contended that government efforts precluded an environment permissive, let alone encouraging, of free speech in the period leading up to the national referendum on the legislation. The organization also took issue with the relatively short time between Bouteflika's unveiling of the Charter and the scheduled popular vote on the measure.[30] Once again, the opacity of state judicial procedures regarding the repentant ones meant that Algerians could not be sure whether the state meted out punishment to suspected rapists and murderers that was in any way commensurate with the crimes they may have committed.

Algeria's state undertook this peace process exactly as more and more scholars and media outlets were paying attention to the virtues or drawbacks of truth and reconciliation commissions as well as transitional justice. Algeria's reconciliation measures were shaped against a backdrop of similar processes that had taken place or were still underway since 1973.[31] The tail end of Algeria's peace process coincided with neighboring Morocco's revisiting of the repressive Years of Lead through the Equity and Reconciliation Commission put in place by Mohammed VI.

Citing the South African example, critics from inside and outside of Algeria expressed their belief that the country's government was failing to provide for a more transparent peace process.[32] Algeria's conflict was unique to the country, and truth and reconciliation commissions in a number of contexts have faced criticism for being unable to provide justice or to offer adequate opportunity for all survivors to speak about their experiences.[33] Such committees have in some cases been shown to provide little more than credence to a political authority rather than actual meaningful justice to those who have been wronged in the past. Justice can sometimes be only partially delivered, with certain perpetrators not being prosecuted.[34] Even with these caveats, Algeria's reconciliation and amnesty processes appear thinner and less rigorous than many others that have been overseen in other societies emerging from conflict.

In the Algerian case, a lack of open dialogue about the conflict besides that available in its robust, if still monitored, media landscape proved the rule. The government whose agents were also suspected of crimes and human rights violations unilaterally brokered the peace agreement and opted to focus almost all of its attention on horrendous acts committed by rebel agents rather than state ones. While some reparations were paid, no forum was provided for individuals who had suffered to address their experiences, and a greater confrontation with the horrors of the previous years did not occur. As previously mentioned, the human rights committees (the National Human Rights Observatory, which later became the National Consultative Commission for the Promotion and Protection of Human Rights) that the government set up to oversee parts of the reconciliation process investigated some cases of forced disappearances. Those organizations along with the military released some numbers concerning the overall death toll and the rate of forced disappearances.[35] But other investigations into crimes committed by armed parties did not take place as had occurred in, for instance, Peru and Argentina. Unlike in other instances as well, Algeria's reconciliation process did not result in legal proceedings against any public figures considered to be responsible for the conflict. Institutions potentially behind some of the violence were also not held accountable and did not undergo any major change, a pattern that held true for other reconciliation processes, especially where militaries and police were concerned.[36]

Therefore, organizations and individuals interested in attempts to achieve justice or construct more truthful narratives have had to do so outside of official processes and organizations.[37] For instance, while the terms of the Charter make direct criticism of the state's actions during the war illegal, some organizations dedicated to the conflict's memory and the pursuit of justice for crimes committed during the violence have been able to advocate at least semiopenly for change. These include SOS Disparus (SOS the disappeared), among other groups.[38]

The period of debate, however limited, on the Civil Concord and the Charter provided a ripe environment for Algeria's most influential cartoonists to intervene and express their opinions on official peace measures. Despite Human Rights Watch's negative evaluation of free speech during the Charter campaign, caricaturists seem to have been able to liberally communicate their thoughts on the reconciliation measures without much fear of repression, at least at the time the measures were being passed through the referendum. These cartoonists voiced sharp, articulate, and at times searing opinions concerning the terms of the peace agreements and reminded readers of ongoing and past violence, implying that deals with the armed groups would not bring peace. Instead, they would violate the memory of Algerians who had perished in the conflict, a memory that cartoonists kept alive for readers. In this regard, Algeria's caricaturists kept in step—knowingly or unknowingly—with creators of humor from other parts of the globe where reconciliation processes took place that they considered to be inadequate or incomplete.[39]

BAKHTIN'S CARNIVAL, VIRTUAL JUSTICE, AND SOCIAL MEMORY FORMATION IN RECONCILIATION CARICATURES

Russian philosopher Mikhail Bakhtin's writings regarding medieval European carnival and its influence on Renaissance literature offer some ideas for interpreting many Algerian caricaturists' responses to the reconciliation process. Bakhtin may have derived his thoughts on carnival from his experiences living in Stalin's Soviet Union, lending a more modern applicability to the work.[40] Bakhtin defined carnivals as popular celebrations with several distinctive characteristics. They were medieval festivals, initially for Lent, that authorities had to sanction; popular appetite for these affairs overpowered any objections rulers could raise. Everyone at the carnival could be subjected to the public's humor.[41] By the very nature of the drive toward upholding carnival traditions against rulers' desires, revelers highlighted the constraints and limits of those authorities' power. Furthermore, medieval revelers during carnival strove to create a world that upended the normal structure of things for the purpose of regeneration.[42] Toward the end of establishing an alternate hierarchy of power, the regenerative factor of Bakhtinian carnival often involved "grotesque realism." Fools or carnival participants carried out grotesque realist acts by showcasing genitalia and by associating leaders or higher-ups with the ground or dirt.[43]

Caricatures from the late 1990s and early 2000s that questioned the government's handling of the peace process built on earlier patterns of ridicule and jest in the country while also crafting work similar to the conventions of carnival in Bakhtin's view. The regime further seemed incapable of quelling the force of this art given the persistence of critical jabs at the regime in cartoons even when caricaturists faced judicial proceedings for their work. Thus, as with carnival, the government may have been powerless to stop the inertia of caricatures. "Kings" and other individuals singled out by cartoonists for derision may have witnessed a decline in citizens' actual belief in their prowess. Reactions on the part of the regime to illustrations from this time suggest that it viewed these sketches as powerful enough to undercut its legitimacy.

Cartoons may have helped preserve Algerian social memories of the Black Decade in the face of official amnesia. Jacob Mundy has noted that Algeria's reconciliation process was aimed at concluding the conflict without ascribing it a history, a collective story, or narratives that the nation as a whole could use in the future when referring to events. Into this void entered several Algerian artists (in Mundy's study, filmmakers) who tried to fill in this blank part of

Algeria's history.[44] Yet, the government has not truly cast a veil over the time that the Black Decade occupied in Algeria's history. Regardless of who occupied the *kursī* ("chair" in Arabic and a term Algerians use for the highest position in the regime when discussing politics), the state had spent years curating specific articulations of what was happening during the Time of Terrorism. Its insistence on the country "turning the page and moving forward" without investigations into the conflict's armed actors meant that it wanted its previous versions of the violence to stand uncorrected.[45] This issue of preservation versus alteration of voices and stories came to a prominent head in the work of the country's most popular caricaturists, who had long been pushing back against official government narratives of the violence by the late 1990s.[46]

Through preserving and potentially shaping social memories, Algerian cartoonists appeared to try to use their oeuvres as a means of achieving public recognition of the 1990s horrors. They persisted in detailing recent and past violence, to the chagrin of the state seeking both reconciliation and acceptance of its official version of affairs (namely, that the military and citizens valiantly combatted armed terrorists). Films such as 2004's *Viva Laldjérie* constituted rare public acknowledgments of the conflict's horrors.[47] Cartoons similarly kept memories of the war alive and attested to its more horrendous aspects, but on a daily basis and as political decisions to resolve the conflict were being made. This art seems to have drummed up memory for concrete political purposes. Its consumers may have formed social non-movements of memory activists against official forgetting of the Time of Terrorism.

Indeed, cartoons' carnival spirit sought to undermine state peace efforts and to engender what Ranjana Khanna has called "virtual justice" in an Algerian setting.[48] Through this humor, artists intended to critique the state and rebels in overt ways, leaning toward the types of satire contained within carnival: a drawing down of those on high to keep them closer to the population. In other words, they sought to preserve and mobilize social memories surrounding the conflict and, in the process, hold belligerents accountable for the bloodshed, with symbolic lowering and humiliation their punishment. The verdicts handed down by Algeria's leading satirists in a court of public opinion on Islamists/rebels and on reconciliation measures and their proponents proved so strong that the state at several points attempted to curb their influence. While it is difficult to determine whether this body of art held sway over Algerian communities, regime retaliation indicated that the state feared that it did. Cartoonists such as Dilem, Ayoub, and Le Hic would determine what would be remembered and who would be held responsible for their crimes—if not in reality, then in their (regenerated) worlds and the minds of their readers.

THE RAGE, RANCOR, AND REVELRY OF ALI DILEM

Of the three cartoonists investigated here due to their popularity and activism against reconciliation, Dilem most stridently employed carnivalesque humor to seek justice not otherwise attainable for the Black Decade's victims and survivors. He further attacked the reconciliation process as too lenient toward individuals suspected of harming the populace and not effective enough at halting the then-continuing violence. His comedy transformed at this moment into a force that no longer aligned with state narratives as it had earlier in the 1990s, when the prevailing sections of the government, like many artists, opposed dialogue with rebels. As a result, unlike the revelers of medieval carnival whom Bakhtin contemplates, Dilem found himself a target of the regime.

By the time of the reconciliation process, Dilem had had nearly a decade to refine his style and to age from a young fine arts student to a seasoned veteran of Algeria's cartooning industry. He stood, in fact, as the only artist to continuously publish in Algerian dailies throughout the 1990s conflict. From a maelstrom of events that coalesced to rob the caricaturist of his mentor, his neighborhood, his friends, and, arguably, his youth, emerged a pen singularly capable of contesting reconciliation policies toward the armed groups with scathing, farcical skill.

Dilem's cartoons unabashedly called into question the validity of and the justice present (or absent) in the government's late 1990s and early 2000s peace. Arguably, among all of the country's caricaturists, Dilem most strongly contested the facet of the Law of Civil Concord and the Charter that granted immunity to former members of the armed groups, thereby permitting them to reintegrate into society. The terms of the peace agreements were designed to help the repentant ones, mainly AIS militants and later members of other groups, be seamlessly reabsorbed into the population. It appears that in Dilem's eyes, however, the repentant militants should remain distinguished and apart from the rest of society. His body of work from the late 1990s through 2005 or so echoes this viewpoint by marking them as fundamentally different from civilians and still a threat to the latter.

For instance, while Bouteflika's regime and its supporters wanted to turn the page on the recent turmoil in the country, Dilem kept the memory of the conflict alive by referencing the purported past wrongdoings of the amnestied insurgents in his cartoons. He accomplished this task in carnivalesque ways that stressed the former rebels' debased and material character. Figure 5.2 exemplifies this broader trend in his work. The caricaturist published it on January 11, 2000, two days before Bouteflika's amnesty of the AIS came into effect and the

Figure 5.2. "The repentant ones return home." Dilem, *Liberté*, January 11, 2000, 24.

group's adherents were scheduled to turn themselves in to state authorities. The title reads, "The 'repentant' ones return home." The cartoon's action takes place in a domestic setting. One of Dilem's run-of-the-mill terrorists is standing outside of a home with the door open. He carries a sack on his shoulder instead of a smoking gun, a sign that he is indeed one of the ex-members of a rebel organization coming back to his homestead for the first time since the start of the conflict. A woman in a *niqāb* (a black face covering) is in front of the door with her hand on a little boy's head. Presumably, she is the man's spouse who has come out to meet her long-absent husband. The man points to the boy and asks, "This is my son?" The woman replies, "There's a possibility. Which false checkpoint were you in in 1995?" The wife's response implies that the son resulted from her being raped by a member of the armed groups, perhaps from the same organization that her husband had spent years fighting in.[49]

Dilem turned the supposed crimes of the armed insurgents back on them. The returning Islamist/rebel, the usual harbinger of horror in Dilem's world, finds himself the injured party of an insurgent tactic that his own wife believes he employed: another rebel raped his wife, and he now has to raise a son who is most likely not his own. Dilem often played with social codes and stigmas, so it would not be unfathomable that, by suggesting that repentant ones' wives may themselves have been the victims of rape while their spouses were away, he meant to ridicule them for no longer having wives who exclusively had sex with them. As in some other parts of the world, certain parts of Maghribi societies considered the rape of a woman a source of shame not only for the survivor but for her family and husband. Rape during the Black Decade was discussed, but many communities still viewed the subject as taboo.[50] Furthermore, the group overwhelmingly benefiting from Bouteflika's amnesty agreements at the time, and the one to which this man most likely belonged given his *repenti* status, was the AIS. This group had always insisted that it never attacked civilian targets. Therefore, this man would not have been present at a fake checkpoint according to the AIS line. Yet, the wife's suspicion that her husband could have manned one of these traps that targeted civilians undercuts this claim. It also goes against the assertion of Bouteflika's regime that the Concord's terms would not be extended to rapists. In this image, the woman expresses her belief that her husband, a *repenti*, could have raped women. With this carefully crafted piece of satire, Dilem questions the truthfulness of the AIS and the government while also, once again, delivering a stinging put-down of the repentant ones. He likewise attests to one of the most horrific aspects of the Time of Terrorism.

The carnivalesque, furthermore, enters into the boundaries of this illustration's frame. The drawing alludes to the genitalia as well as the fecundity of both the man returning home and his wife. The debased action of rape has borne fruit, but the child, according to well-documented contemporary social standards in Algeria that Dilem's readers would recognize, would struggle to survive both the government's bureaucracy and socially determined stigma. Children born out of wedlock were not allotted certain rights under Algeria's legal system and faced social discrimination.[51] Despite the man's decision to give up his weapons, a fly still circles the figure. Dilem persists in associating the man with base, earthly filth, as though the stain of the armed groups would continue to color him for the foreseeable future.

This drawing likewise mixes the profane and the sacred: a former rebel who was supposedly fighting in the name of his religion completely violated its tenets by raping a woman. The caricature additionally testifies to the reality that many assailants in the war were masked and unidentifiable to their victims; even a wife may have been unable to recognize that her assailant was her husband. By emphasizing the ambiguities of the crimes reportedly committed by the armed rebel groups, Dilem perhaps meant to call attention to one of the major flaws of the peace agreements: the impossibility of knowing for certain which armed rebel had committed what crime in the absence of more thorough investigative processes. Finally, the cartoon reminds readers that, regardless of the amnesty agreements and the reassimilation of former Islamist combatants into Algerian society, the consequences of the conflict are ongoing; the son exists, he is there, and he will have to be taken care of from now on. Such an assertion challenged the notion that the amnesty agreements could fully permit Algerians to turn the page on their recent, bloody past.

As illustrated in his cartoon of rebels descending the mountain, Dilem's reconciliation art often referenced the bowels, lower-stratum bodily functions, and orifices through which the body digests and expels material or procreates. Dilem's work, indeed, entered the realm of grotesque realism by pointing to bodily functions of individuals involved in the reconciliation process. Other examples of grotesque realism in Dilem's cartoons abound. After Bouteflika's first election to the presidency in April 1999, Dilem drew a ballot box as a toilet seat, complete with bathroom tissue to the side. Each individual square had the new president's name etched onto it.[52] These symbols collectively represent a clear, scatological effort to denounce the candidate who was running on a pro-peace platform. At various points in Dilem's repertoire of satirical drawings, the artist drew generals naked with their genitals and anuses rubbing up against newspapers, depicted water spouts as penises, and alluded to the sexuality of Algerian politicians.[53] One cartoon implied that Bouteflika had slept with Boumediene when he served "under" the former head of state. Rumors did exist asserting that Bouteflika had served as a receptive partner in anal sex with Boumediene, a way for the latter to exact submission from the younger politician. The cartoon's content evokes the libido and particularly the anal cavity of the then president while also signaling that he might have been gay, a strong accusation in an Algerian context and a hefty one to lob at the unmarried Bouteflika among Algerian communities.[54] Later in the 2000s, Ali Dilem described a potential scenario to the journalist Mustapha Benfodil in which he would draw the general Mohamed Mediene called "Toufik" wiping his mouth with an Always-brand maxi pad.[55]

Beyond bodily fluids, Bakhtin associated corporeal bulk with grotesque realism as well.[56] Dilem conjured generals with stomachs so girthy that they could dance like women with scarves around their lower bodies, a common way of dancing at Maghribi weddings, upon learning the happy news that petroleum prices were rising.[57] Thus, Dilem dabbled in the world of what Bakhtin would consider popular carnival through allusions to the grotesque to communicate his message of distaste for peace initiatives as well as figures of power.

Death also appears as an occasion for laughter and joy, however perverse, in the world of Dilem's drawings and in line with carnivalesque portraits of demise.[58] Dilem battled the idea that the Concord had put the country on the path toward tranquility through ironically joyful references to death; carnivalesque tropes, once again, proved critical tools of his arsenal in a war against the regime's terms of peace. The caricaturist reminded readers that agents continued carrying out horrific acts in the country and that, perhaps like the rape survivor in the cartoon that we have just examined, Algerians were in no position to put the past squarely behind them.

On August 16, 1999, Dilem published a cartoon (fig. 5.3) that echoed a common message in his work as well as the editorial line of his paper, *Liberté*, in the weeks leading up to the Concord referendum. For the paper and its cartoonist, it was strange to expect Algerians still traumatized by past crimes and threatened by potential future ones to vote rationally on whether to forgive suspected assailants. On that day, mere weeks before Algerians cast their ballots, newspapers announced that a massacre two nights before at the town of Bechar had left twenty-nine people dead and three injured. Dilem's picture that day showed the town awash in blood and human body parts, with vultures circling the carnage's remnants. Words above the strewn corpses proclaimed, "Bechar: survey on the intentions of the population concerning the vote on Bouteflika's Civil Concord." One of Dilem's Islamists/rebels stands to the left side of the picture and seems to answer what the results of such a survey would be, observing, "Here, the people are really divided." This assertion contains an obvious play on words since the landscape is covered with dismembered body parts and the man is holding a bloodied knife. In contrast to supporters of Bouteflika's Law of Civil Concord, including papers lionizing the president's efforts and presenting an optimistic outlook for reconciliation, Dilem offered a vision of the country still deadlocked in turmoil with no end in sight and with deadly results for civilians. In short, the work appears to underscore the artist's conviction that reconciliation would prove fruitless, that violence would persist unabated, and that civilians were not yet secure enough to make informed decisions about peace.[59]

Furthermore, through this cartoon, Dilem crafts his own folk world that replicates the real one but festively points to death to harness what Bakhtin might consider a "second life."[60] The latter implies a new environment wherein structures are overturned and all individuals are made equally ridiculous. While not necessarily allowing the bounds of reality to be discarded or disrupted (except that readers gain access to horrific scenes whose images were strongly controlled by the government), the armed man bearing a bloodied knife still manages to deliver an excoriatingly honest pun.[61] This pun further relates to the deaths of the individuals, a sign of gaiety even amid tragedy that was hardly visualized in other media during this period.

Figure 5.3. "Here, the people are really divided [on the referendum]."

Additionally, in this sketch and others like it, Dilem did not hesitate to imply that one of the reasons the violence had yet to cease was the purportedly intractable criminal nature of Islamists/rebels. As with his work from earlier in the 1990s, Islamists/rebels showed themselves time and again in drawings to be innately violent.[62] In pictures concerning amnestied former insurgents, the men still retain their earlier physical appearance allotted to them by Dilem when drawing them in active rebellion. They are short with dark beards and hair, and all appear alike (see figs. 5.1 and 5.2).

Other drawings by the famed artist from El-Harrach communicated that the state under Bouteflika's charge was erring in its handling of the Black Decade's resolution. It seems as though the architect of Algeria's most well-known news caricature series entrusted the task of calling out the president and the problematic terms of his reconciliation proceedings to one specific character in his arsenal of Algerian every-people. Time and again, Dilem mobilized his Madame Algeria character in the late 1990s and early 2000s to have her upbraid politicians over reconciliation. She stands among a wider array of Dilem characters, which includes visa-hungry youth and *hittistes* (wall-holders, a pun for unemployed youth), epitomizing the supposed simplicity of Algerian civilians, an example of ever-present self-derision in Algerian humor and comedy.[63] For instance, as Algerians were about to express their confidence for Bouteflika's vague plan for peace in the September 1999 referendum, Dilem portrayed Madame Algeria ridiculously swooning over the single Bouteflika, a mark of her lack of decorum and how her decisions could be driven by libido. The drawing may have reflected the artist's frustration that his fellow citizens voted in favor of the plan.[64]

Madame Algeria may have even functioned as a ridiculous version of the famed and mythologized War of Independence *mujāhidāt* (written as *moudjahida*, plural *moudjahidat* in French). These women worked for national independence between 1954 and 1962 as part of the FLN, with some earning national and international attention. The haik (*ḥāyak*) headscarf that Dilem's character unfailingly dons had earned a reputation for evoking an authentic Algeria that many after independence believe the female War of Independence participants embodied.[65] Contrary to nationally celebrated heroines such as real *mujāhidāt* Djamila Bouhired and Zohra Drif, dynamic figures and well-educated university students at the time of the revolution, Dilem's readers never witness Madame Algeria in another attire, nor does she possess a formal education. The *mujāhidāt* symbolized the supposedly courageous, steadfast, and serious demeanor of Algerian women when confronted with the violence of a colonial regime. The *mujāhidāt* had also come out to protest policies such as the 1984 Family Code that they saw as noxious to the nation.[66] While equally a patriot, Madame Algeria can show herself a fool, as when she fawns over the single Bouteflika, her interest in romance causing her to support his September 1999 referendum.[67]

Dilem invented his Madame Algeria as early as 1992 in the pages of *Le Matin* when he initially anointed her with this moniker.[68] Dilem employed Madame Algeria in the mid-1990s only once every few weeks or months. Beginning in January 1999, though, that pattern changed. Amid a presidential election where Bouteflika appeared as virtually the only candidate and the one unabashedly favored by the regime, the artist started using the character with mounting frequency.[69] She had become so omnipresent in Dilem's work during Bouteflika's presidency and reconciliation that, in his 2008 book on the artist, Benfodil notes that the he "serves up" "episode after episode" of "the adventures of this Lady of the Haïk, the heroine of this sitcom full of love and of hatred that is the House of Algeria."[70] Once a student so interested in Algerian humor that he tried to write a master's thesis on the topic, Benfodil compared this haik-clad figure to Palestinian cartoonist Nājī al-'Alī's Handala or Algerian writer Kateb Yacine's Nedjma, characters who symbolized their nations.[71] Dilem's turn to a character intended to speak for the nation at a moment when Bouteflika, a new, pro-reconciliation president, was coming to power may have been purposeful. Her sudden movement to the center stage of Dilem's carnivalesque rendition of the world may have signaled that the artist considered the state to be in confrontation with the people precisely because it was embracing peace with the armed groups.

Yet, as with her creator and his fellow artists, the character of Madame Algeria did not go after the state as a whole. Rather, she singled out specific figures in the government for purportedly betraying the Algerian every-person whom she emblemized. She wagged her finger at cronies of the regime: corrupt, pot-bellied generals; ineffective bureaucrats; and, regularly, Bouteflika himself.[72] Quite significantly, Madame Algeria, and by extension her creator, refrained from attacking or calling out foot soldiers in the army or blue-collar police officers; in fact, Dilem only rarely went after the rank and file of the army or police.[73] Dilem distinguished between government elites such as the generals and members of the state occupying its lower strata. In sum, the artist used Madame Algeria as an emblem of the nation, potentially a slanted take on the mujāhidāt, to harass certain state figures at the moment of reconciliation. She therefore echoes earlier humorous products in the country that represented or spoke for the nation or a national every-person, such as Slim's Bouzid character.[74]

For instance, Dilem's caricature that "commemorated" the first anniversary of the referendum (fig. 5.4) showcased an angry Madame Algeria yelling at "Boutef," the artist's nickname (along with the more feminine "Atika") for the then-new president.[75] In the wake of persistent violence sown purportedly by the remaining armed groups (violence did continue into 2000), she admonishes, "In the end, you didn't bring peace to Algerians, but left the terrorists in peace!" To the right of the image, two of Dilem's "bearded ones" were up to their old tricks, hacking away at a poor civilian.[76] Her words relate a truth that Dilem insinuates Bouteflika is ignoring: violence is still underway in Algeria. Bakhtin remarked that insight from representations of carnivals often hailed from the "mouths of fools."[77] Like the former female War of Independence fighters whose image of valor she may be upending, the sometimes foolish, sometimes wise Madame Algeria spoke truth to powerful individuals whom Dilem seems to have wanted to hold responsible for hurting the nation through reconciliation.

Beyond the use of a potential fool, this particular drawing engages with the carnivalesque in other ways. Bouteflika carries a ballot box and, very significantly, gazes past an enraged (based on her furrowed brow and eyes as well as her words) Madame Algeria to lock eyes with the men slaughtering the civilian. Hearts float around the pair of terrorists as well as the president's head.[78] They most likely insinuate in a humorous fashion that the president's ill-founded rapprochement with the AIS stems from his being duped or falling prey to his own unfounded sentiments, as Dilem equates romantic feelings with silliness.

Figure 5.4. "One year ago, Algerians voted for the Civil Concord."
Dilem, *Liberté*, September 17, 2000, 24.

The ballot box in Bouteflika's hands represents his possession of authority, a symbolic crowning or nod to his power, albeit one that sits on illegitimate grounds given Dilem's penchant for criticizing elections during this period. Through this cartoon, the reader once again witnesses death juxtaposed with joy and allusions to romantic love that Algerians would typically deem inappropriate. The image is full of carnivalesque material intended to ridicule both the armed groups and the president while questioning the Civil Concord's vitality.[79]

Bouteflika's peace efforts were so integral to the politician's overall political platform that many of Dilem's drawings on the increasingly unpopular figure into the early 2000s indirectly debated the value of his reconciliation measures.[80] Indeed, during this period after the referendum, Dilem arguably went after Bouteflika with more vigor than that with which he had targeted previous presidents, including Ali Kafi and Liamine Zeroual. And, as with the folk carnival traditions of medieval western Europe, his daily sketches had possibly gathered too much strength for the state to oppose them.

That seems to have been the case at least until international attention shifted away from the country after Bouteflika's first election to the presidency.[81] During the late 1990s and early 2000s reconciliation period, Dilem severed Bouteflika, the head generals in his government (including Mohamed Mediene and Khaled Nezzar), and repentant ones from the nation to reconfigure these actors as the people's enemies. These messages seem to have resonated too strongly for the regime's taste. In May 2001, after the country had concluded the Civil Concord referendum, Algeria's National Assembly, the government's major legislative body, passed a series of amendments to the country's penal code regarding freedom of expression. Articles 144 and 146 clarified the punishment for persons found guilty of "harming" either the republic's president or members of a number of its institutions, including the army, "in terms containing injury, insult, or defamation, whether by writing, by drawing, or by declaration, whatever medium used: audio, electronic, digital, or otherwise." The code authorized sentences of three to twelve months and 50,000 to 250,000 dinars (then the equivalent of approximately several hundred to several thousand dollars) to its violators. Fines and prison sentences were to be doubled for recidivists.[82]

It is challenging to trace precisely when and by whom these measures were first connected to Dilem, but, in June of that year (2001), the artist went on a hunger strike to denounce these restrictions on freedom of speech in the country.[83] Very early on, in popular parlance, these statutes collectively became known as the "Dilem amendment." This moniker may have especially gained popularity after the government first used the legislation to crack down on the cartoonist.[84] As the decision to adopt this language in the penal code proved too sensitive for me to investigate with official sources, it is difficult to know whether Dilem's direct work haranguing the state inspired this legislation, as the artist's supporters believed. What is known is that it was only after his campaign against the Concord and his sketches against Bouteflika that the artist was crowned "the *pouvoir's* [regime's] nightmare" by *Le Monde*, the world's most widely read French-language newspaper.[85]

Authorities first used the amendments to respond to a Dilem cartoon that they believed attacked the country's military elite in January 2002. The November 29, 2001, drawing in question displayed Dilem's version of the country's generals condescendingly handing out money to residents of Algiers's Bab El-Oued neighborhood after a spate of floods. The picture insinuated that the generals were corrupt.[86] However, the second caricature that resulted in Dilem's appearance before the tribunal of Algiers engaged directly in matters linked to the ongoing security situation in the country as well as the legacy of the Time of Terrorism. The piece implicated Khaled Nezzar, one of Algeria's leading generals in the early 1990s, and another general in the ultimately successful plot to assassinate Boudiaf, Algeria's fourth president, who was killed only months after he returned to the country in 1992 to helm the state following the end of the democratic transition.[87] His death is broadly deemed a key episode in Algeria's ultimate descent into the armed struggle of the 1990s.[88] A courtroom speech to a judge and lawyers representing the Ministry of National Defense revealed the caricaturist's own view on the power of his art to effect change or influence ideas.[89]

When asked about the meaning of the cartoon in question, Dilem's lawyer retorted that the judge would have to ask the plaintiff, the Ministry of National Defense as represented by Colonel Ammar Boussis and two lawyers, why it was so "damaged" by the image. The artist went on to insist, "I have nothing to explain. My interpretation is there [in the drawing]. Where do you see that I accused the army of liquidating Boudiaf? There are people who said it, his son Nacer [Boudiaf] said it. Me, I am a caricaturist. I take facts, declarations, and I comment on them in my own way." When asked about the source of information that incriminated Nezzar in the fourth Algerian president's death, the artist responded, "But I don't have a source, I am a caricaturist. I draw inspiration from the events that I read about, the declarations of one person or another. Then, I make my *mickey* [a term derived from the Disney character for a silly product that Algerians widely use to debase someone or something, often their own country, as absurd]. The plan [to challenge someone politically] doesn't exist, it's a fiction."[90] His lawyer, Khaled Bourayou, added, "Dilem is an artist, not a journalist. His source of information is his spirit." Later, the attorney directly challenged the representative of the Ministry of National Defense, Colonel Amar Boussis, on his understanding of what precisely a caricature was and could be. When the latter declared that such knowledge was beyond his expertise, the counsel questioned why the trial was taking place at all.[91]

Here, Dilem and his counsel vehemently rejected the notion that his art truly added any information or discourse to general discussions of events underway in Algeria and around the world; he simply provided his own humorous, unserious perspective of these current affairs. Furthermore, according to this testimony, the impact of his work depended on others' reading. Of course, the context of these exchanges mattered; Dilem and his lawyer were working in the courtroom to avoid the full weight of the penal code amendments. His very presence in the courtroom indicated the power of Dilem's art to provoke controversy and conversation as well as the government's suspicions that the small square dedicated each day to the cartoonist's "mickey" resonated far beyond its limited space. Dilem continued to face trials for the first several years of the new millennium, thirty-eight in total. By 2006, he had earned nine years of prison sentences, although all were suspended so that he avoided an actual extensive stay in jail.[92] His long sessions in court nonetheless deprived him of time and resources, even if he managed to pursue his art undeterred.

Although his insistence that he only represented preexisting ideas holds validity in this case, his drawings amplified messages circulating around the country and found an audience with his readers. This is not to suggest that the Ministry of National Defense's attacks on Dilem and *Liberté* had merit. Instead, they point to a real fear on the part of the government of the power of Dilem's work to chip away at their legitimacy or reputation, particularly as it pertained to an incident of violence often considered part of the Black Decade. The Ministry of Defense's decision to pursue the artist in court may have also reflected a desire to illustrate the strength of the state in front of a cartoonist who had often employed his art to, in the cartoonist's words, "demystify this *'pouvoir'* [an Algerian term for the regime]."[93] To make Dilem cower or waste time and energy in court would be to show that the government could interrupt his work and equally ideologically hail the artist in an Althusserian sense, forcing him to respond to their authority, and, in the process, attempt to demean him as his work did them.[94]

Moreover, the Dilem affair arrived at a moment between elections and peace legislation referendums, when the country was not drawing significant international attention. His arrests at this time suggest that the state may have wanted to move earlier to try to muzzle the artist but had to refrain until the country was no longer under as much external observation. Dilem's appearances before the court took place against a larger backdrop of state repression of the private press in the early 2000s but between Bouteflika's major peace initiatives.[95] As lead human rights advocate and lawyer Ali Yahia Abdennour stated in a 2004 interview with Moroccan news outlet *TelQuel*, "Newspapers obey [the regime] without receiving orders, not for reasons that the editors deem good, but out of fear of judicial proceedings."[96] In other words, the new legal code permitted the military to suppress incendiary speech from private newspapers by rendering the defense of such discourse in court too draining to undertake.

This intimidation does not appear to have worked in Dilem's case. In addition to deftly sidestepping prosecutors' questions about the intentions of his work, Dilem's habit of challenging the state's narrative of conflict ending due to its reconciliation procedures extended into the period of the 2005 Charter for Peace and Reconciliation campaign. Figure 5.5 attests to this continued inclination in his work. The drawing's caption states, "My hand is extended." Rather than putting forth an open hand for a gracious handshake, though,

Figure 5.5. "Madani Mezrag supports the Charter for Peace [and Reconciliation]."

AIS leader Madani Mezrag gives the Algerian equivalent of a middle finger. The gesture is a vulgar one that evokes a phallus. Mezrag shows this grotesque display associated with genitalia, the lower body, to no one in particular. It consequently seems that Dilem meant for readers to believe that Mezrag was giving them, or the government or the Algerian people, a sign of disrespect. Mezrag, a figure proclaiming to represent the sacred, indulges in the profane, a clear means for Dilem to degrade the AIS emir's offer of peace.[97] This cartoon symbolically lowers Mezrag and his authority in other ways that call into question the feasibility of the Charter by insinuating that the man will not give up his bloody mission and that the government's efforts may be disingenuous. What is more, the word *peace* is inscribed on a dog food dish on the ground behind the AIS leader. Mezrag treats actual peace as a dog, an insult in some Islamic and Maghribi societies due to the association of dogs with filth that requires extra cleaning. Mezrag abuses peace like Bouteflika mistreats the Algerian people in Dilem's art, where he often placed a similar bowl bearing the word *people* next to the president's desk. To further emphasize Mezrag's dirty undertakings and in line with the artist's general rendering of Islamists, flies and a bat buzz around the figure. Dilem further assigns to Mezrag, a man who was embracing a laying down of arms, the typical symbols that the artist gave rebels to signify their purportedly violent character: a recently used weapon along with a subdued civilian victim behind the dog dish.[98] The caricaturist once again implies that the Algerian people cannot anticipate that the repentant ones will prove peaceful.

Finally, through his drawings of this period, Dilem appears to have sought to keep the memory of the victims of the 1990s fresh in his readers' minds while criticizing the state for its reconciliation policies. Through a cartoon (fig. 5.6) printed on October 27, 2005, the artist expressed his view that continued overtures made to armed insurgents insulted the conflict's victims. The piece addressed a report that the government was negotiating with Hassan Hattab, a former leader of the GIA who had founded the Salafist Group for Preaching and Combat. That organization embraced connections to international jihadis and eventually declared allegiance to Al-Qaeda. Dilem sketched his Madame Algeria figure enraged as she held up a newspaper to another citizen with the headline, "The government [*pouvoir*] is negotiating with Hattab." The title of the image announces, "200,000 graves desecrated [*profanées*]."[99] The artist produced this drawing after the Charter had been approved, but its heading reminds readers of the stakes still at play, that Algerians had died en masse and that some of the elements behind their deaths were still loose and might be pardoned. Hattab had actually been condemned to death in absentia by a court in 2003, a detail the caricaturist leaves out, but negotiations could have bought the rebel leader clemency. The artist also critically reproduces the number of dead from the war that the government emphasized during Bouteflika's second term. That number was double the one that officials had touted only a few years previously while violence had actually waned.[100] The bloodshed was devastating, according to Dilem. Its victims merited better forms of remembrance through the punishment of their tormentors, a message that kept the memory of the conflict alive for readers. Playing with similarities between the words *amnesia* and *amnesty*, the cartoonist had also drawn armed militants celebrating the earlier Concord as "a general amnesia for the victims of terrorism" instead of a general amnesty for the AIS.[101] Dilem named and fought against this amnesia when it came to the Charter as well.

During both peace legislation campaigns, Dilem persisted in challenging the terms of reconciliation and dialogue through practices that Bakhtin associated with carnival. He was not alone in this endeavor.

Figure 5.6. "200,000 graves desecrated."

LE HIC'S AND AYOUB'S SYMBOLIC LOWERING OF THE ARMED GROUPS AND THE STATE IN LIGHT OF RECONCILIATION

By the time of Bouteflika's campaign for the Civil Concord Law, another cartoonist had begun to occupy a prime spot on the country's French-language caricaturing scene. Le Hic, a pseudonym for Hicham Baba Ahmed, took over for Slim at *Le Matin* in 1999.[102] While the paper was not published at the time of the referendum for the Charter, Le Hic confronted the question of the Civil Concord in 1999. At this time, like Dilem, he used carnivalesque work to ridicule the agents behind the reconciliation efforts, to judge them through unofficial means, and to stress that the population was not behind Bouteflika's platform to restore peace in the country.

On the whole, the young caricaturist's work contained many of the same messages that Dilem's did. He made it clear through his daily drawings that the soldiers of the AIS were dark, angry, volatile creatures; amnesty and

"DANCING ON COFFINS" AND DRUMMING UP MEMORY 217

Figure 5.7. The "repentant ones" from the AIS sing the national anthem with skulls pinned to their chests in place of medals.

reintegration into Algerian society could not transform them into peaceful civilians and magically undo their supposed past crimes. Le Hic had drawn his armed men as short with black hair and flies floating around them, not too distinct from Dilem's grotesque and carnivalesque versions except in the style in which the newer artist depicted them.

Furthermore, his portrayal of these men did not shift with their impending reentry into Algerian civil society. Figure 5.7 graced the cover of *Le Matin*'s

January 12, 2000, edition. It shows AIS men, now repentant, still in their *qamīs* and beards. They stand on an athletes' podium, the kind used for medal ceremonies after a major sporting event. The reader knows that these armed men belonged to the AIS because the headline of the cover reads, "Bouteflika Amnesties the AIS." They join their voices together in a resounding "Kassaman," the title of Algeria's national anthem, meaning "I pledge." Of course, as with other national anthems, this song would be played for Algerian athletes who had won some great championship as medals hung around their necks. In place of the medals, though, the reader sees skulls, a testament to their previous violent behavior and possibly a sign that the cartoonist thinks of the amnesty as the state's celebration of the rebels' clearly deadly achievements.

The national anthem of Algeria holds deep and sacred ties to the War of Independence. An FLN partisan and poet, Moufdi Zakaria, composed the song's lyrics in the notorious Algiers Barberousse/Serkadji prison, the site of numerous executions of pro-independence militants. Lacking ink, in the stuff of nationalist myth, Zakaria etched the words on the wall with his own blood. In this drawing, then, Le Hic profanes or has the AIS militants seemingly profane this song, performed as a sign of allegiance to the nation and state. They sing the hallowed tune while filthy and surrounded by flies. Through these associations, Le Hic shows the Civil Concord reducing a performance of Algerian nationalism to a carnivalesque farce. This cartoon shows a world turned upside down, in which supposed perpetrators of atrocities are held up as national heroes while civilians are absent from the festivities. Le Hic, like Dilem, did not perceive Bouteflika's amnesty as granting the militants a moral blank slate; here, he assigns the former members of the AIS physical attributes that distinguish them from civilians who never took up arms. Like contemporary joke-tellers, he portrays the lines between combatants and noncombatants as clear and persisting after rebels turned in their arms. These familiar touchstones perhaps serve as a sign of his lack of faith that the men from the armed groups will be able to come back completely from their rebellion.[103]

Furthermore, again like Dilem, Le Hic could overtly insult the repentant ones. For International Women's Day in 2000, similar to his more established and long-standing colleague, in figure 5.8 Le Hic hinted at supposedly inappropriate sexual conduct of the former armed rebels. The cartoon displays two women in haiks confiding to one another. The conversation follows formulas popular in orally passed jokes, including incongruity in a punchline.[104] The woman to the left tells her friend, "Yesterday, my neighbor . . . you know, the wife of the 'repentant one!' . . . she caught her husband in bed

Figure 5.8. "First March 8th of the Civil Concord."

with his mistress ... she shot at point-blank range ..." The other woman questions, "And then?" "Well ... the goat was immediately killed!" The cartoonist thereby implied that the repentant ones had a particular penchant for having sex with animals. Since the title of the drawing announces, "The first March 8th of the Civil Concord," his purpose appears to be to ridicule the former rebels along with the general idea that they were readmitted into society.[105] The artist also celebrates International Women's Day by depicting civilian women indulging in gossip and a joke at the repentant ones' expense. In line with the carnivalesque, Le Hic here references sexuality or the lower stratum of the body when dealing with an agent of power to debase him and, by extension, the former rebels as a whole. Once more, rebels or repentant ones are engaging in socially reprehensible sexual acts (bestiality).

Other drawings also reflected Le Hic's belief that the peace process was a failure. Similar to Dilem, he suggested a romantic link in some of his work between members of the armed groups and the state. Such a comment on romantic, potentially sexual love between the regime's leaders and terrorists, while far from reality, anchored these political figures to the earthly.[106] Later on in the first decade of the 2000s, Le Hic gave Bouteflika (who continued to profit from his reconciliation legacy) a crown, which arguably lent the leader a ridiculous demeanor and may have attested to his lack of credibility as the leader of a supposedly democratic state.[107] Le Hic carnivalesquely raised up and toppled Algeria's politician leading the attempt to usher the country beyond the violence of the 1990s. And, like Dilem, he paid a price: between the Concord and Charter, Le Hic experienced indirect censure for a cartoon of the generals in 2002 and faced nine lawsuits for drawings that offended authorities.[108]

As with Dilem and Le Hic, Algeria's reigning Arabic-language caricaturist, Ayoub, wielded his art to denounce the reconciliation. He designated the armed men as incapable of peace and even beyond the point of being human. Toward this end, the artist also used bestiality as a way of proverbially and carnivalesquely lowering the rebels down to earth. Numerous drawings show emirs (leaders of armed groups) having donkeys as wives, a clear sign that the artist wished to deride them. Figure 5.9 was one such image.[109] Here, an emir wistfully confides in his companion, a she-ass, referring to her as his "beloved one." He says, "Thankfully you are in my life because I was going to die alone in this mountain." His loneliness may stem from his former comrades taking advantage of the Civil Concord. Indeed, while the beast/man offers readers no sign that he is moving to leave his newer homestead, *El Khabar* printed the drawing in the days after the successful 1999 referendum backing Bouteflika's yet-to-be-specified plans for peace.

Figure 5.9. "My friend the cobbler asked for news about the emir [the name given to armed groups' leaders] and his beloved one." Ayoub, *El Khabar*, August 4, 1999, 24.

Like Dilem and Le Hic, Ayoub wished not only to publicly denigrate the members of the armed groups but also to associate them with aberrant sexual behavior. While the man here is himself a beast, he represents humans and engages in sex with an animal from another species. This association further marked insurgents as outsiders just as they were supposed to be seamlessly rejoining civil society. The donkey, a symbol of stupidity in the Middle East and North Africa, looks back at the artist's transmogrified rebel with loving eyes, hearts swirling around her head. His art was aimed at an Arabic-language audience, and Ayoub turned armed insurgents into fearsome ogre-like creatures that engaged in the activities that were supposed to render them ineligible for amnesty. Indeed, if the Civil Concord were followed to the letter, such beings would most likely not make excellent candidates for forgiveness under the law that had just been supported through a popular referendum.

The monsters that the rebel groups embody in Ayoub's world also sport grotesquely large bellies. In one cartoon, rebel actors behind the violence in

Ayoub's world place a call to an unknown large-gutted man who appears to be running the group. The image suggests that secret coconspirators of the rebel groups are also turning a large profit from the war. Ayoub derides this shady figure (who holds a cordless or cell phone, a sign of his wealth) in a carnivalesque manner through reference to his extended belly.[110] Ayoub especially criticized the reconciliation process for the way that it reportedly provided resources for surrendering men and their families but not for the communities devastated by the fighting. The government offered surrendering armed militants some employment, housing, and financial support. Ayoub juxtaposed the fat stomach that his rebels sport with the thin bodies he assigned ordinary peaceful civilians.[111] In the cartoonist's view, the conflict has worsened inequalities and the lot of average Algerians.

THE POWER OF CARTOONS TO EVOKE A STATE RESPONSE: THE WORK OF PRO-STATE CARTOONISTS DURING THE RECONCILIATION DEBATES

The carnivalesque creations of Dilem, Ayoub, and Le Hic that questioned reconciliation measures were so vituperative that it seems the state assigned artists working in its employ to directly counter them. As Dilem, Ayoub, and Le Hic questioned the soundness of the Concord and Charter, state cartoonists seemingly sought to subvert narratives of their more popular counterparts on the war and peace measures. For example, in a caricature dating to the weeks leading up to the Charter referendum, cartoonist Gharez depicted a member of an armed group offering a flower to a civilian (fig. 5.10). Behind his back, he holds a present, presumably one that he will give to the man in front of him. Whereas in one of Dilem's or Le Hic's drawings we could expect the hand to bear a bomb or a fuse to be poking out of the present to signal its danger, here it appears as if the "bearded one's" offer of peace is sincere. As if to make the picture of reconciliation more idyllic, hearts float above the bearded one's head as he extends the flowers. The individual standing in for Islamists/rebels shares many physical attributes with Dilem's or Le Hic's terrorists: dark, spiky beard and hair, large and prominent teeth and nose, and so on. The title at the top of the image states, "From national arms to national reconciliation." *Arms* here is misspelled in Arabic (with a letter *mīm*, m, and an extra letter *alif*, ā, *musāllaḥa*), but it is because the artist is trying to play with the word *reconciliation*, and how he spells *arms* differs only in one letter from this word (the use of *sīn* instead of *ṣād*).[112] Consequently, the work encourages readers to believe in the capacity of the reconciliation to end the conflict. Quite possibly, the cartoonist

Figure 5.10. "From national arms to national reconciliation." While this drawing may seem tongue-in-cheek, the rest of the newspaper in which it appeared lauded reconciliation measures, a sign that the work was sincere. Gharez, *Echa'ab*, September 19, 2005, 32.

was directly responding to Dilem's or Le Hic's negative notions regarding the Charter and their portrayals of the repentant ones. Flowers here invert the grotesque; the bearded figure is clean and dignified rather than disgusting and thereby debased.

Not one sketch but two produced for the Arabic-language *Echa'ab* displayed an upright Civil Concord, personified as the word in Arabic for "concord," lifting up the nation. Another portrait showed the referendum as a shovel burying terrorism in a grave. An artist likewise envisioned better times for Algeria's intelligentsia as their surroundings evolved from an area filled with trash to one filled with flowers and where they were able to circulate with ostensibly no fear of attack, a break from the 1990s. Repeated associations between seemingly Islamist/rebel figures, as well as the reconciliation more generally, and flowers may have subverted the auras of filth and earthliness in which caricaturists in the private press immersed armed rebels.[113] In a mid-2000s interview with

Benfodil, Dilem explicitly embraced the grotesque when, addressing the Time of Terrorism, he declared, "When you speak about a massacre, you are not going to talk about flowers, *ya errab* [my God]!"[114] Flowers were precisely what state-backed caricaturists drew to signify that the dark scenes that artists such as Dilem, Le Hic, and Ayoub depicted the reconciliation portending for the country were false.

Artists operating at state-run papers grounded their support for reconciliation measures in terms that upended the vastly negative rhetoric concerning the same legislation contained in most private-press caricatures. Along with this body of pro-regime/pro-reconciliation work, the Algerian government's decision between peace legislation campaigns to prosecute the country's lead cartoonists for attacks "on the President of the Republic" lends credence to the notion that their cartoons held sway over the population. At the very least, caricaturists' art was perceived by authorities as having the power to do so. That response, along with the incorporation of referendum-positive caricatures into state-run papers, points to a government calculation that the popularity of these artists and their work was worthy of attack.

CONCLUSION

> It was the humor of despair. I was dancing on coffins, because writing a column is a little like dancing. Nobody comes through an experience like this unscathed. As an Algerian, I'm entitled to laugh at the horror in order to distance myself from it.[115]
>
> —Algerian editorialist Y.B. on writing humorous pieces at the height of violence in the 1990s

In an interview with journalist Thierry Oberlé, Algerian newspaper editorialist Y.B. expressed these words to explain why his writing took a turn toward the satirical in the wake of the summer 1997 massacres. Y.B.'s reason for rendering his compositions more humorous at a moment of profound mourning for his nation is echoed in the reconciliation-era works of the country's major caricaturists. These artists brought out mirth amid the horror. Yet, rather than distancing themselves or their audiences from the violence, they looked at it head-on. And they had important political motivations for doing so.

As with earlier in the 1990s, illustrations offered Algerian cartoonists (and, by extension, their avid readers) a way to reimagine their world. Often, this process involved fashioning scenarios that were unlikely or impossible: a simple, ordinary woman upbraiding the president, a rebel transformed into a beast, and an insurgent getting his comeuppance upon returning home. Time and again, the nation's principal caricaturists depicted instances in which they felt that criminals were being allowed to go free. All the while, their art insisted that civilians were continuing and would continue to suffer as a result of the armed groups' actions. On paper in images that would be printed upward of four hundred thousand times and at the moment of events, these illustrators held agents suspected of extreme violence toward mostly unarmed populations accountable for their crimes in ways unattainable in reality.[116] As they railed against amnesia, Dilem, Le Hic, and Ayoub might have also bound their readers together in a social non-movement against official forgetting of the conflict. Indeed, their work kept the war alive for their followers and might have shaped social memories of the war as it wound down, potentially forging communities with similar visions of the conflict.

The work of Algeria's major cartoonists outside of a revived run of *El Manchar*, which supported Bouteflika's peace initiatives, comprised a complete indictment of the official justice system and its ability to deliver closure to embattled communities across the country. The critiques contained in caricaturists' art reminded the state and wider public of the dubious behavior of powerful actors. Cartoonists such as Dilem, Ayoub, and Le Hic moved judgment of the armed groups out of the courtroom, out of spaces of secret dealings, and into the public sphere. These artists stirred up a popular morality for public view, much in the way the medieval carnival of Bakhtin's focus did.[117] In this way, virtual justice reigned in their work as real justice seemed out of reach.

To spread their stark messages, like Y.B., Dilem, Ayoub, and Le Hic merged levity and gravity to produce laughter amid death and new order amid chaos, spinning out of ink imagined acts of justice and a leveling of powerful figures. Their work cast or reinforced doubt about the legitimacy of the post–Black Decade regime as well as Bouteflika's leadership as it undertook peace initiatives. It certainly attached negative characteristics to or buttressed existing negative attitudes toward insurgents, whether they accepted or declined peace offers. Through their individual work and as suggested by the state's reaction to it, Dilem, Ayoub, and Le Hic shaped views and social memories concerning the conflict's warring sides through their carnivalesque "dancing on the tombs" of some one hundred thousand fellow citizens who perished in the Time of Terrorism. In the process, they created a virtual court of public opinion to seek justice for victims and survivors of the 1990s bloodshed, then still ongoing, that was otherwise unattainable in reality. This justice-seeking, memory-shaping humor built on earlier humorous practices in the country but was still distinctive to this moment and attested to a desire for Islamists/rebels to be held accountable for the Black Decade violence. Once again, humor was a powerful tool that Algerians turned to as they sought to decipher what civil violence and the manner in which it was ending meant for their country. This humor had powerful implications for the nation.

NOTES

1. See chap. 4.

2. January 13, 2000, the day that this cartoon appeared in the daily paper *La Liberté*, was the deadline for members of the Islamic Salvation Army to put down their arms and reintegrate into civil society. An October 1997 peace truce along with the Law of Civil Concord permitted the members of this particular insurgent organization who laid down their arms to reenter civil society.

3. Dilem, "Dilem," *La Liberté*, January 13, 2000, 24. Image also reprinted in *Boutef président*.

4. For examples of pro-reconciliation legislation cartoons, see Chawki Amari's work in *La Tribune* until 1996. While opposing earlier peace initiatives, *El Manchar* came out in favor of the 1999 Civil Concord. "Pour la Concorde Civile," *El Manchar*, August 28–September 3, 1999, 2. See also the cartoon in *El Manchar*, September 25–October 1, 1999, 6.

5. See M. M. Bakhtin, *Rabelais and His World*, trans. Helene Iswolsky (Bloomington: University of Indiana Press, 1984).

6. Asef Bayat, *Life as Politics: How Ordinary People Change the Middle East*, 2nd ed. (Palo Alto: Stanford University Press, 2013).

7. I am using Geoffrey Cubbit's definition of social memories to stress how social contexts influence the ways that events are remembered and how those memories are created and transmitted. See Geoffrey Cubbit, *History and Memory* (Manchester: Manchester University Press, 2007).

8. I owe this observation of caricatures as commenting in real time to the 1990s violence to Sandra Rousseau.

9. Interview with Hicham Baba Ahmed, June 25, 2013.

10. Dilem, *Liberté*, January 16, 2000, 24.

11. See chap. 3.

12. See the previous chapter. On some occasions, Dilem cartoons appear to have borrowed wording from popular jokes, and one was a direct extension of a joke.

13. George Joffé, "National Reconciliation and General Amnesty in Algeria," *Mediterranean Politics* 13, no. 2 (2008): 215.

14. The massacres of 1996–1998 are thought to have stemmed in part from the GIA increasing attacks as AIS members were readying to surrender to the state. See Jacob Mundy, *Imaginative Geographies of Algerian Violence* (Palo Alto: Stanford University Press, 2015), 62–82.

15. Martin Evans and John Phillips, *Algeria: Anger of the Dispossessed* (New Haven, CT: Yale University Press, 2007), 214, 244–245, 259. Other forces, such as the state's possible need to bring soldiers who had infiltrated rebel groups back into society, were also likely at play.

16. Evans and Phillips, *Algeria*, 214, 244–245, 259.

17. See Human Rights Watch, *Algeria: Impunity Should Not Be Price of Reconciliation*, August 31, 2005, https://www.hrw.org/news/2005/08/31/algeria-impunity-should-not-be-price-reconciliation.

18. José Garçon, "Algérie: Bouteflika joue l'amnistie," *Libération*, July 5, 1999, https://www.liberation.fr/planete/1999/07/05/algerie-bouteflika-joue-l-amnistie-le-president-annonce-la-liberation-de-milliers-d-islamistes_278448/; text of the Civil Concord, Algeria Watch, December 13, 2009, https://algeria-watch.org/?p=55415.
19. Evans and Phillips, *Algeria*, 263.
20. Joffé, "National Reconciliation," 216.
21. Joffé, "National Reconciliation." See Joffé's article along with Abderrahmane Moussaoui's work on the reconciliation for more information concerning the general amnesty accords and peace agreements in Algeria in the late 1990s through the mid-2000s. Joffé, "National Reconciliation," 213–228; Abderrahmane Moussaoui, "Algérie, la réconciliation entre espoirs et malentendus," *Politique étrangère* 72, no. 2 (2007): 339–350.
22. Human Rights Watch, *Algeria*.
23. See, for example, Nesroulah Yous and Selima Mellah, *Qui a tué à Bentalha? Chronique d'un massacre annoncé* (Paris: Découverte, 2000).
24. "La charte pour la paix et la réconciliation nationale," *Journal officiel de la République Algérienne*, February 28, 2006, 6.
25. "La charte pour la paix," 7.
26. Human Rights Watch, *Algeria*.
27. See, for example, James Le Sueur, *Algeria since 1989: Between Terror and Democracy* (London: Zed Books, 2010), 195–206; Benjamin Stora, "L'amnésie algérienne," Histoire coloniale et postcoloniale, August 6, 2006, https://histoirecoloniale.net/l-amnesie-algerienne-par-Benjamin.html. In a cartoon published just as the Concord was taking hold, Ali Dilem depicted reconciliation as imposing amnesia over victims' testimonies and realities. See Dilem, *Liberté*, January 13, 2000, 2.
28. See Joffé, "National Reconciliation."
29. Evans and Phillips, *Algeria*, 290.
30. Human Rights Watch, *Algeria*.
31. For an overview of some of these reconciliation processes, see Kevin Avruch and Beatriz Vejarano, "Truth and Reconciliation Commissions: A Review Essay and Annotated Bibliography," *Online Journal of Peace and Conflict Resolution* 4, no. 2 (2002): 37–76.
32. Mundy, *Imaginative Geographies*, 25; Joffé, "National Reconciliation," 217.
33. Avruch and Vejarano, "Truth and Reconciliation Commissions," 38–39; Mundy, *Imaginative Geographies*, 138.
34. Mundy covers the various drawbacks of truth and reconciliation commissions, pulling upon literature such as Susan Thomson's *Whispering Truth to Power*. Mundy, *Imaginative Geographies*, 25, citing Susan Thomson, *Whispering Truth to Power: Everyday Resistance to Reconciliation in Post-genocide Rwanda* (Madison: University of Wisconsin Press, 2013).
35. See Mundy, *Imaginative Geographies*, 42–43.
36. Avruch and Vejarano, "Truth and Reconciliation Commissions," 42.
37. See, for instance, Cynthia E. Milton, "At the Edge of the Peruvian Truth Commission: Alternative Paths to Recounting the Past," *Radical History Review* 98 (2007): 3–33.
38. For more about these organizations, see Soraya Laribi, "Les mobilisations des associations de familles et proches des disparus de la décennie noire en Algérie," *Confluences Méditerranée* 114, no. 3 (2020): 177–188.
39. Milton, "At the Edge."
40. Specialists in his treatises, including one of his major translators, have declared that through his study of carnival and its subversive properties Bakhtin may have wanted

to undermine Soviet power. Katerina Clark and Michael Holquist, *Mikhail Bakhtin* (Cambridge, MA: Belknap, 1984), 307–314; Sue Vice, *Introducing Bakhtin* (Manchester: Manchester University Press, 1997), 152–154.

41. Bakhtin, *Rabelais and His World*, 5–9.

42. See Bakhtin, *Rabelais and His World*, especially 10–11.

43. Bakhtin, *Rabelais and His World*, 18–27.

44. Jacob Mundy, "Visualising National Reconciliation after the Algerian Civil War: Violence, Gender and 'Virtual Justice' in Film," in *Spectacles of Blood: A Study of Masculinity and Violence in Postcolonial Films*, ed. Swaralipi Nandi and Esha Chatterjee (Chicago: University of Chicago Press, 2012), 33.

45. In 2017, a documentary on the Black Decade, *Ḥatā lā nansā* (So that we will not forget), was aired on a government-controlled television station to mark the Charter's twelfth anniversary. That documentary contained explicit scenes of violence and sparked outrage among sectors of the public, who thought the government was playing up the dangers of a return to the Time of Terrorism for political gain and were upset at the film's disturbing content. The production and showing of this film suggest that the government has not historically sought to move past the conflict but has sought to control the narrative surrounding it. See ʿAbd al-Ḥamīd Bin Muḥammad, "Hal ḥaqqan arādat," *al-Jazeera*, October 11, 2017, https://www.aljazeera.net/news/reportsandinterviews/2017/10/11/%D9%87%D9%84-%D8%AD%D9%82%D8%A7-%D8%A3%D8%B1%D8%A7%D8%AF%D8%AA-%D8%A7%D9%84%D8%B3%D9%84%D8%B7%D8%A7%D8%AA-%D8%A7%D9%84%D8%AC%D8%B2%D8%A7%D8%A6%D8%B1%D9%8A%D8%A9-%D8%AA%D8%AE%D9%88%D9%8A%D9%81.

46. See chap. 4.

47. Chap. 4; Mundy, *Imaginative Geographies*, 137–160.

48. Ranjana Khanna, *Algeria Cuts: Women and Representation, 1830 to the Present* (Palo Alto: Stanford University Press, 2008), 96–97.

49. Dilem, *Liberté*, January 11, 2000, 24.

50. For more on women, rape, and shame during the Black Decade, see, for instance, Abderrahmane Moussaoui, "Pertes et fracas: Une décennie algérienne meurtrière," *NAQD* 18, no. 2 (2003): 135–138.

51. See Abderrahmane Moussaoui, "Enfants du maquis en Algérie: Un héritage explosif," *Anthropology of the Middle East* 12, no. 1 (2017): 20–37.

52. Cartoon in *Boutef président*.

53. See, for instance, some of the cartoons in *Boutef président*.

54. Conversation with Martin Evans, a historian of modern Algeria and France; cartoon contained in *Boutef président*.

55. Mustapha Benfodil, *Dilem président: Biographie d'un émeutier* (INAS, 2008), available at http://www.argotheme.com/dilempres%5B1%5D.pdf, 83.

56. Bakhtin, *Rabelais and His World*, 19.

57. Dilem, *Liberté*, December 5, 1999, 24. In an exchange with Benfodil, Dilem defended his practice of drawing generals as "ugly, fat, and corrupt," quipping, "The day I meet some generals who are handsome, skinny, and poor, I will draw them as well, I promise you." Benfodil, *Dilem président*, 86.

58. Bakhtin, *Rabelais and His World*.

59. Dilem, *Liberté*, August 16, 1999, 24. See also contemporary cartoons from *Echaʿab*.

60. See Bakhtin, *Rabelais and His World*, 6–8.
61. See chap. 4; Mundy, *Imaginative Geographies*.
62. See chap. 4.
63. See chap. 1.
64. Dilem, "Dilem," *Liberté*, September 6, 1999, 24; Dilem, "Dilem," *Liberté*, September 9, 1999, 24.
65. See Edward McAllister, "Yesterday's Tomorrow Is Not Today" (PhD diss., Oxford University, 2015), especially 193–203; Natalya Vince, "Saintly Grandmothers: Youth Reception and Reinterpretation of the National Past in Contemporary Algeria," *Journal of North African Studies* 18, no. 1 (2013): 32–52; Natalya Vince, "Colonial and Postcolonial Identities: Women Veterans of the 'Battle of Algiers,'" *French History and Civilization* 2 (2009): 162. McAllister notes the association between the indigenous form of veiling in Algeria and authenticity among communities in working-class Bab El-Oued, while Vince found during interviews with female veterans from the War of Independence that these women contrasted the haik with foreign types of veiling.
66. See, for example, Vince, "Colonial and Postcolonial Identities."
67. Dilem, *Liberté*, September 6, 1999, 24.
68. See Dilem, *Le Matin*, 1992.
69. Evans and Phillips, *Algeria*, 255–259.
70. Benfodil, *Dilem président*, 16.
71. Literary critics consider that Handala, portrayed as a refugee, stood in for the Palestinian people forced to bear witness to immense atrocities and suffering, and, according to Naji himself, he used the small child as a "signature" for his drawings. In a similar vein, some scholars contend that the eponymous character of Kateb Yacine's most famous work represents Algeria. Consequently, with this statement, Benfodil conceives of Madame Algeria as an analogous stand-in for the national community. Benfodil, *Dilem président*, 15; interview with Mustapha Benfodil, July 24, 2013. See Charles Bonn, "Kateb Yacine," *Research in African Literatures* 23, no. 2 (1992): 67.
72. See, for example, cartoons from *Liberté* in *Boutef président*.
73. See his cartoons from *Liberté* from this period.
74. See chap. 1.
75. See his work from *Liberté* and *Boutef président*.
76. Dilem, *Liberté*, September 17, 2000, 24.
77. Bakhtin, *Rabelais and His World*, 2.
78. See Dilem's *Liberté* pieces from this period.
79. Dilem, *Liberté*, September 17, 2000, 24.
80. Evans and Phillips note that Bouteflika and the peace measures lost popularity by 2001. Evans and Phillips, *Algeria*, 270.
81. See Mundy, *Imaginative Geographies*, where international interest appears to spike during the 1997 and 1998 massacres.
82. Code as published in *Journal officiel de la République Algérienne*, June 27, 2001, 14–15.
83. See, for example, Benfodil, *Dilem président*, 5.
84. Benfodil, *Dilem président*, 5.
85. Florence Beaugé, "Dilem le caricaturist: Le cauchemar du pouvoir, mais une revanche pour la jeunesse," *Le Monde*, May 18, 2001.
86. Benfodil, *Dilem président*, 5, 131; Dilem, *Liberté*, November 29, 2001, 24.

87. Benfodil, *Dilem président*, 131.
88. For instance, cartoonist Slim cited Boudiaf's assassination as a turning point for him. He left the country shortly afterward for Morocco. Interview with Slim, August 20, 2014.
89. Benfodil, *Dilem président*, 143–144, transcribing actual court record of trial.
90. Benfodil, *Dilem président*, 143–144.
91. Benfodil, *Dilem président*, 143–144.
92. Benfodil, *Dilem président*, 143–144, citing *Paris-Match*, February 16–22, 2006, 29.
93. Benfodil, *Dilem président*, 3.
94. Louis Althusser, "Ideology and Ideological State Apparatuses," in *Lenin and Philosophy and Other Essays*, trans. Frederic Jameson (New York: NYU Press, 2001), 115–120.
95. See, for instance, the Mohammed Benchicou affair, in which the editor of *Le Matin* was imprisoned for illegally handling currency. Journalists considered the charges trumped up and vengeance for Benchicou's public denunciations of Bouteflika. Benfodil, *Dilem président*, 55, 82.
96. Driss Ksikes, "Algérie: Le printemps de la presse, c'est bien fini," *TelQuel*, November 23, 2005, https://www.courrierinternational.com/article/2005/11/24/le-printemps-de-la-presse-c-est-bien-fini.
97. Dilem, *Liberté*, August 24, 2005, 24.
98. Dilem, *Liberté*, August 24, 2005, 24.
99. Dilem, *Liberté*, October 27, 2005, 24.
100. Mundy, *Imaginative Geographies*, table on 41 and text on 42.
101. See Dilem, *Liberté*, January 13, 2000, 2.
102. It should be noted that Le Hic also occasionally contributed to *El Manchar* around the time of the Civil Concord. Interview with Hicham Baba Ahmed, June 25, 2013.
103. Le Hic, *Le Matin*, January 12, 2000, 1.
104. Incongruity, in which objects or people are out of place or behave as they should not, is recognized by humor specialists as one of its key elements. John Morreall, "Philosophy of Humor," in *Stanford Encyclopedia of Humor*, last modified November 12, 2012, http://plato.stanford.edu/entries/humor/#SupThe.
105. Le Hic, *Le Matin*, March 9, 2000, 24.
106. See, for example, Le Hic, *Le Matin*, April 9, 2000, 24.
107. See his drawings from later on in the 2000s and 2010s in publications such as *El Watan*.
108. Farid Alilat, "Algérie: La pique du Hic," *Jeune Afrique*, April 30, 2015, https://www.jeuneafrique.com/230577/societe/alg-rie-la-pique-du-hic/; Benfodil, *Dilem président*, 113–114.
109. See, for example, Ayoub, *El Khabar*, September 27, 1999, 24.
110. Ayoub, *El Khabar*, August 4, 1999, 24.
111. See, for instance, Ayoub, *El Khabar*, August 30, 1999, 24. Ayoub often depicted families as suffering food shortages and accordingly thin. See Abderrahmane Moussaoui, "La Concorde Civile en Algérie: Entre mémoire et histoire," in *Où va l'Algérie*, ed. Ahmed Mahiou and John-Robert Henry (Aix-en-Provence: Karthala—Institut de recherches et d'études sur les mondes arabes et musulmans, 2001), 71–92.
112. Gharez, *Echa'ab*, September 19, 2005, 32.
113. Anonymous artist, *Echa'ab*, August 31, 1999, 32; anonymous artist, *Echa'ab*, August 18, 1999, 32; anonymous artist, *Echa'ab*, August 22, 2005, 32; Oussama, *Echa'ab*, September 11, 2005, 32.

114. The artist repeats references to flowers and how he could never draw them in his work because of the grim circumstances in Algeria, including the Black Decade, at least five times. See Benfodil, *Dilem président*, 7, 41, 83, 85, 119. Benfodil's transliteration.

115. Thierry Oberlé, "Like He Said: A Vitriolic Chronicle of Algeria," *Grand Street* 65 (Summer 1998): 51.

116. Numbers of daily printed copies for the most popular papers from the 1990s cited in Fatima Zohra Taiebi Moussaoui, "Le développement de la presse électronique en Algérie: Des dispositifs aux pratiques journalistiques," *L'Année du Maghreb* 15 (2016): 61–76.

117. Bakhtin, *Rabelais and His World*.

CONCLUSION

Remembering Algeria's 1990s Conflict and Humor over Time

ON A HOT SUMMER DAY in 2016, I walk down to Hassiba Ben Bouali, one of the major boulevards and shopping centers in downtown Algiers.[1] Amblers around me proceed at various paces, with some moving more quickly and others more slowly as they stop to look at boutiques' offerings, meet with friends, or enter stores. While this street serves as a key site for shopping, eating and drinking out, and fun, it does not attract many foreign visitors. In the middle of this lively artery, off toward the side of the road facing the bay, stands Place de la Liberté de la Presse / Sāḥat ḥurriyyat al-ṣaḥāfa, the Square of Press Freedom.

There are no photo-snapping tourists like the ones who gather at the foot of Maqām al-Shahīd (Monument of the Martyr), the great structure dedicated to Algeria's storied revolutionary struggle against France amid a backdrop of Cold War–era intrigues and actors. Maqām al-Shahīd sits atop one of the highest hills of the capital not very far from the street that residents refer to simply as "Hassiba," recognizable immediately as having been named after the murdered heroine of the Battle of Algiers. Visitors convene below the grandiose architectural mark to the sacrifice that the state often claims more than one million Algerian men and women made in the struggle for freedom from France. Ambassadors have trod that sacred ground, acknowledging the struggle that millions of Algerians racialized by settler colonialism as "Muslims" and their allies undertook to rid their country of that same brutal administration.[2]

Far below the dizzying heights of Maqām al-Shahīd and along commercial, bustling Hassiba, the Square of Press Freedom draws a sharp contrast to the larger War of Independence memorial. Unlike the monument, the square is not set apart from the street. Stairs leading down to another road hosting Algiers's major train station lie opposite the structure. Its positioning makes the entire space less a place for pause and reflection and more a thoroughfare, although benches do offer visitors an opportunity for rest. Similarly unlike Maqām al-Shahīd and its elaborate, emotive museum, only a small plaque exists on the bottom level of the Square of Press Freedom to guide visitors and indicate that they are occupying the public area that the state has dedicated to the fight for free journalism. A stele does stand atop the square's adjacent tunnel. It bears the names and assassination/kidnapping dates of the 105 media workers who were killed or forcefully disappeared during the Black Decade only twenty years earlier. However, during my visit, one that I purposefully conducted to evaluate efforts to commemorate Algeria's lost intellectuals, I did not see it; it seems that I missed stairs or a pathway leading to the top of the tunnel, under which a street passes. This section of the monument contains a brief explanation of its meaning alongside the list of names, all written in Arabic script. Absent is any mention of the other losses that individuals tasked with keeping Algerians and the international community apprised of happenings in the country endured during that trying period: time spent away from loved ones, who feared that any day could bring their demise; lingering health problems; or a persistent tendency to sit in public establishments facing the door lest a killer suddenly come in for them, more than twenty years after the last assassination of a newsperson.[3] Even the central point of the square, a green-and-blue globe, bears no words. Its inclusion suggests that Algeria is a leader in the global fight for press freedom despite authorities continuing to curb liberty of expression in the country.[4]

Throughout the modern history of this North African territory, communities and individuals have had to fight for the ability to express themselves freely. With laws enacted during the colonial and postindependence eras, liberties surrounding freedom of speech and the press have never fully taken hold in Algeria for the Muslim-majority population.[5] Even the limited press freedom marked by the democratic opening of 1989–1992 was fleeting. Police and military forces across the pre- and postindependence divide have rounded up individuals for breaking such policies or expressing ideas anathema to governments or power structures in place. Sides with stakes in promoting ideological divisions rendered language and discourse veritable battlegrounds at various points during the country's history.

This trend of discourse as a site of conflict was never stronger than during the Black Decade. This globe and stele function as one of the few publicly funded monuments dedicated to the idea of press freedom in the country. Monuments for other groups beyond writers and journalists highly impacted by Black Decade violence are rare, including for the victims of the 1996–1998 massacres. This lacuna contrasts sharply with omnipresent mentions of the War of Independence and lives lost to colonial brutality around the country (such as Hassiba Ben Bouali). Bentalha, Raïs, and other centers where hundreds of Algerians perished during the 1990s conflict are only places and dots on maps, unlike earlier sites of horror considered worthy of official acknowledgment and remembrance.

Activists step in to fill this void. The martyrs of the Black Decade are very often seen in Algeria only in identification photos displayed with powerful implications by groups devoted to the remembrance of the disappeared.[6] Social memory organizations such as Al-Ajouad (The Finest) group and SOS Disparus (SOS the Disappeared) regularly publish photos of the dead and the still missing and unaccounted for through social media and offline demonstrations. These pictures likewise grace the signs that SOS Disparus protestors hold weekly and, since early 2019, have been incorporated into their displays at weekly marches for regime transition.[7]

For a country whose history and historiography have centered tensions involving voice versus silence, inclusion versus exclusion, and remembrance versus forgetting or amnesia, the Black Decade represents the ultimate enigma. Narratives surrounding most events are contested. Sources can be hard to acquire and are often contradictory. Presently, state policies, especially Article Forty-Six of the Charter for Peace and Reconciliation, discourage not only the collection of data surrounding the Black Decade but also its evocation outside of state circles for political purposes.[8]

History and remembrance are not necessarily a panacea for the present, as Jacob Mundy reminds us.[9] The ultimate question of commemorating or letting go of the atrocities of the 1990s is one that Algerian communities themselves will answer, as they possibly have already done through the 2005 referendum on the charter. Yet, a better understanding of the 1990s and their impact on Algerians through scholarship may be able to correct misunderstandings of the war and its import for Algerian communities while also unraveling myths about these events that persist abroad, most significantly the image of civilians as passive victims during this period. Indeed, in a conversation with historian of modern Algeria James McDougall, Judith Scheele lamented the foreign coverage of the country's Black Decade / Time of Terrorism / civil conflict / war of the 1990s that rendered the territory a site of horror that seemed devoid of actual people.[10] Years later, narratives of the conflict that have circulated abroad and made their way into foreign accounts center mainly on the actions and motivations of the state and armed rebel groups, even to the neglect of other Islamist agents and organizations.

The circumstances of the Black Decade followed patterns similar to other instances, both past and present, in different regional as well as global contexts, particularly the post–Arab Spring trajectories of some countries—namely, Egypt with the suppression of the Muslim Brotherhood, as well as other instances of internal power struggles resulting in armed conflict in the wake of the 2010–2011 uprisings. Dozens of African nations transitioned from one-party to multiparty systems by the mid-1990s, as Algeria did.[11] Regarding the Arab world, Algeria experienced a comparatively early move toward a democratic regime after its 1988 Revolution. All of these similar events render more knowledge about the Black Decade and how at least some Algerian communities experienced it fruitful terrain for comparison to other contexts around the region and world.

Humor provides a pathway for researchers to see how various actors in the postindependence era articulated often competing visions of what exactly was taking place whenever circumstances were murky. Jokes and cartoons hold critically needed glimpses into the stories of how some civilians lived or responded to events during the political crisis of the 1990s. Tracing political humor and how it changes over time reveals shifts in attitudes toward national-level events while also unearthing humorous tactics for altering them. Shifts in the use or content of humor also prove a worthwhile subject of historical inquiry. The Black Decade, a pivotal conflict for the region and the world, one of the deadliest of the late twentieth century, was no exception in this regard. Political humor in Algeria from the interwar period to the 1980s permitted actors of different backgrounds to imagine and build different communities that could represent the nation. Continuing in this vein, in the period spanning the October 1988 Revolution to the January 1992 interruption of legislative elections, humor permitted the formation of in- and out-groups based on political position. The 1990s conflict saw humor become a means for a beleaguered population to express critical ideas about the war and its actors as well as the peace processes that ultimately resolved the war but at the cost of justice for its victims. This book has also considered efforts to understand the war through political humor, taking into consideration how humorous practices of the 1990s compared to those of earlier eras.

The humorous heritage of the Black Decade continues to inspire joke-tellers in Algeria and beyond. Terrorism-era jokes appear to have best resisted the passing of time and geographic boundaries set by national borders. For instance, the ever-popular fake checkpoint jokes of the 1990s have entered into the wider region's humorous repertoire.[12] There has additionally been a recent surge in interest among intellectuals in humorous traditions in Algeria throughout the twentieth century, resulting in some Algerian communities expressing a strong sense of pride in their humorous heritages.[13] This reality may not be surprising; wit and humor are associated in some cultural contexts with increased intelligence, especially when the joke's formula depends on the listener being in the know.[14]

The significance of this so-called Algerian humor burst onto international news channels and digital forums in February 2019.[15] For years before this moment, Algerian activist citizens had published humorous commentary on the country's political affairs through burgeoning online and social media outlets. Abdelaziz Bouteflika's absence from the political arena following a 2013 stroke stirred particular mockery. Caricaturists made him out to be a puppet, while the online satirical site *El Manchar* (not related to, but borrowing its name from, the earlier satirical newspaper) pointed out the absurdity of the most powerful man in the country not truly having power.[16] In many ways, his absence permitted imaginings of what he might be doing and who was really in charge of the country to run wild. On February 22, 2019, and during weekly meetings thereafter, protesters around the country crowded the streets of major towns and cities to denounce then-president Abdelaziz Bouteflika's bid for a fifth term after two previous constitutional alterations allowed him to stay head of state. The demands of protesters were by no means limited to their desire for new leadership. Chants arose from the weekly crowds declaring that the time had come for the "fall of the regime," a throwback to the chant par excellence of Arab Spring crowds, or the end to the *'iṣāba* ("gang") that they saw as having plundered the country. Protesters infused signs and slogans with humor. Humor and a general sense of levity and community have so marked this movement that it has become known as the "Revolution of Smiles."[17] Furthermore, this revolution has now morphed into a greater call for a transition from military to civilian rule in Algeria.

Beyond signaling the capacity of Algerian humor to demonstrate peaceful resistance and common national culture, the Algerian Ḥirāk has brought together citizens who had been engaged in atomized resistance and discussions about the country's past, present, and future.[18] In this more visible grassroots-level dialogue, conversations about the Black Decade have flourished. Analysts of contemporary Algeria have advanced unfounded claims that the younger generations who have driven the popular movement for regime change in the country do not recall the Black Decade or interface with social memories surrounding it.[19] Yet, younger protesters have called for more official transparency and more open dialogue about what took place during the country's bitter civil conflict. Their adept use of slogans, symbols, and references to the violence likewise evinces their awareness of—and potential desire for—official investigations into or remembrance of this past.[20] Observers of the country even believe that the regime has crafted its protest management strategies to try to prevent a collective questioning of its actions during the Black Decade.[21] The embattled state leadership may also have initially refrained from violently repressing the Ḥirāk to avoid claims that it was inflicting the same kind of brutality on the population that it had in October 1988 and critical moments of the 1990s conflict.

Algeria's past humorous traditions have made their reappearance during outpourings of national pride, communal love, and desire for a better Algerian future. Indeed, demonstrators, many of whom belong to the country's majority youth population, have mobilized laughter as a sign of both the peacefulness of their organizing and the ridiculousness of the present state of affairs in the country. In doing so, they are drawing on past iterations of Algerian humor.[22] For example, one *tifo* (a large visual display associated with soccer culture) hung in the Ḥirāk hotspot of Tizi Ouzou reproduced a cartoon by Ali Dilem featuring his infamous general figure.[23] In his work, the large-girthed figure is a sign of the military's persistent intervention into the nation's political affairs and top government officials' squandering of its resources.[24] Tifo culture had already been present in the country's soccer stadiums as fans made them to support their teams. These fifty-foot-long cloth posters caricature political figures in ways similar to contemporary cartoons. Tifo makers critically draw the nation just as trailblazers of Algerian cartooning Slim, Dilem, Le Hic, and others have, and they seem at times to have been inspired by the latter.[25] The same can be said for some of the posters and signs that protestors are hoisting not just for the eyes of their fellow demonstrators but also for the international media covering events.

Other examples of Ḥirāk protesters paying homage to earlier forms of Algerian comedy abound. In downtown Algiers in late spring 2019, a vendor of pins sold a series of his work showcasing comedian Rouiched's famous character Hassan Terro (Hassan the Terrorist). Pins are popular emblems that Ḥirāk participants have worn and that even made their way onto the Cannes red carpet in 2019.[26] As mentioned in chapter 1, the character of Hassan Terro satirizes fake War of Independence fighters, detestable villains in metanarratives of the country's past and present, involved as they supposedly are in the betrayal of revolutionary principles reflecting the desires of the Algerian people. This pin, then, when bought and worn by protesters, treats the regime as ridiculous and members of this hypocritical class as illegitimate with no right to rule in the name of the revolution. In the early weeks of the protest, a demonstrator held aloft a poster on which someone had drawn the likeness of famed Algerian stand-up comedian Mohand Fellag from his beloved show, *Djudjurassique bled*. The humorist is depicted menacing the regime by saying, "*Bla din yemakoum* [transliteration on poster] *vous* [*n'*]*allez pas dormir*" / "Without the religion of your mother [an expression encapsulating frustration with the person or group to whom it is expressed], you will not go to sleep." Fellag pronounced these words at one point in the routine to talk about Amazigh populations supposedly hounding ancient Roman invaders.[27] Based on the context of the protests, where youth were earnestly imploring the older generation of leaders to abdicate their positions, the poster bearer most likely wanted to tell Bouteflika and other elderly politicians that it was time to go and rest.[28]

Regional observers should not be surprised at this mobilization of the country's earlier humorous traditions along with new forms of humor for Algeria's Revolution of Smiles. Political humor has long served as a critical venue for political expression and a site for debating what it meant to be part of different identity-based communities (Algerian, Muslim, etc.). Historians and other scholars postulate that certain national identities, invented, malleable, and reiterated over time as they are, possess "natural" or trumped-up characteristics or collective emotions, such as the British "stiff upper lip."[29] Humor, especially of the self-deprecating variety, may be such an emotion that some writers, artists, and members of communities in Algeria have wanted to cultivate as representative of a so-called national character. Indeed, as an analysis of the history of Algerian humor demonstrates, various actors have worked to employ humor in the service of nationalism or to advance ideologies and key notions surrounding power in the country. Such was the case with theatrical works from the interwar period, *bandes dessinées* from the immediate postindependence era, slogans from October 1988, and caricatures and jokes from the 1990s.

Yet, in the sense of political humor proving to be widespread, Algeria is not unique; political humor is a practice present in many societies around the world. Precisely because of restrictions on free speech and media for expressing dissent in both pre- and postindependence Algeria, humor stood as one of the few ways of channeling emotion into shareable and accessible discourse. Cartoonists such as Dilem and Ayoub are celebrated in Algeria as veritable rock stars, whose status as informed commenters on in-country affairs translated to foreign diplomats using their art as a source of intelligence.[30] Humorous movies and the country's rich *bandes dessinées* and cartoon cultures have morphed into nostalgic touchstones of different moments in the country's history. Characters from earlier moments of Algerian comedy such as Slim's Bouzid, Rouiched as Hassan Terro, and Hadj Abderrahmane as the Inspector Tahar bring back fond memories for Algerians that they see as being connected to a part of the nation.³¹ These comedic art forms additionally valorize Algerian ways of speaking, the rich practice of code-switching between all of the country's spoken languages—Tamazight, the Algerian dialect of Arabic (*darja*), French, and others—in ways that literature generally does not (although the plastic arts are increasingly doing so).³²

Moreover, reconstructing the ways in which Algerian communities have employed humor and how these practices have shifted over time reveals how political attitudes among at least some Algerians may have changed in tandem with events. A break from earlier humorous traditions, Black Decade humor indicates a desire on the part of some citizens to contemplate newfound dangers and uncertainty about what their nation was in light of the bloodshed. As a case study for the use of humor under competing authoritarian regimes or in times of war, humor commenting on politics linked to the national level in 1990s Algeria demonstrates humor's capacity to work as resistance or counter-resistance according to the context and who is speaking.

A longer-term approach to humor allows significant and revelatory patterns to become clear. Possibly didactic, possibly impelling serious actions on the part of its consumers (for instance, rebellion in the case of October 1988 in Algeria), humor can be used by agents to effect change. However, the degree of change possible depends on several factors. Authorities ruling Algeria across the twentieth century have significantly recognized the capacity of humor to alter power structures. It is for this reason that states crossing the pre- and postindependence divides have at times encouraged, surveilled, co-opted, feared, suppressed, and prosecuted humor and its creators.

Products of humorous expression (jokes, cartoons, etc.) in turn furnish scholars of different contexts with an archive that reveals aspects of these communities' pasts that may not otherwise be available. In the case of Algeria, political sensitivities have rendered access to archives concerning different phases of the territory's past, especially the Black Decade, difficult.³³ At the same time, historians and other scholars must be careful when working with humorous archives. The existence, persistence, and popularity of Algerian political humor should not lead to the conclusion that this humor holds the key to some sort of collective Algerian national consciousness or shared emotional response to events. Such thinking would involve an essentialization of communities that suffered and still suffer from stereotyping that reinforced and reinforces colonial/neocolonial power structures. Instead, these products should be understood within the contexts in which they were produced, and I have tried to present them as codes that certain subsections of the population have used to comment on national politics.

Humor itself, though, is a cultural product filled with connotations that actors can exploit to advance their own agendas. It is also important to note, especially as Ḥirāk activists tout political humor as a pacifist creative tool of grassroots resistance, that over different eras of the country's past humor may in its own right have come to symbolize a practice of the well informed, the clever, the creative, and the resistant. Yet, certain (but not all) moments associated with conflict were commented on with laughter, while others seem to have proved too sacred or too painful. Therefore, certain groups, such as communities caught between opposing sides of the War of Independence, appear by all accounts not to have expressed their experiences through humor. When and where humor is absent and present, especially in the social memories of groups surrounding certain events, can likewise be revealing for historians. In this study, the inability of oral history narrators specializing in either producing or writing on Algerian humor to recount War of Independence jokes or humor may attest to the solemn terms in which this past has been and continues to be constructed.[34]

At times, the task of mapping out instances of past humor or its absence in Algeria has involved speculation on my part. It is, after all, incredibly difficult to retroactively try to evaluate what kind of impact a joke or a cartoon had on the diverse, heterogeneous communities that reside in Algeria. Wherever possible throughout this volume, I have tried to approximate the potential reception of Algerian humorous products through the use of theories developed for dissecting humor and popular culture both in the region and elsewhere. In chapter 1, ideas of interpellation and humor as a mechanism for creating in- and out-groups assist in understanding nationalizing humor in Algeria from the 1920s through the 1980s. Bayat's concept of social non-movements similarly helps show how humor may have helped foment dissent during October 1988 and brought populations together, even informally, in the lead-up to postindependence Algeria's first multiparty legislative elections. Theories from a variety of scholars on humor's efficacy to either support or thwart authoritarian power informs the third chapter. In the fourth chapter, I think again about the ability of humor to build community, this time with cartoons helping shape shared visions of the conflict and its drivers among readers. Finally, ideas of social memory formation, social non-movements, and Mikhail Bakhtin's thoughts on carnival prove useful for understanding how cartoonists attempted to forge opposition to reconciliation measures from the late 1990s through the middle of the first decade of the 2000s.

I have presented sources indicating that humor across the precolonial and postcolonial divide worked as a critical tool for fostering a sense of belonging to a larger community. From the interwar period through the 1980s, Algerian populations used humor to envision Algeria as independent or part of a larger French nation or to conversely challenge French control and then rebuild a nation after independence. Humor from both before and after independence was used by citizens as well as states to create in-groups and out-groups based on who should belong to the nation and their notions concerning what characteristics the ideal national community should have. Artists such as Ksentini and Bachtarzi hoped their works would hail fellow members of their community to share in their vision for the nation and its future. Self-derision by Algerian joke-tellers and producers of other humorous products (songs, drawings, etc.) especially morphed into an action associated with performing Algerian-ness. Citizens told jokes to bypass state censorship and repressive environments in place from the interwar period through the 1980s. These jokes sometimes functioned, according to their contexts, as methods of resisting powerful elites or conversely imagining the average citizen as the main national figure. This was a further way of centering the nation in the voice of the people and alienating individuals in power from the national community. Correctly noted by Ameziane Ferhani as the first art form to emerge and gain traction in postindependence Algeria, *bandes dessinées* and cartoon culture were constructed by artists, along with state backers, over the first three decades after the dismantling of the colonial regime.[35] Despite working in state outlets, cartoonists were able to create work that challenged official discourse but generally had to do so in subtle ways to avoid the sharp blade of the censor. Other forms of state-supported comedy existed in the immediate postindependence era as well, a sign that the government considered humor to be an excellent method of shoring up Algerian-ness among the population and distracting from disunity among communities and political elites like.

Humor appears to have then morphed into a space of multisided criticism once the FLN's monopoly on power was broken, at least in a limited way, following Algeria's bloody October 1988 Revolution. Humor itself might have motivated protesters to take to the streets during the movement of mainly young men speaking out against their disenfranchisement by the country's lead figures. Indeed, the events of Black October themselves were not bereft of humor or lightheartedness, at least not in the beginning. Protestors and rioters mocked power as they claimed public spaces such as theaters for their expressions of outrage at a political system that allowed the country's kleptocrats to flaunt wealth while they suffered. October 1988 participants drew on preexisting humorous tropes surrounding the "cauliflower president" and his cronies to attack the group as unfit to rule the country.

In the wake of October 1988, the presidency along with reform-minded FLN leaders chose, under pressure from Islamist and Amazigh-rights activists, to allow a multiparty system to form for the first time in the country's history. After this moment, different political parties, their followers, and their opponents used political satire to distinguish between various groups' rhetoric and stances on key issues. This humor broke with previous humorous practices by attesting more to divisions within the national body politic than to the sharing of a national culture or character. The period additionally marked a loosening of the state's single-handed control over print culture. Newfound openness and freedom meant that more groups channeled humor as a means of cementing solidarity around similar worldviews and toward common political goals just when Algerian civilians were promised a stronger role in shaping their government than ever before. Groups that employed humor during this period included the FIS.

During the Black Decade, media outlets both at home and abroad painted the country as a grim landscape, turning victims into universal symbols of suffering at the hands of shrouded and unshrouded actors. Beyond work focusing on writers and artists, literature on the conflict has overwhelmingly examined the experiences and motivations of the leading figures—state, military, and rebels—whose actions led to or possibly perpetuated the armed struggle. Amid this bloodshed, though, civilians, the largest contingency in the country, lived through and attempted to understand what was happening around them, a story that has gone woefully underexamined. Jokes and cartoons worked as sites that permitted at least some civilians to digest the horrors of the 1990s, to spread news and rumors about events (especially as to who was driving the violence and their motivations), and to rethink the Algerian national community in light of shifting circumstances. Quite significantly and in direct contravention of narratives surrounding their country in foreign media, at least some civilians used humor to refute the idea that the Black Decade violence was in any way Algerian.[36] This humor was equally not without consequence. At least one senior armed forces official thought that a cartoonist attacked the insurgents' cause more vehemently than the military did.[37] In the battle for the hearts and minds of Algerian citizens during the civil conflict, humor may have helped turn the tide against the rebel armed groups.

Of course, across all these periods, humor labeled as Algerian or dealing with Algerian national politics did not necessarily hail solely from Algerian citizens, nor did humor circulating around Algeria stay within the country's borders. Instead, Algerians both borrowed from and influenced humor around the region and the world. Algeria's Black Decade fake checkpoint jokes have seemingly spread to different parts of the Middle East and North Africa.[38] Of course, the original Black Decade joke from Algeria's October 1988 Revolution, one of the first mass popular uprisings against a postcolonial regime in the region, was adapted from a popular humorous anecdote from then-communist-ruled central Europe.[39] Nevertheless, through borrowing, localizing, and exporting humorous codes, Algerians demonstrated their integration into wider global and regional networks and their creativity as world citizens existing outside the limiting colonial-postcolonial framework in which analysts often place them. Humor also attests to multidirectional exchanges between Algeria and other parts of the world besides former colonizer France, a polarity that scholarship continues to emphasize. Along with other emerging literature on Algeria and other parts of the Maghrib, this study has had as one of its principal goals the illumination of connections between North Africa and various parts of the world.[40] Humor in the periods discussed here could transcend political boundaries as other forms of culture could not, demonstrating the flexibility and capacity of humor to be adapted to fit local circumstances.

Above all, this work has highlighted political humor as a crucial means of thinking through, defining, and testing the limits of belonging to the Algerian nation and how political humor commenting on Algeria's national politics has changed over time. This humor seems to have itself altered the outcomes of critical events. Shifts in political satire engaging with national identity and politics also spoke to changing trends in attitudes across at least some Algerian populations toward key political players and institutions. Twentieth-century connections of power and humor in Algeria reveal diverse responses to particular yet not unique circumstances (life under a colonial regime, decolonization and the construction of a new nation, authoritarianism, rebellion, civil conflict, brutal and unexpected violence, etc.). Humor and power have been intimately linked phenomena in Algeria. Humor has historically served as a site of significant political engagement when regimes have curtailed other outlets for civilians' political expression, almost a constant throughout the territory's modern history. Above all, through the creative harnessing of humor, Algerians have expressed competing visions of unity in a divided colonial society, channeled and processed emotions surrounding a brutal war of decolonization and the forging of a new nation, and demonstrated resilience in the face of an abjectly horrific civil conflict.

NOTES

1. For the beginning of this conclusion, I take inspiration from the introduction to Natalya Vince, *Our Fighting Sisters: Nation, Memory and Gender in Algeria, 1954–2012* (Manchester: Manchester University Press, 2015), 1–3.

2. For instance, the American ambassador visited the monument in 2017. See video posted by US Embassy of Algiers on October 31, 2017, at https://www.youtube.com/watch?v=Z13d3EWzXt4. Muriam Haleh Davis's book on capitalism and development in Algeria explores how "Muslim" became a racialized category under French imperialism. See Muriam Haleh Davis, *Markets of Civilization: Islam and Racial Capitalism in Algeria* (Durham, NC: Duke University Press, 2022).

3. The lasting impact of the Black Decade came up in a number of interviews—for example, interview with *El Watan* director Omar Belhouchet, July 20, 2013.

4. See "Algeria: Repressive Tactics Used to Target Hirak Activists Two Years On," Amnesty International, February 22, 2021, https://www.amnesty.org/en/latest/news/2021/02/algeria-repressive-tactics-used-to-target-hirak-activists-two-years-on/.

5. Arthur Asseraf, "Charlie Hebdo and the Limits of the Republic," *Jadaliyya*, January 11, 2015, https://www.jadaliyya.com/Details/31658/Charlie-Hebdo-and-the-Limits-of-the-Republic.

6. Jennifer Howell, "Investigating the Enforced Disappearances of Algeria's 'Dark Decade,'" *Journal of North African Studies* 21, no. 2 (2016): 213–234.

7. See the Facebook pages for both groups: https://www.facebook.com/groups/1477903382515971/ and https://www.facebook.com/sos.disparus.

8. Article Forty-Six, "La charte pour la paix et la réconciliation nationale," *Journal officiel de la République Algérienne*, February 28, 2006, 7.

9. Jacob Mundy, *Imaginative Geographies of Algerian Violence* (Palo Alto: Stanford University Press, 2015), 154–155.

10. James McDougall, *A History of Algeria* (Cambridge: Cambridge University Press, 2017), 292n5.

11. Michael Bratton and Nicholas van de Walle, *Democratic Experiments in Africa: Regime Transitions in Comparative Perspective* (Cambridge: Cambridge University Press, 2017).

12. Conversation with Moroccan scholar concerning *faux barrage* jokes in Morocco.

13. See, for instance, Amnay Idir, "Rachid Ksentini: Le rire pour supporter la misère," *El Watan*, September 13, 2005.

14. See, for instance, Jody Baumgartner and Jonathan S. Morris, "The *Daily Show* Effect," *American Politics Research* 34, no. 3 (2006): 341–367.

15. Hiyem Cheurfa, "The Laughter of Dignity," *Jadaliyya*, March 26, 2019, https://www.jadaliyya.com/Details/38495/The-Laughter-of-Dignity-Comedy-and-Dissent-in-the-Algerian-Popular-Protests.

16. See, for instance, the work of Ali Dilem and Le Hic from this period along with the *El Manchar* Facebook page accessible at https://www.facebook.com/ElMancharOfficiel. I am indebted to Idriss Jebari for his observation that absurd humor reflects the absurd nature of politics at times in Algeria.

17. Ḥirāk is Arabic for "movement." See also El-Mahdi Acherchour, ed., *La révolution du sourire* (Tizi-Ouzou: Frantz Fanon, 2019).

18. I am indebted to feminist activist Saadia Gacem, among others, for this insight.

19. See, for instance, George Joffé, "The Arab Spring in North Africa," *Journal of North African Studies* 16, no. 4 (2011): 507–532.

20. Elizabeth Perego, "Beyond Paralyzing Terror: The 'Black Decade' in the Algerian Hirak," *JadMag* 7, no. 3 (2019); Faouzia Zeraoulia, "The Memory of the Civil War in Algeria," *Contemporary Review of the Middle East* 7, no. 1 (2020): 25–53.

21. This conversation came up at the "Special Session: Hirak—Algeria's New Revolution?" panel during the 2019 Middle East Studies Association Annual Meeting.

22. For more on laughter as a way of signaling peacefulness, see Cheurfa, "Laughter of Dignity."

23. See "Vendredi 14," Tout sur l'Algérie, May 24, 2019, https://www.tsa-algerie.com/direct-14e-vendredi-alger-quadrille-la-manifestation-prend-de-lampleur/.

24. See chap. 5.

25. See, for instance, tifos included in "Vendredi 15," Tout sur l'Algérie, May 31, 2019, https://www.tsa-algerie.com/direct-15e-vendredi-forte-mobilisation-les-manifestants-disent-non-au-dialogue-avec-les-2b/. On tifos and other facets of football culture in Algeria, see Sihem Benmalek, "Les stades, ces tribunes politiques," Liberté, July 12, 2018.

26. Elsa Keslassey, "Oscars: Algeria's Papicha Stays in International Feature Race but Can't Get Released at Home," Variety, October 11, 2019, https://variety.com/2019/film/global/oscars-papicha-canceled-release-algeria-1203367239/. Author's observation from the May 2019 protests.

27. Poster seen via social media in spring 2019, photographer unknown. See also Mohand Fellag, "Djurdjurrasique bled," recording published by MLP Music, YouTube, October 9, 2012, https://www.youtube.com/watch?v=otZUYttO1ok&t=3169s.

28. Poster seen via social media in spring 2019, photographer unknown.

29. See "AHR Conversation: The Historical Study of Emotions," American Historical Review 117, no. 5 (2012): 1492–1493.

30. Interview with Hichem Baba Ahmed, known as "Le Hic," June 24, 2013. US State Department employees, including then–US ambassador to Algeria Robert Ford, sent cables mentioning Ali Dilem and Le Hic that were eventually revealed by WikiLeaks. The US diplomatic corps in Algeria appear to have used the cartoonists' freedom, work, and statements as evidence of the state of affairs in the country at the time. See US diplomatic cable available through WikiLeaks, "Form over Function: Surviving as a Newspaper in Algeria Today," sent May 5, 2008, https://wikileaks.org/plusd/cables/08ALGIERS504_a.html. A weekly roundup of Algerian media developed by the embassy and distributed among its employees reportedly includes cartoons.

31. See, for instance, Omar Zelig, Slim, le gatt, et moi (Algiers: DALIMEN, 2009).

32. Muriam Haleh Davis and Ziad Bentahar, among others, have discussed how Algerian populations are embracing and taking pride in local dialects of Arabic through the Ḥirāk. See Muriam Haleh Davis, Hiyem Cheurfa, and Thomas Serres, "A Hirak Glossary: Terms from Algeria and Morocco," Jadaliyya, June 13, 2019, https://www.jadaliyya.com/Details/38734; and Ziad Bentahar, "'Ytnahaw Ga,'" Journal of African Cultural Studies 33, no. 4 (2020): 471–488. See also works by various Algerian artists included in the exhibit Waiting for Omar Gatlato, curated by Natasha Marie Llorens, Wallach Art Gallery of Columbia University, New York City, October 2019 to March 2020.

33. See, for instance, Todd Shepard, "'Of Sovereignty': Disputed Archives, 'Wholly Modern' Archives, and the Post-decolonization French and Algerian Republics," American Historical Review 120, no. 3 (2015): 869–883.

34. See chapter 1.

35. Ameziane Ferhani, 50 ans de bande dessinée algérienne et l'aventure continue (Algiers: Dalimen, 2012), 15.

36. For work addressing stereotypes about Algerians as "violent," see James McDougall, "Savage Wars? Codes of Violence in Algeria, 1830s–1990s," Third World Quarterly 26, no. 1 (2008): 117–131.

37. Mustapha Benfodil, Dilem président: Biographie d'un émeutier (INAS, 2008), http://www.argotheme.com/dilempres%5B1%5D.pdf, 111.

38. Based on the author's observations and conversations with a Moroccan scholar concerning checkpoint jokes in Morocco and with a Somali national.

39. See chap. 2.

40. See M'hamed Oualdi's critiques of previous Maghribi historiography, including comments about relations with France and the region getting the lion's share of historians' attention, in M'hamed Oualdi, *A Slave between Empires: A Transimperial History of North Africa* (New York: Columbia University Press, 2020).

BIBLIOGRAPHY

SECONDARY SOURCES

Abedinifard, Mostafa. "Humor and Gender Hegemony: The Panoptical Role of Ridicule vis-à-vis Gender." PhD diss., University of Alberta, 2015.

———. "Reply to Davies." *Humor* 30, no. 2 (2017): 247–253.

———. "Structural Functions of the Targeted Joke: Iranian Modernity and the Qazvini Man as Predatory Homosexual." *Humor* 29, no. 3 (2016): 337–357.

Abu-Sarah, Christiane Marie. "To Drink a Cup of Fire: Morality Tales and Moral Emotions in Anti-colonial Activism." PhD diss., University of Maryland, 2019.

Acherchour, El-Mahdi, ed. *La révolution du sourire*. Tizi-Ouzou: Frantz Fanon, 2019.

Adams, Bruce. *Tiny Revolutions in Russia: Twentieth-Century Soviet and Russian History in Anecdotes*. London: Routledge, 2005.

Ageron, Charles-Robert. *Histoire de l'Algérie contemporaine*. Paris: Presses Universitaires de France, 1964.

"AHR Conversation: The Historical Study of Emotions." *American Historical Review* 117, no. 5 (2012): 1486–1531.

Aissaoui, Rabah. "Politics, Identity, and Temporality in Colonial Algeria in the Early Twentieth Century." *Journal of North African Studies* 22, no. 2 (2017): 182–204.

Aït-Aoudia, Myriam. *L'expérience démocratique en Algérie (1988–1992)*. Algiers: Koukou, 2016.

Allman, Jean. "Phantoms of the Archive." *American Historical Review* 118, no. 1 (2013): 104–129.

Althusser, Louis. *Lenin and Philosophy and Other Essays*. Translated by Frederic Jameson. New York: NYU Press, 2001.

Amer, Amar Mohand. "Les wilayas dans la crise du FLN de l'été." *Insaniyat* 65–66 (2014): 105–124.

Amine, Khalid, and Marvin Carlson. *The Theatres of Morocco, Algeria, and Tunisia: Performance Traditions of the Maghrib*. New York: Palgrave Macmillan, 2012.

Amnesty International. *Algeria: Fear and Silence—a Hidden Human Rights Crisis*. November 28, 1996. https://www.amnesty.org/download/Documents/172000/mde280111996en.pdf.

Amrane, Djamila. *Des femmes dans la guerre d'Algérie: Entretiens*. Paris: Karthala, 1994.

Anagondahalli, Deepa, and Sahar Khamis. "Mubarak Framed! Humor and Political Activism before and during the Egyptian Revolution." *Arab Media and Society* 19 (2014): 1–16.

Anderson, Benedict. *Imagined Communities*. 2nd ed. London: Verso, 1991.

Arezki, Saphia. "Les camps d'internement du sud en Algérie (1991–1995): Contextualisation et enjeux." *L'Année du Maghreb* 20 (2019): 225–239.

Armbrust, Walter. *Mass Culture and Modernism in Egypt*. Cambridge: Cambridge University Press, 1996.

Asseraf, Arthur. "Charlie Hebdo and the Limits of the Republic." *Jadaliyya*, January 11, 2015. https://www.jadaliyya.com/Details/31658/Charlie-Hebdo-and-the-Limits-of-the-Republic.

———. *Electric News in Colonial Algeria*. Oxford: Oxford University Press, 2019.

———. "Khoualdia Salah and the Networks of Pan-Islamic News around 1900." Paper presented at the Middle East Studies Association's Annual Meeting, New Orleans, LA, November 15, 2019.

Astapova, Anastasiya. *Humor and Rumor in the Post-Soviet Authoritarian State*. London: Lexington Books, 2021.

Avruch, Kevin, and Beatriz Vejarano. "Truth and Reconciliation Commissions: A Review Essay and Annotated Bibliography." *Online Journal of Peace and Conflict Resolution* 4, no. 2 (2002): 37–76.

Bakhtin, M. M. *Rabelais and His World*. Translated by Helene Iswolsky. Bloomington: University of Indiana Press, 1984.

Bakr, 'Abd al-Raḥman. *al-Ṣaḥāfa al-sākhiriyya fī Miṣr*. Giza: Arab Press Agency, 2018.

Baumgartner, J. C. "The *Daily Show* Effect." *American Politics Research* 34, no. 3 (2006): 341–367.

Bayart, Jean-François. *The Illusion of Cultural Identity*. 2nd ed. Translated by Steven Rendall, Janet Roitman, Cynthia Schoch, and Jonathan Derrick. Chicago: University of Chicago Press, 2005.

Bayat, Asef. *Life as Politics: How Ordinary People Change the Middle East*. 2nd ed. Palo Alto: Stanford University Press, 2013.

Beaugé, Florence. "Dilem le caricaturiste: Le cauchemar du pouvoir, mais une revanche pour la jeunesse." *Le Monde*, May 18, 2001.

Becker, Cynthia. "Exile, Memory, and Healing in Algeria: Denis Martinez and La Fenêtre du Vent." *African Arts* 42, no. 2 (2009): 24–31.
Bencheneb, Rachid. "Allalu et les origines du théâtre algérien." *Revue des mondes musulmans et de la Méditerranée* 24 (1977): 29–37.
———. "Les mémoires de Mahiéddine Bachtarzi ou vingt ans de théâtre algérien." *Revue des mondes musulmans et de la Méditerranée* 9 (1971): 15–20.
Benfodil, Mustapha. *Dilem président: Biographie d'un émeutier*. INAS, 2008. http://www.argotheme.com/dilempres%5B1%5D.pdf.
Benmalek, Sihem. "Les stades, ces tribunes politiques." *Liberté*, July 12, 2018.
Benrabah, Mohammed. "Competition between Four World Languages in Algeria." *Journal of World Languages* 1, no. 1 (2014): 38–59.
Bentahar, Ziad. "'Ytnahaw Ga.'" *Journal of African Cultural Studies* 33, no. 4 (2020): 471–488.
Ben Yahmed, Marwane. "Présidentielle algérienne: Bouteflika devant un théâtre d'ombres." *Jeune Afrique*, March 19, 2014. http://www.jeuneafrique.com/Article/JA2774p022.xml0.
Bergson, Henri. *Le Rire*. Paris: Félix Alcan, 1900.
Berlant, Lauren. *Cruel Optimism*. Durham, NC: Duke University Press, 2011.
Blazy, Olivier. "La presse militaire française à destination des troupes indigènes." Translated by Robert A. Doughty. *Revue historique des armées* 271 (2013): 51–59.
Bonn, Charles. "Kateb Yacine." *Research in African Literatures* 23, no. 2 (1992): 61–70.
Boskin, Joseph. "American Political Humor: Touchables and Taboos." *International Political Science Review* 11, no. 4 (1990): 473–482.
Bozzini, David M. "The Catch-22 of Resistance: Jokes and the Political Imagination of Eritrean Conscripts." *Africa Today* 60, no. 2 (2013): 38–64.
Branche, Raphaëlle. *La torture et l'armée pendant la Guerre d'Algérie, 1954–1962*. Paris: Gallimard, 2001.
Bratton, Michael, and Nicholas van de Walle. *Democratic Experiments in Africa: Regime Transitions in Comparative Perspective*. Cambridge: Cambridge University Press, 2017.
Brule, J. C., and J. Fontaine. "Géographisme dans l'islamisme politique en Algérie." *Bulletin de l'association de géographes français* 74, no. 1 (1997).
Brummett, Palmira. *Image and Imperialism in the Ottoman Revolutionary Press, 1908–1911*. Binghamton: SUNY Press, 2000.
Bryant, Chad. "The Language of Resistance? Czech Jokes and Joke Telling under Nazi Occupation, 1943–1945." *Journal of Contemporary History* 41, no. 1 (2006): 133–151.
Burgat, François, and William Dowell. *The Islamic Movement in North Africa*. Austin: University of Texas Press, 1993.
Byrne, Jeffrey James. *Mecca of the Revolution: Algeria, Decolonization, and the Third World Order*. Oxford: Oxford University Press, 2016.

Bytwerk, Randall. *Julius Streicher: Nazi Editor of the Notorious Anti-Semitic Newspaper.* Der Stürmer. New York: Copper Square Press, 2001.
Charef, Abed. *Algérie: Autopsie d'un massacre.* Paris: Editions de l'Aube, 1998.
———. *Algérie: Le grand dérapage.* Paris: Editions de l'Aube, 1994.
———. *Octobre.* 2nd ed. Algiers: Laphomic, 1990.
Chaulet-Achour, Christiane, and Dalila Morsly. "Plus d'un siècle de rire en Algérie." In *2000 ans de rire*, 55–65. Franc-Comtoises: Université de Franc-Comtoises, 2002.
Cheniki, Ahmed. *Le théâtre en Algérie.* Paris: Edisud, 2002.
Cheurfa, Hiyem. "The Laughter of Dignity." *Jadaliyya*, March 26, 2019. https://www.jadaliyya.com/Details/38495/The-Laughter-of-Dignity-Comedy-and-Dissent-in-the-Algerian-Popular-Protests.
Clark, Katerina, and Michael Holquist. *Mikhail Bakhtin.* Cambridge, MA: Belknap, 1984.
Cole, Joshua. "A chacun son public." Translated by Stéphane Bouquet. *Sociétés et représentations* 38, no. 2 (2014): 21–51.
Connolly, Matthew. *A Diplomatic Revolution.* New York: Oxford University Press, 2002.
Courreye, Charlotte. "L'Association des oulémas musulmans algériens et la construction de l'état indépendant algérien." PhD diss., Université Sorbonne Paris, 2016.
Crowley, Patrick, ed. *Algeria: Nation, Culture, and Transnationalism, 1988–2005.* Liverpool: Liverpool University Press, 2017.
Cubbit, Geoffrey. *History and Memory.* Manchester: Manchester University Press, 2007.
Dallet, J. M. *Dictionnaire français-kabyle.* Vol. 2. Paris: SELAF, 1985.
Davies, Christie. "Humour and Protest: Jokes under Communism." *International Review of Social History* 52 (2007): 291–306.
———. "Reply to Abedinifard, Jokes Have No Consequences." *Humor* 30, no. 2 (2017): 239–246.
Davis, Muriam Haleh. *Markets of Civilization: Islam and Racial Capitalism in Algeria.* Durham, NC: Duke University Press, 2022.
Deriabin, Peter, and Frank Gibney. *The Secret World.* Garden City, NY: Doubleday, 1959.
Djaout, Tahar. *Le dernier été de la raison.* Paris: Editions du Seuil, 1999.
Douglas, Allen, and Fedwa Malti-Douglas. *Arab Comic Strips: Politics of an Emerging Mass Culture.* Bloomington: Indiana University Press, 1994.
Draitser, Emil. *Forbidden Laughter: Soviet Underground Jokes.* Los Angeles: Almanac, 1978.
———. "Soviet Underground Jokes as a Means of Entertainment." *Journal of Popular Culture* 23 (1989): 117–125.

Dris, Cherif, "La nouvelle loi organique sur l'information de 2012 en Algérie." *L'Année du Maghreb* 8 (2012): 303–320.

Durand, Monique. "Le combat des Algériennes." *Gazette des femmes*, last modified March 5, 2005. https://www.gazettedesfemmes.ca/2853/le-combat-des-algeriennes/.

El Shakry, Omnia. "'History without Documents.'" *American Historical Review* 120, no. 3 (2015): 920–934.

Evans, Martin. "Contextualising Contemporary Algeria: June 1965 and October 1988." *Open Democracy*, May 25, 2012. https://www.opendemocracy.net/en/contextualising-contemporary-algeria-june-1965-and-october-1988/.

Evans, Martin, and John Phillips. *Algeria: Anger of the Dispossessed*. New Haven, CT: Yale University Press, 2007.

Fahmy, Ziad. *Ordinary Egyptians: Creating the Nation through Popular Culture*. Palo Alto: Stanford University Press, 2011.

Falola, Toyin. *Nationalism and African Intellectuals*. Rochester, NY: University of Rochester Press, 2001.

Faraiḥa, Anīs. *al-Fukāha 'and al-'arab*. Beirut: Maktaba Ra's Beirut, 1962.

Farrell, Jeremy. "Comic Authority." In *Words That Tear the Flesh*, edited by Alan Baragona and Elizabeth L. Rambo, 85–117. Berlin: De Gruyter, 2018.

Fel, Alison S., and Nina Wardleworth. "The Colour of War Memory: Cultural Representations of *Tirailleurs Sénégalais*." *Journal of War and Culture Studies* 9, no. 4 (2016): 319–344.

Ferhani, Ameziane. *50 ans de bande dessinée algérienne et l'aventure continue*. Algiers: Dalimen, 2012.

Foucault, Michel. *Discipline and Punish: The Birth of the Prison*. Translated by Alan Sheridan. New York: Vintage Books, 1979.

———. *Power/Knowledge: Selected Interviews and Other Writings, 1972–1977*. Edited by Colin Gordon. New York: Pantheon Books, 1980.

Gafaïti, Hafid. "Power, Censorship, and the Press: The Case of Postcolonial Algeria." *Research in African Literatures* 30, no. 3 (1999): 51–61.

Geiger, Susan. "Tanganyikan Nationalism as 'Women's Work': Life Histories, Collective Biography, and Changing Historiography." *Journal of African History* 37, no. 3 (1996): 456–478.

Gèze, François, and Sahra Kettab. *Dossier 7: Les violations de la liberté de la presse*. Comité Justice pour l'Algérie. Accessed August 17, 2015. http://www.algerie-tpp.org/tpp/pdf/dossier_7_presse.pdf.

Ghanem-Yazbeck, Dalia. "Challenging Fieldwork." *Anthropology Matters Journal* 17, no. 2 (2017): 28–56.

———. "Sociologie de la violence extrême en Algérie." PhD diss., Versailles Saint-Quentin-en-Yvelines University, 2012.

Göçek, Fatma Müge, ed. *Political Cartoons in the Middle East*. Princeton, NJ: Markus Wiener, 1998.

Goodman, Jane E. "Acting with One Voice: Producing Unanimism in Algerian Reformist Theater." *Comparative Studies in Society and History* 55, no. 1 (2013): 167–197.

Groensteen, Thierry. "The Impossible Definition." In *A Comic Studies Reader*, edited by Jeet Heer and Kent Worcester, 124–131. Jackson: University of Mississippi, 2009.

Hamūda, 'Ādel. *al-Nukta al-sīyāsīya*. Cairo: al-Firsān lil-Nashar, 1999.

Hannoum, Abdelmajid. *Violent Modernity: France in Algeria*. Cambridge, MA: Harvard University Press, 2010.

Helmy, Mohamed M., and Sabine Frerichs. "Stripping the Boss: The Powerful Role of Humor in the Egyptian Revolution 2011." *Integrative Psychological and Behavioral Science* 47, no. 4 (2013): 450–481.

Høigilt, Jacob. "Egyptian Comics and the Challenge to Patriarchal Authoritarianism." *International Journal of Middle East Studies* 49, no. 1 (2017): 111–131.

Howell, Jennifer. "Investigating the Enforced Disappearances of Algeria's 'Dark Decade.'" *Journal of North African Studies* 21, no. 2 (2016): 213–234.

Hūfī, Aḥmad Muḥammad. *al-Fukāha fī al-'adab*. Cairo: Dār Nahḍa Miṣr, 1967.

Human Rights Watch. *Algeria: Elections in the Shadow of Violence and Repression*. June 1, 1997. https://www.refworld.org/docid/3ae6a7d1c.html.

———. "Algeria: Impunity Should Not Be Price of Reconciliation." August 31, 2005. https://www.hrw.org/news/2005/08/31/algeria-impunity-should-not-be-price-reconciliation.

Idir, Amnay. "Rachid Ksentini: Le rire pour supporter la misère." *El Watan*, September 13, 2005.

Jarvis, Jill. *Decolonizing Memory: Algeria and the Politics of Testimony*. Durham, NC: Duke University Press, 2021.

Joffé, George. "The Arab Spring in North Africa." *Journal of North African Studies* 16, no. 4 (2011): 507–532.

———. "National Reconciliation and General Amnesty in Algeria." *Mediterranean Politics* 13, no. 2 (2008): 213–228.

Jones, Christa Catherine. "Female Tricksters." In *Women and Resistance in the Maghrib: Remembering Kahina*, edited by Nabil Boudraa and Joseph Ohmann Krause, 123–140. New York: Routledge, 2022.

Kadi, Amine, Denise Ammoun, and Benjamin Barthe. "Dossier: Dérision et religion." *La Croix*, February 2, 2006, 5.

Kalyvas, Stathis. "Wanton and Senseless? The Logic of Massacres in Algeria." *Rationality and Society* 11, no. 3 (1999): 243–285.

Kepel, Gilles. *Jihad*. 2nd ed. Paris: Gallimard, 2003.

Khadda, Naget, and Monique Gadant. "Mots et choses de la révolte." *Peuples méditerranéens* 52 (July–December 1990): 19–24.

Khanna, Ranjana. *Algeria Cuts: Women and Representation, 1830 to the Present.* Palo Alto: Stanford University Press, 2008.

Khelladi, Aïssa. "Rire quand même: L'humour politique dans l'Algérie d'aujourd'hui." *Revue des mondes musulmans et de la Méditerranée* 77–78 (1995): 225–237.

Kishtainy, Khalid. *Arab Political Humor.* London: Quartet Books, 1985.

Kuipers, Giselinde. "The Politics of Humour in the Public Sphere." *European Journal of Cultural Studies* 14, no. 1 (2011): 63–80.

———. "The Sociology of Humor." In *The Primer of Humor Research*, edited by Victor Raskin, 382–385. Berlin: Mouton de Gruyter, 2008.

Kutz-Flamenbaum, Rachel V. "Humor and Social Movements." *Sociology Compass* 8, no. 3 (2014): 294–304.

Labat, Séverine, and Malik Aït Aoudia. *Algérie, 1988–2000: Autopsie d'une tragédie.* Paris: Compagnie des Phares et Balises, 2005.

Labter, Lazhari. *Journalistes algériens, 1988–1998.* Algiers: Chihab, 2005.

———. *Panorama de la bande dessinée algérienne.* Algiers: Lazhari Labter, 2009.

Laineste, L. "Can Stripping the Boss Be More Than a Joke?" *Integrative Psychological and Behavioral Science* 47 (2013): 482–491.

Laribi, Soraya. "Les mobilisations des associations de familles et proches des disparus de la décennie noire en Algérie." *Confluences Méditerranée* 114, no. 3 (2020): 177–188.

Lawrence, William. "Representing Algerian Youth." PhD diss., Tufts University, 2005.

Leperlier, Tristan. *Algérie, les écrivains et la décennie noire.* Paris: CRNS, 2018.

Le Sueur, James D. *Algeria since 1989: Between Terror and Democracy.* London: Zed Books, 2010.

Lipman, Steve. *Laughter in Hell: The Use of Humor during the Holocaust.* Northvale, NJ: J. Aronson, 1991.

Lorcin, Patricia. "Imperialism, Colonial Identity, and Race." *History of Science Society* 90, no. 4 (1999): 653–679.

Lounes, Abderrahmane. *Djeha.* Algiers: Casbah, 2009.

Maddy-Weitzman, Bruce. "Contested Identities." *Journal of North African Studies* 6, no. 3 (2001): 23–47.

Mahmood, Saba. "Religious Reason and Secular Affect: An Incommensurable Divide?" *Critical Inquiry* 35 (2009): 836–862.

Martinez, Luis. *The Algerian Civil War.* New York: Columbia University Press, 2000.

Mbembe, Achille. "La 'chose' et ses doubles dans la caricature camerounaise" [The "Thing" and its doubles in Cameroonian caricatures]. *Cahiers d'études africaines* 36, no. 141/142 (1996): 143–170.

McAllister, Edward. "Immunity to the Arab Spring?" *New Middle Eastern Studies* 3 (2013).

———. "Yesterday's Tomorrow Is Not Today: Memory and Place in an Algiers Neighbourhood." PhD diss., Oxford University, 2015.
McClintock, Anne. "Family Feuds: Gender, Nationalism, and Family." *Feminist Review* 44 (1993): 61–80.
McCulloch, John. *Black Peril, White Virtue: Sexual Crime in Southern Rhodesia, 1902–1935*. Bloomington: Indiana University Press, 2000.
McDougall, James. *History and the Culture of Nationalism in Algeria*. Cambridge: Cambridge University Press, 2006.
———. *A History of Algeria*. Cambridge: Cambridge University Press, 2017.
———. "Savage Wars? Codes of Violence in Algeria, 1830s–1990s." *Third World Quarterly* 26, no. 1 (2008): 117–131.
McKinney, Mark. "The Frontier and the Affrontier: French-Language Algerian Comics and Cartoons Confront the Nation." *European Comic Art* 1, no. 2 (2008): 175–200.
Messaoudi, Khalida. *Unbowed*. Translated by Anne C. Vila. Philadelphia: University of Pennsylvania Press, 1998.
Mestyan, Adam. *Arab Patriotism: The Ideology and Culture of Power in Late Ottoman Egypt*. Princeton, NJ: Princeton University Press, 2017.
Mills, Brett. *Television Sitcom*. London: British Film Institute, 2005.
Milton, Cynthia E. "At the Edge of the Peruvian Truth Commission: Alternative Paths to Recounting the Past." *Radical History Review* 98 (2007): 3–33.
Mitchell, Timothy. "The Limits of the State: Beyond Statist Approaches and Their Critics." *American Political Science Review* 85, no. 1 (1991): 77–96
Morreall, John. "Humor in the Holocaust: Its Critical, Cohesive, and Coping Functions." Holocaust Teacher Resource Center, November 22, 2001. http://www.holocaust-trc.org/humor-in-the-holocaust/.
———. "Philosophy of Humor." In *Stanford Encyclopedia of Humor*. Last modified November 12, 2012. http://plato.stanford.edu/entries/humor/#SupThe.
Morsly, Dalila. "Humour d'Algériennes, Hanan-El-Maz'ouka et Daïffa." In "Armées d'humour: Rires au féminin," edited by J. Stora and E. Pillet, special issue, *Humoresques* 11 (2000): 187–208.
Moussaoui, Abderrahmane. "Algérie, la réconciliation entre espoirs et malentendus." *Politique étrangère* 72, no. 2 (2007): 339–350.
———. *De la violence en Algérie*. Paris: Actes Sud, 2006.
———. "Enfants du maquis en Algérie: Un héritage explosif." *Anthropology of the Middle East* 12, no. 1 (2017): 20–37.
———. "La Concorde Civile en Algérie: Entre mémoire et histoire." In *Où va l'Algérie*, edited by Ahmed Mahiou and John-Robert Henry, 71–92. Aix-en-Provence: Karthala—Institut de Recherches et d'Études sur les Mondes Arabes et Musulmans, 2001.

———. "Pertes et fracas: Une décennie algérienne meurtrière." *NAQD* 18, no. 2 (2003): 135–138.
Mundy, Jacob. *Imaginative Geographies of Algerian Violence*. Palo Alto: Stanford University Press, 2015.
———. "Visualising National Reconciliation after the Algerian Civil War: Violence, Gender and 'Virtual Justice' in Film." In *Spectacles of Blood: A Study of Masculinity and Violence in Postcolonial Films*, edited by Swaralipi Nandi and Esha Chatterjee, 31–50. Chicago: University of Chicago Press, 2012.
Obadare, Ebenezer. *Humor, Silence, and Civil Society in Nigeria*. Rochester, NY: University of Rochester Press, 2016.
Oberlé, Thierry. "Like He Said: A Vitriolic Chronicle of Algeria." *Grand Street* 65 (Summer 1998): 47–63.
Obrdlik, Antonin J. "'Gallows Humor,' a Sociological Phenomenon." *American Journal of Sociology* 47, no. 5 (1942): 709–716.
Orwell, George. "Funny but Not Vulgar." In *Funny, but Not Vulgar and Other Selected Essays and Journalism*. London: Folio Society, 1968.
Oualdi, M'hamed. *A Slave between Empires: A Transimperial History of North Africa*. New York: Columbia University Press, 2020.
Pearson, Lyle. "Four Years of North African Film." *Film Quarterly* 26, no. 4 (1973): 18–26.
Perego, Elizabeth. "Beyond Paralyzing Terror: The 'Black Decade' in the Algerian Hirak." *JadMag* 7, no. 3 (2019).
———. "Emasculating Humor from Algeria's 'Dark Decade,' 1991–2002." *International Journal of Middle East Studies* 52, no. 1 (2020): 67–86.
Pi-Sunyer, Oriol. "Political Humor in a Dictatorial State: The Case of Spain." *Ethnohistory* 24, no. 2 (1977): 179–190.
Prochaska, David. "History as Literature, Literature as History." *American Historical Review* 101, no. 3 (1996): 670–711.
Qarlifa, Hamid. "al-Nukta al-siyāsiyya fī al-Jazā'ir: dirāsa muqārana bayn al-'ahdatayn al-ra'īsiyyatayn, 1978–1992." Master's thesis, Université Abou Elkacem Saad Allah d'Alger 2, 2008.
Rahal, Malika. "Fused Together and Torn Apart: Stories and Violence in Contemporary Algeria." *History and Memory* 24, no. 1 (2012): 118–151.
Rahnama, Sara. *The Future Is Feminist*. Ithaca: Cornell University Press, forthcoming.
Raskin, Victor, ed. *The Primer of Humor Research*. Berlin: Mouton de Gruyter, 2008.
Rea, Christopher G. *The Age of Irreverence: A New History of Laughter in China*. Oakland: University of California Press, 2015.
Rees, Phil, and Philip Tibenham. *Algeria's Hidden War*. London: BBC Worldwide, 1994.

Roberts, Hugh. *The Battlefield: Algeria, 1988–2002, Studies in a Broken Polity*. New York: Verso, 2003.
Rose, Alexander. "When Politics Is a Laughing Matter." *Policy Review* 110 (2001–2002): 59–72.
Rosenthal, Franz. *Humor in Early Islam*. Leiden: Brill, 2011.
Ross, Kristin. *Fast Cars, Clean Bodies*. Cambridge, MA: MIT Press, 1996.
Roth, Arlette. *Le théâtre algérien de langue dialectale, 1926–1954*. Paris: François Maspero, 1967.
Rouadjia, Ahmed. *Les frères et la mosquée*. Paris: Karthala, 1989.
Rousseau, Sandra. "Une drôle de mémoire: relations franco-algériennes et mémoire comique, 1954–2012." PhD diss., Pennsylvania State University, 2015.
Ruedy, John. *Modern Algeria*. 2nd ed. Bloomington: Indiana University Press, 2005.
Saïd, Edward W. *Orientalism*. New York: Pantheon Books, 1978.
Sakthivel, Vish. "The Movement for a Society of Peace." PhD diss., Oxford University, 2019.
Salhi, Kamal. "Morocco, Algeria and Tunisia." In *A History of Theatre in Africa*, edited by Martin Banham, 37–76. Cambridge: Cambridge University Press, 2004.
Samraoui, Mohamed. *Chronique des années de sang*. Paris: Denoël, 2003.
Sanos, Sandrine. "The Sex and Race of Satire." *Jewish History* 32 (2018): 33–63.
Scott, James C. *Weapons of the Weak: Everyday Forms of Peasant Resistance*. New Haven, CT: Yale University Press, 1985.
Semati, Mehdi. "The Geopolitics of *Parazit*, the Iranian Televisual Sphere, and the Global Infrastructure of Political Humor." *Popular Communication* 10, no. 1–2 (2012): 119–130.
Serres, Thomas. *L'Algérie face à la catastrophe suspendue*. Tunis: Karthala, 2019.
Shehata, Samer. "The Politics of Laughter." *Folklore* 103, no. 1 (1992): 75–91.
Shepard, Todd. *The Invention of Decolonization*. Ithaca, NY: Cornell University Press, 2006.
———. "'Of Sovereignty': Disputed Archives, 'Wholly Modern' Archives, and the Post-decolonization French and Algerian Republics." *American Historical Review* 120, no. 3 (2015): 869–883.
Siblot, Paul. "'Cagayous antijuifs': Un discours colonial en proie à la racisation." *Mots: Les langages du politique* 15 (1987): 59–75.
Sidhoum, Salah-Ed-dine, and Algeria Watch. *Les milices dans la nouvelle guerre d'Algérie*. December 13, 2009. Updated June 3, 2018. https://algeria-watch.org/?p=48532.
Silver, Christopher. *Recording History: Jews, Muslims, and Music across Twentieth-Century North Africa*. Palo Alto: Stanford University Press, 2022.
Silverstein, Paul A. "An Excess of Truth: Violence, Conspiracy Theorizing, and the Algerian Civil War." *Anthropological Quarterly* 75, no. 4 (2002): 643–674.

Slyomovics, Susan. "Sex, Lies and Television: Algerian and Moroccan Caricatures of the Gulf War." In *Women and Power in the Middle East*, edited by Suad Joseph and Susan Slyomovics, 72–98. Philadelphia: University of Pennsylvania Press, 2001.

Speier, Hans. "Wit and Politics: An Essay on Laughter and Power." *American Journal of Sociology* 103, no. 5 (1998): 1352–1401.

Stokker, Kathleen. *Folklore Fights the Nazis: Humor in Occupied Norway, 1940–1945*. Madison: University of Wisconsin Press, 1997.

Stone, Martin. *The Agony of Algeria*. New York: Columbia University Press, 1997.

Stora, Benjamin. *La guerre invisible*. Paris: Presses des Sciences Po, 2001.

———. "L'amnésie algérienne." Histoire coloniale et postcoloniale. August 6, 2006. https://histoirecoloniale.net/l-amnesie-algerienne-par-Benjamin.html.

———. *Les trois exils: Juifs d'Algérie*. Paris: Stock, 2006.

Sukys, Julija. *Silence Is Death: The Life and Work of Tahar Djaout*. Lincoln: University of Nebraska Press, 2007.

Summerfelt, Hannah, Louis Lippman, and Ira E. Hyman Jr. "The Effect of Humor on Memory." *Journal of General Psychology* 137, no. 4 (2010): 376–394.

Swart, Sandra. "'The Terrible Laughter of the Afrikaner': Towards a Social History of Humor." *Journal of Social History* 42, no. 4 (2009): 889–917.

Taiebi Moussaoui, Fatima Zohra. "Le développement de la presse électronique en Algérie: Des dispositifs aux pratiques journalistiques." *L'Année du Maghreb* 15 (2016): 61–76.

Tamer, Georges, ed. *Humor in der arabischen Kultur* [Humor in Arabic culture]. Berlin: De Gruyter, 2009.

Tamimi, Hammadi. *al-Fukāha fī shi'r al-Tūnisī*. Tunis: Dar Bou Salamah, 1986.

Thénault, Sylvie. "1881–1919: L'apogée de l'Algérie française et les débuts de l'Algérie algérienne." In *Histoire de l'Algérie à la période coloniale, 1830–1961*, edited by Abderrahmane Bouchène, Jean-Pierre Peyroulou, Ouanassa Siari Tengour, and Sylvie Thénault, 159–184. Paris: La Découverte, 2012.

Thomson, Susan. *Whispering Truth to Power: Everyday Resistance to Reconciliation in Post-genocide Rwanda*. Madison: University of Wisconsin Press, 2013.

Thurston, Robert W. "Social Dimensions of Stalinist Rule: Humor and Terror in the USSR, 1935–1941." *Journal of Social History* 42, no. 3 (1991): 541–562.

Vice, Sue. *Introducing Bakhtin*. Manchester: Manchester University Press, 1997.

Vince, Natalya. "Colonial and Postcolonial Identities: Women Veterans of the 'Battle of Algiers.'" *French History and Civilization* 2 (2009): 153–168.

———. "Dangerous Shortcuts: Paris Attacks and the War of Independence." *Textures du Temps / Ḥakabāt al-Zaman*, November 22, 2015. https://textures dutemps.hypotheses.org/1754.

———. *Our Fighting Sisters: Nation, Memory and Gender in Algeria, 1954–2012*. Manchester: Manchester University Press, 2015.

———. "Saintly Grandmothers: Youth Reception and Reinterpretation of the National Past in Contemporary Algeria." *Journal of North African Studies* 18, no. 1 (2013): 32–52.

Webber, Sabra. *Romancing the Real*. Berkeley: University of California Press, 1991.

Wedeen, Lisa. *Authoritarian Apprehensions*. Chicago: University of Chicago Press, 2019.

———. "Ideology and Humor in Dark Times: Notes from Syria." *Critical Inquiry* 39, no. 4 (2013): 841–874.

Willis, Michael. *The Islamist Challenge in Algeria*. New York: New York University Press, 1996.

Wyrtzen, Jonathan. "Performing the Nation in Anti-colonial Protest in Interwar Morocco." *Nations and Nationalism* 19, no. 4 (2013): 615–634.

Younsi, Rochdi Ali. "Caught in a Colonial Triangle: Competing Loyalties within the Jewish Community of Algeria, 1842–1943." PhD diss., University of Chicago, 2003.

Yous, Nesroulah, and Selima Mellah. *Qui a tué à Bentalha? Chronique d'un massacre annoncé*. Paris: Découverte, 2000.

Zelig, Omar. *Slim, le gatt, et moi*. Algiers: DALIMEN, 2009.

Zelizer, Craig. "Laughing Our Way to Peace or War: Humour and Peacebuilding." *Journal of Conflictology* 1, no. 2 (2010): 1–9.

Želvys, V. I. "Obscene Humor: What the Hell?" *Humor* 3, no. 3 (1990): 323–332.

Zeraoulia, Faouzia. "The Memory of the Civil War in Algeria." *Contemporary Review of the Middle East* 7, no. 1 (2020): 25–53.

Zirem, Youcef. *Algérie la guerre des ombres*. Brussels: Complexe, 2002.

Žižek, Slavoj. *The Sublime Object of Ideology*. 2nd ed. London: Verso, 2008.

PRIMARY SOURCES—ARCHIVAL

National Library of Algeria, Algiers, Algeria (Frantz Fanon and El Hamma Locations)

    Algérie-Actualité
    Alger républicain
    al-Ṣaḥḥ Āfa
    Baroud
    Echa'ab
    El-Khabar
    El Monquidh
    El Moudjahid
    Journal officiel de la République Algérienne
    La Nation
    La Tribune
    Le Matin

Le Quotidien d'Oran
L'Expression
L'Hebdo libéré
L'Opinion
Tenani, Mustapha. *Hommes du djebel.* Algiers: ENAL, 1985.

Les Glycines Centre d'Etudes Diocésain, Algiers, Algeria

Lounes, Abderrahmane, text, and Rachid Marai, drawings. *Histoires extra et ordinaires du cimetièr-monde.* Algiers: SNED, 1983.

Archives of El Khabar *Newspaper, Algiers, Algeria*

El Khabar

Archives of El Watan *Newspaper, Algiers, Algeria*

El Watan

Archives of Liberté *Newspaper, Algiers, Algeria*

Dilem, Ali. *Boutef président.* Algiers: self-published, 2000.
La Liberté

Private Collections of Narrators

Personal library of anonymous (journalist): pamphlets and documents from armed rebel groups during Algeria's "Black Decade"
Personal library of Lazhari Labter: documents concerning opening up of the press in the late 1980s
Personal library of Mahfoud Aïder: copies of *El Manchar*

Library of the Algerian Cultural Center, Paris, France

Abtroun, Samy, text, and Ali Dilem, drawings. *Golfe: La guerre des Boushés.* Algiers: ENAG, 1991.
El Manchar
El Watan
La Tribune
Various artists. *Le journal de M'Quidèch.* Algiers: ENAG, 2003.

French National Library- François Mitterrand, Paris, France

Le Turco

France's National Overseas Archive (Archives Nationales d'Outre-Mer), Aix-en-Provence, France

ANOM Archives du Département d'Alger 4I/183

ANOM Archives du Département d'Alger 9H37
ANOM Library B 400
ANOM Library B 2151
ANOM Library B 2152
ANOM Library B 3494

France's Defense Historical Service (Service Historique de la Défense), Ministry of the Armed Forces, Vincennes, France

1 H 1715
1 H 2588
1 H 2589
1 H 2590
1 H 4458

Other

Alleg, Henri. *La question*. Paris: Editions de Minuit, 1958.
Bachtarzi, Mahieddine. *Mémoires, 1919–1939*. Vol. 1. Algiers: SNED, 1968.
Bencheneb, Saaddedine. "Chansons satiriques d'Alger." *Revue Africaine* 74 (1933): 75–117, 296–352.
Bouzaher, Hocine. *Des voix dans le Casbah: Théâtre algérien militant*. Paris: François Maspero, 1960.
Dahak, Bachir. *Les Algériens: Le rire et la politique de 1962 à nos jours*. Algiers: Frantz Fanon, 2018.
Dahmani, Lounis. *Algérie: L'humour au temps du terrorisme*. Paris: Bethy, 1998.
———. *Blagues: Made in Algéria*. Paris: Dahmani, 2007.
Desparmet, Joseph. "La chanson d'Alger pendant la Grande Guerre." *Revue africaine* 73 (1932): 54–83.
Fellag, Mohand. *Djurdjurassique Bled*. Paris: J. C. Lattès, 1996.
———. "Djurdjurrasique bled." Recording published by MLP Music, YouTube, October 9, 2012. https://www.youtube.com/watch?v=otZUYttO1ok&t=3169s.
———. "Sos Labess." DailyMotion, performed March 8, 1990, published 2014, https://www.dailymotion.com/video/x1zvikv.
Lakhdar-Hamina, Mohamed, dir. *Hassen Terro*. Algiers: Office des Actualités Algériennes / Office of Algerian News, 1968.
Mekbel, Said. *Ce voleur qui*. Algiers: Dalimen, 2002.
———. *Dix ans déjà*. Algiers: Dalimen, 2005.
Nadia, and Baya Gacemi. *I, Nadia, Wife of a Terrorist*. Translated by Paul Cote and Constantina Mitchell. Lincoln: University of Nebraska Press, 2006.
Sahnine, Rachid. *Mémoires de Rouiched*. Algiers: Editions el-Adib Chihab, 1993.
Samraoui, Mohammed. *Chroniques des années de sang*. Paris: Denoël, 2003.

Semiane, Sid Ahmed. *Octobre, ils parlent*. Alger: *Le Matin*, 1998.
Slim. *Moustache et les frères Belgacem* [Mustache and the Belgacem brothers]. Slim via Lulu.com, 2011.
———. *Une loubia pour un marsien naïf*. Slim via Lulu.com, 2011.
Souaïdia, Habib. *La sale guerre*. Paris: Découverte, 2001.

PRIMARY SOURCES—ORAL HISTORY INTERVIEWS (SELECTED)

Interviews with Mahfoud Aïder, June 13, 2013, June 18, 2013, April 2, 2014, Algiers, Algeria
Interview with Malik Aït-Aoudia, December 19, 2014, Paris, France
Interview with Mohamed Ali Allalou, December 17, 2014, Paris, France
Interviews with Chawki Amari, June 23, 2013, July 3, 2013, Algiers, Algeria
Interview with Redouane Assari, June 4, 2013, Paris, France
Interview with Tayeb Belghiche, July 15, 2013, Algiers, Algeria
Interview with Omar Belhouchet, July 20, 2013, Algiers, Algeria
Interview with Mustapha Benfodil, July 24, 2013, Algiers, Algeria
Interview with Lounis Dahmani, August 11, 2013, Algiers, Algeria
Interview with Saïd Djaafer, July 27, 2013, Algiers, Algeria
Interview with Ihsane El Kadi, July 28, 2013, Algiers, Algeria
Interview with Ameziane Ferhani, March 15, 2015, Algiers, Algeria
Interview with Hacène Ferhat, January 20, 2014, Algiers, Algeria
Interview with Salima Ghezali, January 21, 2014, Algiers, Algeria
Interview with Gyps, September 24, 2014, Algiers, Algeria
Interview with Mustapha Hammouche, August 4, 2013, Algiers, Algeria
Interview with Haroun, June 30, 2013, Algiers, Algeria
Interview with Séverine Labat, December 16, 2014, Paris, France
Interview with Lazhari Labtar, June 22, 2013, Algiers, Algeria
Interview with Amine Labter, July 26, 2013, Algiers, Algeria
Interview with Le Hic (Hichem Baba Ahmed), June 13, 2013, Algiers, Algeria
Interview with Badreddine Manaa, October 6, 2014, Algiers, Algeria
Interviews with Mohamed Mazari, June 13, 2013, July 9, 2013, Algiers, Algeria
Interview with Adlène Meddi, September 21, 2014, Algiers, Algeria
Interview with Nazim Mekbel, August 9, 2013, virtual
Interview with Dalila Morsley, December 27, 2015, Algiers, Algeria
Interview with Abrous Outoudert, January 19, 2014, Algiers, Algeria
Interview with Rym from the Chaîne Trois/Station Three Radio, March 29, 2015, Algiers, Algeria
Interview with Saad, March 5, 2015, Algiers, Algeria

Interview with Zineb Sedira, March 29, 2015, Algiers, Algeria
Interviews with Sid Ahmed Semiane, July 13, 2013, October 12, 2014, Algiers, Algeria
Interview with Ali Silem, December 27, 2015, Algiers, Algeria
Interviews with Slim, July 1, 2013, August 20, 2014, Algiers, Algeria
Interview with Mustapha Tenani, June 13, 2013, Algiers, Algeria
Interview with Omar Zelig, November 12, 2013, Algiers, Algeria

INDEX

2015 Terrorist Attacks in Île de France (Paris), 14

Abbas, Ferhat, 44
Abdennour, Ali Yahia, 213
'Abduh, Muhammad, 44
Abedinifard, Mostafa, 9
Abtroun, Samy, 107
Afghanistan, 91, 166, 168–170
Al-Ajouad (group for preserving Black Decade memories), 17, 234
Ageron, Charles-Robert, 36
Agrarian Revolution (under Boumediene), 63, 65
Ahmed, Kaïd. *See* slimaneries
Aïder, Mahfoud, 162–163
Aissaoui, Rabah, 36
Aït Ahmed, Hocine, 56–57
Aït Aoudia, Malik, 20, 152
Aït-Aoudia, Myriam, 89
Aït Djaffer, Djamel, 52
alcohol, 42, 47, 93, 107, 126, 135–136, 171, 177–178
Algerian Arabic (*darija, darja*), 21, 42, 52, 67, 154, 172, 239
Algerian Islam (concept). *See* Muslimness
algerianité. *See* Algerianness
Algerian National Movement (Mouvement algérien national, MNA), 53, 56
Algerianness (*jazā'iriyya/ algerianité*), 33, 36, 43, 59, 153–155
Algerian People's National Army (Armée nationale populaire, ANP), 4, 11, 16–17, 19–22, 82, 84–85, 89, 95, 110, 118–124, 127–131, 139, 140, 142–143, 151, 157–158, 160, 162–164, 168–169, 176–180, 183, 194–197, 199, 201, 209, 211, 213, 233, 236–237, 242
Algerian People's Party (Parti du peuple algérien, PPA), 51
Algerian Revolution of 1954–1962 (War of Independence/Liberation): in general, 11, 12, 90; humor during, 51–55, 240; nationalist fighters (*maquisards, moudjahidines*), 20, 63, 170, 237; representations of, 63, 233–234; revolution "stolen," 59, 237
Algerian War. *See* Algerian Revolution of 1954–1962
Algérie: Autopsie d'une tragédie (documentary), 17
Algérie-Actualité, 59, 63–64
Alger républicain, 2–3, 98–103, 106, 159
Al-'Alī, Nājī, 208
Allalou (Algerian interwar performer), 43
Allalou, Mohamed Ali, 83–85
Alleg, Henri, 2, 55
Allied Powers, 49–51. *See also* World War II
Allman, Jean, 14
Althusser, Louis, 35, 66–67, 213

Amari, Chawki, 159–161
Amnesty Law 95–12 of February 25, 1995, 195
Anderson, Benedict, 33
An-nisā' (Bachtarzi play), 44–46
Antisemitism. *See* Jews
Arabic: in general, 52, 80, 90, 105; importance to nationalism, 47. *See also* Algerian Arabic; Arabization
Arabization, 57, 90
Arab Spring: in general, 9, 11, 14, 79–81, 83, 235; October 1988 imagined as precursor to, 11, 14, 79–80, 83
archives: challenges in postcolonial contexts, 14–15; interpretation of, 19; oral history, 16–18; used for this project, 16–18
Armed Islamic Group (Groupe islamique armée, GIA), 119, 124, 127, 133–134, 151, 155, 164–166, 172, 183, 195, 215
Armed Islamic Movement (Mouvement islamique armée, MIA), 91, 118–119
Army General Staff (Etat-major général of the National Liberation Army), 56
Asseraf, Arthur, 39
Association of Algerian Muslim Ulama (L'Association des oulémas musulmans algériens, AUMA), 42, 44, 47, 90. *See also* Muḥibbī al-fann
authoritarianism, 5, 9, 12, 23, 117–118, 122, 133–134, 143, 239, 240, 243. *See also* censorship
Ayoub (Abdelkader Aboud), 155, 161–162, 167, 170–173, 176–180, 183, 201, 216, 220–222, 224–226, 238

Bachtarzi, Mahieddine, 42–47, 49, 52, 241
Bakhtin, Mikhail, 194, 200, 202, 205, 206, 209, 215, 225, 240. *See also* carnival
bandes dessinées: definition, 52; disruption in the 1990s, 23, 152; early history in Algeria, 52, 59–63; legacy in Algeria, 101, 105, 238. *See also* cartoons
Barberousse Prison. *See* Serkadji Prison
Bayat, Asef, 78, 240. *See also* social non-movements
Belhadj, Ali, 81, 91, 97, 103, 117–118
Belhouchet, Omar, 127–128
Belkacem, Krim, 56
Ben Badis, 'Abd Al-Hamid, 44

Ben Bella, Ahmed, 56–58
Ben Bouali, Hassiba, 232, 234
Bencheneb, Rachid, 43
Bencheneb, Saadeddine, 41–42
Benfodil, Mustapha, 167–168, 205, 208, 223–224
Benjedid, Chadli, 66, 78, 80–82, 84–86, 89–80, 97, 99–101, 103, 241. *See also* Chadli jokes
Les Benis Oui Oui (Bachtarzi play), 45–46, 49
Benmiloud, Yassir. *See* Y.B.
Bentalha massacre, 163, 176, 234
Berber: ethnicity. *See* Imazighen; Tamazight (Berber) languages.
Berber Spring of 1980, 58
Berlant, Lauren, 80
Beskri, Djilali, 102
Betchine, Mohamed, 159
Black Decade: ambiguity of violence, 12, 15; belligerents, 20–21, 118–120; civilians' views of, 13–14; different terms for, 19–20, 132–133; "Islamization" of, 165, 178; place in world history, 235; the problem of periodization, 21–22; remembrance of, 232–234; the start of the conflict, 118–120; supposed fear of return to, 13–14
bled mickey ("country of mickey"), 67
Blum-Violette reform, 44–45
Boudiaf, Mohamed, 56, 120, 125, 211–212
Bouhired, Djamila, 208
Boumediene, Houari, 31–32, 56–57, 65–66, 80, 86, 90, 96
Bouteflika, Abdelaziz, 22, 56, 176–177, 191–192, 195–198, 204–211, 213–216, 218, 220, 225, 236
Bouyali, Mustapha, 91
Bozzini, David, 123
Bryant, Chad, 9, 140

Cagayous, 36, 38
camps du sud (concentration camps in Saharan desert), 118, 156
carnival (Mikhail Bakhtin), 194, 200–202, 204–205, 209–210, 216–218, 220, 222, 225, 240
cartoons: from Algerian Revolution, 15; literature on power of cartoons, 6;

scandals surrounding (Algeria and elsewhere), 6, 97, 152, 162. *See also* *bandes dessinées* and names of individual cartoonists

censorship, 5, 33–34, 48–49, 58, 101, 155–161, 167, 213, 220, 233

Chadli jokes, 66, 80–81, 84–86. *See also* Chadli Benjedid

Charef, Abed, 84

Charlie Hebdo, 6, 97

Charter for Peace and National Reconciliation (2005): Article Forty-Six, 17, 197, 234; in general, 17, 22, 196–199, 202, 213–216, 222–223

chi chis/tchés-tchés, 83, 103–104

Christianity, 108–109

cinema, 59, 60, 67, 89, 103, 200–201

Civil Concord Law of 1999, 195–196, 199, 202, 204, 206, 210–211, 215–223

clothing as symbol of identity, 61, 84–85, 93, 96, 102–103, 105–106, 126, 134–135, 166, 168, 170–172, 191–192, 208

Code de l'Indigénat (Indigenous Code), 34

conciliator/eradicator divide (position related to question of dialogue between the state and the Islamic Salvation Front and armed groups), 119–120, 158–160, 177–178, 180–181

conspiracy theories/rumor, 7, 19, 81, 121, 123–124, 130, 143, 151–152, 157–158, 171. *See also "qui tue qui"*

Crémieux Decree, 34. *See also* Jews

Cultural Revolution (in Algeria), 57

Dahak, Bachir, 32

Dahmani, Lounis, 159

Dahmoun, 42

darija/darja. *See* Algerian Arabic

dark humor. *See* humor

Davies, Christie, 122

de Gaulle, Charles, 54–55

democratic transition in Algeria (1988 to 1992), 14, 76–79, 89–111, 117–119, 233, 235

Department of Intelligence and Security (Département du renseignement et de la sécurité, DRS), 157–158

Desparmet, Joseph, 38–40

Dilem, Ali, 8, 85, 98–101, 105, 107, 152, 155, 160–171, 173–179, 182, 191–194, 201–216, 220–226, 237–238

disparus (forcefully disappeared persons). *See* forced disappearances

Djaballah, Abdallah, 91

Djaout, Tahar, 138

Dorbane, Mohammed, 4, 153

Drif, Zohra, 208

DRS. *See* Department of Intelligence and Security

Eastern Europe humor. *See* Soviet/socialist humor

Echa'ab, 222–224

education, 90–91. *See also* literacy in Algeria

Egypt, 6, 44, 47, 90, 122–123, 235

elections: in general, 90, 101–102, 106, 118–119; referendum, 196–199, 206–211. *See also* democratic transition in Algeria

Ennahda Party. *See* Islamic Renaissance Party

eradicator (position related to the Islamic Salvation Front and armed groups). *See* conciliator/eradicator divide

Etat-major général of the ALN. *See* Army General Staff

Evans, Martin, 88, 92

Fahmy, Ziad, 33

fake checkpoints (*faux barrages*): in general, 203–204; and jokes, 12, 98, 117–118, 128–130, 135–136, 138, 141, 153, 235, 243–244

Family Code (1984), 90

Fāqū, 41–42, 47, 49

Fathy, 101–103

faux barrages. *See* fake checkpoints

faux moudjahidines (fake Algerian Revolution nationalist fighters), 59, 170

Fellag, Mohand, 76–77, 93, 101, 238

Ferhani, Ameziane, 142, 241

Ferzat, Ali, 6

films. *See* cinema

First Gulf War (1990–1991), 96, 106–107

First World War. *See* World War I

Fisk, Robert, 14

folklore, 1–4, 37, 48
football, 9, 41
forced disappearances, 118, 160, 197, 199, 233–234
Free France. *See* Allied Powers
French language, 43, 52–53, 105, 153–154, 239
Front des forces socialistes (FFS). *See* Front of Socialist Forces
Front of Socialist Forces (Front des forces socialistes, FFS), 57, 92–93, 180

Gadant, Monique, 85–86
gender, 86, 90, 96, 102, 128, 165–166, 168, 170–171, 203–205. *See also* humor: gender and humor; masculinity
Ghezali, Salima, 158–159
El Ghoul, *Alger républicain*, 3. *See also* Saïd Mekbel
Ghozali, Sid Ahmed, 56
Guerroui, Brahim, 4, 153

Hadj, Messali, 44, 53
Hadj Guillaume song, 38–40, 49
haik/haïk (*ḥāyak*), 61, 102–103, 170–171, 208, 218
Hamrouche, Mouloud, 99, 156
ḥarkīs, 60–61
Haroun (Ahmed Haroun), 62
Hassan terro (*Hassan the Terrorist* film), 59, 237–238
Hattab, Hassan, 215–216
L'Hebdo libéré, 159
Le Hic (Hichem Baba Ahmed), 162–163, 194, 201, 216–225, 237
Ḥijāb. *See* veiling
Ḥirāk (2019, Algeria), 14, 236–240
hittistes ("those who hold up the walls"), 80, 83–84, 110, 207
Holocaust, 52, 133–134
homosexuality, 86, 140, 205
humor: ability to cross social groups and border, 34, 242; comparison with comedy and satire, 21; as coping mechanism, 137–140; to create in-groups/out-groups, 183, 241; dark humor (humor and trauma) 12, 142; definition, 21; gender and humor, 18, 86, 92–94, 96, 102, 168, 170–171, 203–205, 207–210, 218–222; as historical source, 8–9, 239; incongruity theory of, 40, 70, 135, 176, 218; intertextuality and, 7, 12, 194; multifunctionality of, 9, 239; nationalizing humor or national personalities, 15, 58–66, 238, 240; political vocabulary and practices in Algeria and, 9, 238–239; "pressure valve" theory/tension relief, 5, 142; related terms in Arabic and French, 21; rumor and, 171–176; superiority theory of, 8–9, 34–35; as a thermometer of public opinion, 5; typology of Algerian humor, 18–19, 36
humorists under threat, 1–4

Imazighen; 57–58, 92. *See* Berber Spring; Tamazight (Berber) languages
Indigenous Code. *See* Code de l'Indigénat
interpellation (Louis Althusser), 35, 42, 66–67, 240
Iran, 91, 168
Iraq, 106. *See also* First Gulf War
Islamic Renaissance Party (Ennahda), 91
Islamic Salvation Army (Armée islamique du salut, AIS), 119, 124, 151–153, 165, 180, 182–183, 191, 195, 202, 204, 209, 214–218
Islamic Salvation Front (Front islamique du salut or FIS, *al-Jabha al-islāmiyya lil inqādh*): as broad movement, 91; connection to AIS, 119; elections, 11, 21, 92; in general, 11, 77, 101, 117–119, 180, 183, 195; humor for or against, 13, 77, 92–97, 103–109, 117–119, 165; leadership, 91, 117–188; policies, 91, 93
Islamophobia, 6, 165

January 1992 cancellation of electoral elections, 11, 21, 78, 118–119, 235
Jarvis, Jill, 9
jazā'iriyya. *See* Algerianness
Jews: antisemitism, 6, 36, 47–48, 52, 133–134; connections with Muslim communities, 39, 41–43, 45; humor and, 38–40, 41, 133; legal status in Algeria under colonization, 11, 34, 51–52; performers and troupes, 41–44; persecution under Vichy France,

52; status after independence, 55–56. *See also* Holocaust
J'ha. *See* Juḥā; Mesmar J'ha
Jonnart Law (1919), 41. *See also* Muslims
journalism: in general, 99, 101, 150–163, 232–233; state sponsorship of, 99, 152–153, 155–156, 222
journalists: dark humor used by, 127–128; in general, 99, 101, 212; importance in the 1990s, 157; jokes about, 121, 141–142; threats against in 1990s, 1–4, 121, 127–128, 138, 141–142, 157
Juḥā: in general, 2–4, 43, 50–51, 65, 97; tale of the "nail" (*mismār*/mesmar) of Juḥā, 3, 97

Kabylia, 57–58
Kafi, Ali, 210
Kaiser Wilhelm II, 38. *See also* Hadj Guillaume song
Karagüz. See Karakouz
Karakouz (puppetry), 37–38, 49
Kateb Yacine, 208
El Khabar, 151–161, 172–173, 220–222
Khadda, Naget, 85–86
Khanna, Ranjana, 201
Khelladi, Aïssa, 13, 48, 120
Kishtainy, Khalid, 8
Ksentini, Rachid, 41–42, 47, 52, 77, 241

Labter, Lazhari, 59, 62
Lacoste, Robert, 15, 55
Lawrence, William, 81
Liberté, 152, 174–180, 202–216
Libya, 169
literacy in Algeria, 33, 52, 67, 162
Lounes, Abderrahmane, 67

Madani, Abassi, 90–91, 95–97, 104, 107, 117–118
maddaḥ. See oral storytelling
Maghrib, definition, 10
Mahdi, 39
Mahmood, Saba, 6
malḥūn. See poetry
El Manchar (satirical newspaper), 104–106, 155, 161, 163, 168, 180, 193, 225, 236
El Manchar (satirical website), 236

m'ānī, 40
Martinez, Denis, 98
Martinez, Luis, 16, 120
masculinity, 86, 96, 128, 205
Mashriq, 10
Le Matin, 1–4, 8, 37, 107, 151–152, 161, 163, 166–167, 175, 216–217
Maz (Mohamed Mazari), 62, 162, 182
Mbembe, Achille, 7–8, 123
McClintock, Anne, 33
McDougall, James, 36, 234
McKinney, Mark, 160
Meddi, Adlène, 105, 138
Media Code of 1990, 99, 101
Mediene, Mohamed (Toufik), 205, 211
Mehri, Abdelhamid, 102
Mekbel, Saïd (El Ghoul, Mesmar J'ha), 1–5, 8, 24, 37, 98–99, 152–153, 161
Melouah (Sid Ali Melouah), 105–106
Merabtene, Menouar. *See* Slim
Mesmar J'ha (Saïd Mekbel editorial), 1–4. *See also* Juḥā *and* Saïd Mekbel
Metaoui, Fayçal, 158
Mezrag, Madani, 214
military. *See* Algerian People's National Army; National Liberation Army
moderate Islam/Islamists, 165–167
El Monquidh (FIS newspaper), 107–109
Morocco, 10, 43, 51, 56, 169, 198, 213
El Moudjahid, 31–32, 34, 53, 62–63
Mouffouk, Ghania, 158
Moussaoui, Abderrahmane, 13, 15, 87, 88, 126, 136–137, 152, 155
Moustache et les frères Belgacem, 60–61
Movement for the Triumph of Democratic Liberties (MTLD), 49
Movement of Algerian Journalists (Mouvement des journalistes algériens), 99
Movement of Society for Peace (Mouvement de la societé pour la paix, MSP, also known as Hamas formerly Movement of the Islamic Society), 91, 166
Movement of the Islamic Society. *See* Movement of Society for Peace
El Moutribia (musical group), 41, 43
M'Quideche (children's review), 60, 62

Mubarak, Hosni, 6, 122–123
Muḥibbī al-fann, 47
mujāhidāt (*moudjahidat*, female pro-nationalist participants in the Algerian Revolution), 208
multi-party political system (*multipartisme*) in Algeria. *See* democratic transition in Algeria
Mundy, Jacob, 16, 78, 164, 200–201, 234
music, 38–49
Muslimness, 155, 168, 170–172, 182
Muslims: political status under French colonialism, 11, 34, 41, 44–47, 51–52; as a racialized category under French imperialism, 10–11, 34, 232. *See also* Muslimness

Al-Nahdha (cultural renaissance across the Middle East and North Africa), 47
Nahnah, Mahfoud, 91
La Nation, 160
National Liberation Army (Armée de libération nationale, ALN), 55–56, 88
National Liberation Front (Front de libération nationale, FLN): in general, 11, 53–55, 102; one-party control, 11, 56–58, 78, 89–90
Nazi Germany: in general, 49–51; humor under, 12, 126
newspapers. *See* print cultures
Nezzar, Khaled, 180, 211–212
North African Star (l'Étoile nord-africaine), 44

OAS. *See* Secret Armed Organization
October 1988 Revolution: Arab Spring comparisons, 11, 14, 79–80, 83, 235, 237, 239–240; in general, 4, 11, 14, 77–90
oral history methodology (including use of term "narrator"), 16–18
orality: and cartoons, 141–142, 152, 155–156, 162–163; and humor, 10, 37; importance to nationalism, 33; and newspapers in Algeria in the 1990s, 151–152
oral storytelling (*guwwāl, maddaḥ, ḥakawātī*), 37

Organisation armée secrète (settler terrorist group). *See* Secret Armed Organization
Orientalism, 38–39, 153–154, 164–165, 183
Orwell, George, 123
Ottoman Empire, 10, 35–40
Oujda Clan, 56
Outoudert, Abrous, 162

Palestine, 81
Parti de l'avant-garde socialiste (PAGS). *See* Socialist Vanguard Party
patriots (civilians armed by the state to fight off rebel organizations), 118, 177–178
personal status laws in Algeria, 11, 34, 41. *See also* Jews; Muslims
petroleum, 32, 109, 194, 205
Phillips, John, 88, 92
pieds-noirs. *See* settlers
poetry, 36–37
Pravda (Soviet Union newspaper), 31
Press Code of 1990. *See* Media Code of 1990
print cultures: circulation numbers, 105, 161–162; in general, 45–48, 52, 53–55, 150–152; satirical publications, 47–48, 102–106, 156, 161
Prophet Muhammad cartoon scandals, 8, 97
psychological warfare, 162
puppetry, 37–38

Al Qaeda of the Islamic Maghrib, 119
al-Qiyam al-islāmiyya (Islamic Values Society) 58, 90
La question (1958). *See* Henri Alleg
"*qui tue qui*" ("who is killing whom"), 130, 153, 172–176, 182. *See also* conspiracy theories/rumor

racism, 10–11, 34, 48, 51
Rahal, Malika, 14
Raïs massacre, 234
Rally for Culture and Democracy (Rassemblement pour la culture et la démocratie, RCD), 92–93, 97–98
Rassemblement pour la culture et la démocratie (RCD). *See* Rally for Culture and Democracy

reconciliation process in Algeria (1994 to 2005), 12, 15, 191–199. *See also* Charter for Peace and National Reconciliation; Civil Concord Law
reforms, 11, 44–45, 52, 78, 81–82, 89–91, 242
repentis (repentant ones), 191–192, 194, 198, 202–204, 211, 217–221, 223
Résistance algérienne, 52
Roberts, Hugh, 20, 82, 90, 94, 132
Rouiched (Ahmed Ayad), 59, 237–238
Ruedy, John, 36, 165
rumor. *See* conspiracy theories/rumor

Al-Saḥḥ Āfa, 102–104, 156, 168–169
Sakthivel, Vish, 19–20
Salafist Group for Combat and Preaching, 119, 208
Samraoui, Mohamed, 157, 172
Sant'Egidio peace conference, 166, 180–181
Saudi Arabia, 95–96, 106–107, 109. *See also* First Gulf War
Scheele, Judith, 234
Scott, James C., 9. *See also* weapons of the weak
Second World War. *See* World War II
Secret Armed Organization (*Organisation armée secrete*, OAS), 56, 159
self-censorship. *See* censorship
Semiane, Sid Ahmed, 85
Sénatus-Consulte Law of 1865, 34. *See also* Jews; Muslims; personal status
Serkadji Prison (also known as Barberousse Prison), 53, 218
Sétif Massacre (also in Guelma and Kherrata), 51–52
settlers (European in Algeria during colonialism): departure from Algeria, 56; legal status in settler colonial system, 11, 34; use of racial slur by some against Muslim women, 92; theater and, 41–42
al-Shabaab, 6
El Shakry, Omnia, 14
Silverstein, Paul, 123
El-Sisi, Abdel Fattah, 6
Si Slimane (Kaïd Ahmed). *See* slimaneries

Slim (Menouar Merabtene), 60–64, 99, 105, 155, 165–166, 176–177, 179–180, 209, 216, 237
slimaneries (mistakes by Kaïd Ahmed, known by *nom de guerre* Si Slimane), 66
Socialist Vanguard Party (Parti de l'avant-garde socialiste, PAGS), 92, 101
social non-movements (Asef Bayat), 78–79, 83, 101, 110, 194, 201, 225, 240
soccer. *See* football
songs. *See* music
SOS Disparus (group for preserving Black Decade memories), 17, 199, 234
SOS Labess, 76–77
Soussan, Marie, 42
South African reconciliation process, 197–198
Soviet/socialist humor, 12, 31–32, 80, 243
Soviet Union, 12, 31–32, 91
Stand-up comedy, 77–78

Takfir wa'l hijra (Excommunication and Exodus), 119
Tamazight (Berber) languages, 17, 52, 57, 92, 154, 239
tchés–tchés. *See* *chi chis/tchés-tchés*
Tenani, Mustapha, 162, 180–181
al-thawra (Algerian Revolution/War of Independence). *See* Algerian Revolution of 1954–1962
theater, 41–47, 49, 52–53
Time of Terrorism. *See* Black Decade
torture, 2–3, 55, 82, 197
Touri, Mohamed, 52
La Tribune, 163, 166, 181
Tripoli Program, 57
Tunisia, 10, 36, 47–48, 53, 56, 169
Le Turco (settler newspaper), 48

veiling (any type of head or face covering), 61, 85, 93, 102–103, 105, 126, 134–135, 170–171, 208. *See also* haik
Vichy France, 49–51, 61
virtual justice (Ranjana Khanna), 200–201, 225
visual cultures, 67, 151, 153–154. *See also* *bandes dessinées*; cartoons
Viva Laldjérie (film), 201

El Watan, 127, 142, 151, 157–158, 161, 182
weapons of the weak (James C. Scott), 9, 13
Wedeen, Lisa, 35, 123
women: in general, 43, 92–93; humor and, 18, 64, 78, 88, 92–93, 134–135, 168, 170–171, 203–205, 207–210, 218–220; in the interwar period, 41, 45; Islamism and, 77, 90, 92–93, 96, 102, 105, 170–171; storytelling and, 37. *See also* Family Code; gender; masculinity
World War I, 11, 38–41
World War II, 49–52

Wyrtzen, Jonathan, 33

Y.B. (pen name of Yassir Benmiloud), 224–225

Zanoun, Saïd, 52
Zeroual, Liamine, 125, 132, 161, 178–180, 195, 210
Zid ya Bouzid, 62–63, 105, 238
Zirem, Youcef, 158
Zitouni, Djamel, 124
Žižek, Slavoj, 88
Zouabri, Antar, 133

ELIZABETH M. PEREGO is Assistant Professor in the Department of History at Appalachian State University. Her work has appeared in the Journal of North African Studies and the International Journal of Middle East Studies.

For Indiana University Press

Tony Brewer, Artist and Book Designer
Brian Carroll, Rights Manager
Emma Getz, Editorial Assistant
Sophia Hebert, Assistant Acquisitions Editor
Samantha Heffner, Marketing and Publicity Manager
Brenna Hosman, Production Coordinator
Katie Huggins, Production Manager
Nancy Lightfoot, Project Editor and Manager
Bethany Mowry, Acquisitions Editor
Dan Pyle, Online Publishing Manager
Jennifer Witzke, Senior Artist and Book Designer